HUMAN–COMPUTER INTERACTION AND U.S. LAW

The core topics at the intersection of human–computer interaction (HCI) and U.S. law – privacy, accessibility, telecommunications, intellectual property, artificial intelligence (AI), dark patterns, human subjects research, and voting – can be hard to understand without a deep foundation in both law and computing. Every member of the author team of this unique book brings expertise in both law and HCI to provide an in-depth yet understandable treatment of each topic area for professionals, researchers, and graduate students in computing and/or law. Two introductory chapters explaining the core concepts of HCI (for readers with a legal background) and U.S. law (for readers with an HCI background) are followed by in-depth discussions of each topic.

Jonathan Lazar, PhD, LLM, is Professor in the College of Information at the University of Maryland, where he is the executive director of the Maryland Initiative for Digital Accessibility (MIDA) and a faculty member in the Human-Computer Interaction Lab (HCIL). He has been teaching and researching about human–computer interaction (HCI), accessibility, and the intersections between law, policy, and HCI, for over 25 years. He has previously authored or edited 18 books and published over 200 refereed articles in journals, conference proceedings, edited books, and magazines. He has received research funding from the U.S. National Science Foundation, the U.S. National Institute on Disability, Independent Living, and Rehabilitation Research (NIDILRR), Google, and Adobe. He has served as an expert witness in many legal cases, has given legislative testimony at the state and federal level over 20 times, regularly teaches legal research methods to nonlawyers, and is a member of the Disability Rights Bar Association.

Casey Fiesler, PhD, JD, is Associate Professor in Information Science at the University of Colorado Boulder, where she is also affiliated with the law school's Silicon Flatirons Center for Law, Technology, and Entrepreneurship. She is a social computing researcher and legal scholar whose research addresses internet law and copyright, online governance, and research ethics. She is also a member of the SIGCHI Research Ethics Committee and the Legal Committee for the Organization for Transformative Works, which helps protect the rights of fan creators. She holds a JD from Vanderbilt Law School and a PhD in Human-Centered Computing from Georgia Tech.

Brian Wentz, ScD, MSL, is Professor of Information Systems and Analytics at Shippensburg University, Pennsylvania. His research interests include how the accessibility and usability aspects of human–computer interaction affect business, education, employment, public policy, and societal inclusion. He has been involved in a variety of projects related to web accessibility and usability for people with disabilities, including working as a contractor on the regulatory process for website accessibility under the ADA for the Civil Rights Division of the U.S. Department of Justice. He has published over 40 refereed articles in journals, books, and conference proceedings.

Raja Kushalnagar, PhD, JD, LLM, is Professor in the School of Science, Technology, Accessibility, Mathematics and Public Health at Gallaudet University in Washington, DC. With over 20 years of experience in the accessible technology field, he brings a wealth of experiential research in information and communication accessibility for people with diverse hearing abilities. He also advocates for laws and regulations to incorporate accessible computing advances such as automatic captioning/subtitling. He has mentored over 100 students, including over 60 who are deaf or hard of hearing, and has published over 100 articles in collaboration with these students. Raja focuses on increasing the number of people with diverse hearing abilities in the computing pipeline through community involvement. He serves on the NSF-funded AccessComputing Leadership Corps, and as a board member for the New York School for the Deaf, and Computing Research Association Widening Participation (CRA-WP). He earned a PhD in Computer Science and an LLM in Intellectual Property and Information Law from the University of Houston, and a JD from Texas Southern University.

This book is an important and thoughtful treatment of a fast-moving area, balancing the technical and legal aspects in an impressive way.

Michael Waterstone, *Dean and Professor of Law, UCLA School of Law*

Authored by leading multidisciplinary experts in technology and law, this book offers an invaluable resource for professionals working in human–computer interaction (HCI). Clear examples and explanations demystify how U.S. law impacts numerous domains of HCI, including interface design, digital accessibility, privacy, and AI.

Paul Heaton, *Professor and Academic Director of the Quattrone Center for the Fair Administration of Justice, University of Pennsylvania Law School*

At the intersection of human-computer interaction and law, this essential text illuminates how legal frameworks inform design, regulate use, and protect user rights. From AI ethics to dark patterns, from accessibility to algorithmic bias, it equips practitioners with critical knowledge of U.S. law and dimensions of interactive technologies that shape everyday life. A vital resource that not only clarifies current legal+tech landscapes but also charts compelling paths for the next generation of human-centered design.

Elizabeth D. Mynatt, *Dean and Professor, Khoury College of Computer Sciences, Northeastern University*

Whether you're a lawyer, a technologist, or just curious about tech policy, *Human–Computer Interaction and U.S. Law* has something to teach. The collection covers the basics while delving into depth in all the right places. This is interdisciplinary scholarship done right.

Ryan Calo, *Lane Powell and D. Wayne Gittinger Professor, University of Washington School of Law*

Human–Computer Interaction and U.S. Law

JONATHAN LAZAR
University of Maryland

CASEY FIESLER
University of Colorado Boulder

BRIAN WENTZ
Shippensburg University of Pennsylvania

RAJA KUSHALNAGAR
Gallaudet University

With a Foreword by
LORRIE CRANOR
Carnegie Mellon University, Pennsylvania

Shaftesbury Road, Cambridge CB2 8EA, United Kingdom

One Liberty Plaza, 20th Floor, New York, NY 10006, USA

477 Williamstown Road, Port Melbourne, VIC 3207, Australia

314–321, 3rd Floor, Plot 3, Splendor Forum, Jasola District Centre, New Delhi – 110025, India

103 Penang Road, #05–06/07, Visioncrest Commercial, Singapore 238467

Cambridge University Press is part of Cambridge University Press & Assessment, a department of the University of Cambridge.

We share the University's mission to contribute to society through the pursuit of education, learning and research at the highest international levels of excellence.

www.cambridge.org
Information on this title: www.cambridge.org/9781009096270

DOI: 10.1017/9781009093989

© Jonathan Lazar, Casey Fiesler, Brian Wentz, and Raja Kushalnagar 2026

This publication is in copyright. Subject to statutory exception and to the provisions of relevant collective licensing agreements, no reproduction of any part may take place without the written permission of Cambridge University Press & Assessment.

When citing this work, please include a reference to the DOI 10.1017/9781009093989

First published 2026

Cover image: cnythzl/DigitalVision Vectors via Getty Images

A catalogue record for this publication is available from the British Library

Library of Congress Cataloging-in-Publication Data
NAMES: Lazar, Jonathan, author.
TITLE: Human-computer interaction and U.S. law / Jonathan Lazar, University of Maryland, College Park; Casey Fiesler, University of Colorado Boulder; Brian Wentz, Shippensburg University of Pennsylvania; Raja Kushalnagar, Gallaudet University, Washington DC; Lorrie Cranor, Carnegie Mellon University, Pennsylvania.
OTHER TITLES: Human-computer interaction and US law
DESCRIPTION: Cambridge, United Kigndom ; New York, NY : Cambridge University Press, 2026. | Includes bibliographical references and index.
IDENTIFIERS: LCCN 2025025425 (print) | LCCN 2025025426 (ebook) | ISBN 9781009098458 (hardback) | ISBN 9781009093989 (ebook)
SUBJECTS: LCSH: Computers – Law and legislation – United States. | Computer networks – Law and legislation – United States. | Intellectual property – United States. | Artificial Intelligence – Law and legislation – United States. | Human-computer interaction – United States.
CLASSIFICATION: LCC KF390.5.C6 H86 2026 (print) | LCC KF390.5.C6 (ebook) | DDC 343.7309/99–dc23/eng/20250524
LC record available at https://lccn.loc.gov/2025025425
LC ebook record available at https://lccn.loc.gov/2025025426

ISBN 978-1-009-09845-8 Hardback
ISBN 978-1-009-09627-0 Paperback

Cambridge University Press & Assessment has no responsibility for the persistence or accuracy of URLs for external or third-party internet websites referred to in this publication and does not guarantee that any content on such websites is, or will remain, accurate or appropriate.

For EU product safety concerns, contact us at Calle de José Abascal, 56, 1°, 28003 Madrid, Spain, or email eugpsr@cambridge.org

Contents

Foreword by Lorrie Cranor		*page* xi
Preface		xv
Table of Cases		xix

1 Introduction to Law for Human–Computer Interaction 1
  1.1 History of the U.S. Legal Structure 1
  1.2 Statutes and Judicial Precedent 3
  1.3 Constitutional versus Statutory versus Administrative Law 4
  1.4 Federal versus State Law 8
  1.5 U.S. Court System 8
  1.6 The Appellate Process 9
  1.7 U.S. Circuits and Their Impact on U.S. Law 11
  1.8 Substantive versus Procedural Criminal Law 13
  1.9 Executive Orders in the U.S. 14
  1.10 Sovereign Immunity and U.S. Law 14
  1.11 Understanding Court Opinions and Case and Statutory Citations 15
  1.12 How to Find Legal Sources 17
  1.13 Applying U.S. Legal Basics to HCI Research 19

2 Introduction to Human–Computer Interaction for Law 21
  2.1 Definition and Origin of HCI 21
  2.2 Research and HCI 28
  2.3 Practical Intersection between HCI, Law, and Policy 29

3 Accessibility 31
  3.1 Introduction 31
  3.2 What Is Digital Accessibility in HCI? 35
  3.3 Understanding the Core Legal Theories Underpinning Digital Accessibility Law in the U.S. 40
  3.4 Sources of Legal Rules 44

	3.5	What Legal Procedures or Remedies Are Specific to Accessibility?	64
	3.6	Legally Speaking: What Is Clear, What Is Still Ambiguous, and What Often Causes Confusion?	65
	3.7	Future Legal Questions	65
	3.8	HCI Work Areas That Could Help Support the Legal Side, and Vice Versa	69
	3.9	Summary	70
4	**Privacy**		71
	4.1	Introduction	71
	4.2	Evolution	74
	4.3	Privacy from HCI Point of View	76
	4.4	Privacy from a Legal Point of View	82
	4.5	Sources of Legal Rules	87
	4.6	State Laws	97
	4.7	International Laws	102
	4.8	Privacy Laws from an HCI Perspective	103
	4.9	Legal Procedures or Remedies Unique to Privacy	106
	4.10	What Are the Legal Questions That May Be Decided in the Future?	108
	4.11	What Are the HCI Work Areas That Could Help Support the Legal Side, and Vice Versa?	109
5	**Human Subjects Research Regulation**		111
	5.1	Introduction	111
	5.2	What Is Human Subjects Research in HCI?	111
	5.3	Background and Sources of Legal Rules	114
	5.4	Regulatory Challenges for HCI Research	128
	5.5	Critiques and Opportunities	133
	5.6	Conclusion	135
6	**Intellectual Property**		136
	6.1	Introduction	136
	6.2	Sources of Legal Rules	138
	6.3	Patent	140
	6.4	Copyright	147
	6.5	Trademark	163
	6.6	Conclusion	171
7	**Telecommunications**		173
	7.1	Introduction	173
	7.2	The Intersection of HCI with Telecommunications Law	174
	7.3	Telecommunications Law Is National, but HCI Is Global	176

	7.4	U.S. Telecommunications Statutes and Regulations	178
	7.5	The Federal Communications Commission	188
	7.6	Net Neutrality	188
	7.7	International Telecommunications Policy and Standards	191
	7.8	World Wide Web Consortium	192
	7.9	Legal Aspects Unique to U.S. Telecommunications Law	193
	7.10	Future Legal Questions	196
8	**Artificial Intelligence**	198
	8.1	Introduction	198
	8.2	Deepfakes	201
	8.3	Bias and Discrimination	204
	8.4	Generative AI and Intellectual Property	207
	8.5	What's Next?	211
9	**Dark Patterns**	212
	9.1	Introduction	212
	9.2	Types of Dark Patterns	213
	9.3	Legal Rules for Dark Patterns	216
	9.4	What Are the Next Steps?	229
10	**Voting Interfaces and U.S. Law**	230
	10.1	Introduction	230
	10.2	Legal History of Voting Procedures and Mechanisms	233
	10.3	Current Legal Requirements	241
	10.4	How Can the HCI Community Contribute to This Discussion?	247
	10.5	Summary	248
11	**International Laws, Treaties, and HCI**	249
	11.1	What Is an International Treaty?	249
	11.2	U.S. Adoption of International Treaties	250
	11.3	Ratification and the Impact on Binding National Law	250
	11.4	The Impact of International Treaties on HCI	251
	11.5	International Laws That Impact HCI in the U.S.	258
	11.6	Technology and Indirect International Impact	260

Index 263

Foreword

As an industry researcher in the late 1990s with a doctorate in engineering and public policy, I worked on some of the pressing internet policy issues of the time, including online privacy and ways to protect children online without trampling on the rights of adults. I repeatedly encountered thorny issues related to the law and human–computer interaction (HCI). I worked collaboratively with lawyers and HCI experts and did my best to learn from them. By the time I joined the computer science faculty at Carnegie Mellon University (CMU) in 2003, I positioned my research squarely in the newly evolving multidisciplinary area of usable privacy and security: a nice mix of security, privacy, HCI, and design, with a dollop of law and public policy. From my early career through the present, I've frequently navigated law and HCI issues in tandem, and thus, I appreciate the urgent need for this book.

I've done a lot of research related to privacy "nutrition labels" in various forms and for a variety of applications, including websites, mobile apps, and IoT devices. I've worked on systems for using machine-readable metadata to create privacy labels, and I've researched how to present labels to end users most effectively. Privacy labels can be thought of as legal commitments, the user-facing abbreviated version of the corporate privacy policy (see Chapter 4). In my work on a machine-readable privacy standard called P3P, I was regularly involved in discussions with both corporate and public interest lawyers about the nuances of the words used in the standard, for example, the use of the word "may" to signal that a data practice was permittable but might not actually take place. I argued to French data protection officials who did not want the standard to allow for the disclosure of practices prohibited under French law that such disclosures were important so that automated tools would be able to detect them and alert French users or potentially even block noncompliant websites in France. I learned that in the absence of strong U.S. privacy laws, the U.S. Federal Trade Commission (FTC) had successfully interpreted its authority as including privacy enforcement when violations could be considered a form of fraudulent or deceptive practice. My subsequent research with CMU colleagues on automating the analysis of natural language privacy policies benefited tremendously from collaborations with lawyers, including the late Joel Reidenberg, a law professor who had a deep appreciation for the ways that technology and design work together with law to govern information policy.

I often encounter poor privacy-related user interfaces that likely came to exist due to misguided efforts to comply with the law. Cookie banners are an all-too-prevalent example of this. I have reached out to several nonprofit organizations that do not appear to be monetizing their website visitors' data to ask them why their sites sport annoying pop-up banners that offer no choices but require visitors to acknowledge their use of cookies for unspecified purposes. The organizations' responses confirm their web designers were attempting to comply with laws they did not fully understand and had mostly just copied bad banner designs from other websites that also likely didn't understand the legal situation (they should have read Chapter 1). More troubling, I have seen similar banners from large corporations that presumably have lawyers on staff, but perhaps their lawyers and their web designers are not in communication. (I am not a lawyer, but I am not aware of a law that would require websites to obtain a vague acknowledgment of their use of cookies without offering visitors a choice.) On the positive side, I have seen an improvement in cookie banners over time, perhaps in part due to guidance from European regulators that has become increasingly specific, for example, making clear that it needs to be as easy to reject cookies as it is to accept them. This is a case where law and policy experts would benefit from talking with HCI experts more to find ways to comply with the law and protect privacy without negative usability consequences (or they could read Chapter 2).

In 2016, I spent a year at the FTC in the role of chief technologist and got to see firsthand how FTC staff think about HCI issues in their enforcement actions. First, it is important to note that the FTC staff is largely made up of attorneys: There are only a small number of technologists and even fewer people with HCI expertise on staff. The staff does include some economics researchers, some of whom have a behavioral economics background that is sometimes relevant to the HCI issues that play a role in the FTC's regulations. The FTC hires consultants from time to time, including HCI and design consultants who have provided insights into HCI issues in their cases. While I was there, I observed multiple instances of complaints against companies for websites that allegedly mislead users into agreeing to terms against their interests, sometimes related to privacy. These sorts of interfaces have more recently come to be referred to as "dark patterns" or "deceptive patterns" (see Chapter 9). When the FTC staff looked into these complaints, they would consider whether a case could be made that a website user would reasonably expect something other than the website's actual practices based on the information it had presented to visitors. The staff would get opinions from experts and could potentially commission a user study. The FTC cases are usually settled before they end up in court, and settlement agreements in these sorts of cases frequently include terms requiring companies to change the language in their user interfaces so as to eliminate any deception. However, I observed that the settlement terms were sometimes vague, with no metrics for assessing whether the revised interfaces had succeeded in eliminating deception. After my year at the FTC concluded and I returned to CMU, I focused some of my research on developing ways of measuring usability issues associated with privacy choice interfaces, including the extent to which they include deceptive patterns.

Even when I am not directly examining law-related issues, as a researcher conducting human subjects research studies, I run into legal issues all the time and I have become a frequent visitor to the office of my university's general counsel. In one of our early research studies at CMU, my students created a fake phishing website with a domain name similar to a major brand so that they could observe study participants' susceptibility to simulated phishing attacks in our lab. After lawyers for the brand reached out to university lawyers to discuss potential intellectual property violations (see Chapter 6), I had to find a way to achieve our research goals that would not trigger legal issues. In this case, since we were doing the entire study in our lab, we did not need to expose our fake domain to the public Internet. Once the fake website existed only in the physical confines of our lab, we were able to proceed with our research.

A few years later my students proposed a study of web browser certificate warnings in which they wanted to expose lab study participants to warnings when they visited the website of a major bank. The students planned to trigger the warning by performing what is known as a "man-in-the-middle" attack, which would intercept communications between the lab computer used in the study and the bank. The university lawyers would not let us proceed with the project, as they were concerned that this could violate wiretap laws (see Chapter 7). My students and I got up to speed on wiretap laws, thought through study details, and eventually came up with a way to trigger the warnings without actually performing an attack.

More recently, university lawyers raised concerns about my lab's use of an international crowd working platform to recruit participants in Europe and the UK for an online user study. Their concerns stemmed from a careful reading of the platform's terms of use, which they argued could put the university at risk under the European General Data Protection Regulation laws when conducting research using this platform (see Chapter 5). Once again, I had to familiarize myself with the relevant laws to help find a path forward.

Throughout my career, I have experienced in multiple contexts the need for HCI practitioners and researchers to be familiar with the law and for lawyers to be familiar with HCI. This dual understanding is needed to produce products that are both legally compliant and usable, to conduct HCI research without taking on unnecessary legal risk, or to propose or enforce policies where human factors play a role. While lawyers and HCI practitioners will ideally work together to address these issues, it is helpful for all involved to have some background on both sides. That is what this book provides.

This book is authored by four leading experts in HCI and law, all of whom have a rare combination of both technical PhDs and law degrees. These authors speak the language of lawyers as well as of HCI practitioners and researchers. Together, they have written a timely and important book that will fill a critical gap for those of us who have been educated in either HCI or the law but need to understand both.

Lorrie Cranor, Bosch Distinguished Professor and
FORE Systems University Professor, Carnegie Mellon University

Preface

If you search for the phrase "human–computer interaction and U.S. law" using a search engine, the AI-generated response is "There isn't much information about human-computer interaction (HCI) and U.S. law, but here's some information about HCI and standards." Even a generative AI response makes note of the lack of information about the intersection of HCI and U.S. law. Efforts in the recent past to connect the broader computing community and the legal community (such as the ACM Symposium on Computer Science and Law) are often missing any representation from or topics within the HCI community. Our goal is to fill that gap, providing information about the various intersections of HCI and U.S. law.

Practitioners and researchers within HCI often face legal issues related to their HCI work. For instance, there are legal requirements for making websites and technologies accessible for people with disabilities, questions related to the intellectual property of interface designs, and requirements related to the privacy of user data. Yet outside of more commonly discussed areas, very little has been published in the HCI literature about the intersections of law and HCI. Conversely, U.S. legal practitioners and researchers often find it challenging to understand HCI and apply it to legal situations. Part of this stems from the fact that HCI itself is at the intersection of computer science, psychology, sociology, and design, and draws upon all of them. One of the most eloquent calls for more examination of the intersection of HCI and law comes from Judge David Hamilton in a recent 7th circuit case, *Domer v. Menard, Inc.* (116 F.4th 686, 703 (7th Cir. 2024)). In his concurrence with the majority opinion, Judge Hamilton writes:

> *Start from the intuition that there is something odd about judges looking at online user interfaces with magnifying glasses and debating font color and size and the placement of hyperlinks ... Because user-interface design is technical and empirically testable, it should be possible for judges or juries to evaluate evidence as to whether or not real-life consumers are on fair notice that they have agreed to a long list of legal terms every time they complete a purchase online or download a new application on their devices. At heart, the way a reasonable consumer responds to a particular user interface is a factual issue. A plaintiff willing to present the necessary*

> evidence may be able to show genuine disputes of material fact that can then be tried before a jury ... If businesses like Menards invest in designing their user interfaces "to influence the behavior of real consumers," courts should not allow them to enforce hidden contract terms with arguments that "assume consumer behavior in idealized markets with 'perfect information, perfect competition, and no transactions costs.'" ... These empirical studies on consumer behavior in response to a particular user interface are exactly the type of evidence an expert could present to a jury to show that a consumer did or did not have notice of the terms and conditions found on a digital website. The evidence might show, for example, that the interface has been designed to distract or mislead the consumer, or at least to manipulate the consumer into proceeding without bothering to look at the terms of the contract of adhesion ... As Justice Kagan said recently, "we're a court. We really don't know about these things. You know, these are not like the nine greatest experts on the internet." Transcript of Oral Argument at 45–46, Gonzalez v. Google, 598 U.S. 617 (2023). The same is true of the judiciary as a whole. More specific to this case, judges are not experts in the highly specialized and technical fields of user-interface design and human-computer interaction. I suspect few judges know much about the fields beyond our experience as consumers. Rather than debating among ourselves our impressions about font size and color, the placement of hyperlinks, and the choice between click-wrap and browse-wrap agreements, we should start treating these issues about user-interface design as questions of fact. We should invite sufficiently motivated parties to test alternative designs and to conduct discovery into merchants' actual design choices.

It would be hard to find a stronger statement from a judge for the importance of examining the intersection of HCI and law, and we thank Judge Hamilton for this recognition.

Three of the coauthors of this book proposal taught an innovative course at the CHI (Computer–Human Interaction) 2019 conference in Glasgow, Scotland, related to the intersections of HCI and Law, which was well attended and received high evaluation scores. After the conference, Lauren Cowles, an editor at Cambridge University Press, reached out to us and asked whether we might be interested in doing a book on this topic. There is clearly a need for more published work and discussion at the intersection of HCI and law, so we eagerly said yes and began a journey together. We are a unique authoring team, as all four coauthors of the book have earned both doctorates focusing on HCI, and also some form of legal degree: Jonathan Lazar has an LLM from the University of Pennsylvania Law School, Casey Fiesler has a JD from Vanderbilt Law School, Raja Kushalnagar has an LLM from the University of Houston and a JD from Texas Southern University, and Brian Wentz has an MSL from Pennsylvania Western University. The Author team has a diverse set of legal experiences, including serving on federal agency advisory committees, serving as an expert witness in litigation, authoring law review articles, teaching legal research methods for non-law students, and drafting bill text for legislation.

It's important to start with a common question: Why a book only on U.S. law? Like many research communities in STEM, the HCI community (and its twin practitioner community, often called user experience) is an international community. While language and culture have a great influence on HCI, you would not find many differences between the type of HCI research taking place in the U.S., Canada, the United Kingdom, and Australia. Yet the laws in each one of these countries are completely different. And even within a single country ... the laws in the Canadian province of Ontario are vastly different from the laws within the Canadian province of Quebec. So, while much HCI work easily transfers across international borders, the legal framework for each HCI topic is inherently specific to jurisdictional borders. And those legal requirements impact the interfaces, for instance, in terms of requirements for privacy and accessibility. It wouldn't be possible to write a book about "HCI and Law" and cover the laws of every country, as well as every province and state within that country, unless we wanted to talk about overall legal theories and concepts but not actually discuss specific legal rules that apply in a specific situation. Our book focuses only on HCI and U.S. law. We hope that in the future, those with expertise in both HCI and law in other countries write similar books exploring the legal frameworks for HCI topics in their countries. In writing this book, our approach has been to try and serve both the HCI and legal communities. Our first two chapters are "boot camp introductions" – a grounding in the basics of HCI designed for lawyers, and a grounding in the basics of law designed for those working in HCI. We acknowledge that it would be impossible to give a comprehensive introduction to each topic in only one chapter, but we've tried our best to provide sufficient information for the remaining topical chapters to be useful to both sets of readers. And we hope that over time, the number of people who have a background in both HCI and law will continue to grow.

As an author team, we want to acknowledge the encouragement, support, and ongoing enthusiasm from Lauren Cowles at Cambridge University Press. This book would not have come to fruition without her efforts. We also want to acknowledge the administrative work of Arman Chowdhury at Cambridge University Press. We greatly appreciate the reviewers who gave generously of their time to provide feedback on earlier versions of chapter drafts: Amy Bruckman, Sai Shruti Chivukula, Lorrie Cranor, Josh Dehlinger, David Ferleger, Juan Gilbert, Harry Hochheiser, Paul Jaeger, J. Bern Jordan, Clayton Lewis, Kathy McCoy, Whitney Quesenbury, Blake Reid, Annie Ross, Katie Shilton, Abigail Stangl, Andy Stefik, Michael Stein, Kathryn Summers, Christian Vogler, and Michael Zimmer. The book is greatly enhanced because of your shared wisdom. The authors also want to thank Shaun Kane, who originally introduced Jonathan Lazar and Casey Fiesler somewhere in the mid 2010s, noting that both were interested in legal topics, and that we probably could find something cool to collaborate on (Shaun, you were right!). And the authors want to thank all of our various mentors in the HCI and legal communities, who often encouraged us to be different and be creative and expand our impact by studying both topics.

Finally, we want to note that while everything in the book is technically and legally accurate at press time, both the technical topics and the legal topics change rapidly. As an example, whether "net neutrality" was the prevailing legal rule nationally changed multiple times since we first taught the course at the CHI 2019 conference! By the time that you are reading this book, it's likely that there's a new statute, regulation, or court ruling that may modify the legal framework on one of these topics, or a new technology that may render some of what we said as being dated (this is especially true of AI). That's the nature of working on a book at the intersection of two fast-moving fields. As authors, we hope that you enjoy reading the book, that you find it useful, and that it helps expand your horizons and you become as passionate about the intersections of HCI and law, as we are.

Table of Cases

A&M Records, Inc. v. Napster, Inc., 239 F.3d 1004 (9th. Cir., 2001), 150, 160
Alice Corp. v. CLS Bank International, 573 U.S. 208 (2014), 143
Allen v. Milligan, 599 U. S. 1 (2023), 234
Am. Ass'n of People with Disabilities v. Harris, 647 F.3d 1093 (11th Cir. 2011), 242
Andersen v. Stability AI Ltd., 3:23-cv-00201, (N.D. Cal.); (2023, December 1), 150, 208
Apple Computer, Inc. v. Microsoft Corporation, 35 F.3d 1435 (9th Cir. 1994), 159
Apple Inc. v. Samsung Electronics Co., 580 U.S. 53 (2016), 144, 170
Apple Inc. v. Samsung Electronics Co., Ltd., 786 F.3d 983 (Fed. Cir. 2015), 167
Attorney General v. Google LLC and YouTube, LLC, Case No. 1:19-cv-02642 (D.D.C. 2019), 104
Auer v. Robbins, 519 U.S. 452 (1997), 7
Authors Guild v. OpenAI Inc., 1:23-cv-08292, (S.D.N.Y.); (2023, September 21), 150, 208
Baker v. Selden, 101 U.S. 99 (1879), 148
Bilski, 561 U.S. 593 (2010), 143
Braun v. HHS, 983 F.3d 1295 (Fed. Cir. 2021), 122
Bush v. Gore, 531 U.S. 98 (2000), 237
Carparts Distribution Ctr., Inc. v. Auto. Wholesaler's Ass'n of New England, Inc., 37 F.3d 12 (1st Cir. 1994), 42
Carpenter v. United States, 585 U.S. 296 (2018), 181
Cetacean Community v. Bush, 386 F.3d 1169 (9th Cir. 2004), 207
Chevron U.S.A., Inc. v. Natural Resources Defense Council, Inc., 467 U.S. 837 (1984), 6
Chicago Mercantile Exchange v. Deaktor, 410 U.S. 113, 93 S.Ct. 705, 35 L.Ed. 2d 147 (1973), 16
DDR Holdings, LLC v. Hotels.com, L.P., 773 F.3d 1245 (Fed. Cir. 2014), 143
Diamond v. Diehr, 450 U.S. 175 (1981), 142
Digital Equip. Corp. v. Altavista Tech., Inc., 960 F. Supp. 456 (D. Mass. 1997), 169

Dobbs v. Jackson Women's Health Org., 597 U.S. 215, 142 S. Ct. 2228, 213 L. Ed. 2d 545 (2022), 4, 8, 75, 87
Doe v. Internet Brands, Inc., 824 F.3d 846 (9th Cir. 2016), 185
Domer v. Menard, Inc., 116 F.4th 686, 703 (7th Cir. 2024), xv
Domer v. Menard, Inc., 116 F.4th 686, 706–07 (7th Cir. 2024), 218
Dominguez v. Banana Republic, LLC, No. 1:19-CV-10171-GHW, 2020 WL, 68
Domino's Pizza, LLC v. Robles, 140 S. Ct. 122 (2019), 57
Eisenstadt v. Baird, 405 U.S. 438 (1972), 74
Eldred v. Ashcroft, 537 U.S. 186, 151, 155
Elliott v. Google (9th Cir. 2017), 166
Enfish LLC v. Microsoft Corp., 822 F.3d 1327 (Fed. Cir. 2016), 144
Fair Housing Council of San Fernando Valley v. Roommates.com, LLC, 521 F.3d 1157 (9th Cir. 2008), 185
Fed. Trade Comm'n v. Amazon.com, Inc., No. 2:23-CV-00932-JHC, 2024 WL 2723812 (W.D. Wash. May 28, 2024), 217, 218
Fed. Trade Comm'n v. Amazon.com, Inc., No. 2:23-CV-00932-JHC, 2024 WL 2723812 (W.D. Wash. Aug. 1, 2024), 217, 218
Federal Radio Commission v. Nelson Brothers Bond & Mortgage Co., 289 U.S. 266 (1933), 178
Federal Trade Commission v. Facebook, Inc., Case No. 1:19-cv-02184 (D.D.C. 2019), 104
Folsom v. Marsh, 9 F. Cas. 342 (C.C.D. Mass. 1841), 149, 150
Fry v. Napoleon Cmty. Sch., 137 S. Ct. 743, 197 L. Ed. 2d 46 (2017), 61
Getty Images (US), Inc. v. Stability AI, Inc., 1:23-cv-00135, (D. Del.); (2023, February 7), 150, 208
Gil v. Winn-Dixie Stores, Inc., 21 F.4d 775, 776 (11th Cir. 2021), 56
Gil v. Winn-Dixie Stores, Inc., 257 F. Supp. 3d 1340 (S.D. Fla. 2017), 55, 56
Gonzalez v. Google, 598 U.S. 617 (2023), xvi
Google v. Oracle, 593 U.S. 1 (2021), 150
Griswold v. Connecticut, 381 U.S. 479 (1965), 71, 74, 85, 86
Gucci Am., Inc. v. Hall & Assocs., 135 F. Supp. 2d 409, 413 (S.D.N.Y. 2001), 186
Hidalgo-Semlek v. Hansa Med., Inc., 498 F. Supp. 3d 236 (D.N.H. 2020), 122
Hindel v. Husted, 875 F.3d 344 (6th Cir. 2017), 245
Katz v. United States, 389 U.S. 347 (1967), 74, 86
Keyishian v. Board of Regents, 385 U.S. 589 (1967), 134
Lawrence v. Texas, 539 U.S. 558 (2003), 75
Loper Bright Enterprises v. Raimondo, 603 U.S. 369, 144 S. Ct. 2244 (2024), 6, 7, 44, 189
Lotus Development Corp. v. Borland International, Inc., 516 U.S. 233 (1996), 160
McClure v. Youth and Family Services of Solano County, No. C 14–5629 MMC (N.D. Cal. Apr. 24, 2015), 120
Medellin v. Texas, 552 U.S. 491 (2008), 250

Meyer v. Nebraska, 262 U.S. 390 (1923), 85
MGM Studios v. Grokster, 545 U.S. 913 (2005), 161
Microsoft Corp. v. Lindows.com, Inc., 319 F. Supp. 2d 1219 (W.D. Wash. 2004), 169
Missert v. Trustees of Boston Univ., 73 F. Supp. 2d 68 (D. Mass. 1999), 122
Mohamed v. Palestinian Authority, 566 U.S. 449 (2012), 208
Moore v. Harper, 600 U. S. 1 (2023), 234
Multi Time Machine, Inc. v. Amazon.com, Inc., 804 F.3d 930 (9th Cir. 2015), 169
Naruto v. Slater, 888 F.3d 418 (9th Cir. 2018), 207
Nat'l Ass'n of the Deaf v. Netflix, Inc., 869 F. Supp. 2d 196 (D. Mass. 2012), 42
Nat'l Fed'n of the Blind of Alabama v. Allen, No. 2:22-CV-721-CLM, 2023 WL 2533049 (N.D. Ala. Mar. 15, 2023), 246
Nat'l Fed'n of the Blind v. Target Corp., 582 F. Supp. 2d 1185 (N.D. Cal. 2007), 16
Nat'l Fed'n of the Blind v. Lamone, 813 F.3d 494 (4th Cir. 2016), 245
National Broadcasting Co. v. United States, 319 U.S. 190 (1943), 179
National Federation of the Blind v. Target, Corp., 452 F. Supp. 2d 946 (N.D. Cal. 2006), 55
NetChoice, LLC v. Bonta, 113 F.4th 1101, 1123 (9th Cir. 2024), 222
New v. Lucky Brand Jeans (Apr. 10, 2014), 6, 43, 44
The New York Times Company v. Microsoft Corporation, 1:23-cv-11195, (S.D.N.Y.), 209
Nintendo of America Inc. v. Lewis Galoob Toys, Inc., 964 F.2d 965 (9th Cir. 1992), 159
Ohio Telecom Ass'n v. FCC, No. 24–3449 (6th Cir. 2025), 190
Orozco v. Garland, 60 F.4th 684 (D.C. Cir. 2023), 47
Panavision International L.P. v. Toeppen, 141 F.3d 1316 (9th Cir.1998), 169
People of the State of NY v. Sirius XM Radio Inc. (2023), 213, 218
Perfect 10 v. Google, 508 F.3d 1146 (2007), 150
Pierce v. Society of Sisters, 268 U.S. 510 (1925), 85
Red Lion Broadcasting Co. v. FCC, 395 U.S. 367 (1969), 180
Reinoehl v. Ctrs. for Disease Control & Prevention, No. 22–1401 (7th Cir. Oct. 25, 2022), 120
Rendon v. Valleycrest Prods., Ltd., 294 F.3d 1279 (11th Cir. 2002), 41, 42
Reno v. American Civil Liberties Union, 521 U.S. 844 (1997), 183
Riley v. California, 573 U.S. 373 (2014), 86
Robles v. Domino's Pizza, LLC, 913 F.3d 898, 907 (9th Cir. 2019), 57
Robles v. Domino's Pizza LLC, No. CV 16–6599 JGB (EX), 2021 WL 2945562 (C.D. Cal. June 23, 2021), 36, 57
Robles v. Domino's Pizza LLC, No. CV 16–06599 SJO (SPx), 2017 WL 1330216, at *1 (C.D. Cal. Mar. 20, 2017), 55, 56
Roe v. Wade, 410 U.S. 113 (1973), 75, 86
Seagull v. WinRed, Inc., No. X07HHDCV226154527S, 2023 WL 4322714, at *4 (Conn. Super. Ct. June 28, 2023), 218

Sega Enterprises Ltd. v. Accolade, Inc., 977 F.2d 1510 (9th Cir. 1992), 159
Skidmore v. Swift & Co., 323 U.S. 134 (1944), 7
Smith v. Maryland, 442 U.S. 735 (1979), 181
Sony v. Universal, 464 U.S. 417 (1984), 150
Tennessee v. FCC, 832 F.3d 597 (6th Cir. 2016), 195
Thaler v. Hirshfeld, 559 F. Supp. 3d 238 (E.D. Va. 2021), 200
Thaler v. Vidal, 42 F.4th 597 (Fed. Cir. 2022), 200
Touma v. Gen. Counsel of the Regents, Case No. SA CV 17–01132-VBF-KS (C.D. Cal. Jul. 6, 2018), 120
Troxel v. Granville, 530 U.S. 57 (2000), 85
Turner Broadcasting System, Inc. v. FCC, 512 U.S. 622 (1994), 179
Ultramercial, LLC v. Hulu, LLC, 772 F.3d 709 (Fed. Cir. 2014), 143
United States v. American Library Association, 539 U.S. 194 (2003), 91
United States v. Harriss, 347 U.S. 612 (1954), 85
United States v. Miller, 425 U.S. 435 (1976), 181
United States v. Rumely, 345 U.S. 41, 47 (1953), 85
United States v. Southwestern Cable Co., 392 U.S. 157 (1968), 179
United States v. Warshak, 631 F.3d 266 (6th Cir. 2010), 181
U.S. v. Brandt, 196 F.2d 653 (2d Cir. 1952), 114
Viacom International Inc. v. YouTube, Inc., 676 F.3d 19 (2d Cir. 2012), 186
Whitlock v. Duke University, 637 F. Supp. 1463 (M.D.N.C. 1986), 120
WinRed, Inc. v. Ellison, 59 F.4th 934, 936 (8th Cir. 2023), 218
Zeran v. America Online, Inc., 129 F.3d 327 (4th Cir. 1997), 184, 185
Zurcher v. Stanford Daily, 436 U.S. 547 (1978), 93

1

Introduction to Law for Human–Computer Interaction

Human–computer interaction (HCI) and User Experience (UX) professionals can benefit from having a basic understanding of law and the legal system in the United States. Technology design significantly impacts many areas of life and work, sometimes requiring regulation and other times indirectly or more directly influencing laws and policies. Technology itself can also be designed and used to implement or enforce regulations and policies. Laws can impose requirements on some areas of technology design. For example, in design areas where user data and privacy might be involved, legal compliance and regulation can easily become a necessity. Design that impacts the securing of user information, design of health-related systems, and design of systems that interact with government services all illustrate the value that HCI and UX professionals can find in understanding U.S. law. This chapter will cover the history of U.S. law, the basic constructs of the U.S. legal system, the differences between law and policy at the federal versus state level, the use of legal resources, and how to apply basic legal principles to HCI research. It should be noted that new executive branch leadership, changes in court opinions, and new or revised legislation can have a significant impact on the legal topics discussed in this chapter.

1.1 HISTORY OF THE U.S. LEGAL STRUCTURE

The U.S. legal structure was heavily influenced by the backgrounds of the immigrants who made up the early English and European colonial population in the U.S., combined with the factors that motivated the original states to break away from England.[1] The Declaration of Independence was predicated by a restriction of freedoms and compounded by a desire to protect what were considered to be "natural" human rights, which are rooted in the philosophies of those such as John Locke, St. Thomas Aquinas, and many before them.[2] The idea of

---

[1] Friedman, L. M. (2019). *A History of American Law* (4th ed.). Oxford University Press, pp. 1–73.
[2] Kaplan, D. S. (2015). *An Introduction to the American Legal System, Government, and Constitutional Law*. Aspen, p. 3.

natural rights acquired by birth actually comes from a framework of natural law that, ironically, would have also influenced the legal system of England. The emergence of a new government and therefore formalized U.S. law was also influenced by the idea of "federalism," where there exists a national (or federal) level of government as well as a state level of government in the U.S., carrying with that structure a certain amount of state government power and independence from the federal government in certain matters.[3] Similar tensions and struggles between state power and federal power that were present at the time of the original creation of the U.S. Constitution are still present today. The structure of the U.S. government in its conception also has significantly dictated the structure of U.S. law. A core aspect of that structure is the separation of powers through the executive (U.S. president and executive agencies), judicial (federal court system), and legislative (Congress) branches of government.[4] As such, the U.S. Constitution established the basis for legislative power for creating laws, the executive power to veto legislation and enforce laws, and the judicial power afforded by the creation of the U.S. Supreme Court and lower federal courts. This government design was intended to balance out the power of the U.S. federal government.[5]

1.1.1 Basis for U.S. Law

Civil law is law that is based primarily on laws that have been codified through enacted legislation, while common law is derived primarily from prior judicial rulings and precedent.[6] Many legal traditions and inherent assumptions on legal basics come from common law tradition and precedent that has evolved over almost 1,000 years, dating back to the early royal judges in England. By the time of the Declaration of Independence, the traditions of English common law were well established in various forms throughout the North American colonies.[7] While this resulted in a legal tradition that in general is common law, there are a number of aspects of U.S. law that have been codified through constitutions, statutes, international treaties, court rules, and the regulations from administrative agencies at both the federal and state levels.[8]

---

[3] Friedman, L. M. (2019). *A History of American Law* (4th ed.). Oxford University Press, pp. 99–102.
[4] Currier, K. A., Eimermann, T. E., & Campbell, M. S. (2020). *The Study of Law: A Critical Thinking Approach*. Wolters Kluwer, p. 29.
[5] Burnham, B. (2016). *Introduction to the Law and Legal System of the United States*. West, pp. 9–19.
[6] Ibid., pp. 42–43.
[7] Friedman, L. M. (2019). *A History of American Law* (4th ed.). Oxford University Press, pp. 77–85.
[8] Rosen, D., Aronson, B., Litt, D. G., McAlinn, G. P., & Stern, J. P. (2017). *Introduction to American Law* (3rd ed.). Caroline Academic Press, p. 4.

1.1.2 *The U.S. "Adversarial" System of Law*

At the international level, many countries follow an "inquisitorial" system of law, which means that the judge can ask questions and call witnesses, rather than the attorneys.[9] In the U.S., there is an "adversarial" system of law which has as one of its hallmarks a neutral decision-making party to passively decide the case and two opposing parties who present arguments and evidence, with equal opportunity to argue their case before the passive party, which would be the judge and sometimes a jury.[10] It is believed to be essential that the primary decision-maker (judge) does not actively gather evidence and engage in the arguments but rather has a more passive role in evaluating the evidence. This type of legal structure is considered to be "adversarial" because there is an opposing clash of conflicting arguments and evidence by both sides of the case (plaintiff and defendant). A jury is a common component of the adversarial system because it is another passive component (like the judge) without prior knowledge of the facts and not actively engaged in the investigation or questioning process.[11] For criminal cases where the criminal charge has a potential for incarceration for six months or longer, the Seventh Amendment to the U.S. Constitution provides a right to a trial by jury.[12] For lesser crimes, a trial by jury is not required; however, some states (e.g., Virginia) provide the right to a trial by jury in all cases – with the caveat that the plaintiff has to pay for the costs if they lose the case.[13] Many juvenile courts (e.g., Illinois) view nonviolent juvenile cases as civil rather than criminal, so there is no trial by jury,[14] and the majority of civil cases do not have trials by jury.[15]

1.2 STATUTES AND JUDICIAL PRECEDENT

At the federal level, the U.S. Congress creates and enacts a statute (law), and the courts are left to interpret the law.[16] There is often vagueness or insufficient details from Congress as to how to interpret what they have enacted. If Congress does not agree with how a law is being interpreted by the courts, it has the option to later revise the law to add clarity to any ambiguity. Over time, as courts interpret laws that have been passed, future court decisions are based on those prior court decisions by applying a particular rule of law when there is similarity between a current case and a prior ruling – this is the concept of judicial precedent, known as *stare*

---

[9] Ibid., pp. 121–122.
[10] Ibid.
[11] Ibid., p. 122.
[12] U.S. Const. amend. VII.
[13] VA Code § 8.01–643.
[14] 102 N.E.3d 149, 161 (Ill. 2017).
[15] Diamond, S. S. & Salerno, J. M. (2020). Reasons for the Disappearing Jury Trial: Perspectives from Attorneys and Judges. *Louisiana Law Review*, 81(1), pp. 120–163.
[16] Burnham, W. (2016). *Introduction to the Law and Legal System of the United States.* West, pp. 40–44.

decisis.[17] *Stare decisis* is considered to be "horizontal" when a court is deferring to its own decisions, while "vertical" *stare decisis* is a court deferring to the decisions from higher courts. This concept of a strict judicial precedent is the approach that holds current legal decisions to unambiguous aspects of past legal decisions, regardless of whether the current court agrees with the prior decision.[18] The contemporary approach of what seems to be a "relaxed" interpretation of judicial precedent allows for flexibility in a judge's decision in that they do consider legal precedent, but they can override precedent if they think that the earlier decision(s) was incorrect.[19] In 2022, the U.S. Supreme Court illustrated that *stare decisis* can quickly disappear in a single court decision.[20]

1.3 CONSTITUTIONAL VERSUS STATUTORY VERSUS ADMINISTRATIVE LAW

The various sources of U.S. law are relevant to a good understanding of how to interpret and apply the law. Constitutions exist at the federal and the state levels across the U.S. The highest source for U.S. law is the Constitution of the United States, and adherence to constitutional content takes precedence over any other law or regulation. In fact, the structure set forth by the U.S. Constitution is what outlines the authority given separately to the federal government and the individual states.[21] The U.S. Constitution also outlines the core protection of individual rights, provides the framework for courts to review laws that might conflict with the Constitution, and creates the U.S. division of government that is separated as the executive, legislative, and judicial branches. Most legal cases do not directly involve constitutional law and instead involve statutory law, administrative law, and questions regarding the resulting regulations.[22] The first ten amendments (the Bill of Rights) that were adopted two years after the U.S. Constitution were considered to be a condition attached to the initial approval of the Constitution, which is why those rights are considered to be so connected to the U.S. Constitution rather than a revision or change of direction.[23]

A very influential level of legal authority is the administrative law level, which refers to the regulations from and administration from federal and state agencies, and because administrative agencies can dictate regulations and rules that directly involve business and everyday life, administrative law can impact HCI and technology. Administrative law finds its source in both federal and state agencies and

---

[17] Burnham, W. (2016). *Introduction to the Law and Legal System of the United States*. West, pp. 70–72.
[18] Ibid.
[19] Ibid., pp. 374–375.
[20] Dobbs v. Jackson Women's Health Org., 597 U.S. 215, 142 S. Ct. 2228, 213 L. Ed. 2d 545 (2022).
[21] Currier, K. A., Eimermann, T. E., & Campbell, M. S. (2020). *The Study of Law: A Critical Thinking Approach*. Wolters Kluwer, pp. 29–64.
[22] Ibid., pp. 44–45.
[23] Rosen, D., Aronson, B., Litt, D. G., McAlinn, G. P., & Stern, J. P. (2017). *Introduction to American Law* (3rd ed.). Caroline Academic Press, pp. 39–40.

1.3 Constitutional versus Statutory versus Administrative Law

orders, and it is often more directed and narrow in focus.[24] At the federal level, there is no specification in the U.S. Constitution that creates these federal administrative agencies, however, they can be created by the three branches of the U.S. government (usually by the legislative branch – U.S. Congress).[25] Administrative law is derived from statutory law (passed by Congress at the federal level or by various state legislative bodies). Congress creates agencies to focus on and specialize in particular aspects of U.S. statutes or areas of government that require expertise, enforcement, review, and service to the public.[26] Some agencies are primarily focused on social welfare or public service (Social Security Administration, Department of Health and Human Services, etc.), while other agencies are primarily designed for regulatory purposes (Federal Trade Commission, Environmental Protection Agency, etc.).[27] The U.S. Congress often delegates its authority to specific federal agencies, not only to oversee and implement statutes but also sometimes to further act under a form of "quasi-legislative authority" to create rules or regulations.[28] One of the many examples of this would be the REAL ID Act as established by Congress following the recommendations of the 9/11 Commission, where the Department of Homeland Security was subsequently expected to create the standards and implement the statute.[29] So, this is where administrative law would begin. The Department of Homeland Security was created in 2002 as a response to U.S. efforts to prevent future terrorism, following the terrorist attacks on September 11, 2001.[30] The Secretary of Homeland Security would issue proposed rules (administrative law) relating to the implementation of the REAL ID Act, and following a required comment period (where public input is requested), a final rule would be published – essentially becoming administrative law.

If a scenario arises where the interpretation or implementation of a U.S. statute through administrative law presents the possibility for misapplying the intent of the statute, the U.S. Supreme Court sometimes ends up hearing cases related to administrative law. It is not uncommon for an administrative regulation to flow from a U.S. statute that contains ambiguity.[31] Judicial deference refers to courts permitting a certain level of independence in how an agency applies a statute. The U.S. Supreme Court has used three levels of deference to administrative agencies regarding such scenarios. Chevron deference has been the highest level since the

---

[24] Currier, K. A., Eimermann, T. E., & Campbell, M. S. (2020). *The Study of Law: A Critical Thinking Approach*. Wolters Kluwer, pp. 37–41.
[25] Ibid., pp. 37–39.
[26] Burnham, W. (2016). *Introduction to the Law and Legal System of the United States*. West, pp. 210–211.
[27] Rosen, D., Aronson, B., Litt, D. G., McAlinn, G. P., & Stern, J. P. (2017). *Introduction to American Law* (3rd ed.). Caroline Academic Press, pp. 449–450.
[28] Ibid., pp. 38–41.
[29] H.R.418, 109th Cong. (2005), www.congress.gov/bill/109th-congress/house-bill/418.
[30] H.R.5005, 107th Cong. (2002), www.congress.gov/bill/107th-congress/house-bill/5005.
[31] Currier, K. A., Eimermann, T. E., & Campbell, M. S. (2020). *The Study of Law: A Critical Thinking Approach*. Wolters Kluwer, pp. 35–37.

1980s (established with *Chevron U.S.A., Inc. v. Natural Resources Defense Council, Inc.*),[32] used for an agency's interpretation of a statute relating to that agency.

However, in June 2024, the U.S. Supreme Court overturned *Chevron* deference, which will have an unpredictable impact on federal agency regulations.[33] In the written decision another legal concept – *stare decisis* – was noted as not being relevant to maintaining the *Chevron* precedent. This change is especially important to laws that relate to technology because of the fast-moving pace of technology and the frequent reliance on an agency's interpretation of existing law. We acknowledge that this change presents unpredictability in many areas of technology law. This is not a minor shift, in that a plethora of regulations and court cases rely on the *Chevron* structure. In Justice Kagan's dissent, she noted that in areas of technical expertise, this will likely create a significant shift, with the courts and legislature now needing to rely on more specific technical expertise in their cases and proposed legislation.

Of all the various components of the legal framework for digital accessibility, the one that relies most heavily on agency interpretation is the legal requirement for web accessibility under Title III (Public accommodations) of the ADA. Unlike Title II of the ADA, or Section 508 of the Rehabilitation Act, or the Air Carrier Access Act, all of which have regulations that specify in detail the requirements for web accessibility, requirements for Title III (public accommodations) of the ADA rely on an agency interpretation. Among other things, the regulations state: "*A public accommodation shall furnish appropriate auxiliary aids and services where necessary to ensure effective communication with individuals with disabilities. This includes an obligation to provide effective communication to companions who are individuals with disabilities.*" However, neither the statute nor the regulations specifically mention websites. Since 1996, the Department of Justice (DOJ) has stated that websites of public accommodations are covered under the "effective communications" requirement of Title III of the ADA, which exists in both the statute and the regulations. Courts have generally (but with some exceptions) deferred to the DOJ interpretation, applying the effective communications requirement to cover all forms of communication, including websites. Sources of reference for this interpretation usually include the initial letter from Assistant Attorney General for Civil Rights Deval Patrick to Sen. Tom Harkin in 1996[34] and the DOJ Statement of Interest in the *New v. Lucky Brand Jeans* case in 2014 explaining the application of the "effective communications" requirement to websites.[35]

---

[32] Loper Bright Enterprises v. Raimondo (2024) 603 U.S. 369, 144 S. Ct. 2244.

[33] Sherman, M. (June 28, 2024). *The Supreme Court weakens federal regulators, overturning decades-old Chevron decision.* https://apnews.com/article/supreme-court-chevron-regulations-environment-5173bc83d3961a7aaabe415ceaf8d665.

[34] Patrick, D. *Letter from Assistant Attorney General for Civil Rights Deval Patrick to Sen. Tom Harkin, United States Department of Justice* (September 9, 1996), www.justice.gov/crt/foia/file/666366/download.

[35] United States Department of Justice, Statement of Interest in the New v. Lucky Brand Jeans (April 10, 2014), www.ada.gov/briefs/lucky_brand%20_soi.docx.

Auer deference is the next level (established with *Auer v. Robbins*),[36] used for an agency's interpretation of its own regulations.[37] The lowest level is Skidmore deference (established with *Skidmore v. Swift & Co.*),[38] which is used for agency opinions, letters, manuals, and other guidelines related to administrative regulations. The concept of these levels of deference to administrative law does not permit violation of constitutional rights, other clear statutes, or interpretations that are arbitrary and capricious.[39]

The administrative rulemaking process is guided by a law established in 1946, called the Administrative Procedure Act (APA),[40] which together with separate mandates from Congress, outlines the procedures for rulemaking, including the requirement for posting notices of proposed rules and publishing the final rules in the *Federal Register*. The APA also addresses standards for the courts to review administrative rules if a person has been incorrectly affected by the actions of an administrative agency. Agency rules can be categorized as being interpretive, which essentially describes how an agency will implement a statute as written by Congress, or legislative, which carries more weight in that an administrative agency will establish their procedures for carrying out a delegated mandate from a statute.[41]

The legislative rules can be further broken down into substantive versus procedural rules. While procedural rules only impact the procedures by which an agency can enforce and implement a mandate, substantive rules are more like actual statutes, in that they can impact the rights of individuals.[42] The APA outlines three approaches to administrative rulemaking: exempted, formal, and informal. Exempted rulemaking is outlined in the APA and applies to things such as rules regarding the military, foreign affairs, or government grants.[43] The formal rulemaking process is the most extensive and longest approach to rulemaking. As such, it is only used when a statute from Congress specifies that the formal process applies.[44] This extensive process follows the APA procedure with a notice to the public (Notice of Proposed Rulemaking or NPRM), a public hearing (mini trial-like hearing), and finally the official rule, based on a decision from an administrative law judge or other official.[45] The informal rulemaking process applies to any rulemaking where the formal or exempt process does not apply. There is still the requirement for an NPRM, typically published in the *Federal Register*, but after a public comment period (now also available online through Regulations.gov), the

---

[36] 519 U.S. 452 (1997).
[37] Loper Bright Enterprises v. Raimondo (2024) 603 U.S. 369, 144 S. Ct. 2244.
[38] 323 U.S. 134 (1944).
[39] 5 U.S.C. §§ 551–559 (1947).
[40] 5 U.S.C. §§ 551–559.
[41] Hall, D. E. *Administrative Law: Bureaucracy in a Democracy* (7th ed.). Pearson, p. 164.
[42] Ibid., pp. 164–165.
[43] Ibid., p. 164.
[44] Ibid., pp. 165–168.
[45] Ibid., pp. 166–167.

administrative agency can then issue its final rule. Administrative law, even after the final rule, is not absolute.[46] Any administrative agency actions can face judicial review, and an individual who believes that an agency's action should be changed or reversed can file a civil case in the matter, and if there is a potential constitutional issue ("question") in play, it could also be reviewed by a federal court. In order for this to happen, it would have to be proved that a "protected" right has been violated, which is the doctrine of "standing" (validating that federal review is available for the matter).[47]

1.4 FEDERAL VERSUS STATE LAW

The U.S. legal system has a layer of complexity because of there being not only the federal legal system but also separate legal systems for each state. The laws of one state can be slightly or dramatically different from the laws of another state. This can change over time, for example, there is now a dramatic increase in state laws regarding abortion, since the U.S. Supreme Court decision in *Dobbs*.[48] Regardless of which state becomes the venue for a legal case, federal law will always be involved whenever there is a constitutional question, a question of individual freedom that is protected by the Bill of Rights, a federal statute (federal tax law, for example), or the regulations of a particular federal agency involved (such as the FDA). Any of the above automatically makes the legal question a federal legal question.

Because of the way that the federal government has limited itself under the U.S. Constitution,[49] states have significant latitude for issues that do not involve federal questions. States are able to create whatever laws they determine are necessary for their citizenry, and they are only limited by the restrictions of the U.S. Constitution and federal law – in other words, if a particular law is not prohibited by the U.S. Constitution or federal statutes, states are able to create their own statutes in areas such as contract law, tort law, family law, and criminal law. Likewise, state agencies are able to create their own regulations based on state laws, as long as there is no conflict with federal law.

1.5 U.S. COURT SYSTEM

A broad way to consider the court structure in the U.S. is by classifying courts as trial courts (where most cases are initiated) or appellate courts (where cases from

---

[46] Ibid., pp. 168–171.
[47] Burnham, W. (2016). *Introduction to the Law and Legal System of the United States*. West, pp. 376–377.
[48] Dobbs v. Jackson Women's Health Org., 597 U.S. 215, 142 S. Ct. 2228, 213 L. Ed. 2d 545 (2022).
[49] Burnham, W. (2016). *Introduction to the Law and Legal System of the United States*. West, pp. 31–39.

trial courts are "appealed" and reviewed for validity). Just as there are federal and state laws, there are federal and state court systems. The origin and structure of the federal court system is traced back to the U.S. Constitution.[50] The federal court system receives its authority from the U.S. Constitution, which established the U.S. Supreme Court and the Congressional authority to create the lower federal court system. At the federal level in the U.S., the District (trial) courts and Courts of Appeals are organized by thirteen regions (circuits), and each one of those circuits has a Court of Appeals. One of those circuits is considered to be the Federal Circuit, which has federal jurisdiction over international trade, International Property (IP) law (refer to Chapter 6), federal contracts, and similar case topics.[51] There are 94 district courts spread across those circuits, with at least one district court in every U.S. state, the District of Columbia, Puerto Rico, the U.S. Virgin Islands, Guam, and the Northern Mariana Islands. The distribution of these 94 district courts is determined by state populations. Most federal cases and lawsuits begin at the district court level, where a single judge reaches a decision (ruling) or the suit is settled between the two parties.[52] The second federal court level is the appellate level (discussed in Section 1.6). The final (and highest) level of the federal court system is the U.S. Supreme Court, which has discretion to choose a limited number of cases from the U.S. Courts of Appeals. It also has the power to consider decisions from state courts whenever there is a question about the U.S. Constitution or federal law.[53] It is said that 95 percent of all legal activity occurs within state courts.[54] The state court system structure can vary from one state to another. However, there are general similarities across state court systems within the U.S. they generally have a trial court level (the names of the courts can vary by state), an appellate court level, and a final appellate court (often called the state supreme court). Figure 1.1 provides a general depiction of the U.S. court system.

1.6 THE APPELLATE PROCESS

When a legal issue is appealed, the appellate process is used, and the primary arguments are in the form of written briefs that are submitted to an appellate court[55]

---

[50] Kaplan, D. S. (2015). *An Introduction to the American Legal System, Government, and Constitutional Law*. Aspen, pp. 80–83.
[51] Kaplan, D. S. (2015). *An Introduction to the American Legal System, Government, and Constitutional Law*. Aspen, pp. 80–82.
[52] Ibid., pp. 80–82.
[53] Ibid., pp. 82–84.
[54] American Bar Association. (September 9, 2019). *How Courts Work*. www.americanbar.org/groups/public_education/resources/law_related_education_network/how_courts_work/court_role/.
[55] Kaplan, D. S. (2015). *An Introduction to the American Legal System, Government, and Constitutional Law*. Aspen, p. 168.

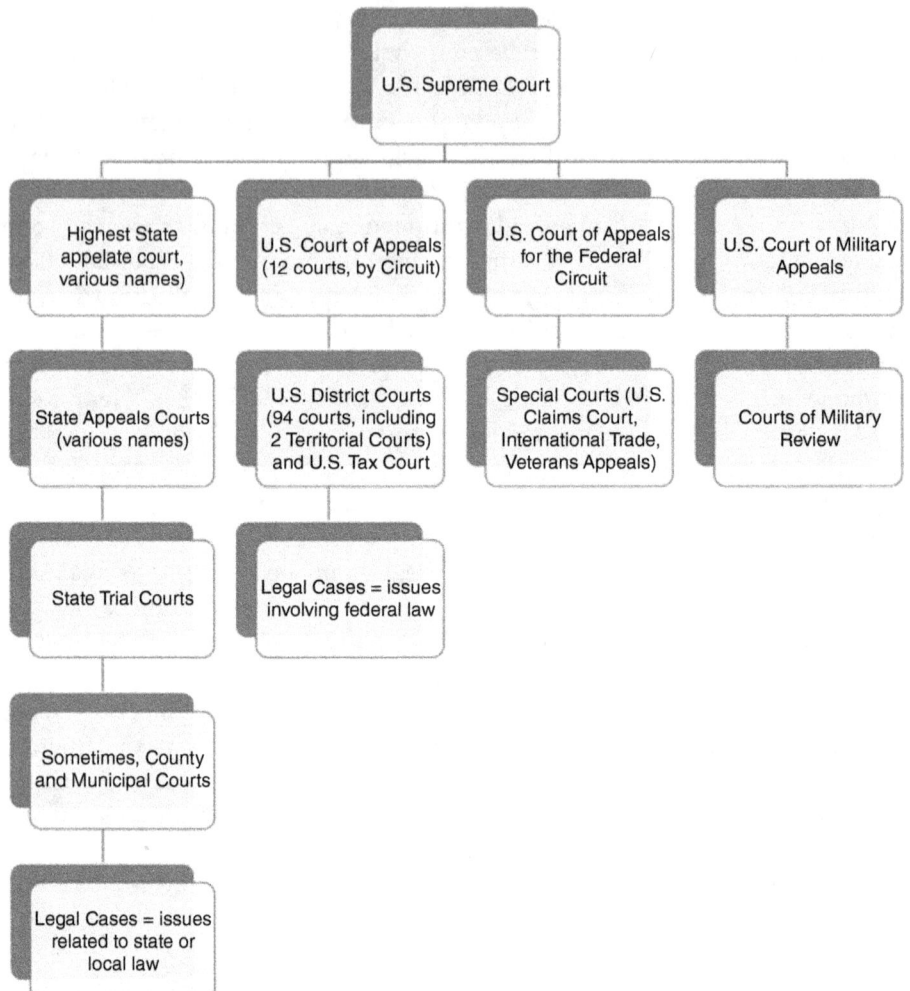

FIGURE 1.1 Diagram of the U.S. court system

(at the state level, there can be different names used for the appellate courts – for example, it is called the Court of Appeals in Virginia,[56] but in Pennsylvania, there are two intermediate appellate courts, one called the Commonwealth Court – for administrative and civil public law – and another called the Superior court – for criminal and private civil law).[57] Appellate courts only address legal issues, not facts (which need to be remanded to trial courts). At the federal level, there are thirteen

---

[56] Virginia's Judicial System. *Courts of Appeals of Virginia*. Retrieved February 4, 2023, from www.vacourts.gov/courts/cav/home.html.
[57] Available at: www.pacourts.us/courts/commonwealth-court.

Circuit Courts of Appeals across the U.S. Unlike the lower trial court level, where arguments and evidence may be presented, the appellate courts focus on the written briefs and then typically a short time of oral arguments, with a much smaller audience (attorneys and their assistants, rarely clients).[58] Generally, there is a right to have your case appealed at a mid-level appellate court. However, the top-level federal and state-level appeals courts in the U.S. also have what is known as discretionary jurisdiction, which means that they can decide whether or not to accept an appeal of a lower court's decision. In fact, very few cases are taken up by the top-level appellate courts. It is important to understand that an appeal is not a second trial of a case with evidence and witnesses. At the mid-level appeals courts, there is often a three-judge panel to review the proceedings of the lower court to evaluate whether or not the decision of the lower court was correct.[59] After a review of the case, an appellate court will either affirm or reject the decision of the lower court. If an appellate court finds that the law was incorrectly decided by the lower court, it may reject and remand (return) the case to the lower court, which then must follow the guidance of the appellate court's decision.[60]

1.7 U.S. CIRCUITS AND THEIR IMPACT ON U.S. LAW

Because the Circuit Courts of Appeals in the U.S. hear cases based on geographic jurisdiction and not collectively,[61] there can be different decisions that have been reached in cases in separate Circuits that may share a common legal question. Essentially this means that there could emerge a difference of opinion on a particular legal issue, and when this occurs, this is referred to as a "circuit split." A circuit split can eventually result in the U.S. Supreme Court ultimately reviewing a particular case.[62] Another unique aspect of the U.S. federal court system is that there is an impact on precedent (recall the prior mention of *stare decisis*) and the order in which decisions are binding to lower courts. The result is that a decision by the U.S. Supreme Court is binding to all lower courts. On the other hand, because of the Circuit structure, Court of Appeals and District Courts in one Circuit are not bound by a decision of a Court of Appeals in a different Circuit, even though they are all U.S. federal courts. Lower courts within that particular Circuit would, however, be bound by that decision. So, the practical result is that a particular legal decision could only impact a particular geographic area within the U.S. Figure 1.2 depicts a map of the U.S. Appeals Courts districts, as provided by uscourts.gov.

---

[58] Burnham, W. (2016). *Introduction to the Law and Legal System of the United States.* West, pp. 178–181.
[59] Ibid., p. 178.
[60] Ibid., p. 181.
[61] Rosen, D., Aronson, B., Litt, D. G., McAlinn, G. P., & Stern, J. P. (2017). *Introduction to American Law* (3rd ed.). Caroline Academic Press, pp. 133–134.
[62] Legal Information Institute. *Circuit Split.* Retrieved February 3, 2023, from www.law.cornell.edu/wex/circuit_split.

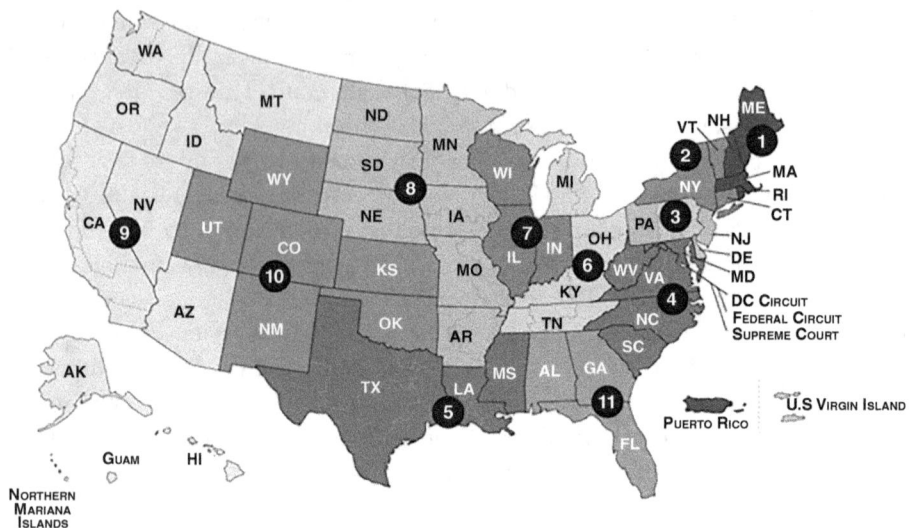

FIGURE 1.2 U.S. Appeals Courts districts, Source: uscourts.gov

The concept of jurisdiction involves whether a particular court has the legal authority to hear a particular case.[63] Courts also cannot hear cases related to events or actions that are in the future (have not yet occurred). For a case to be heard in a federal court, there generally must be a federal statute, treaty, or constitutional question involved. Federal courts have jurisdiction over cases that involve a dispute between two or more states, a case involving U.S. ambassadors or similar public officials, or a dispute between the U.S. federal government and a state. Federal courts also have jurisdiction over cases where the dispute involves an amount greater than $75,000 USD. If the defendant and plaintiff are from different states and the dispute in a case exceeds that threshold, it is considered to be a diversity of citizenship case, where federal jurisdiction can apply.[64] Once general jurisdiction is determined, the decision between several courts that could have jurisdiction is often based on the geographic nature of the case.[65] For example, if an incident occurred closer to a District Court in a particular state, that court may be selected to hear the case. "Subject matter jurisdiction" means that a court is legally permitted to hear the case based on the case type (such as a federal contract issue falling under the jurisdiction of a federal court). "Personal jurisdiction"

---

[63] Currier, K. A., Eimermann, T. E., & Campbell, M. S. (2020). *The Study of Law: A Critical Thinking Approach*. Wolters Kluwer, p. 84.
[64] Ibid., pp. 98–99.
[65] Ibid., pp. 99–100.

means that a particular court has the legal power over a defendant in the case (such as a state court not being able to force a defendant from another state to appear in court).[66] At the federal level, the U.S. Supreme Court only receives cases that have already proceeded through the District Court and appellate court levels. The U.S. Supreme Court then has significant latitude over which cases it elects to hear, and it selects from thousands of cases that are submitted each year, typically through a *writ of certiorari*, which means that the requestor is asking the U.S. Supreme Court to review the case record from the lower court.[67] At least four of the nine Supreme Court Justices must agree to review the case for it to reach the docket (agenda) of the Supreme Court.[68] A refusal to review the case (denial of *cert*) does not mean that the Supreme Court is validating a decision from the lower court but rather that it will not be reviewed. At the state level, a state's highest appeals court (often called a state supreme court) is the final stop for most cases, unless there is a federal issue involved.

1.8 SUBSTANTIVE VERSUS PROCEDURAL CRIMINAL LAW

Criminal law differs from civil law in the U.S., in that its focus is on defining what is considered to be criminal activity and the related penalties for conviction of those activities (such as theft, assault, etc.).[69] Civil law, by contrast, is focused on the rights of individuals in their dealings with other individuals or organizations.[70] As a result, most HCI and technology topics tend to be related to civil rather than criminal law, where the focus is on civil liability rather than criminal guilt and conviction. The resulting remedies (based on the court decision) are related to financial damages and/or an injunction (order from a court) that mandates an action or mandates an action to cease.[71] Most criminal law in the U.S. has its roots in federal- and state-level statutes as well as common law for defining the basics of crimes such as murder and theft. Criminal law carries with it the penalty of fines, imprisonment, or both. And in the U.S., criminal law has evolved to reflect the views of society, by creating or modifying federal and state level statutes.[72] For the U.S. federal government, criminal statutes are confined by the powers explicitly given in the U.S. Constitution. States in the U.S. can also create their own criminal laws, as long as they do not violate

---

[66] Ibid., pp. 125–129.
[67] Ibid., pp. 92–93.
[68] Ibid., pp. 92–93.
[69] Rosen, D., Aronson, B., Litt, D. G., McAlinn, G. P., & Stern, J. P. (2017). *Introduction to American Law* (3rd ed.). Caroline Academic Press, pp. 139–141.
[70] Currier, K. A., Eimermann, T. E., & Campbell, M. S. (2020). *The Study of Law: A Critical Thinking Approach*. Wolters Kluwer, pp. 65–67.
[71] Currier, K. A., Eimermann, T. E., & Campbell, M. S. (2020). *The Study of Law: A Critical Thinking Approach*. Wolters Kluwer, pp. 70–71.
[72] Rosen, D., Aronson, B., Litt, D. G., McAlinn, G. P., & Stern, J. P. (2017). *Introduction to American Law* (3rd ed.). Caroline Academic Press, pp. 112–141.

any of the individual rights provided in the U.S. Constitution. Where things get a bit more complicated and controversial is when both the U.S. federal government and individual states make the same activity a crime by statute, both with prescribed repercussions (the term "overcriminalization" is often used). This ultimately results in a "stacking" of violations where someone can be prosecuted for both federal and state crimes for the same offense. A core common law requirement for something to be considered criminal was based on a knowledgeable intent to commit a crime, using the idea of a criminal act (known as *actus reus*) and a guilty mind (known as *mens rea*), and under this framework, a simple unknowing mistake was not categorized as a crime.[73] With the volume of new statutes covering various aspects of what is determined to be criminal activity, there is the ongoing question of whether each new statute is thoroughly vetted for intent and the necessity of the statute.

1.9 EXECUTIVE ORDERS IN THE U.S.

In the U.S., executive orders and memorandums from the President (at the federal level) or from governors (at the state level) are related to the discussion of administrative law. The orders should be based on delegated authority from U.S. federal statutes.[74] These orders and memos are used to provide specific direction to agencies and government employees regarding either something within the scope of constitutionally provisioned executive power or related to statutes or regulations and how they should be implemented. One example of such an executive order was the 2021 Executive Order on Protecting Americans' Sensitive Data from Foreign Adversaries, which was released as being supported by 50 U.S.C. 1701 (International Emergency Economic Powers Act), 50 U.S.C. 1601 (National Emergencies Act), and 3 U.S.C. § 301 (relating to the delegation of government functions).[75] It is important to note that executive orders are prioritized by courts at a lower level than statutes or regulations, and an executive order cannot overrule a statute or regulation or case law, despite what leaders may sometimes claim.

1.10 SOVEREIGN IMMUNITY AND U.S. LAW

Another concept that the U.S. inherited from English Common Law is the doctrine of "sovereign immunity" for the U.S. federal government and state governments. This was rooted in a tradition of the courts being prevented from suing the king, and it has continued in the U.S. under a structure that requires the U.S. federal government or individual states to permit themselves to be sued for various reasons,

---

[73] Ibid., pp. 112–141.
[74] Currier, K. A., Eimermann, T. E., & Campbell, M. S. (2020). *The Study of Law: A Critical Thinking Approach*. Wolters Kluwer, p. 41.
[75] The White House. (June 9, 2021). *Executive Order on Protecting Americans' Sensitive Data from Foreign Adversaries*. www.whitehouse.gov/briefing-room/presidential-actions/2021/06/09/executive-order-on-protecting-americans-sensitive-data-from-foreign-adversaries/.

yet they have control over what those reasons might be.[76] For example, during the COVID-19 pandemic, many states in the U.S. limited their liability for decisions related to the pandemic by relying on this legal tradition of sovereign immunity.

1.11 UNDERSTANDING COURT OPINIONS AND CASE AND STATUTORY CITATIONS

When your research into legal frameworks leads to a court opinion, the first step in understanding the implications of that opinion is to determine the date of the decision and whether it was decided by a U.S. federal court or a state court. This is important to determine because the date can help determine whether the decision is valid and holds authority today or whether it has been nullified or modified by a more recent decision. Legal databases are mentioned later in this chapter, and many of those databases will provide a notification regarding decisions that are "overturned" (meaning nullified or amended). Determining the type of court is valuable for understanding whether the decision of that court has authority in a particular situation (whether it's "good law") or whether it has been reversed by a higher court. After determining the authority of the court opinion, the next step is to review the facts of the case, which can be found in the first part of the court opinion.[77] The facts of a case begin with the parties in the dispute, the details of the conflict, and what the parties have requested of the court. This is followed by any procedural facts of the case, particularly if the case was already reviewed by lower courts or administrative agencies.[78] Finally, there will be the decision that has been reached by the judge or the majority of the judges on the panel for that court (known as the "holding"). This provides insight into how any laws in question should be interpreted or what the next steps for the case will be. If applicable, it will also detail whether there was a new legal rule created or whether an existing legal rule was modified. Sometimes the decision process means it is remanded (sent back) to a lower court or agency. Sometimes the opinion is that the court agrees with (affirms) a decision made by a lower court or agency. There are also instances where a court will reverse a decision from a lower court or administrative agency.[79]

The case citation itself reveals a little bit about the case. The format of case citations can at first seem a bit cryptic. It is very common for anything that can be abbreviated or shortened to be abbreviated. Behind that format is a way to determine the court that decided the case, the date of the decision for the case, the name of the case, and where it can be located. For example, with *Nat'l Fed'n of the Blind v. Target*

---

[76] Rosen, D., Aronson, B., Litt, D. G., McAlinn, G. P., & Stern, J. P. (2017). *Introduction to American Law* (3rd ed.). Caroline Academic Press, pp. 112–113.

[77] Currier, K. A., Eimermann, T. E., & Campbell, M. S. (2020). *The Study of Law: A Critical Thinking Approach*. Wolters Kluwer, pp. 10–11.

[78] Currier, K. A., Eimermann, T. E., & Campbell, M. S. (2020). *The Study of Law: A Critical Thinking Approach*. Wolters Kluwer, p. 14.

[79] Burnham, W. (2016). *Introduction to the Law and Legal System of the United States*. West, p. 69.

Corp., 582 F. Supp. 2d 1185 (N.D. Cal. 2007), the plaintiff (party filing the case) is the National Federation of the Blind, and the defendant named in the case is Target Corporation. The 582 F. Supp. 2d is the reporter volume number and abbreviation (in this case, it is referring to Volume 582 of the *Federal Supplement*, 2nd series), the 1185 is the first page, and the 2007 is the date the case was decided in the Northern District of California. As another example, a U.S. Supreme Court decision from 1973 might look like this: *Chicago Mercantile Exchange v. Deaktor*, 410 U.S. 113, 93 S.Ct. 705, 35 L.Ed. 2d 147 (1973). This citation would mean that the plaintiff was Chicago Mercantile Exchange, the defendant was Deaktor, the *U.S. Reports* volume was 410, with the first page being 113. For this citation, it is also noted that this was published elsewhere (as is usually the case with U.S. Supreme Court cases), including the *Supreme Court Reporter* and the *Lawyer's Edition*. Note that state cases are published in "regional" reporters based on the geographic location of the state. For example, Massachusetts and New York state cases are published in the *North Eastern Reporter*, which would be abbreviated as N.E. Figure 1.3 shows an illustrated diagram of a federal court case citation (even though states are not always in the geographic reporter that you would expect).

When locating and reading a case or ruling (decision) through a database or online legal reference, the decision begins with the heading area, listing the plaintiff(s) and defendant(s), followed by the case number and court where the case was heard. This is followed by information regarding the particular reporters where the case is published and dates specifying when the case was argued and decided (if it has been decided). If this case has already been heard by prior courts, the next section will list the decisions by those prior courts as well as where those decisions can be found (the citations). The next portion of the case is the "disposition," which describes the final determination (action) by the court. This could be granting or denying a request or (if it is a higher court) it could be affirming or reversing the decision of a lower court or sending the case back (remanding it) to a lower court. Next will be a case summary which provides background information regarding the case, followed by a summary of the court's opinion and a summary of the facts, history, and holding of the court.

Case Name, Plaintiff versus Defendant

9th Circuit Court, Decided in 2019

Robles v. Domino's Pizza, LLC, 913 F.3d 898, 905-06 (9th Cir. 2019)

Official legal publication (law reporter). In this case, volume 913 of the Federal Reporter, 3rd series, starting on page 898

FIGURE 1.3 Diagram of a federal court citation

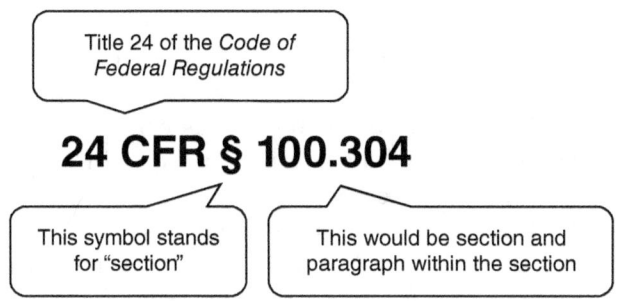

FIGURE 1.4 Diagram of a federal regulation citation

In the court reporters or other databases, there may also be a "syllabus" before the core information from the court, which is another summary of the opinion as added by the court reporter or database. This is supplemental and not part of a court's decision.

Following this will be the information regarding the counsel (attorneys) who represented the parties in the case. Finally, there will be a lengthier opinion, starting with the judge who wrote the opinion, and this portion is where the finer details are included, such as the history of the case facts, relevant legal issues, relevant statutes, and any relevant past decisions (precedent) that can be applied to the current case. The opinion then details the court's analysis and their ruling based on that analysis. For U.S. Supreme Court cases (and sometimes appellate court cases), there will be a majority opinion of the Court, followed by any dissenting opinions of the court for the case (judge(s) who disagree with the majority opinion). Note that the order of the above structure might be slightly rearranged or different based on the court (federal versus state) and the level of the court (District Court versus Supreme Court, for example).

To better understand the parts of a U.S. or state-level Code citation, when examining a citation such as 47 U.S.C. § 618 (2012), the statute is found in Title 47 of the U.S. Code, the symbol represents the word "Section," which is Section 618, in this case, and the 2012 is the year of that particular U.S. code. Things can be even more specific than just the section, and a subsection and paragraph can even be specified with this citation format. For a federal regulation, it would be listed in the *Code of Federal Regulations* and might look like 47 C.F.R. § 216.1. For that regulation, it would be referring to Title 47 in the *Code of Federal Regulations* and section 216.1. Figure 1.4 depicts a diagram of a federal regulation.

For a state-level example, Cal. Civ. Code § 55.61 would be referring to California state civil code, section 55.61.

1.12 HOW TO FIND LEGAL SOURCES

There are some key things to consider when doing research that involves legal sources or trying to find legal sources related to an HCI topic. The first approach to legal research should involve determining jurisdiction as introduced earlier. After identifying statutes or regulations that may apply to a technology or situation, it must be determined whether it is a federal statute/regulation or a state statute/regulation, and whether it can be applied to the specific topic at hand. As previously noted regarding the parts of a court case or a statute, it is important to also know the date of the statute or the court decision. It is possible that the decision is no longer applicable because of a more recent decision.

The next step in legal research is locating the sources for the particular topic. If relevant, a good starting point would be federal or state statutes, as those are the primary source for many laws. The second source for research would be cases that are related to those statutes as well as the technology topic itself. A third source for legal research would be administrative regulations or rulings that relate to your topic. Because of the rapidly changing nature of HCI and technology, this may be the most likely place to find regulations related to a more novel technology, as older statutes and rulings may not address it. Often statutes do not keep up with the pace of technology, and as a result, regulations are the best place to search for legal relevance. Finally, law reviews and other scholarly publications can help point the way to other primary and secondary sources for legal research. While a number of printed sources still exist, most recent (and many older) sources are now available in electronic format.

One thing that becomes evident when reading law reviews is that the citation format looks very different from other formats such as APA[80] and MLA.[81] Most legal citations follow a format known as "Bluebook" format, which is based on a regularly updated handbook called *The Bluebook: A Uniform System of Citation*.[82] Citations from relevant law review articles can often lead to other good sources (both primary and secondary), and popular tools such as Google Scholar can assist you as you uncover legal resources. However, electronic databases such as Westlaw[83] (for secondary sources and copies of primary sources), Lexis/Nexis[84] (for secondary sources and copies of primary sources), or EBSCO Legal Collection[85] (for secondary sources) provide a wealth of legal resources. Unless there is existing access to a library which has subscribed to those resources, a subscription fee is involved to access those resources. The CFR, USC, and other state codes are available free of charge. The "eCFR" provides electronic access to the Code of Federal Regulations as offered by the U.S. National Archives.[86] This tool can be used to easily search by

---

[80] American Psychological Association. *APA Style: Paper Format*. Retrieved February 3, 2023, from https://apastyle.apa.org/style-grammar-guidelines/paper-format.
[81] MLA Style Center. *Using MLA Format*. Retrieved February 4, 2023, from https://style.mla.org/mla-format/.
[82] The Bluebook. *The Bluebook Online*. Retrieved February 4, 2023, from www.legalbluebook.com/.
[83] Thompson Reuters. *Westlaw Sign In*. Retrieved February 1, 2023, from https://1.next.westlaw.com/.
[84] LexisNexis. *Lexis: Online Legal Research*. Retrieved January 29, 2023, from www.lexisnexis.com/en-us/products/lexis.page.
[85] EBSCO. *Full-Text Database Legal Collection*. Retrieved January 29, 2023, from www.ebsco.com/products/research-databases/legal-collection.
[86] National Archives. *Code of Federal Regulations*. Retrieved January 29, 2023, from www.ecfr.gov/.

CFR reference or expand/search through various federal regulations. U.S. Code can also be accessed indirectly online through websites such as the Legal Information Institute website managed by Cornell Law School.[87] Another alternative portal is the Justia.com portal for federal and state codes and statutes.[88] An example at the state level of a primary source, is the Maryland legal code, which can be found online through the Thurgood Marshall State Law Library.[89]

Another good way to continue legal research is to use a relevant case or statute and find other cases or statutes that might be citing that particular case or statute, helping with the expansion of the legal research. A favorite tool for this is Shepherd's United States Citations,[90] which is a feature within LexisNexis that may also be available at select libraries. This resource shows other court decisions that cite the particular case or statute that has already been located (in the legal field, it is referred to as "Shephardizing"). Westlaw provides similar functionality using "flagging" (a red flag on a case means that the case is no longer considered "good law").

1.13 APPLYING U.S. LEGAL BASICS TO HCI RESEARCH

Legal research often follows the "CREAC" (Conclusion, Rule, Explanation, Analysis, Conclusion) approach[91] and in law review articles, there is a noticeable difference in approach as well as citation procedure and format (using the Bluebook format previously mentioned). There is a focus on identifying the laws that apply and the source of those rulings. There is an examination of the history of the law and its current state – is it still undecided, and as noted before about the federal court system, is there a "circuit split" that impacts the law in the U.S.? The legal jurisdiction for the topic is examined, and the distinction between state and federal law is noted, particularly where there may be a conflict between the two. History and historical precedents (if they are good law) have value in law to a certain degree, and on the other hand, computer developments in 1978 have little relevance today. And, as emphasized before, the concept of *stare decisis* is critical to determining the legal answer.

When conducting HCI research that involves legal questions or an aspect of technology that might have an impact on law or public policy, it is good to begin with the question of where the research or technology would be used in the U.S.

---

[87] Cornell Law School. *Legal Information Institute*. Retrieved February 1, 2023, from www.law.cornell.edu/.
[88] Justia. *Justia: Free Law & Legal Information*. Retrieved February 1, 2023, from www.justia.com/
[89] Maryland Courts. *Thurgood Marshall State Law Library*. Retrieved February 6, 2023, from https://mdcourts.gov/lawlib.
[90] LexisNexis. *Shephard's United States Citations*. Retrieved February 5, 2023, from https://store.lexisnexis.com/products/shepards-united-states-citations-master-case-and-statute-edition-skuSKU66103/details.
[91] Columbia Law School, *Organizing a Legal Discussion: IRAC / CRAC / CREAC*. Retrieved February 4, 2023, from www.law.columbia.edu/sites/default/files/2022-06/WC%20Handout%20IRAC%2C%20CRAC%2C%20CREAC.revised%205.22.pdf.

to determine what legal jurisdiction might apply. Once there is a better sense of jurisdiction, the U.S. federal laws and (if relevant) state laws can be examined that might intersect with the research or be impacted by the technology. When exploring potential legal sources, it is good to remember that some sources (e.g., secondary sources such as law reviews) are theoretical versus other sources (court rulings, for example). Court rulings can also be classified as binding precedent (depending on the jurisdiction) versus persuasive precedent (a court opinion that may be considered but is not binding – an opinion on a matter of definition not directly related to the case question, for example). It is also essential to remember that federal law always takes precedence over state law. As discussed previously, on the federal level, a Court of Appeals can overrule a District Court, and the U.S. Supreme Court can overrule a Court of Appeals. At the state level, a mid-level appeals court can overrule a lower-level trial court, and the state's highest-level court of appeals can overrule the mid-level courts. Unlike HCI research, there is no wiggle room in determining whether the source of the information (legal rulings for this discussion) is of lower or higher quality. With law, a strict priority of weighting is based on the source: constitutions (which have the highest priority), statutes, regulations, case law (which has higher priority but is lower than a constitution and can counteract each other), and executive orders (which have lower priority). Refer to Chapter 11 for information on treaties and laws of other countries.

As noted in Section 1.12, it is then essential to identify additional primary and secondary sources of law that relate to the topic. Are there any statutes or court decisions that directly apply to the research or technology? If there are no clear laws or relevant decisions, the next step would be to determine where there might be similarity from other statutes or case law. Because of the novel and evolving nature of HCI and technology, it is likely that this scenario might occur. Laws may easily predate current and emerging technology, and therefore a framework or relevance for the legal question might be developed based on a similar situation, which may not even be technology related. Recent law review articles might be helpful, as there may be similar topics that are being explored from a legal perspective. However, these case materials and other scholarly resources are theories or research but are not the law. Also note that legal theory tends to be a discussion of legal approaches or novel legal arguments, unlike the type of theories encountered in HCI with hypotheses and rigorous methodologies. Court rulings provide the framework for the legal rules, not quantitative research like might be expected with HCI.

2

Introduction to Human–Computer Interaction for Law

2.1 DEFINITION AND ORIGIN OF HCI

Legal professionals whose work and interests interact with technology in any way should have a general understanding of the field/discipline/sub-discipline (depending on who you ask) of human–computer interaction (HCI). For over 40 years, the field of human-computer interaction has worked towards meeting user needs by understanding and designing positive user experiences. Unlike many engineering problems where there is an optimal approach or solution, interface design (and more broadly, HCI) is more of an art. The interaction of users with technology inevitably also creates security, privacy, and ethical concerns that at some point may intersect with law and public policy. Legal experts and policymakers have a vested interest in understanding the underlying history, principles, concepts, and directions of interaction design, as these aspects are increasingly influential in modern legislation, rulemaking, court decisions, and policy considerations.

While the terminology "human–computer interaction" began to be more widely used in the 1980s, the principles behind HCI can be traced back to the study of human tasks as the industrial era emerged, as well as the study of systems that developed during the world wars in the twentieth century, followed by the Ergonomics Research Society in 1949.[1] The field of "human factors" or ergonomics was a key discipline that influenced HCI. This older field focused on making all types of systems efficient, safe, and comfortable by studying human performance and capabilities.[2] Over the decades as the HCI field emerged, it changed from "man–machine interaction" to "human–computer interaction," with the fields of computer science and psychology serving as the core backdrop for that emergence. There has been

---

[1] Carroll, J. M. (2003). Introduction: Toward a Multidisciplinary Science of Human-Computer Interaction. In *HCI Models, Theories, and Frameworks: Toward a Multidisciplinary Science*. Elsevier, pp. 7–8.

[2] MacKenzie, S. I. (2012). *Human-Computer Interaction: An Empirical Research Perspective*. p. 2.

a long-standing interest in the user and, in particular, diversity of users, with the notion that as design of technology includes the widest group of users possible, the quality of that design increases for everyone. As computers moved from mainframes with specialized engineers to personal computers in homes and offices, used by nontechnical people without computing/engineering training, it became important to figure out how to make these machines usable for the person without technical training. In 1982, HCI more formally launched as a discipline, with the first conference on Human Factors in Computing Systems, which grew into CHI and in parallel led to the creation and growth of the Association of Computing Machinery SIGCHI (Special Interest Group on Computer–Human Interaction).

The earlier roots within the ACM are evident as early as the late 1960s, with the ACM SIGSOC (Social and Behavioral Computing) that would ultimately be renamed in 1983 as the focus shifted toward users and human factors.[3] The very fact that the SIGCHI sponsored conferences[4] bringing together both practitioners and researchers illustrates the blended and interdisciplinary nature of the HCI field.[5] The HCI field has continued to evolve from an early focus on basic ergonomics and menu design structures for individual users to contemplating more usable design of touch-based systems, wearable components, haptic feedback, and artificial intelligence today (refer to Chapter 8 for more detail on the Legal Aspects of Artificial Intelligence and HCI). In the 1990s, the field of design increasingly influenced HCI as well. The focus on usable and effective design began with command line interfaces and shifted to graphics-based interfaces (GUI), and web-based and mobile interfaces.

Basic computing requires information to be given to the device (e.g., keyboard or touch screen input) and ultimately something returned from the device (e.g., output on a screen). The input and output aspects of computing are not only crucial to the computing cycle but they also define the primary aspects where humans interact with computers through human senses such as sight, hearing, and touch.[6] This interaction often involves one or more of these senses and depending upon the design, a multifaceted approach to interaction can assist an enhanced interaction or distract and limit interaction with a computer. The information that is accessed and used on systems changed from static text to dynamic content that now relies heavily on multimedia. Data analytics, information visualization, and AI integration are now at the forefront of many systems, and once again HCI is focused on creating interfaces and feedback that are innovative, usable, and effective.

---

[3] Ibid., p. 15.
[4] https://sigchi.org/conferences/.
[5] Hochheiser, H., & Lazar, J. (2007). HCI and Societal Issues: A Framework for Engagement. *International Journal of Human & Computer Interaction*, 23(3), pp. 339–374.
[6] Dix, A., Finlay, J., Abowd, G. D., & Beale, R. (2004). *Human–Computer Interaction* (3rd ed.). Pearson, pp. 12–26.

2.1.1 HCI and the Individual

User-centered design is an approach that emphasizes the role of the actual users and their needs and goals at the center of the design process, rather than constraints of technology or other development needs. The general principles behind this design approach are a focus on people, understanding the actual problem, treating everything as a system (interconnected), and a careful approach to a solution (not rushing to an assumption).[7] True user-centered design has a focus on the user and user-related tasks from the onset of the product development,[8] rather than this being a particular phase or final review later in a project. This requires a thorough knowledge of the user population and their needs prior to the development of the system requirements. The initial concept of user-centered design originated from Donald Norman in the 1980s and focused on the idea that the designer should work with the users to ensure that what is developed is a project that works well for the users and works as intended without a cumbersome learning curve.[9] Prototyping might be used when a baseline of user requirements is needed in order to more finely focus on user needs. User-centered design is an ongoing process from the onset to conclusion of a project, with regular interaction and evaluation that heavily involves users.

Proof of concepts or prototypes are often used as a more interactive and concrete way to obtain user feedback and observational data by providing a device or interface that can be tangibly used or handled. Individual users or organized groups of users can then provide their reaction to the proposed design. While prototypes can be as simple as a sketched paper mockup of an interface, technology (including software and 3D printers) has enabled the more rapid production of more tangible and complex prototypes. Prototype purposes can range from an initial prototype, which has the single purpose of eliciting better requirements and then is discarded, to a prototype that is intended to be used throughout the design process and itself is modified and evolves as the requirements emerge and are refined.[10] Having the ability to interact with something and explore its usability and adequacy can greatly improve the likelihood of producing a design that meets user needs. Prototyping has also gained more traction in the broader technology community due to the change from traditional system and application development with a long, predicted life cycle and planning to a focus on agile development, which requires shorter, more iterative development timeframes and a reliance on regular stakeholder feedback.

---

[7] Interaction Design Foundation – IxDF. (June 5, 2016). What is User Centered Design? Interaction Design Foundation – IxDF. www.interaction-design.org/literature/topics/user-centered-design.

[8] Sharp, H., Preece, J. & Rogers, Y. (2019). *Interaction Design: Beyond Human-Computer Interaction.* John Wiley and Sons, pp. 327–328.

[9] Abras, C., Maloney-Krichmar, D., & Preece, J. (2004). User-centered Design. *Bainbridge, W. Encyclopedia of Human-Computer Interaction. Thousand Oaks: Sage Publications,* 37(4), pp. 445–456.

[10] Dix, A., Finlay, J., Abowd, G. D., & Beale, R. (2004). *Human–Computer Interaction* (3rd ed.). Pearson, pp. 241–242.

HCI has focused on cognition because of the pivotal role that it plays in using an interface and interacting with computing devices. For example, the concept of user attention relies on design from a perspective of visual, auditory, or other sensory cues, and from a design perspective, HCI seeks to present information in a way that enables a user to focus on essential information. With current ubiquitous technology, user attention plays a pivotal role as users tend to perform "quasi-multitasking," where they are essentially moving back and forth between various interfaces and devices. Cognitive aspects of perception and memory are equally relevant to HCI, as it is essential to design systems in a way that they are easy to use, recognize, and understand, as well as recall actions and utility. Cognitive load has also become of increasing concern to HCI as some systems become more complex, there is more multitasking and ubiquitous use of computing devices, and most systems require some sort of authentication, which often requires individuals to recall usernames and passwords. Nothing in HCI is ever an optimization problem where there is one maximized and correct answer – just as in design, there is a lot of creativity and interpretation.

Usability testing (or user testing) is a commonly used data collection technique in HCI. Observation of users completing tasks is a standard technique for usability testing. The users involved with the usability testing study are observed directly (in person) or remotely by the investigator(s) as they are either completing their standard activities or a prescribed number of tasks as requested by the investigator(s). This testing can occur in a structured lab environment that controls the parameters for a standard configuration for each user, or it can be in the user's typical setting (office, home, and school), which results in a less standard configuration but a more natural one for the user.

Observations of users, whether in person or remote (i.e., Zoom or similar technology, as mentioned earlier), have been a method to collect user data regarding particular tasks and activities. One further observational approach in HCI is called the "Think Aloud" method where the participants are asked to describe what they are thinking as they use an interface or complete tasks. This approach can add additional insight to the data so that the researcher does not have to draw as many conclusions as to what users are thinking. Another technique to gather observational user data is a user "diary," where a user is asked to record their activities, why they did what they did, and other thoughts about the task.[11] Keystroke logging and analytics software has also been used to collect observational user data. The emergence of more sophisticated and affordable eye tracking technology has also been integrated as a way to collect observational data of user actions as they use interfaces and complete tasks. Eye tracking in general tracks the movement of the eye or the point of gaze.[12] Eye

---

[11] Sharp, H., Preece, J., & Rogers, Y. (2019). *Interaction Design: Beyond Human-Computer Interaction*. John Wiley and Sons, pp. 263–264.

[12] Olson, J. S. & Kellogg, W. A. (2014). *Ways of Knowing in HCI*. Springer, pp. 326–328.

tracking technology is being used by not only HCI researchers but also psychologists and neuroscientists. While complex equipment and even eye tracking glasses have been developed to gather data, there has been interest in collecting data on a broader scale. With cameras attached to most computing devices, HCI researchers have also been trying to leverage eye tracking through those cameras in ways that could collect data from hundreds (or thousands) of users over more extended periods of time in more natural settings.[13]

2.1.2 Disciplines and "Waves" of HCI

The HCI field evolved by input from a variety of disciplines, not only computer science and information science. Psychology and cognitive sciences, engineering, design, and other disciplines have contributed to and continue to be involved with HCI, making it an interdisciplinary field.[14] Within the history and evolution of HCI, there are often considered to be major changes in direction or emphasis, referred to as "waves." The first wave of HCI refers to the initial engineering, human factors, and ergonomics roots of the discipline, with very practical goals and directions (i.e., to solve an obvious problem between machines and people).[15] The second wave of HCI is viewed as the point at which there was a heavier emphasis on the psychological and social science aspects of design, and with that wave a new focus on integrating theory and a better understanding of users as a way to understand design.[16] The so-called third wave of HCI is viewed as the time where HCI reached beyond the external (organizational and industrial) environment to a more personal level where design met the home and personal lives of individuals along with technology such as augmented reality and tangible interfaces.[17] There has also been discussion within the HCI community of a fourth wave of HCI, with a focus on social justice, environmental justice, racial justice, political values, ethics, and other values as they intersect with technology design.[18] The fourth wave of HCI has a connection to law in that there are many core legal topics associated with human rights, and many of those are discussed throughout this book. For example, a right to privacy, a right to free speech, the right to vote, and intellectual freedom are considered to be core rights firmly established in the U.S.,[19] yet they are also highly related to HCI topics

---

[13] Olson, J. S. & Kellogg, W. A. (2014). *Ways of Knowing in HCI*. Springer, pp. 335–342.
[14] Ibid., pp. 4–5.
[15] Duarte, E. F., & Baranauskas, M. C. C. (2016, October). Revisiting the Three HCI Waves: A Preliminary Discussion on Philosophy of Science and Research Paradigms. In *Proceedings of the 15th Brazilian Symposium on Human Factors in Computing Systems*, pp. 1–4.
[16] Ibid.
[17] Ibid.
[18] Ashby, S., Hanna, J., Matos, S., Nash, C., & Faria, A. (2019, November). Fourth-wave HCI Meets the 21st Century Manifesto. In *Proceedings of the Halfway to the Future Symposium 2019*, pp. 1–11.
[19] Jaeger, P., Lazar, J, Gorham, U., & Greene Taylor, N. (2023). *Foundations of Information Law*. ALA/Neal-Schuman Press, pp. 32–33.

such as legal aspects of accessibility (discussed in Chapter 3), information privacy (discussed in Chapter 4), intellectual property (discussed in Chapter 6), and voting (discussed in Chapter 10).

There has also become increasing awareness of an underlying (so-called "infrastructure") problem in HCI, where the accessibility and usability of interfaces and devices have received the primary focus, while the underlying structure including the preexisting code libraries, design toolkits, protocols, and other underlying and long-established technology structures remains largely inaccessible and lacking in usability.[20] One very common example of this would be the security functions that developers use, which are built upon established libraries of code. It is perceived as a necessary practice to avoid inconsistency and lack of secure code; however, the resulting reliance on an established infrastructure means that any resulting interaction and computing process may have very little flexibility in terms of design.[21] This underlying, extensive, and long-standing "infrastructure" can pose a challenge when HCI attempts to change the design of things. This challenge can also be felt when examining the intersection of design with policy, in the sense that new policies or laws that are enacted are limited by the existing technology framework.[22] There may also be situations where innovation and changes to basic or customized functionality are also restricted by the existing technology infrastructure.[23]

2.1.3 Authority and Organizations in HCI

Because of the diversity and breadth of disciplines that comprise HCI, there is often the question of whether there is one governance or standards body for the general HCI field. The answer to that question depends on the context. Is this HCI practice within the federal or a state government? If so, certain statutes and/or regulations and policies might apply, for example, requirements regarding the procurement process – that is, what is required based on a regulation or statute. Is this HCI within a private organization? If so, it is possible that some other standard applies that was selected by that organization or institution (e.g., something like using a standard such as WCAG to guide accessibility compliance within an organization). Or, a statute might apply to that private entity, as well. In other contexts, regional or international regulations or laws might apply. One such example would be the GDPR

---

[20] Edwards, W. K., Newman, M. W., & Poole, E. S. (2010, April). The Infrastructure Problem in HCI. In *Proceedings of the SIGCHI Conference on Human Factors in Computing Systems*, pp. 423–425.

[21] Edwards, W. K., Newman, M. W., & Poole, E. S. (2010, April). The Infrastructure Problem in HCI. In *Proceedings of the SIGCHI Conference on Human Factors in Computing Systems*, pp. 423–425.

[22] Jackson, S. J., Gillespie, T., & Payette, S. (2014, February). The Policy Knot: Re-integrating Policy, Practice and Design in CSCW Studies of Social Computing. In *Proceedings of the 17th ACM conference on Computer Supported Cooperative Work & Social Computing*, pp. 588–602.

[23] Fiesler, C. (2020, April). Lawful Users: Copyright Circumvention and Legal Constraints on Technology Use. In *Proceedings of the 2020 CHI Conference on Human Factors in Computing Systems*, pp. 1–11.

(General Data Privacy Regulation) in the European Union which specifies how data collected regarding its citizens can be used and must be handled. Regardless of where a company is located, if its transactional data involves EU citizens, that law would apply.

From a professional organization standpoint, there are several different organizations and core conferences that support the discipline. The Association for Computing Machinery (ACM) is the largest of those professional organizations, having been established in 1947 and hosting some of the most respected international conferences related to HCI as well as peer-reviewed journals that focus on HCI.[24] The annual CHI Conference (ACM Conference on Human Factors in Computing Systems) is one of the most widely recognized HCI conferences, and it has been held since 1982.[25] In the proceedings of the 2025 CHI conference, topics ranged from accessible interaction to AI to data privacy, but there was no core session focused on law or policy, with the exception of a session focused on the politics of data.[26] The ACM ASSETS Conference (on Computers and Accessibility) is a primary conference within the ACM to focus on research and design related to people with disabilities.[27] Also, within the special interest group from ACM known as SIGCHI (ACM Special Interest Group on Computer–Human Interaction), there are a number of cosponsored conferences that shed light on many of the current areas of focus within the HCI community.[28]

Separately from SIGCHI, there are at least two other large and ongoing HCI conferences: INTERACT (from IFIP-TC13, which is the International Federation for Information Processing and is a highly respected international committee)[29] and

---

[24] Association for Computing Machinery. *About ACM.* Retrieved January 30, 2024, from www.acm.org/about-acm.

[25] Association for Computing Machinery. *CHI: Conference on Human Factors in Computing Systems.* Retrieved January 30, 2024, from https://dl.acm.org/conference/chi.

[26] ACM Digital Library. *CHI '24: Proceedings of the 2024 CHI Conference on Human Factors in Computing Systems.* Retrieved January 13, 2025, from https://dl.acm.org/doi/proceedings/10.1145/3613904.

[27] Association for Computing Machinery. *ASSETS Conference – Proceedings.* Retrieved February 8, 2024, from https://dl.acm.org/conference/assets.

[28] ACM Special Interest Group on Computer–Human Interaction. *Our Twenty-Six Conferences.* Retrieved February 1, 2024, from https://sigchi.org/conferences/; These include AutoUI (Automotive User Interfaces and Interactive Vehicular Applications), C&C (Creativity and Cognition), Play (Computer–Human Interaction in Play), CI (Collective Intelligence), COMPASS (Computing and Sustainable Devices), CSCW (Computer-Supported Cooperative Work), CUI (Conversational User Interfaces), DIS (Designing Interactive Systems), EICS (Engineering Interactive Computing Systems), ETRA (Eye Tracking Research & Applications), GROUP (Supporting Group Work), HRI (Human–Robot Interaction), ICMI (International Conference on Intermodal Interaction), IDC (Interaction Design and Children), IMX (Interactive Media Experiences), ISS (Interactive Surfaces and Spaces), IUI (Intelligent User Interfaces), MobileHCI (Mobile Human–Computer Interaction), RecSyS (Recommender Systems), SUI (Spatial User Interaction), TEI (Tangible, Embedded, and Embodied Interaction), UIST (User Interface Software and Technology), UMAP (User Modeling, Adaptation, and Personalization), UbiComp/ISWC (Joint Conference on Pervasive and Ubiquitous Computing), and VRST (Virtual Reality Software and Technology).

[29] IFIP-TC13. *INTERACT Conference.* Retrieved February 16, 2024, from https://ifip-tc13.org/interact/.

HCI International (which is a broadly inclusive but not as prestigious conference).[30] Both of these conferences also have published research proceedings. Also, outside of the more well-known HCI spokes of the ACM organization, there is a supported international conference known as "FaccT" that focuses on bringing together both industry and academic scholars from computer science, social sciences, law, and the humanities to address technology and resulting policy changes from socio-technical areas of emerging technology in terms of how it impacts individuals. Examples of recent papers from this conference include topics such as Human–AI decision-making, AI regulation, and targeted advertising discrimination.[31]

2.2 RESEARCH AND HCI

Collecting and evaluating data for research and applied purposes is a common activity within HCI, and it also holds a connection to law and regulatory policies. Within academic, government, or larger corporate environment, an institutional review board (IRB) or some other human subjects or ethics review committee ensures that the data collection will take appropriate steps to ensure the safety, privacy, and security of the data being collected while not exposing participants to any unnecessary risk (refer to Chapter 5 on Research Regulations and HCI for more detail on research regulations).

While following any relevant policies, evaluation first must identify its goals, appropriate participants, and methodology. Within HCI, determining the appropriate research participants (population) is often an essential aspect of collecting data for evaluation. While some evaluation may more broadly evaluate data from a general, less-specific population, it is common for the population to be specific, such as users with unique experience or characteristics (such as employment in a specific industry or job type), people of a certain age or other demographic parameter, or people with disabilities. Beyond the specifics of the population, another decision is how to select the portion (sample) from that population, as it is not likely that an entire population could realistically be involved in a research project. Probability sampling would involve random sampling from that population versus nonprobability sampling, such as using volunteers or convenience sampling.[32] HCI does not view random sampling of participants as a necessary standard, as the disciplines of psychology and sociology do, primarily because of the lack of standardized government datasets for analysis, leaving researchers to collect their own datasets.[33]

---

[30] HCI International. *HCI International 2024*. Retrieved February 16, 2024, from https://2024.hci.international/.

[31] Association for Computing Machinery. *ACM FAccT 2023 Accepted Papers*. Retrieved February 1, 2024, from https://facctconference.org/2023/acceptedpapers.

[32] Sharp, H., Preece, J. & Rogers, Y. (2019). *Interaction Design: Beyond Human-Computer Interaction*. John Wiley and Sons, p. 228.

[33] Lazar, J., Feng, J. H., & Hochheiser, H. (2017). *Research Methods in Human-Computer Interaction*. Morgan Kaufmann, pp. 5–6.

Because evaluation studies within HCI tend to involve novel topics or technology, it is common for pilot studies with a small number of participants to be conducted to gain insight and fine-tune any details prior to a larger data collection study. Details of the recruitment, data collection, storage, and use of the data collected will typically be approved by the review board or ethics review committee, and this will specify details such as the form in which data can be recorded (notes, photographs, audio recording, video, screen or keystroke captures, etc.). The COVID-19 pandemic increased the use of remote user observation for data collection, with tools such as Zoom used to observe or record data.[34] This evolution has increased the potential reach in user sample data while presenting some unique logistical challenges when planning HCI research.

2.3 PRACTICAL INTERSECTION BETWEEN HCI, LAW, AND POLICY

One of the international conferences supported by the ACM (the computing organization mentioned earlier) is the ACM Symposium on Computer Science and Law, which aims to bridge the gap between the two.[35] In reality, very little from this conference currently covers HCI and law, and this underscores the need for more emphasis in this area. There are now examples of HCI people who have served in law and policy positions. This would include Lorrie Cranor, who served as the chief technologist for the U.S. Federal Trade Commission and is also a respected HCI researcher and professor of engineering and public policy at Carnegie Mellon University.[36] A non-U.S. example would be Jan Gulliksen, who is an HCI professor and well-known HCI researcher at the KTH Royal Institute of Technology in Sweden and also is involved in public policy, serving on the European Commission and the Swedish Committee for Digitalization.[37]

As noted in the discussions of HCI "waves," there is a long-standing infrastructure problem (inaccessibility and lack the usability of preexisting libraries and foundational technology infrastructure) that was mentioned earlier in this chapter. This is compounded by a disconnect between technology-related laws and policy and HCI. Law and policy can impact design in ways that HCI professionals may not always be aware of. One example of this would be Digital Rights Management laws (such as the DMCA) that have been implemented to address intellectual property protections and unauthorized use of someone else's work. They can also inadvertently create a

---

[34] Griffith, M., Wentz, B., & Lazar, J. (2022). Quantifying the Cost of Web Accessibility Barriers for Blind Users. *Interacting with Computers*, 34(6), pp. 137–149.
[35] Association for Computing Machinery. *ACM Symposium on Computer Science and Law*. Retrieved February 1, 2024, from https://computersciencelaw.org/.
[36] Carnegie Mellon University. *Lorrie Cranor*. Retrieved February 1, 2024, from www.cylab.cmu.edu/directory/bios/cranor-lorrie.html.
[37] KTH Royal Institute of Technology. *Jan Gulliksen*. Retrieved February 1, 2024, from www.kth.se/profile/jangul.

scenario where personalization, accessibility, innovation, and creativity may be stifled because of this type of legal protection.[38]

The field of HCI has relevance to law in a variety of ways. Probably the most prevalent example would be its connection to intellectual property law in terms of the way software is developed and designed, including issues related to copyright law in terms of the design of technology. Refer to Chapter 6 for a focus on Intellectual Property law and its relationship to HCI. Yet another area of HCI and design that holds connection to areas of law would be that of privacy. The almost universal connectivity of modern applications creates a potential for design to have significant influence over the privacy rights of individuals. Refer to Chapter 4 for a more in-depth discussion of Privacy. Chapter 8 (Artificial Intelligence) and Chapter 9 (Dark Patterns in HCI) also have relevance to the way that interfaces are designed and their legal implications for individuals.

---

[38] Fiesler, C. (2020, April). Lawful Users: Copyright Circumvention and Legal Constraints on Technology Use. In *Proceedings of the 2020 CHI Conference on Human Factors in Computing Systems*, pp. 1–11.

3

Accessibility

3.1 INTRODUCTION

All users should have equal access to digital technologies and content. Designing digital technologies and content so that they can be utilized by the broadest audience, including people with disabilities, should be an obvious design goal. This seems like it would be straightforward, since it is good design (to design for the largest number of users) and good business (because those users are often customers who want to purchase goods and services), right? While people with disabilities deserve equal access to digital technologies and content, in reality, companies, nonprofit organizations, governments, service providers, and professionals often provide technologies and digital content that are inaccessible. And that's why so much of what we discuss in the human–computer interaction (HCI) side of accessibility intertwines with law. For individuals who work in HCI, as researchers or developers, these legal rules for accessibility apply to their design work, regardless of whether they are familiar with the legal rules. This is not unique to HCI; for instance, if you are designing digital healthcare devices, there are many other legal rules (in addition to accessibility) that also apply to one's design work. And furthermore, there are opportunities, for those with expertise in HCI, to get involved with informing law by responding with feedback to regulatory rulemaking, or by giving testimony as bills are under consideration in state legislatures and the U.S. House of Representatives and Senate.

Sometimes the accessibility barriers exist because developers and organizations are simply unaware of accessibility, although the excuses are often inexcusable (e.g., you really can't claim that you didn't know about captioning your video given that video captioning has been going on for television shows for over 50 years).[1] Other times, companies and other organizations do not realize the severity of the problem (i.e., how many consumers they are losing) and perhaps do not know how to fix

---

[1] Lazar, J. (2019). Web Accessibility Policy and Law. In Y. Yesilada & S. Harper (eds.), *Web Accessibility: A Foundation for Research* (2nd ed.). London: Springer-Verlag, pp. 247–261.

accessibility issues (which may be partially due to how little accessibility content is taught in university programs).[2] Inaccessible web content, applications, and devices can lead to societal exclusion, including employment discrimination, pricing discrimination, and exclusion from educational opportunities, commerce, socialization, and creative endeavors.[3]

What causes these organizations to change their ways and move toward making their websites, documents, software applications, operating systems, and hardware devices accessible? The answer is clear: legal requirements for accessibility.[4] Anyone who claims that "the market will take care of it" is unaware of how many companies either are blissfully unaware or actively discriminate against different populations of consumers.[5] A classic example is that of the grocery delivery app Peapod, which was forced by the U.S. Department of Justice (DOJ) to make their website and app accessible for blind users, even though people with disabilities are customers who frequently prefer to use grocery delivery due to transportation concerns, meaning that accessibility would have been a great business opportunity for Peapod.[6] Market forces by themselves frequently do not lead to improved accessibility.[7] Again, that's why the law plays such an important role! This is one of the most obvious areas of HCI where the law directly influences how digital technologies and content need to be designed. Furthermore, legal actions related to digital accessibility also bring attention to the topic and help to educate the public about the importance of digital accessibility, an added benefit.

However, it's important to identify here that there aren't just two viewpoints here, that of HCI and law. People with disabilities currently play various roles in HCI (as developers, codesigners, and users) and in law (as lawyers, advocates, and litigants). People with disabilities (PWD) are the ones most impacted by the outcomes of accessibility work. PWD want to use technology as a tool in their daily life and don't understand why companies, employers, educational institutions, and other

---

[2] See Putnam, C., Dahman, M., Rose, E., Cheng, J., & Bradford, G. (2016). Best Practices for Teaching Accessibility in University Classrooms: Cultivating Awareness, Understanding, and Appreciation for Diverse Users. *ACM Transactions on Accessible Computing (TACCESS)*, 8(4), pp. 1–26, for some best practices in terms of teaching about digital accessibility.

[3] Lazar, J., Goldstein, D., & Taylor, A. (2015). *Ensuring Digital Accessibility through Process and Policy*. Elsevier/Morgan Kaufmann Publishers.

[4] Research by Loiacono and Djamasbi has found that corporations really do act differently when statutes related to web accessibility are present: Loiacono, E. T., & Djamasbi, S. (2013). Corporate Website Accessibility: Does Legislation Matter? *Universal Access in the Information Society*, 12(1), pp. 115–124.

[5] Lazar, J. (2022). Ableist Language in the Web Accessibility Case of Robles v. Domino's Pizza Inc: When "Everyone" Doesn't Include People with Disabilities. *Including Disability*, 1(2), pp. 7–26.

[6] Available at: www.justice.gov/opa/pr/justice-department-enters-settlement-agreement-peapod-ensure-peapod-grocery-delivery-website.

[7] Perhaps this could be a great example of why we need behavioral economics, since ignoring potential customers who actively want your goods or services would not be the decision of a "rational decision-maker."

organizations fail to acknowledge their needs in terms of the user experience. Or, put another way, PWD favor real accessibility that meets their needs, whereas an organizational point of view might favor doing the absolute minimum to meet legal compliance. Yet that viewpoint, of doing the bare minimum to meet legal compliance, misses out on the great opportunities for increased numbers of customers and the great opportunities for technical innovation that accessibility presents. And many organizations are unaware of the existing legal framework, meaning that it is not as effective as it could potentially be.

The United States has a comprehensive yet complex legal framework when it comes to digital accessibility.[8] The United States is a "common law" country (refer to Chapter 1), meaning that the legal tradition views case law, the precedents from court decisions, as being a source of legal rules, with case law having the ability to interpret or overrule statutes and regulations. That means that some legal rules are encoded in statutes or regulations and some legal rules are established by case law. Yet because many of the rules are not encoded in statutes or regulations, they are often hard to find and understand, for people with an HCI background, but no legal background. Put another way, your typical person with extensive experience in HCI may not be familiar with technical standards for accessibility, but likely could read through them and comprehend them. However, even an HCI expert in technical aspects of accessibility may not be able to read through a 60-page court opinion, identify where in the 60 pages the legal rule is described, and determine what jurisdiction that legal rule has based on the court that issued it. Similarly, those trained in law may understand the legal rules and feel comfortable reading through a 60-page court opinion, but not feel comfortable with the technical aspects related to actually implementing accessibility. And chances are good that the lawyers are more comfortable with the idea that law contains many "gray areas" of interpretation, whereas an HCI person may want a 100 percent clear answer in the law which simply doesn't exist.[9]

Accessibility, the idea that everyone deserves equal access to digital technologies and content, is shorthand for a multilayer, complex, and fast-moving area of U.S. law. Just as digital accessibility is often viewed as a subset of the broader area of HCI, the legal aspects of digital accessibility are often viewed as falling under the broad umbrella of civil rights law or the subset of civil rights law known as disability rights law.[10] For instance, in the United States, the Americans with Disabilities Act

---

[8] The Digital Accessibility Rights Evaluation (DARE) Index gives the USA 22.5/25 for the country's laws and regulations on digital accessibility. The USA lost 2.5 points for not having ratified the UN Convention on The Rights of Persons with Disabilities. https://g3ict.org/country-profile/united-states-of-america.

[9] As Annie Ross described it, "As an HCI person, I want a clear answer, and the odds of me getting a clear answer in the law are very slim. I want more clarity than the law can give."

[10] This chapter is only focusing on legal aspects of digital accessibility, not physical accessibility such as ramps, curb cuts, wide door frames, and turnaround radius. If you are interested in learning more about physical accessibility, we suggest consulting with various physical accessibility guidelines from the U.S. Access Board. Available at: www.access-board.gov/.

("ADA") is a key statute at the federal level and is likely the best-known disability rights law. There are other disability rights laws at the federal level, such as the Rehabilitation Act (of which Section 508 requires accessibility for all federal technologies). In many instances, often untapped federal or state constitutional sources of disability rights are underutilized or overlooked.[11] And at least eighteen U.S. states also have state-level statutes related to technology accessibility for government, usually requiring accessible websites for state government services.[12] However, the case law related to digital accessibility primarily relates to federal statutes and federal courts, not state law.[13] And these sources of law frequently separate out technologies based on ownership or industry, or even the relationship between a website and the physical nature of the organization and whether they have a location open to the public to visit. From a computing point of view, a website is a website, running the same technologies and standards, regardless of whether that website is for a (1) federal government agency, (2) online store, (3) supermarket, or (4) airline. Yet from a legal point of view, these are four completely different sets of legal rules for the digital accessibility of these four organizations.

There are many different questions to consider, some of which are primarily HCI questions, and some of which are primarily legal questions.[14] The situation is not as simple as "all digital technologies and content must be accessible for all people with disabilities." The next sections will separate out some of the HCI aspects, and the legal aspects, of digital accessibility. For instance, understanding which types of testing tools and procedures are effective is an HCI topic, whereas understanding what tools or procedures are legally required is a legal topic. Procurement processes can be used to enforce accessibility (a legal topic), but what the procurement contracts specify about accessibility is likely to be an HCI topic. Technical standards are a perfect example of the complexity of digital accessibility law – there are international technical standards, such as the Web Content Accessibility Guidelines (WCAG), which were created with many stakeholders and technologists, including primarily people involved with HCI. Some digital technologies have specific technical standards specified by law, for example, airlines and federal government agencies must conform with WCAG, whereas some state governments (depending on the state) and public accommodations aren't

---

[11] Ferleger, D. (2020). The Constitutional Right to Community Services: Olmstead and Equal Protection. *Journal of Legal Medicine*, 40(1), pp. 101–114. ("Powerful enforcement by the judiciary is limited because thus far the courts have not recognized that the mandate partakes of constitutional liberty interests.").

[12] When Shaheen, N. L. & Lazar, J. (2018). K–12 Technology Accessibility: The Message from State Governments. *Journal of Special Education Technology*, 33(2), pp. 83–97, was published, there were eighteen states with state-level laws requiring digital accessibility.

[13] One notable exception is the use of the Unruh Civil Rights Act, a California civil rights statute, which, unlike Title III of the ADA, provides for damages. Cal. Civ. Code § 51.

[14] Lazar, J. (2019). Web Accessibility Policy and Law. In Yesilada, Y & Harper, S. (eds.), *Web Accessibility: A Foundation for Research* (2nd ed.). London: Springer-Verlag, pp. 247–261.

required to use WCAG (legally) even if that is considered a best practice (from HCI). Legal rules often aren't in line with what is considered to be best practice within the HCI community.

3.2 WHAT IS DIGITAL ACCESSIBILITY IN HCI?

What does it mean to have accessible digital technologies and content? In a nutshell, it means that someone with a disability (or who is perceived to have a disability), whether it is a perceptual disability, a motor disability, a cognitive disability, or some combination of disabilities, can access the same content and the same technologies and engage in the same transactions, as someone without a disability, with a substantially equivalent ease of use. Users with disabilities often use alternate forms of input or output (assistive technologies), such as voice recognition, screen magnification, screen readers, alternate keyboards, captioning, and/or no pointing devices. Websites, applications, operating systems, e-books, and documents (e.g., in Word and PDF format) all need to be designed for maximum flexibility, so that they will work for people who are using all of these different assistive technology approaches. The mechanisms should be created with concepts of "universal design," designing for as many users as possible, in mind. And some people with disabilities don't use any of these assistive technology devices or input/output approaches, but the flexibility helps them as well. For instance, while many people with perceptual or motor impairments use different input or output approaches, people with some cognitive impairments (e.g., Down syndrome) don't use any of these assistive technologies but do heavily utilize features that are already built into the operating system, such as features to autofill forms, word prediction, and "save-my-password" features.[15] The flexibility inherent in digital accessibility actually helps all users, not just users with disabilities. It's just that people without disabilities don't have any legal rights for an interface to be flexible for them, whereas people with disabilities do.

3.2.1 *Defining Digital Accessibility*

From an HCI point of view, there is a question, which in many ways has never been fully answered.[16] When we say accessibility, do we mean compliance with technical standards for accessibility, or do we mean that people with disabilities can actually use the technology? These aren't the same thing. For instance, the best-known technical standard in accessibility is the WCAG. However, it is possible for a website to be in compliance with WCAG and still be incredibly hard for people

---

[15] Schmutz, S., Sonderegger, A., & Sauer, J. (2016). Implementing Recommendations from Web Accessibility Guidelines: Would They Also Provide Benefits to Nondisabled Users. *Human Factors*, 58(4), pp. 611–629.

[16] See www.w3.org/WAI/fundamentals/accessibility-usability-inclusion/ for a great discussion of the differences between accessibility, usability, and inclusion.

with disabilities to use it (and likely hard for people without disabilities to use it as well).[17] If a website meets technical standards but people with disabilities are still unable to use it, does that count as accessible? Or looking ahead to a legal question, if people with disabilities can't use it, but it seems to meet technical standards for accessibility, does that meet the legal requirements? Or what if it takes over an hour for a blind person to get the same type of access, but there is access, does that meet legal muster (spoiler alert: it likely would not meet legal muster).[18] So how does one ensure that a website can be effectively used by someone with a disability? Not only by meeting technical standards but also by including people with disabilities in your design process and doing sufficient evaluation of the technology with users.[19] So when one discusses accessibility, it is important to clearly describe the meaning of accessibility, as definitions may differ. There are narrower meanings of accessibility and broader meanings of accessibility. The narrowest meaning of accessibility is "compliance with technical standards for accessibility," but it may not be effective or useful for end users, even if that seems to be the messaging from some legal rules.

A much broader definition of accessibility involves including people with disabilities in design processes and performing sufficient evaluation of the technology with users with disabilities. If accessibility is the goal, how do you get there from an HCI/design point of view? Disability advocates for years have been requesting and trumpeting the benefits of "born-accessible design." At this point, the knowledge on the born-accessible model seems to revolve around four different activities, which, in an ideal world, should be used together.[20]

3.2.2 *The Born-Accessible Model*

The first activity of the born-accessible model is to involve people with disabilities in the design and development from the start. That makes sure that you fully understand the needs of your users with disabilities, as well as how mixed-ability teams collaborate using technology. There are a lot of ways to involve users. Potentially, if people with disabilities already work at an organization, you might create a

---

[17] Power, C., Freire, A., Petrie, H., & Swallow, D. (2012, May). Guidelines Are Only Half of the Story: Accessibility Problems Encountered by Blind Users on the Web. In *Proceedings of the ACM SIGCHI Conference on Human Factors in Computing Systems*, pp. 433–442.

[18] To justify why it would not, read the court's recent decision in Robles v. Domino's Pizza LLC, No. CV 16-6599 JGB (EX), 2021 WL 2945562 (C.D. Cal. June 23, 2021), where the court states that a 45-minute wait on the phone for a pizza, while technically an accommodation, is not legally sufficient, due to the long wait.

[19] See www.w3.org/WAI/fundamentals/accessibility-usability-inclusion/ or Lazar, J., Goldstein, D., & Taylor, A. (2015). *Ensuring Digital Accessibility Through Process and Policy*. Waltham, MA: Elsevier/Morgan Kaufmann Publishers.

[20] Lazar, J. (2023). A Framework for Born-Accessible Development of Software and Digital Content. *Proceedings of INTERACT 2023*, pp. 333–338. Also, refer to the following keynote speech: www.youtube.com/watch?v=kU142qzMmj8&t=24s.

committee within the organization of employees with disabilities.[21] Similarly, for a company, it would be possible to create an external panel of consumers with disabilities.[22] If no such individuals or relationships already exist, a productive approach would be to reach out to disability rights groups, also known as "consumer groups." These are advocacy groups that likely are well known for their activism in the area of technology, including the National Federation of the Blind (NFB),[23] the National Association of the Deaf (NAD),[24] and the American Association of People with Disabilities (AAPD).[25] The key thing is to involve people with disabilities early on, in the ideation process, to get a better understanding of their needs and also to identify any misperceptions or misunderstandings that the organization building or modifying the technology might have.

The second activity is to have accessibility as a clear design and project goal, up front, so that it is included in all planning and design specifications. Unless it is prioritized and made transparent, accessibility is often forgotten about in the design process. If technologies are being procured rather than built in-house, there are well-established techniques for prioritizing and including accessibility in the procurement process, ensuring that an organization only procures accessible technologies.[26]

The third activity is to build content, applications, or technologies using a well-accepted set of technical standards for accessibility. In each category of technology or content, there is generally one set of guidelines that is well accepted. For web content accessibility, you want to use the WCAG.[27] There are other standards; for instance, for e-books, you want to use the accessible EPUB3 standards.[28] For PDF documents, you want to use PDF/UA.[29] Because the WCAG is the most well-documented, well-accepted set of guidelines for digital accessibility, they can be utilized for non-web content, as well. There is a guidance document, WCAG2ICT,[30]

---

[21] See Lazar, J. & Olalere, A. (2011). Investigation of Best Practices for Maintaining Section 508 Compliance in U.S. Federal Web Sites. *Proceedings of the 2011 Human Computer Interaction International Conference*, pp. 498–506, for an example of a U.S. federal agency that has a committee of employees with disabilities which serves as an ongoing, involved group of users.

[22] See Google's Accessibility Trusted Tester program for an example of this: www.google.com/accessibility/initiatives-research/ (note however that the "Trusted Tester" program from the U.S. Federal government is something completely different).

[23] National Federation of the Blind. (2024). Available at: https://nfb.org/.

[24] National Association of the Deaf. (2024). Available at: www.nad.org/.

[25] American Association of People with Disabilities. Available at: www.aapd.com/.

[26] This procurement approach is commonly used by state and federal government, see www.section508.gov/buy-sell/ or the National Association of State Chief Information Officers (NASCIO) Policy-Driven Adoption for Accessibility: www.nascio.org.

[27] Available at: www.w3.org/TR/WCAG21/.

[28] Available at: http://idpf.org/epub/30/.

[29] Available at: www.pdfa.org/wp-content/until2016_uploads/2013/08/PDFUA-in-a-Nutshell-PDFUA.pdf.

[30] Guidance on Applying WCAG 2.0 to Non-Web Information and Communications Technologies (WCAG2ICT). Available at: www.w3.org/WAI/standards-guidelines/wcag/non-web-ict/.

that describes how to apply these concepts to non-web technologies. Content authors and developers use these standards, yet questions of how to apply them commonly arise during application. For instance, you may find that you are designing a specific type of app, where you don't immediately identify that there are technical standards for your category of technology or content.[31] You should keep looking for domain-specific types of standards, but an important first step is to utilize the concepts of WCAG.

The fourth activity is to do sufficient accessibility evaluations, early on, of prototypes, templates, and working versions. Typically, there are three different types of evaluations. One type is usability testing involving people with disabilities. A second type is expert reviews, also known as a manual inspection, and a third type is using automated accessibility testing tools.[32] These three techniques all have different strengths and weaknesses.

In usability testing, representative users with disabilities attempt representative tasks on an interface. It is important to have a broad representation of people with various types of disabilities. This is best at understanding true usability; however, people with one disability often have trouble identifying barriers for people with other types of disabilities, and this approach is very time intensive and limited in the number of interfaces or screens that can be evaluated. Note that the people with disabilities who evaluate your interfaces need to be different individuals from those who are involved with the design process (using approach one), as it wouldn't make sense to ask people who are involved in codesigning technologies to be the ones who evaluate them.

The second type of evaluation is manual inspections, which are best at determining compliance with technical standards, but given that the experts are often people who themselves do not have disabilities (but do have certifications in accessibility, such as from the U.S. government trusted tester program[33] or IAAP),[34] the expert inspections often miss aspects related to usability. So that means that manual inspections focus on that narrow, compliance-with-standards definition of accessibility.

The third type of evaluation uses an automated accessibility testing tool, which is the only evaluation that scales easily to thousands, or even millions of interfaces; however, current tools fall short of being able to themselves determine even low-level compliance with technical standards. There are many false positives, where the tool identifies things as accessibility barriers that in reality are not accessibility barriers, and the tools often require hundreds of manual checks (e.g., when ALT text is present, but the tool cannot determine if it is useful). None of these evaluation techniques, by themselves, can establish accessibility – it's the combination of

---

[31] For instance, digital libraries. While you can apply the core WCAG concepts to digital libraries, you may also find specialized guidelines, such as those at https://sites.uwm.edu/guidelines/.
[32] Lazar, J., Goldstein, D., & Taylor, A. (2015). *Ensuring Digital Accessibility Through Process and Policy*. Waltham, MA: Elsevier/Morgan Kaufmann Publishers.
[33] Available at: www.dhs.gov/trusted-tester.
[34] Available at: www.accessibilityassociation.org/.

these evaluation techniques that can identify accessibility problems to be fixed and can help determine whether an interface is accessible or not.[35]

3.2.3 Managing Digital Accessibility

Once a new website, software, hardware, or other digital technology is implemented, it should be monitored within the context of well-established organizational and management techniques for accessibility. For instance, there should be ongoing compliance monitoring for all types of digital technology.[36] This includes rules on the frequency of checking for accessibility. For a hardware device, once it is built or procured and is accessible, it does not need to be checked frequently, as it will not change. However, web content changes on a daily basis, so there must be some type of ongoing check to ensure that a website continues to be accessible. Somewhere in the middle of this spectrum is software, which is updated maybe every six months or once a year, and those software rollouts or updates must be evaluated for accessibility.[37] Another best practice is to have an easy way for users to provide feedback so that PWD can flag problems that slip through the monitoring. Having organizational coordinators, someone who is responsible for accessibility in a certain part of an organization and has both responsibility and control, is another useful approach. Many large technology companies now have directors of accessibility, some as high as the vice president level.[38] Multiple U.S. states currently have roles of the Chief Digital Accessibility officer.[39] U.S. federal government agencies have what are known as "Section 508 coordinators," who have responsibility for digital accessibility but often do not have a high profile in the agency and, in many cases, may have this responsibility added onto their existing roles.[40] Using organizational and management approaches can ensure that there are people monitoring accessibility compliance who are given the power and the responsibility for ensuring equal access to digital technologies.

---

[35] Note that there is another category of tool, known as an "overlay" which claims to fix web accessibility problems but the disability community in general is against using these tools because the claims are often exaggerated. See https://overlayfactsheet.com/.
[36] Lazar, J., Goldstein, D., & Taylor, A. (2015). *Ensuring Digital Accessibility Through Process and Policy*. Waltham, MA: Elsevier/Morgan Kaufmann Publishers.
[37] Wentz, B. & Lazar, J. (2016). Exploring the Impact of Inaccessible Redesigns and Updates. In P. Langdon, J. Lazar, A. Heylighen, & H. Dong (eds.), *Designing Around People*. London: Springer-Verlag, pp. 3–12.
[38] For instance, Tom Wlodkowski is the VP of accessibility at Comcast – www.linkedin.com/in/thomas-wlodkowski-b13964b5.
[39] In Pennsylvania, the title is Chief Accessibility Officer; in Massachusetts, Chief Information Technology Accessibility Officer; in Maryland, Director of Accessibility; in Illinois, Chief Information Accessibility Officer; and in Minnesota, Chief Information Accessibility Officer.
[40] Lazar, J., Williams, V., Gunderson, J., & Foltz, T. (2017). Investigating the Potential of a Dashboard for Monitoring U.S. Federal Website Accessibility. In *Proceedings of the 50th Annual Hawaii International Conference on System Sciences (HICSS)*, pp. 2428–2437.

Given the previous descriptions about the differences between a narrow definition of accessibility (compliance with technical standards) and a broad view of accessibility (using a born-accessible approach), the legal frameworks described in later sections of this chapter generally focus on a narrow definition (compliance with technical standards), but are starting to move a bit more broadly, often with the addition of requiring that the digital technologies or content are tested with people with disabilities before implementation. While bringing in users with disabilities to test interfaces before they are released is progress, it's still not the most effective, inclusive, or cost-effective approach, and not the broadest view possible.

3.3 UNDERSTANDING THE CORE LEGAL THEORIES UNDERPINNING DIGITAL ACCESSIBILITY LAW IN THE U.S.

In understanding U.S. legal requirements related to digital accessibility, and before looking at the legal rules themselves, there are three key concepts that are especially important to understand: (1) the type of organization, (2) the nexus theory of the ADA, and (3) the effective communications requirement of the ADA. These core legal theories conceptualize digital technologies using approaches very different from how the HCI community conceptualizes them. We're focusing on the ADA in some of this discussion because it applies everywhere in the U.S., the coverage of public accommodations is very broad, and the considerations in applying it will often be relevant to other laws and regulations, too. But, as we'll see, the ADA is far from the whole story.

3.3.1 Type of Organization

Even though the technologies (the software, the devices, the languages used in website design) may be identical, legal coverage is determined by the type of organization providing the digital technology or content, which may determine which law governs. For instance, a federal government agency, an airline, and a supermarket store may use the same technologies within their respective websites (HTML, JavaScript, Cascading Style Sheets, etc.), yet legal requirements related to the accessibility of the content are covered in three different statutes and/or their associated regulations. The airline website is covered under the Air Carrier Access Act, the federal government website is covered under Section 508 of the Rehabilitation Act, and the supermarket website is covered as a public accommodation under Title III of the ADA (for nonlawyers, Title III is a fancy but technically correct way of saying "Section 3"). Being covered by these different laws impacts which federal agency enforces the legal rules (e.g., airlines are enforced by the FAA, supermarkets are enforced by DOJ, and government websites are enforced basically by no agency, although some agencies now collect data about their lack of compliance with Section 508).

Understanding which statute governs an organization helps in understanding why there are different standards and approaches, depending on the type of organization. For instance, the regulations for both Section 508 and the Air Carrier Access Act specifically require conformance with the WCAG for web content. However, web content is not mentioned in either the statute or the regulations for Title III of the ADA. So if you are an entity covered under Title III of the Americans with Disabilities Act, you *can* use the WCAG to comply with the requirements for effective communication, but you are not limited to using the WCAG. Similarly, Section 508 applies to all technologies in the federal government, both for the public and for federal employees, including kiosks, phones, copier machines, and office equipment. The Air Carrier Access Act specifically mentions only accessibility for airline websites and airport kiosks. The ADA, since it does not specifically mention websites or kiosks, is frequently (and incorrectly) assumed not to apply to websites or point-of-sale terminals. However, the ADA includes some broad mandates, including one for "effective communication," that apply to *any* technologies which currently exist or may exist in the future (see Section 3.3.3 on the effective communications requirement). The Justice Department has been making this point for over 25 years, that creating a new technology does not suddenly give you the right to discriminate simply because that technology is not specifically mentioned in the ADA statute or regulations.[41]

3.3.2 *The Nexus Theory of the ADA*

While the coverage of airlines and the federal government is relatively straightforward, the coverage of private employers (Title I of the ADA) and public accommodations (Title III of the ADA) is a bit more complex because the mandates for inclusion and nondiscrimination are broader (e.g., encompass *everything* including professional services, education, commerce, and not just digital technologies). But there's a logic that's been applied by courts to the law that has influenced, and limited, how courts interpret it, called the "nexus" theory of the ADA. In short, the nexus theory says that a website is covered under Title III of the ADA, only if there is a "nexus" (a connection) between the website, and the physical public accommodation, and the website being inaccessible limits equal access to the public accommodation. The nexus theory predates cases on web accessibility, though it is especially important here. For instance, the nexus theory was used in *Rendon v. Valleycrest Productions*. In *Rendon*, the 11th circuit ruled that an inaccessible telephone selection process for contestants on the "Who Wants to Be a Millionaire?"

---

[41] Patrick, D. *Letter from Assistant Attorney General for Civil Rights Deval Patrick to Sen. Tom Harkin, United States Department of Justice* (September 9, 1966), www.justice.gov/crt/foia/file/666366/download and United States Department of Justice, *Statement of Interest in the New v. Lucky Brand Jeans* (April 10, 2014), www.ada.gov/briefs/lucky_brand%20_soi.docx.

TV show discriminated against potential contestants with disabilities, since the TV show was a place of "public accommodation."[42] One might not think that a TV show is a place, but the nexus theory says it needs to be treated as one. In *Carparts Distribution Ctr., Inc. v. Auto. Wholesaler's Ass'n of New England, Inc.*, the first circuit ruled that:

> Neither Title III nor its implementing regulations make any mention of physical boundaries or physical entry. Many goods and services are sold over the telephone or by mail with customers never physically entering the premises of a commercial entity to purchase the goods or services. To exclude this broad category of businesses from the reach of Title III and limit the application of Title III to physical structures which persons must enter to obtain goods and services would run afoul of the purposes of the ADA and would severely frustrate Congress's intent that individuals with disabilities fully enjoy the goods, services, privileges and advantages, available indiscriminately to other members of the general public.[43]

Despite websites not being an exact match for this early use of the nexus concept, multiple circuit courts have ruled that a website is covered under the ADA, but only if there is a "nexus" between the website and the physical public accommodation. Under this "nexus" theory, the website itself wouldn't be covered, but if the website is a gateway to the public accommodation, if having an inaccessible website blocks you from getting access to the benefits and services of the public accommodation, then the website itself must be accessible under the ADA.[44]

Making the situation more complex, circuit courts of appeals have different interpretations and applications of federal law, causing what is known as a "circuit-split." The 2nd, 3rd, 6th, 9th, and 11th circuits all require a nexus between the website and the physical public accommodation for a website to be covered under Title III of the ADA. By contrast, the 1st circuit and 7th circuit have no such nexus requirement, meaning that a website, by itself, counts as a public accommodation. So, for instance, Netflix, a website which does not have a physical location that consumers visit, is still required to have an accessible website and content according to the 1st circuit.[45] If you are wondering why are there different rules in different parts of the country (again, called a circuit-split!) and why a website wouldn't need to be accessible if there was no physical location to visit but would need to be accessible if there is a physical location to visit, you're not alone. There have been many different law articles written about the nexus theory and the weaknesses inherent in

---

[42] Rendon v. Valleycrest Prods., Ltd., 294 F.3d 1279 (11th Cir. 2002).
[43] Carparts Distribution Ctr., Inc. v. Auto. Wholesaler's Ass'n of New England, Inc., 37 F.3d 12 (1st Cir. 1994).
[44] "[n]o individual shall be discriminated against on the basis of disability in the full and equal enjoyment of the goods, services, facilities, privileges, advantages, or accommodations of any place of public accommodation by any person who owns, leases (or leases to), or operates a place of public accommodation." – 42 U.S.C. § 12182(a).
[45] Nat'l Ass'n of the Deaf v. Netflix, Inc., 869 F. Supp. 2d 196 (D. Mass. 2012).

the nexus theory.[46] For instance, during the COVID-19 pandemic, requirements for web accessibility would appear or disappear depending on the weekly decisions of a public health authority on COVID shutdowns, due to the nexus rule requiring a physical location.[47] Despite these weaknesses, for now, the nexus rule governs web accessibility under Title III of the ADA in a large part of the U.S.

3.3.3 The Effective Communications Requirement of the ADA

"Effective communications" is a legal concept under Title III of the ADA that is necessary for understanding digital accessibility. Among other things, the regulations state: "*A public accommodation shall furnish appropriate auxiliary aids and services where necessary to ensure effective communication with individuals with disabilities. This includes an obligation to provide effective communication to companions who are individuals with disabilities.*"[48] However, neither the statute nor the regulations for Title III specifically mention websites. Since 1996, the DOJ has stated that websites of public accommodations are covered under the "effective communications" requirement of Title III of the ADA, which exists in both the statute and the regulations.[49] The DOJ and courts have interpreted the effective communications requirement to cover all forms of communication, including websites. Sources of reference for this interpretation usually include the initial letter from Assistant Attorney General for Civil Rights Deval Patrick to Sen. Tom Harkin in 1996[50] and the DOJ Statement of Interest in the *New v. Lucky Brand Jeans* case in 2014 explaining the application of the "effective communications" requirement to websites.[51] In their Statement of Interest[52] the DOJ explained that

---

[46] This is just a sampling of articles criticizing the nexus test: Albani, A. (2017). Equality in the Age of the Internet: Websites under Title III of the Americans with Disabilities Act. *Journal of Business and Technology Law*, 13(97), pp. 115–116; Nikki D. Kessling (2008). Why the Target "Nexus Test" Leaves Disabled Americans Disconnected: A Better Approach to Determine Whether Private Commercial Websites Are "Places Of Public Accommodation", *Houston Law Review*, 45(991), p. 995; Johanna Smith & John Inazu (2021). Virtual Access: A New Framework for Disability and Human Flourishing in an Online World, WIS. L. REV, 21(719), pp. 721–722; Lazar, J., & Ferleger, D. (2022). A Reconceptualization of Website Accessibility Under the ADA: Resolving the Inter-Circuit Conflict Post-Pandemic. *Santa Clara High Technology Law Review*, 39(1), pp. 63–90.

[47] Lazar, J. & Ferleger, D. (2022). A Reconceptualization of Website Accessibility Under the ADA: Resolving the Inter-Circuit Conflict Post-Pandemic. *Santa Clara High Technology Law Review*, 39(1), pp. 63–90.

[48] 28 C.F.R. § 36.303(c)(1).

[49] 42 U.S.C. § 12182(b)(2)(A)(iii); 28 C.F.R. § 36.303.

[50] Patrick, D. *Letter from Assistant Attorney General for Civil Rights Deval Patrick to Sen. Tom Harkin, United States Department of Justice* (September 9, 1996), www.justice.gov/crt/foia/file/666366/download.

[51] United States Department of Justice, *Statement of Interest in the New v. Lucky Brand Jeans* (April 10, 2014), www.ada.gov/briefs/lucky_brand%20_soi.docx.

[52] You can think of a "statement of interest" at a trial court level as playing the same role as an "amicus curiae" filed at an appellate level.

the ADA cannot predict in advance every potential technology that could be used in a public accommodation, so regardless of what type of technology or communication, the general ADA requirements of equal access, and specifically the "effective communications" requirement under Title III (Public Accommodations), still apply.[53] Note that because this is an agency interpretation of their own statute and regulation, and not a statute or regulation per se, there is a "hierarchy" of how courts prioritize or defer to (or do not defer to) these agency rules, and this is known as "deference." Up until June 2024, there were three levels of deference: Chevron/Auer/Skidmore (see Chapter 1 for an explanation of the legal concept of deference). However, in the *Loper Bright Enterprises v. Raimondo* case (2024), the U.S. Supreme Court overturned the concept of Chevron Deference. As this book is being published in late 2025, it is unknown how this will impact the legal framework for accessibility.

3.4 SOURCES OF LEGAL RULES

The legal framework for digital accessibility comes through a patchwork of legal rules specific to web and broader technologies, based on statutes, regulations, case law, and administrative interpretations, with differing requirements for technical conformance and organizational type. For simplicity's sake, the next sections will be organized by the statutes from which the legal rules originate. In some places, a statute provides detailed information about digital accessibility. In some places, the statute authorizes a regulation which provides detailed information about accessibility. In some places, absent those clear requirements in statutes or regulations, courts (case law) or federal agencies may be interpreting the statutes or regulations to require accessibility.

Unlike other areas at the intersection of HCI and law where there may be a constitutional basis for some legal rules (e.g., privacy, intellectual property, or voting), currently, the U.S. Constitution and the state constitutions do not provide any explicit legal rules related to digital accessibility, although there may be protections which are present by implication and will be interpreted by courts at some point in the future. We suggest to the reader to consult Waterstone's future-looking article[54] to learn more about the potential use of constitutional law for disability rights in the future.

3.4.1 *Section 508 of the Rehabilitation Act*

We will start by describing a statute that focuses on digital accessibility, but only in the federal government, Section 508 of the Rehabilitation Act:

---

[53] United States Department of Justice, Statement of Interest in the New v. Lucky Brand Jeans (April 10, 2014), www.ada.gov/briefs/lucky_brand%20_soi.docx.

[54] Waterstone, M. E. (2013). Disability Constitutional Law. *Emory Law Journal*, 63, pp. 527–580.

3.4 Sources of Legal Rules

> When developing, procuring, maintaining, or using electronic and information technology, each Federal department or agency, including the United States Postal Service, shall ensure, unless an undue burden would be imposed on the department or agency, that the electronic and information technology allows, regardless of the type of medium of the technology
>
> (i) individuals with disabilities who are Federal employees to have access to and use of information and data that is comparable to the access to and use of the information and data by Federal employees who are not individuals with disabilities; and
> (ii) individuals with disabilities who are members of the public seeking information or services from a Federal department or agency to have access to and use of information and data that is comparable to the access to and use of the information and data by such members of the public who are not individuals with disabilities.[55]

In summary, Section 508 requires accessibility for all types of federal technologies (including websites, software, operating systems, and electronic documents in Word and PDF format) used by both the public and also by federal employees. The technical standards cited in the regulations for Section 508 are the WCAG and the regulations were updated in 2017 to require the use of WCAG 2.0.[56] It is important to note that WCAG is designed to be technology-agnostic, so it can be useful for non-web technologies as well (the WCAG2ICT document describes how to apply the WCAG concepts to non-web technologies).[57]

Section 508 of the Rehabilitation Act differs from many of the other statutes and regulations discussed here in that (1) 508 only addresses the U.S. federal government, (2) 508 covers all types of technologies – websites, operating systems, copier machines, and telephones, and (3) 508 clearly covers both federal employees with disabilities using internal systems as well as the general public accessing government information or services. Many of the other legal rules are more limited in the coverage (e.g., covering only websites or covering only public access, not internal employee-facing systems).

A major weakness of Section 508 of the Rehabilitation Act is that no federal agency has the authority to enforce the rules, only to collect data on compliance. The U.S. Access Board has the authority to promulgate regulations (meaning, to start and manage the rulemaking process) related to Section 508, but not to enforce them.[58] Each federal agency is essentially on the "honor system," as the Attorney General is supposed to prepare and issue a report on the state of compliance with

---

[55] 29 U.S.C. § 794d(a)(1)(A).
[56] 36 C.F.R. § 1194.
[57] Web Accessibility Initiative (2024). WCAG2ICT Overview. Available at: www.w3.org/WAI/standards-guidelines/wcag/non-web-ict/.
[58] 29 U.S.C. § 794d (a)(2)(A).

Section 508 in the federal government[59] and will request materials as needed from federal agencies to prepare the report,[60] but the Attorney General had not issued such a report in over a decade. After twelve years, the Attorney General finally issued a Section 508 report again in 2023.[61] There is no enforcement authority, and there are virtually no consequences.

Compliance with Section 508 within the federal government has generally been poor, although that recently has been changing. In many ways, Section 508, because there is no enforcement mechanism, is subject to the political winds in ways that the other legal rules listed in this chapter are not. When an individual or group in the federal government feels that they have political capital that they can spend bringing attention to Section 508, they do, but they do so without formal enforcement jurisdiction. For instance, when the White House has had a disability policy liaison (2010–2016, 2021–Jan 2025), that person would often take a central role in bringing attention to Section 508. From 2022 to 2024, the U.S. Senate Special Committee on Aging, chaired during that time by then Senator Casey (PA), had taken a leading role in bringing attention to Section 508 compliance, holding hearings in July 2022,[62] and September 2023,[63] and putting out a report in 2022.[64]

It went almost unnoticed that in the Consolidated Appropriations Act of 2023, section 752 required that:

> ... the Director of the Office of Management and Budget (in this section referred to as the "Director"), in coordination with the Architectural and Transportation Barriers Compliance Board and the Administrator of General Services (in this section referred to as the "Administrator"), shall disseminate amended or updated criteria and instructions to any Federal department or agency (in this section referred to as an "agency") covered by section 508 of the Rehabilitation Act of 1973 (29 U.S.C. 794d) for the evaluation required pursuant to paragraph (3)(B).[65]

Most notably in this new public law (in sec 752(a)(2)(A)) was the requirement to:

> (A) include, at minimum, requirements that information technologies and digital services must... (ii) be accessible to and usable by individuals with disabilities as

---

[59] 29 U.S.C. § 794d (d)(2).
[60] 29 U.S.C. § 794d (e).
[61] U.S. Department of Justice. (2023). Section 508 Surveys and Reports. Available at: www.justice.gov/crt/section-508-home-page-0.
[62] U.S. Senate Special Committee on Aging. (2022). Click Here: Accessible Federal Technology for People with Disabilities, Older Americans, and Veterans. Available at: www.aging.senate.gov/hearings/click-here-accessible-federal-technology-for-people-with-disabilities-older-americans-and-veterans.
[63] U.S. Senate Special Committee on Aging. (2023). Unlocking the Virtual Front Door: Ensuring Accessible Government Technology for People with Disabilities, Older Adults, and Veterans. Available at: www.aging.senate.gov/hearings/unlocking-the-virtual-front-door-ensuring-accessible-government-technology-for-people-with-disabilities-older-adults-and-veterans.
[64] U.S. Senate Special Committee on Aging. (2022). Unlocking the Virtual Front Door: An Examination of Federal Technology's Accessibility for People with Disabilities, Older Adults and Veterans. Available at: www.aging.senate.gov/imo/media/doc/unlocking_the_virtual_front_door_-_full_report.pdf.
[65] Consolidated Appropriations Act, 2023, 136 STAT. 4459 PUBLIC LAW 117–328, DEC. 29, 2022.

determined from consultation with individuals with disabilities, including those with visual, auditory, tactile, and cognitive disabilities, or members of any disability organization.... (author's note: the new requirement to involve people with disabilities and disability rights groups, is similar to the requirements in the Air Carrier Access Act, listed in a later section).

This requirement from the Consolidated Appropriations Act of 2023 (section 752) led to the Office of Management and Budget (part of the White House), putting out a seventeen-page memo in December 2023 on "Strengthening Digital Accessibility and the Management of Section 508 of the Rehabilitation Act."[66] Most notably among the guidance in this memo are requirements and guidance on how to manage a 508 program within an agency (section A), is an encouragement to use born-accessible design approaches due to the cost savings (section C, which includes guidance on involving people with disabilities as described in the previous paragraph), an encouragement to use HTML instead of PDF and Word formats in communications (section D), guidance on how to prioritize testing and remediation efforts (section E), as well as a list of upcoming milestones and deadlines in 2024 (under "Immediate Agency Actions").

The recent attention on Section 508 has not been limited to the executive and legislative branches. In February 2023, the DC Circuit (a federal Appellate Court), in a case of first impression, ruled that, *"The plain text of Section 794d [of Section 508] extends a private right of action to all persons with disabilities who file administrative complaints requesting accessible technology and who seek only injunctive and declaratory relief."*[67]

This means that both private citizens and government employees, if they have not gotten satisfaction from the administrative complaint that they are authorized to file first under Section 508, then have the ability to use the courts for Section 508 enforcement.

It seems that 25 years after the 1998 amendments to the Rehabilitation Act that we generally refer to as "Section 508" were signed into law, Section 508 is finally starting to get the attention that it deserves.

3.4.2 The Air Carrier Access Act

The Air Carrier Access Act[68] prohibits discrimination against people with disabilities in air transportation. While the statute is broad, the implementing regulations provide more specific requirements about websites and airport kiosks. Specifically,

---

[66] U.S. Office of Management and Budget. (2023). Strengthening Digital Accessibility and the Management of Section 508 of the Rehabilitation Act. Available at: www.whitehouse.gov/wp-content/uploads/2023/12/M-24-08-Strengthening-Digital-Accessibility-and-the-Management-of-Section-508-of-the-Rehabilitation-Act.pdf.

[67] Orozco v. Garland, 60 F.4th 684 (D.C. Cir. 2023).

[68] 49 U.S.C. § 41705. Note that the Air Carrier Access Act has a lot of requirements related to physical accessibility and provision of services. However, since this is a book on human–computer interaction and law, we are limiting our discussion to ICT including websites and kiosks.

an airline website must conform to the WCAG[69] and, more uniquely, to the Air Carrier Access Act, there is a requirement for usability testing involving people with disabilities:

> *Your primary web site must be tested in consultation with individuals with disabilities or members of disability organization(s) who use or want to use carrier Web sites to research or book air transportation in order to obtain their feedback on the Web site's accessibility and usability before the dates specified in paragraph (c)(1) of this section. Collectively, such individuals must be able to provide feedback on the usability of the Web site by individuals with visual, auditory, tactile, and cognitive disabilities. Consultation is required to ensure that your Web site is usable by individuals with disabilities by the date specified in paragraph (c)(1).*[70]

It's also important to note that the regulation also requires specific features on the website, *"as a carrier covered under paragraph (c) of this section, you must provide a mechanism on your primary Web site for persons with disabilities to request disability accommodation services for future flights, including but not limited to wheelchair assistance, seating accommodation, escort assistance for a visually impaired passenger, and stowage of an assistive device."*[71]

The Air Carrier Access Act also has a requirement for airport kiosks provided by airlines, although the requirement is only that 25 percent of the kiosks utilized by an airline (either owned by the airline or jointly leased by the airline) be accessible by the end of 2022.[72] While the minimal "25 percent" requirement is disappointing, it is important to note that the regulation provides detailed technical specifics on kiosk accessibility, which are often lacking in other statutes and regulations and are important because kiosks combine hardware and software.[73] These technical guidelines, while not legally binding on non-airline entities, can provide useful advice for other organizations who want to implement accessible kiosks. For the Air Carrier Access Act, the enforcement remedies are orders to compel issued by the Secretary of Transportation and, occasionally, civil fines for the air carrier.[74]

3.4.3 *The Americans with Disabilities Act (Broadly)*

The ADA is probably the best-known of the U.S. federal statutes that relate to digital accessibility. While the ADA doesn't specifically mention websites or our present-day digital technologies and content in statutes, the power of the ADA in applying to these technologies is the breadth of the ADA. As has already come up in this

---

[69] 14 C.F.R. § 382.43(c).
[70] 14 C.F.R. § 382.43(c)(2).
[71] 14 C.F.R. § 382.43(d).
[72] 14 C.F.R. § 382.57(a).
[73] 14 C.F.R. § 382.57 (c).
[74] 14 C.F.R. § 383.2(a).

chapter, there are three main sections of the ADA – Title I (employment), II (state and local government), and III (public accommodations). To help understand the broad scope of the ADA, the legal rules from each title are listed below.

> *No covered entity shall discriminate against a qualified individual on the basis of disability in regard to job application procedures, the hiring, advancement, or discharge of employees, employee compensation, job training, and other terms, conditions, and privileges of employment.*[75] (Title I)
>
> *No qualified individual with a disability shall, by reason of such disability, be excluded from participation in or be denied the benefits of the services, programs, or activities of a public entity, or be subjected to discrimination by any such entity.*[76] (Title II)
>
> *No individual shall be discriminated against on the basis of disability in the full and equal enjoyment of the goods, services, facilities, privileges, advantages, or accommodations of any place of public accommodation by any person who owns, leases (or leases to), or operates a place of public accommodation.*[77] (Title III)

For many years, defendants who have been sued for inaccessible technologies (such as websites or point-of-sale terminals) often have made the argument that their technologies are not addressed by the ADA because the ADA does not specifically mention their technologies. Unlike with the regulations from Section 508 of the Rehabilitation Act and the Air Carrier Access Act (and as of early 2024, state and local government under Title II of the ADA), websites and technologies are generally not mentioned in the statutes or regulations related to public accommodations in Title III of the ADA. The reason why this is an important distinction is that the legal rules which are based in statutes and regulations (Section 508 of the Rehabilitation Act and the Air Carrier Access Act) provide specific guidance on the technical guidelines to use (such as WCAG or the kiosk guidelines in ACAA), while the legal rules based on case law or administrative guidelines (such as those emanating from case law related to Title III of the ADA) do *not* yet provide specific guidance related to technical guidelines and only require nondiscrimination, effective communication, inclusion, or a similar high-level goal but leave more flexibility for covered entities on how to reach that goal.

The DOJ has been refuting this claim of "our technologies aren't listed in the ADA so I can discriminate using them" for many years, and a majority of courts (with some exceptions) have interpreted the ADA to include digital technologies for covered entities within the ADA. Because neither the ADA statute nor the regulations in Title III mention digital technologies, the major source of legal rules covering websites, kiosks, and software for public accommodations covered under Title III has been case law at the federal level.

---

[75] 42 U.S.C. § 12112.
[76] 42 U.S.C. § 12132.
[77] 42 U.S.C. § 12182.

3.4.4 State and Local Government: Title II of the ADA

Title II of the ADA focuses on the inclusion of people with disabilities in the "services, programs, or activities of a public entity." In practice, when it comes to digital accessibility, there are two and potentially three overlapping statutes that apply to state and local government. First, Title II regulations did not specifically mention websites, software applications, or other technologies, until April 2024. Title II coverage had applied due to the "effective communications" requirement discussed in earlier sections. A rulemaking process to clarify regulations for website accessibility for entities covered under Title II began in 2010 but ended in 2017 without a proposed rule being issued. The U.S. DOJ put out a notice of proposed rulemaking in August 2023, which closed in October 2023.[78] The notice of proposed rulemaking received 345 public comments, and the DOJ issued the regulation (known as a final rule) for Title II in April 2024.[79] The DOJ, prior to the 2024 rule, had issued a great deal of guidance on Title II coverage, and in Sept 2025, indicated that they may refine the 2024 rule in the future.

Second, because nearly all state and local governments receive some form of federal funding, the broad nondiscrimination requirements of Section 504 of the Rehabilitation Act (described in Section 3.4.7) also apply.

Third, depending on the state or local jurisdiction of the website, a state-level statute equivalent to Section 508 (sometimes known as mini-508s) may apply. Almost half of U.S. states have such statutes, which nearly always require accessible websites for state government and may also require accessible operating systems and application software for state employees, as well as require procurement of only accessible technology using state funds.[80]

Even without a specific regulation in place, the Civil Rights Division of the U.S. DOJ and the Office for Civil Rights at the U.S. Department of Education, had been taking actions, for instance, issuing a joint "Dear Colleague" letter in 2010. Such a guidance letter is a source of a legal rule, but according to the "hierarchy of deference" discussed in Chapter 1, courts may not give as much deference to these agency interpretations as they do to actual regulations, statutes, or case law. This guidance letter from 2010 states that inaccessible e-book readers cannot be used at colleges and universities without providing an accessible equivalent

---

[78] Notice of Proposed Rulemaking: Nondiscrimination on the Basis of Disability: Accessibility of Web Information and Services of State and Local Government Entities. (Docket: DOJ-CRT-2023–0007): US Department of Justice. Available at: www.regulations.gov/document/DOJ-CRT-2023-0007-0001.

[79] The final rule is available at: www.federalregister.gov/documents/2024/04/24/2024-07758/nondiscrimination-on-the-basis-of-disability-accessibility-of-web-information-and-services-of-state and can be found in the Code of Federal Regulations at: 28 C.F.R. § 35.200 – Requirements for web and mobile accessibility.

[80] Shaheen, N. L., & Lazar, J. (2018). K-12 Technology Accessibility: The Message from State Governments. *Journal of Special Education Technology*, 33(2), pp. 83–97, was published in 2018, and at that time, eighteen states had state-level laws requiring digital accessibility.

and discouraged colleges and universities from purchasing, requiring, or recommending these inaccessible technologies.[81] This statement is considered one of the agency interpretations related to applying coverage of accessible technology to Title II entities, and the joint statement from DOJ and DOE also notes previously existing settlement agreements related to inaccessible technology and mentions:

> As officials of the agencies charged with enforcement and interpretation of the ADA and Section 504, we ask that you take steps to ensure that your college or university refrains from requiring the use of any electronic book reader, or other similar technology, in a teaching or classroom environment as long as the device remains inaccessible to individuals who are blind or have low vision. It is unacceptable for universities to use emerging technology without insisting that this technology be accessible to all students.[82]

A further DOJ/DOE Dear Colleague letter from 2014 describes similar requirements for accessible technology in K-12 schools.[83] In that letter, it notes the overlapping coverage between statutes, and because K-12 education is covered by the Individuals with Disabilities Education Act (IDEA), that statute is mentioned as well:

> Three Federal laws – the Individuals with Disabilities Education Act (IDEA), Title II of the Americans with Disabilities Act of 1990 (Title II), and Section 504 of the Rehabilitation Act of 1973 (Section 504) – address the obligations of all public schools to meet the communication needs of students with disabilities, but do so in different ways. In particular, the IDEA requires that schools make available a free appropriate public education (FAPE), consisting of special education and related services, to all eligible children with disabilities (including those with disabilities that result in communication needs). Title II requires schools to ensure that students with disabilities receive communication that is as effective as communication with others through the provision of appropriate auxiliary aids and services.[84]

The DOJ's stand on website requirements for Title II entities had been as follows until the April 2024 Title II regulation:

> Although the language of the ADA does not explicitly mention the Internet, the Department has taken the position that title II covers Internet Web site access. Public entities that choose to provide services through web-based applications (e.g., renewing library books or driver's licenses) or that communicate with their constituents or provide information through the Internet must ensure that individuals with disabilities have equal access to such services or information, unless doing so would result in an

---

[81] U.S. Department of Justice. (2010). Dear College or University President. Available at: www2.ed.gov/about/offices/list/ocr/letters/colleague-20100629.html.
[82] Ibid.
[83] U.S. Department of Justice. (2014). Dear Colleague Letter. Available at: www.ada.gov/doe_doj_eff_comm/doe_doj_eff_comm_ltr.htm.
[84] Ibid.

undue financial and administrative burden or a fundamental alteration in the nature of the programs, services, or activities being offered.[85]

DOJ had recently updated their guidance specific to websites for state and local government:

> Title II of the ADA prohibits discrimination against people with disabilities in all services, programs, and activities of state and local governments. State and local governments must take steps to ensure that their communications with people with disabilities are as effective as their communications with others. Many state and local government services, programs, and activities are now being offered on the web. These include, for example, things like:
>
> > Applying for an absentee ballot;
> > Paying tickets or fees;
> > Filing a police report;
> > Attending a virtual town meeting;
> > Filing tax documents;
> > Registering for school or school programs; and
> > Applying for state benefits programs.
>
> A website with inaccessible features can limit the ability of people with disabilities to access a public entity's programs, services and activities available through that website – for example, online registration for classes at a community college.
>
> For these reasons, the Department has consistently taken the position that the ADA's requirements apply to all the services, programs, or activities of state and local governments, including those offered on the web.[86]

So, at a high level, the legal rules for Title II coverage of technology were previously based on administrative interpretations of Title II, until the April 2024 rule was issued. Now there is a clear regulation for Title II:

> (a) General. A public entity shall ensure that the following are readily accessible to and usable by individuals with disabilities:
> (1) Web content that a public entity provides or makes available, directly or through contractual, licensing, or other arrangements; and
> (2) Mobile apps that a public entity provides or makes available, directly or through contractual, licensing, or other arrangements.[87]

One key aspect of the new Title II rule is that it requires conformance with WCAG, putting it in lockstep with Section 508 of the Rehabilitation Act and the Air Carrier Access Act in being specific when it comes to technical standards.[88]

---

[85] 28 C.F.R. § Pt. 35, App. A.
[86] U.S. Department of Justice. (2022). Guidance on Web Accessibility and the ADA. Available at: www.ada.gov/resources/web-guidance/.
[87] 28 C.F.R. § 35.200.
[88] 28 C.F.R. § 35.200(b).

Given the newness of the Title II regulations for web and mobile app accessibility, and given the phase-in period of the rule (it takes effect on April 24, 2026, for public entities with a total population of 50,000 or more, and April 24, 2027, for public entities with smaller populations),[89] it may take a while to see the impact of this new regulation. The new rule provides broad coverage of any digital content posted on a website or utilized with a mobile app, with only five exemptions: (1) archived web content; (2) preexisting conventional electronic documents, unless such documents are currently used to apply for, gain access to, or participate in the public entity's services, programs, or activities; (3) content posted by a third party, unless the third party is posting due to contractual, licensing, or other arrangements with the public entity; (4) conventional electronic documents that are about a specific individual, their property, or their account and that are password protected or otherwise secured; and (5) preexisting social media posts.[90]

Because state and local entities often have so many overlapping requirements for nondiscrimination, when there is no compliance, usually, a settlement or consent decree is the appropriate legal action, so there is limited case law on this topic. That can be both good and bad: A settlement can be good in resolving a specific conflict, but bad because no trial means no court decision, which means no case law, which means that the situation may remain unclear for other disputes. It is important to note that, because voting is an activity run by state and local government, Title II of the ADA also covers voting technologies. However, there are special considerations that apply, so voting technologies will be covered separately in Chapter 10.

3.4.5 *Public Accommodations: Title III of the ADA*

Of all of the statutes, Title III of the ADA is the one in the news most when it comes to website accessibility. Title III of the ADA covers twelve broad categories of public accommodations:

(A) *an inn, hotel, motel, or other place of lodging, except for an establishment located within a building that contains not more than five rooms for rent or hire and that is actually occupied by the proprietor of such establishment as the residence of such proprietor;*
(B) *a restaurant, bar, or other establishment serving food or drink;*
(C) *a motion picture house, theater, concert hall, stadium, or other place of exhibition or entertainment;*
(D) *an auditorium, convention center, lecture hall, or other place of public gathering;*

---

[89] Ibid.
[90] 28 C.F.R. § 35.201.

(E) *a bakery, grocery store, clothing store, hardware store, shopping center, or other sales or rental establishment;*
(F) *a laundromat, dry-cleaner, bank, barber shop, beauty shop, travel service, shoe repair service, funeral parlor, gas station, office of an accountant or lawyer, pharmacy, insurance office, professional office of a health care provider, hospital, or other service establishment;*
(G) *a terminal, depot, or other station used for specified public transportation;*
(H) *a museum, library, gallery, or other place of public display or collection;*
(I) *a park, zoo, amusement park, or other place of recreation;*
(J) *a nursery, elementary, secondary, undergraduate, or postgraduate private school, or other place of education;*
(K) *a day care center, senior citizen center, homeless shelter, food bank, adoption agency, or other social service center establishment; and*
(L) *a gymnasium, health spa, bowling alley, golf course, or other place of exercise or recreation.*[91]

With the exception of private homes and private clubs, most nongovernmental places that an individual is likely to visit will fall under the list of public accommodations. If you have read news stories about lawsuits against businesses for having inaccessible websites, and the increase in lawsuits over time, you likely are reading about ADA Title III entities. These public accommodations are covered by ADA Title III for any organization, regardless of whether they receive any federal funding (i.e., if an organization gets no federal funds, the requirements described below for Section 504 would not apply). Title III clearly requires accessibility for physical accommodations. However, Title III was implemented before the introduction of websites. As described in Section 3.3.3 of this chapter, the DOJ has stated as early as 1996 that websites must be accessible for public accommodations under Title III of the ADA, under the effective communications requirement. However, as described in Section 3.3.2 of this chapter, some courts have limited coverage of websites, to only be required to be accessible when there is a nexus between the website and the physical location. It is first important to note that this nexus requirement only exists in some circuits and only within the Title III legal framework. There is no nexus concept under Title II of the ADA, Section 504, the Air Carrier Access Act, and the like. It's also important to note that in no way do the Title III lawsuits or administrative guidance from DOJ currently require conformance with any specific technical guidelines.

While there are possibly thousands of legal cases related to web accessibility (which cannot be said for any other statute listed in this chapter), we will briefly discuss the earliest case in which a court ruled that the ADA Title III applies to websites, and two of the recent and well-known cases. One of the best-known cases, and

---

[91] 42 U.S.C. § 12181(7).

the first case where a court ruled that ADA Title III applies to websites, is *National Federation of the Blind v. Target Corp*. In the 2006 court decision in the case, the court wrote:

> The ADA prohibits discrimination on the basis of disability "in the full and equal enjoyment of the goods, services, facilities, privileges, advantages or accommodations of any place of public accommodation." 42 U.S.C. § 12182(a) (emphasis added). The statute applies to the services *of* a place of public accommodation, not services *in* a place of public accommodation. Id. To limit the ADA to discrimination in the provision of services occurring on the premises of a public accommodation would contradict the plain language of the statute.[92]

Note one line (with bolding added by the author, not the court): **"The statute applies to the services of a place of public accommodation, not services in a place of public accommodation"** That line is quoted often in discussions about Title III website accessibility, although in later parts of the same court decision in the *National Federation of the Blind v. Target*, the court does note the limitations of ADA Title III coverage due to the nexus.

> In sum, the court finds that to the extent that plaintiffs allege that the inaccessibility of Target.com impedes the full and equal enjoyment of goods and services offered in Target stores, the plaintiffs state a claim, and the motion to dismiss is denied. To the extent that Target.com offers information and services unconnected to Target stores, which do not affect the enjoyment of goods and services offered in Target stores, the plaintiffs fail to state a claim under Title III of the ADA. Defendant's motion to dismiss this portion of plaintiffs' ADA claim is granted.[93]

Two of the more recent high-profile cases related to web accessibility under Title III of the ADA, both of which had appellate court decisions, are *Gil v. Winn-Dixie Stores, Inc.* and *Robles v. Domino's Pizza*. Both are long-running cases, which have recently been resolved, although in different and unique ways.

Juan Gil, a Blind man, sued Winn-Dixie for their inaccessible website. The district court ruled for plaintiff Gil in 2017 and stated:

> The factual findings demonstrate that Winn–Dixie's website is inaccessible to visually impaired individuals who must use screen reader software. Therefore, Winn–Dixie has violated the ADA because the inaccessibility of its website has denied Gil the full and equal enjoyment of the goods, services, facilities, privileges, advantages, or accommodations that Winn–Dixie offers to its sighted customers.... Winn–Dixie

---

[92] Nat'l Fed'n of the Blind v. Target Corp., 452 F. Supp. 2d 946 (N.D. Cal. 2006). Please note that in the original court decision, "(emphasis added)" was a part of the court decision, where the court emphasized, using italics, words that were not emphasized in the original statute. Because all parts of a court decision are put in italics according to the style guide for our book, we have instead used bolding for those three words that the court used italics for.

[93] Nat'l Fed'n of the Blind v. Target Corp., 452 F. Supp. 2d 946 (N.D. Cal. 2006).

has presented no evidence to establish that it would be unduly burdensome to make its website accessible to visually impaired individuals. To the contrary, its corporate representative unequivocally testified that modifying the website to make it accessible to the visual impaired was feasible. Remediation measures in conformity with the WCAG 2.0 Guidelines will provide Gil and other visually impaired consumers the ability to access Winn–Dixie's website and permit full and equal enjoyment of the services, facilities, privileges, advantages, and accommodations provided through Winn–Dixie's website. Gil has proven that he is entitled to injunctive relief.[94]

However, Winn-Dixie appealed to the 11th Circuit Court of Appeals and in April 2021, the 11th circuit created a new standard, more stringent than the nexus standard (which was later withdrawn), *"accordingly, we hold that Winn-Dixie's website does not constitute an 'intangible barrier' to Gil's ability to access and enjoy fully 'the goods, services, facilities, privileges, advantages or accommodations of' a place of public accommodation (here, a physical Winn-Dixie store). Consequently, Gil's ability to access the website does not violate Title III of the ADA in this way."*[95]

This "intangible barrier" standard no longer exists in the 11th circuit, as the 11th Circuit Court of Appeals, nonlegally speaking, "changed its mind." Gil, the plaintiff in the case, had appealed the April 2021 ruling which included the "intangible barrier," requesting an *en banc* rehearing in the Eleventh Circuit.[96] An *en banc* hearing is when an appellate case, which usually has a panel of three judges, gets a rehearing with all of the judges in that circuit taking part in the case.[97] Then on December 28, 2021, the Eleventh Circuit granted the *en banc* rehearing but stated that the appeal was rendered moot: "We vacate our opinion and the underlying judgment, dismiss the appeal, and remand for the district court to dismiss the case as moot."[98] So the Gil case isn't no longer a valid source of legal rules; as lawyers would say, it's "no longer good law."

In another case, *Robles v. Domino's Pizza*, Robles, a blind individual, sued Domino's Pizza because he could not order pizza through their inaccessible website and mobile app.[99] Domino's claimed that Robles could not request compliance with a specific technical standard, such as WCAG, because no standard is cited in

---

[94] Gil v. Winn-Dixie Stores, Inc., 257 F. Supp. 3d 1340 (S.D. Fla. 2017), vacated and remanded, 993 F.3d 1266 (11th Cir. 2021), opinion vacated on reh'g, 21 F.4th 775 (11th Cir. 2021), and appeal dismissed and remanded, 21 F.4th 775 (11th Cir. 2021).

[95] Gil v. Winn-Dixie Stores, Inc., 257 F. Supp. 3d 1340 (S.D. Fla. 2017), vacated and remanded, 993 F.3d 1266 (11th Cir. 2021), opinion vacated on reh'g, 21 F.4th 775 (11th Cir. 2021), and appeal dismissed and remanded, 21 F.4th 775 (11th Cir. 2021).

[96] Gil v. Winn-Dixie Stores, Inc., 257 F. Supp. 3d 1340 (S.D. Fla. 2017), vacated and remanded, 993 F.3d 1266 (11th Cir. 2021), opinion vacated on reh'g, 21 F.4th 775 (11th Cir. 2021), and appeal dismissed and remanded, 21 F.4th 775 (11th Cir. 2021).

[97] For point of reference, as of January 1, 2024, the 11th circuit has a total of 21 judges, twelve of which are classified as active judges and nine of which are classified as senior judges.

[98] *See* Gil v. Winn-Dixie Stores, Inc., 21 F.4d 775, 776 (11th Cir. 2021) (per curiam).

[99] Robles v. Dominos Pizza LLC, No. CV 16–06599 SJO (SPx), 2017 WL 1330216, at *1 (C.D. Cal. Mar. 20, 2017).

3.4 Sources of Legal Rules

the regulations or the statute, and website accessibility itself isn't mentioned in the statute or regulations (as previously discussed in this chapter, many defendants say that, and DOJ has been saying for decades that it's not a valid defense). The district court ruled that requiring compliance with a specific standard such as WCAG would violate the due process rights of Domino's:[100]

> Plaintiff alleges neither Dominos.com nor the Mobile App are in compliance with version 2.0 of W3C's Web Content Accessibility Guidelines ("WCAG 2.0"), and further alleges that "simple compliance with the WCAG 2.0 Guidelines would provide Plaintiff and other visually-impaired consumers with equal access" to these access portals ... Plaintiff seeks to impose on all regulated persons and entities a requirement that they "compl[y] with the WCAG 2.0 Guidelines" without specifying a particular level of success criteria and without the DOJ offering meaningful guidance on this topic. (Cf. Compl. ¶ 36.) This request flies in the face of due process.

Such a ruling was not in line with most other court decisions. The Ninth Circuit later reversed and remanded, noting that use of the WCAG is a question of remedy, not of liability.[101] In other words, the 9th circuit in their decision explains that Domino's isn't liable in the case because their website doesn't comply with WCAG; they are liable because the website and mobile app aren't accessible and therefore violate Title III of the ADA, and the use of WCAG is a potential option for the 9th circuit as a way to remedy that inaccessibility, but that follows the rules of remedies (what will fix the accessibility barriers) rather than the rules of liability. No circuit has claimed that the WCAG are required for public accommodations under Title III (the legal point of view), even though WCAG are the only internationally accepted guidelines for web content accessibility (the HCI point of view).

After the 9th circuit decision, rather than going back and having a trial, Domino's filed a writ of certiorari to the U.S. Supreme Court (a request for the Supreme Court to hear the case, since the court has discretionary jurisdiction), which the court declined.[102] After the case was remanded back to the district court and discovery took place, the court granted summary judgment in favor of plaintiff Robles on the question of the website's accessibility.[103] Because it was unclear at the time whether the mobile app was accessible, a trial to address the issue of accessibility of the mobile app was pending. However, Domino's Pizza decided to settle the remaining parts of the case, relating to the mobile app, rather than go through a trial (at that point, the trial had lasted nearly six years long).

Notably, no circuit has claimed that the WCAG are required for public accommodations under Title III, even though WCAG are the only internationally

---

[100] Ibid.
[101] Robles v. Domino's Pizza, LLC, 913 F.3d 898, 907 (9th Cir. 2019).
[102] Domino's Pizza, LLC v. Robles, 140 S. Ct. 122 (2019) (Mem.).
[103] Robles v. Domino's Pizza LLC, No. CV 16-6599 JGB (Ex), 2021 WL 2945562, at *9 (C.D. Cal. June 23, 2021).

accepted guidelines for web content accessibility. It is even more important to note that basically, in both the *Robles* case and the *Gil* case, companies were stubborn and decided that they would prefer to fight the case rather than make their websites and/or mobile apps accessible. In the Gil case, the litigation lasted five years. In the Robles case, the litigation lasted six years.

In the end, both companies made their websites and/or mobile apps accessible. Yet they wasted countless hours of time and money fighting against accessibility and fighting against the potential of new customers, rather than simply making their websites accessible. Why? It doesn't make sense from a strict financial point of view. The Robles case is instructive: Despite expert witness estimates that it would cost no more than $20,000 to remediate Domino's website and $20,000 to remediate the Domino's Mobile App (a total of $40,000), Domino's instead spent six years and six years of lawyer time fighting the case. Given that preparing a cert petition to the U.S. Supreme Court means hiring some of the most expensive lawyers out there, there is real evidence here of companies simply discriminating against people with disabilities rather than making the most cost-effective decision (which is to make their website accessible).[104] Perhaps these companies were simply against regulations, and so fought back even when that regulation could increase their sales.

Where does that leave us with the legal rules for website accessibility under Title III of the ADA? For now, the DOJ says that websites are fully covered under the ADA, and courts are split on the question of whether a nexus to a physical accommodation is required, yet there is no guidance or requirements on whether to utilize WCAG or not. Because of this potentially confusing requirement, there are a lot of lawsuits, and there is hope that perhaps the DOJ will eventually start a rulemaking to create regulations for Title III to clarify the situation, similar to how the DOJ has created regulations for Title II.

3.4.6 Employment: Title I of the ADA

Title I of the ADA focuses on disability discrimination in employment and covers any employers with "*15 or more employees for each working day in each of 20 or more calendar weeks in the current or preceding calendar year.*"[105] Unlike nearly all of the disability rights laws described in this chapter, Title I of the ADA has an "exhaustion" requirement.[106] "The doctrine of exhaustion of administrative remedies says that a person challenging an agency decision must first pursue the agency's

---

[104] Lazar, J. (2022). Ableist Language in the Web Accessibility Case of Robles v. Domino's Pizza Inc: When "Everyone" Doesn't Include People with Disabilities. *Including Disability*, 1(2), pp. 7–26.
[105] 42 U.S.C. § 12111 (5)(A).
[106] Here is Westlaw's short yet complex explanation in a headnote: "Title I of ADA incorporates the administrative procedures of Title VII, and thus, a plaintiff alleging a Title I violation must first exhaust administrative remedies before filing an action in court. Civil Rights Act of 1964, § 706, 42 U.S.C.A. § 2000e–5; Americans with Disabilities Act of 1990, § 107, 42 U.S.C.A. § 12117."

available remedies before seeking judicial review .... Congress has since written exhaustion requirements into many statutes to ensure and guide its application."[107] That means that before being able to file a complaint in a court and sue, a plaintiff must first use the government agency's complaint and remediation process, and in the case of Title I of the ADA, that means using the Equal Opportunity Employment Commission (EEOC). In practice, that also means litigation on this topic of "what counts as a reasonable accommodation related to assistive technology and accessibility?" is limited.[108]

Issues of the cost of assistive technology and/or selection of accessible workplace software, and whether the interactive process of discussion took place between employer and employee, are issues that may involve assistive technology and accessible workplace software, but really aren't about the design of the technologies themselves, and so may be perceived as outside of the scope of HCI, so we will only give a basic description of Title I of the ADA (and if you're wondering why Title I is listed in this chapter after Title II and Title III, that's why). Disability discrimination in employment is certainly a topic involving many issues which have nothing to do with technology or digital accessibility, but given this chapter's focus on digital accessibility, at a basic level, this can be split into two major topics: technology used in the job application procedures, and technology used in the actual employment.

If an employment application process includes accessibility barriers, this can be a violation of Title I of the ADA by: "*limiting, segregating, or classifying a job applicant or employee in a way that adversely affects the opportunities or status of such applicant or employee because of the disability of such applicant or employee.*"[109] Most employment applications are now required to be submitted electronically. If a job application process has accessibility barriers (either where portions or the entire application process is unavailable to a user of assistive technology), this means that the person with a disability can't even apply for a job, at least, without contacting the hiring organization and asking for an accommodation (and potentially being forced to "out" themselves as having a disability).[110] The same is true of any computerized assessment tests that are a part of the employment application process. Accessibility barriers have been previously documented in both the actual employer websites[111] and the job "aggregator" websites that offer employment opportunities and applications from

---

[107] Devlin, P. A. (2018). Jurisdiction, Exhaustion of Administrative Remedies, and Constitutional Claims. *NYU Law Review*, 93, pp. 1234–1270.

[108] Lazar, J., Goldstein, D., & Taylor, A. (2015). *Ensuring Digital Accessibility Through Process and Policy*. Waltham, MA: Elsevier/Morgan Kaufmann Publishers.

[109] 42 U.S.C. § 12112 (b)(1).

[110] Lazar, J., Olalere, A., & Wentz, B. (2012). Investigating the Accessibility and Usability of Job Application Web Sites for Blind Users. *Journal of Usability Studies*, 7(2), pp. 68–87.

[111] Lazar, J., Olalere, A., & Wentz, B. (2012). Investigating the Accessibility and Usability of Job Application Web Sites for Blind Users. *Journal of Usability Studies*, 7(2), pp. 68–87; Reuschel, W., McDonnall, M., & Burton, D. (2023). The Accessibility and Usability of Online Job Applications for Screen Reader Users. *Journal of Visual Impairment & Blindness*, 0145482X231216757.

multiple employers[112] (Weissburg has a law review article that provides a sampling of legal cases on this topic).[113] It has also been documented that when applicants with disabilities face inaccessible job aggregator websites and call asking for the equivalent information, they often are not given equivalent information.[114] Unlike Title II (state and local government) and Title III (public accommodations) of the ADA, where the DOJ has taken a proactive policy stance on digital accessibility (even without regulations present yet), the Equal Employment Opportunity Commission, which has jurisdiction over both rulemaking and enforcement of Title I of the ADA, has not taken a similar proactive policy stance on this topic.[115]

In terms of the employment itself, Title I of the ADA applies to any "... *individual who, with or without reasonable accommodation, can perform the essential functions of the employment position that such individual holds or desires.*"[116] Title I requires employers, within the context of technologies used for work, the "*acquisition or modification of equipment or devices, appropriate adjustment or modifications of examinations, training materials or policies, the provision of qualified readers or interpreters, and other similar accommodations for individuals with disabilities.*"[117] This is all subject to the limitation of an undue hardship, which is evaluated among other things, "*(i) the nature and cost of the accommodation ... (ii) the overall financial resources of the facility or facilities involved in the provision of the reasonable accommodation [and] (iii) the overall financial resources of the covered entity.*"[118] Again, these are issues that intersect with employment law and are about the specific nature of an individual employee and their needs for assistive technology or accessible software, rather than global mandates on what is required to be or is not required to be accessible or what technical standards to meet, so this is outside of the scope of the chapter. For more information about Title I of the ADA and employment for people with disabilities (which also involves other statutes such as the Rehabilitation Act of 1973), we suggest reading the excellent disability rights law textbooks by either Bagenstos[119] or Blanck et al.[120]

---

[112] Lazar, J., Wentz, B., Biggers, D., DeLair, J., Donnelly, M., Eludoyin, K., Henin, A., Markakis, J., Matos, A., McNichol, A., Nixon, J., Osbourne, R., Postnova, T., Raja, J., Roberts, R., Rothbard, J., Serra, H., Sfakianoudis, V., Tyler, V., & Yun, J. (2011). Societal Inclusion: Evaluating the Accessibility of Job Placement and Travel Web Sites. *Proceedings of the INCLUDE 2011 Conference (proceedings online)*.

[113] Weissburg, H. (2021). Are You There, EEOC? It's Me, Title I: Using Title I to Improve Web Accessibility under the ADA. *Boston University Law Review*, 101, pp. 1917–1951.

[114] Lazar, J., Goldstein, D., & Taylor, A. (2015). *Ensuring Digital Accessibility Through Process and Policy*. Waltham, MA: Elsevier/Morgan Kaufmann Publishers.

[115] Weissburg, H. (2021). Are You There, EEOC? It's Me, Title I: Using Title I to Improve Web Accessibility under the ADA. *Boston University Law Review*, 101, pp. 1917–1951.

[116] 42 U.S.C. § 12111 (8).

[117] 42 U.S.C. § 12111 (9)(B).

[118] 42 U.S.C. § 12111 (10)(B).

[119] Bagenstos, S. (2020). *Disability Rights Law: Cases and Materials*, 3rd ed., Foundation Press.

[120] Blanck, P., Waterstone M., Myhill, W., & Siegal, C. (2014). *Disability Civil Rights Law and Policy, Cases and Materials*, 3rd ed., West Academic Publishing.

3.4.7 Section 504 of the Rehabilitation Act

While Section 504 of the Rehabilitation Act may sound as if it would be similar to Section 508 of the Rehabilitation Act, Section 504 is much older than the newer Section 508, and structurally it is very different. Section 504 doesn't specifically mention technology, rather, its nondiscrimination coverage is very broad: any organizations that receive federal funding.

Under Section 504 of the Rehabilitation Act,

> *No otherwise qualified individual with a disability in the United States, as defined in section 705(20) of this title, shall, solely by reason of her or his disability, be excluded from the participation in, be denied the benefits of, or be subjected to discrimination under any program or activity receiving Federal financial assistance or under any program or activity conducted by any Executive agency or by the United States Postal Service.*[121]

It is important to note that the statute expressly notes the broad organizational coverage for Section 504, *"the term 'program or activity' means all of the operations of ... a State or of a local government ... a college, university, or other postsecondary institution, or a public system of higher education ... an entire corporation, partnership, or other private organization, or an entire sole proprietorship ... any part of which is extended Federal financial assistance."*[122]

Section 504 doesn't prescribe any technical guidelines or even mention digital accessibility. The power of Section 504 is in the coverage occurring anytime that an organization has received a federal dollar. Courts have generally interpreted this to mean that if an organization has received even one dollar of federal funding, the protections of Section 504 against nondiscrimination apply.[123] So that means that if an organization (such as a university, a professional society, or a private organization) receives federal funding, the nondiscrimination protections of Section 504 apply, regardless of whether ADA coverage exists for state or local government or a public accommodation. This is important, as there are many organizations that may not be legally covered by the ADA, which are "reached" by Section 504.

3.4.8 The Twenty-First Century Communications and Video Accessibility Act

Most of the statutes previously discussed involve either the information/content provided via websites, or the purchasers of technology (e.g., universities

---

[121] 29 U.S.C. § 794(a).
[122] 29 U.S.C. § 794(b).
[123] For instance, see a recent U.S. Supreme Court ruling, Fry v. Napoleon Cmty. Sch., 137 S. Ct. 743, 197 L. Ed. 2d 46 (2017), where Section 504 protections applied to children with disabilities in schools, even though other statutes (such as IDEA) may at first seem to preclude the filing of Section 504 claims.

and government agencies who are required to procure only accessible technology) and not the technology companies who build technology. For instance, as discussed in the earlier "Dear Colleague" letter about e-book readers, the DOJ focused on the purchasers of the technologies, not Amazon, who had built the inaccessible Kindle (it was inaccessible at that time). But there is one statute that is a major exception to this general approach in other legal rules: the Twenty-First Century Communications and Video Accessibility Act (CVAA).[124] The CVAA, which might be categorized more as a telecommunications statute than a disability rights statute, nonetheless provides that, "... *a manufacturer of equipment used for advanced communications services, including end user equipment, network equipment, and software, shall ensure that the equipment and software that such manufacturer offers for sale or otherwise distributes in interstate commerce shall be accessible to and usable by individuals with disabilities, unless the requirements of this subsection are not achievable.*"[125]

And there is a similar rule for providers of communications services, "... *a provider of advanced communications services shall ensure that such services offered by such provider in or affecting interstate commerce are accessible to and usable by individuals with disabilities, unless the requirements of this subsection are not achievable.*"[126]

So, for manufacturers of telecommunications equipment, and providers of communications services, the onus is on them to only build accessible networks, devices, and services. This shift in the requirement is noteworthy.

3.4.9 *State Laws about Digital Accessibility*

Given that almost half of U.S. states have at least one statute or regulation related to digital accessibility, it's important to at least mention the types of legal rules that one may find at a state level. Obviously, a thorough analysis of all state statutes related to digital accessibility is outside of the scope of this chapter. Maryland, which has one of the more detailed legal frameworks, can provide an example of what is possible at the state level.

There are two major Maryland statutes related to digital accessibility: one is known as the *Nonvisual access clause for use in procurement of information technology*,[127] although it is a general-purpose accessibility statute, it doesn't only cover access by blind users. Two notable aspects of this statute are that it has penalties for vendors and requires vendors to indemnify the state:

---

[124] 47 USC §§ 615c, 616 to 620.
[125] 47 U.S.C. § 617.
[126] 47 U.S.C. § 617.
[127] Md. Code Ann., State Fin. & Proc. § 3.5–311.

3.4 Sources of Legal Rules

if the vendor fails to modify the information technology to meet the nonvisual access standards within 12 months after the date of the notification, the vendor:

(1) *may be subject to a civil penalty of:*
  A. *for a first offense, a fine not exceeding $5,000; and*
  B. *for a subsequent offense, a fine not exceeding $10,000; and*
(2) *shall indemnify the State for liability resulting from the use of information technology that does not meet the nonvisual access standards.*[128]

The definition of accessibility and the technical standards used are defined:

[definition of accessibility] provide an individual with disabilities with nonvisual access in a way that is fully and equally accessible to and independently usable by the individual with disabilities so that the individual is able to acquire the same information, engage in the same interactions, and enjoy the same services as users without disabilities, with substantially equivalent ease of use; and

[technical standards] are consistent with the standards of § 508 of the federal Rehabilitation Act of 1973.[129]

The fact that state statute references Section 508 of the Rehabilitation Act is a sign that this is Maryland's state-level equivalent to Section 508, and most other states which have statutes, while not having the same civil penalties and indemnification clauses of Maryland, do have some level of procurement requirements and usually reference the technical standards of Section 508.

Maryland also has a similar statute that applies to K-12 Education: *Equivalent Access Requirements for Students with Disabilities.*[130] Some of the same requirements are present in the K-12 statute, as in the previously mentioned statute: procurement requirements, indemnification clauses, civil penalties, and the technical standards of Section 508. But there are some new twists, including public transparency:

(1) *On or before October 1, 2023, and each October 1 thereafter, each local school system shall submit a report to the Department on the accessibility of the digital tools the local school system developed or purchased for use during the immediately preceding fiscal year.*
(2) *The Department shall compile the information received under paragraph (1) of this subsection and make the information available on the Department's website, including the status of the accessibility of the digital tools used in each local school system.*[131]

and qualifications for who is qualified to evaluate digital technologies for accessibility, *"the evaluation process established under subparagraph (i) of this paragraph shall*

---

[128] Ibid.
[129] Md. Code Ann., State Fin. & Proc. § 3.5-303.
[130] Md. Code Ann., Educ. § 7-910.
[131] Ibid.

include evaluation of the digital tool for equivalent access and nonvisual access by an employee or a contractor of the local school system who:

1. *Specializes in accessibility and Web Content Accessibility Guidelines; or*
2. *Is a blindness specialist who is knowledgeable in accessibility.*"[132]

There is not yet a Maryland statute which has similar requirements for digital accessibility in higher education. However, digital accessibility is briefly mentioned in a number of other (sometimes surprising) Maryland statutes related to: virtual learning,[133] for-hire driving services,[134] advanced health care documents,[135] voting,[136] and the Maryland Park Service.[137]

3.5 WHAT LEGAL PROCEDURES OR REMEDIES ARE SPECIFIC TO ACCESSIBILITY?

One of the unique aspects of most of the disability rights statutes discussed in previous sections is that a plaintiff can generally sue for injunctive relief (fixing the existing accessibility barriers or stopping new accessibility barriers from being created) but not for damages. So, if a court rules for a plaintiff, generally the injunctive relief sought would be to remove a barrier, to make a website, or software, or another technology accessible. For ADA Title III, generally, an individual cannot sue for damages, only injunctive relief[138] and attorney's fees.[139] However, if the DOJ files a lawsuit, the DOJ can request damages in the form of civil penalties.[140] And certainly within the realm of the ADA, the DOJ often does take action in the area of digital technology; however, that usually comes in the form of a settlement agreement, not a lawsuit.[141] And many of these lawsuits and settlement agreements related to digital accessibility originate in complaints filed with the DOJ by disability rights activists. There generally are no administrative hurdles in the area of digital accessibility (e.g., where an administrative complaint must be filed and evaluated before a lawsuit can be filed, as with Section 508). That means that individual plaintiffs and disability rights activists (if they have standing to sue) can

---

[132] Ibid.
[133] Md. Code Ann., Educ. § 7–1002.
[134] Md. Code Ann., Pub. Util. § 10–403.
[135] Md. Code Ann., Health-Gen. § 19–145.1.
[136] Md. Code Ann., Elec. Law § LAW § 9–102.
[137] Md. Code Ann., Nat. Res. § 5–2A-04.
[138] 28 C.F.R. § 36.501.
[139] 28 C.F.R. § 36.505; also note the use of the California Unruh Civil Rights Act, a California civil rights statute, which, unlike Title III of the ADA, provides for damages. Cal. Civ. Code § 51.
[140] 28 C.F.R. § 36.503–504.
[141] See www.justice.gov/crt/disability-rights-cases and https://archive.ada.gov/enforce_current.htm for a list of DOJ cases and settlement agreements involving disability rights.

go ahead and file a complaint in court whenever they are ready, although most choose to first reach out to the offending organization and request that the accessibility barrier be fixed.

3.6 LEGALLY SPEAKING: WHAT IS CLEAR, WHAT IS STILL AMBIGUOUS, AND WHAT OFTEN CAUSES CONFUSION?

The biggest confusion right now for organizations and individuals surrounds how the broad "effective communication" requirements apply to web accessibility for ADA Title III entities. First, the nexus requirement is not well defined (there's no legal test to determine whether a nexus exists), not understood, and entities (and courts) have trouble determining whether a nexus exists between the website and the physical accommodation. Whether the nexus requirement present in some circuits even makes sense is an entirely separate question (and the COVID-19 pandemic made it even more confusing).

Second, neither a performance standard nor a technical standard is defined in some of the legal rules. A performance standard (e.g., 90 percent of users with disabilities can complete the task within three minutes), or a technical standard (e.g., WCAG), or both, would help provide more structure, a clear goal for organizations that are trying to ensure that they are legally compliant. While a certain amount of flexibility is good as it encourages innovation, many companies can't understand why, for instance, WCAG as a technical standard is a requirement for airlines and the federal government, and now with the new ADA Title II rule for state and local government, but not for the companies. Organizations need more guidance, a clearer roadmap, on how to achieve accessibility.

3.7 FUTURE LEGAL QUESTIONS

Because accessibility to digital technologies and content is not yet encoded into either the ADA statute or regulation for Title III, it is likely that there will be efforts to do so. As previously mentioned, there is a rulemaking process that recently completed related to websites and mobile apps under Title II of the ADA for state and local government, with a new regulation issued. Given that the Title II and Title III rulemaking were linked in the past, there is a possibility that since the Title II rule has now been finalized, there may be efforts to introduce a rulemaking process for Title III entities (public accommodations) as well!

A bill was introduced in Sept 2023 in the 118th Congress, and then re-introduced in May 2025 in the 119th congress, called *the Websites and Software Applications Accessibility Act*. At press time, no further actions have been taken. The purpose of the bill (in current draft) is as follows:

(1) to affirm that the ADA and this Act require that websites and applications used by any covered entity to communicate or interact with applicants, employees, participants, customers, or other members of the public be readily accessible to and useable by individuals with disabilities, whether the entity has a physical location or is digital only;
(2) to require the Department of Justice and the Equal Employment Opportunity Commission to set and enforce standards for websites, electronic documents, and software applications and to periodically update such standards;
(3) to address and remedy the systemic nationwide problem of inaccessible websites and applications that exclude individuals with disabilities from equal participation in and equal access to all aspects of society; and
(4) to create effective mechanisms to respond to emerging technologies and to ensure that such technologies do not impair the rights and abilities of individuals with disabilities to participate in all aspects of society.[142]

It is important to note that the definition of accessible in the draft bill:

The term "accessible" or "accessibility", used with respect to web content or an application, means a perceivable, operable, understandable, and robust web content or an application that enables individuals with disabilities to access the same information as, to engage in the same interactions as, to communicate and to be understood as effectively as, and to enjoy the same services as are offered to, other individuals with the same privacy, same independence, and same ease of use as, individuals without disabilities.[143]

incorporates the four core concepts of WCAG: perceivable, operable, understandable, and robust. Aside from introducing the bills, no further actions (including hearings) were taken in the 118th Congress. The bill was recently introduced as H.R. 3417 in the 119th Congress, but at press time, no further actions have been taken.[144] It is important to note that *The Websites and Software Applications Accessibility Act* does not limit a private right of action:

CIVIL ACTION BY OTHERS. – *An individual, class, or entity, described in paragraph (1)(A), including a covered entity described in paragraph (1)(A) alleging a violation by a commercial provider, may bring a civil action alleging a violation of paragraph (2) or (3) of subsection (a), or subsection (c), as the case may be, of section 4 (including a related provision of the final rule issued under section 5(a)) in an appropriate State or Federal court without first filing a complaint with the Department or exhausting any other administrative remedies.*

---

[142] U.S. Congress (2023). Websites and Software Applications Accessibility Act of 2023 (S. 2984). 118th Cong. (2023). Available at: www.congress.gov/bill/118th-congress/house-bill/5813/text?s=2&r=1&q=%7B%22search%22%3A%22The+Websites+and+Software+Applications+Accessibility+Act%2C%22%7D

[143] Ibid.

[144] https://www.congress.gov/bill/119th-congress/house-bill/3417/all-actions?s=4&r=5&q=%7B%22search%22%3A%22Websites+and+Software+Applications+Accessibility+Act%22%7D

It is important to note that a previous effort in the U.S. House of Representatives that would encode website accessibility within the ADA, the Online Accessibility Act (introduced in the 117th Congress), would have removed the right to sue for web accessibility without first overcoming multiple procedural hurdles.[145] Because of the addition of procedural hurdles, disability rights groups were not in favor of that previous bill. This new bill introduced in the 118th and 119th congress is therefore likely to have more support from disability rights groups if reintroduced in a future Congress.

Two potential actions that may take place in the future:

(1) There may be efforts in the future to target accessibility requirements more towards the manufacturers and creators of technologies, rather than only the purchasers, perhaps using the legal approach of the *Twenty-First Century Communications and Video Accessibility Act (CVAA)*. Six years ago, an author of this book had previously proposed that consumer protection laws might be a vehicle for improving digital accessibility.[146] Recently, a legal case, and a related settlement agreement for $2 million, used a new legal theory, claiming that a contractor who created an inaccessible website (but stated that it was accessible) for the California Department of Parks and Recreation, had violated the California False Claims Act.[147] There may be more efforts in the future, to go after the creators of inaccessible technologies. Furthermore, different areas of law may be utilized to advance the rights of people with disabilities. One could imagine that there are other areas of law – employment law, education law, fair housing law, and health law, which while not primarily focused on disability, could be written in ways that advance or limit the rights of people with disabilities in ways that may not immediately be obvious. For instance, computer interfaces that identify or reveal the disability status of an individual without their permission in health care or employment, may lead to forms of discrimination not identified in this chapter (e.g., in extreme circumstances during the COVID-19 pandemic, people with disabilities were deprioritized for getting

---

[145] U.S. Congress (2021). Online Accessibility Act (H.R. 1100), 117th Cong. (2021). Available at: www.congress.gov/bill/117th-congress/house-bill/1100/text.

[146] Lazar, J. (2019). The Potential Role of US Consumer Protection Laws in Improving Digital Accessibility for People with Disabilities. *The University of Pennsylvania Journal of Law and Social Change*, 22(3), pp. 185–204.

[147] See Nelson, K. (2023). Blind Leader Wins $2 Million Settlement Over Inaccessible California Parks Website. Available at: https://trelegal.com/posts/cfca-unruh-settlement/ and Gibson, D. (2023). $2M Bashin Settlement Holds Web Developers Accountable for WCAG Compliance. Available at: www.accessibility.works/blog/bashi-california-accessibility-lawsuit-2m-settlement-web-developers/?utm_campaign=&utm_content=2%20Recent%20Digital%20ADA%20Cases%20Impact%20Website%20Owners%20and%20Web%20Agencies&utm_medium=email&utm_source=getresponse.

health care).[148] More work needs to be done to understand the intersections of various areas of law combined with digital accessibility, especially how privacy violations (where an individual is "outed" as having a disability without their permission) can especially lead to civil rights violations.

(2) There may be efforts in the future to limit a type of nuisance lawsuit, where lawyers who are not involved with disability rights, file many lawsuits a day for web accessibility, using essentially a cut-and-paste approach and without actually evaluating the website for accessibility.[149] The goal of these unethical lawyers is to take advantage of the lack of existing knowledge and unclear standards related to web accessibility, by threatening as many people as possible, and seeing if they can reach a few financial settlements from defendants who are not knowledgeable about web accessibility and are scared of a lawsuit. These "drive-by" or "click-by lawsuits" often have no previous communication between plaintiff and defendant, the complaint filed has no details about what makes the defendant's website inaccessible, and lack detail, instead essentially saying, "that's your problem as the defendant, to figure out what's wrong." Scholars have predicted that this might be resolved with heightened pleading standards, where complaint documents filed about web accessibility to begin a lawsuit process, are required to have more details.[150] The cut-and-paste nature of some of these nuisance lawsuits is evident in a web accessibility case where the court mocked the plaintiff for referring to Banana Republic, a clothing store, as a food establishment:

Computers have made a lot of things in life easier. Copy-and-paste litigation is one of them. The pitfalls of such an approach is [sic] evident here where, among other things, Plaintiff's opposition responds to arguments never made by its opponent … and failed to even correctly identify what Defendant sells … (referring to Banana Republic as a "food establishment"). Although it features the fruit in its name, Banana Republic does not sell bananas.[151]

---

[148] See Andrews, E. E., Ayers, K. B., Brown, K. S., Dunn, D. S., & Pilarski, C. R. (2021). No Body Is Expendable: Medical Rationing and Disability Justice during the COVID-19 Pandemic. *American Psychologist*, 76(3), p. 451 or Panocchia, N., D'ambrosio, V., Corti, S., Presti, E. L., Bertelli, M., Scattoni, M. L., & Ghelma, F. (2021). COVID-19 Pandemic, the Scarcity of Medical Resources, Community-Centred Medicine and Discrimination against Persons with Disabilities. *Journal of Medical Ethics*.

[149] See Elizabeth A. Harris, Galleries from A to Z sued over websites that the Blind can't use, *N.Y. Times* (February 18, 2019). Available at: www.nytimes.com/2019/02/18/arts/design/blind-lawsuits-art-galleries.html.

[150] Lazar, J., Jordan, J. B., & Wentz, B. (2022). Incorporating Tools and Technical Guidelines into the Web Accessibility Legal Framework for ADA Title III Public Accommodations. *Loyola Law Review*, 68(2), pp. 305–341.

[151] Dominguez v. Banana Republic, LLC, No. 1:19-CV-10171-GHW, 2020 WL 1950496, at *30 (S.D.N.Y. April 23, 2020).

The *Online Accessibility Act* bill mentioned in the last section also attempted to address this with heightened pleading standards in Section 603, proposing, "[i]n any action filed under this title, the complaint shall plead with particularity each element of the plaintiff's claim, including the specific barriers to access a consumer facing website or mobile application."[152]

3.8 HCI WORK AREAS THAT COULD HELP SUPPORT THE LEGAL SIDE, AND VICE VERSA

Accessibility is really a multifaceted situation. Not enough people and organizations are aware of digital accessibility. Not enough people and organizations are aware of the legal framework for digital accessibility. And the legal framework could be clearer and provide more guidance. Given that, there are multiple roles for the HCI community to play in improving the current situation.

For instance, clearly, more universities need to teach about digital accessibility in their courses related to computing. Approaches such as injecting accessibility content into every core computing course could lead to students understanding the fundamental nature of accessibility and how it isn't just an add-on after a system has already been built.[153]

There also needs to be more research on which management approaches lead to more effective digital accessibility. This would need to account for the interplay of social, cultural, and political factors with technology and consider social dynamics and power structures.

Obviously, because the legal framework is so intertwined with technical standards, any HCI research that can help to inform technical standards, for example, research pointing to best practices in accessibility for emerging technologies, would be helpful to law. In addition, since multiple rulemaking processes are underway to help more clearly define regulatory requirements for digital accessibility, each of these will need to undergo what is known as a regulatory impact analysis (which is very similar to a cost-benefit analysis for the regulation). Data on how people with different types of disabilities are impacted by accessibility barriers is needed for input into the economic models that calculate the costs and benefits of new regulatory requirements. For HCI researchers to collect such data would be immensely helpful. Similarly, having data on the costs of accessibility, and different methods to reduce the costs (such as the born-accessible model mentioned earlier in the chapter) could also feed into the regulatory impact analyses.

---

[152] See Online Accessibility Act, H.R. 1100, 117th Cong. (2021). Available at: www.congress.gov/bill/117th-congress/house-bill/1100/text.

[153] Waller, A., Hanson, V. L., & Sloan, D. (2009, October). Including Accessibility within and beyond Undergraduate Computing Courses. In *Proceedings of the 11th international ACM SIGACCESS Conference on Computers and Accessibility*, pp. 155–162.

3.9 SUMMARY

The basic concepts of digital accessibility have existed for almost 50 years, since the beginnings of video captioning and the foundations of the personal computer. The legal framework for disability rights in the U.S. has similarly existed for around 50 years, since some of the earliest federal statutes, such as the Rehabilitation Act of 1973 and the Architectural Barriers Act (ABA) of 1968. Yet at the beginning, the legal framework for disability rights didn't incorporate digital technologies, and to be fair, many of these digital technologies didn't exist when these statutes were originally implemented. However, over time, the two independent strands of technology and law for people with disabilities have started to intertwine. The first statutes that specifically address technology for people with disabilities appeared in the 1980s and 1990s, as the first technical standards for web accessibility appeared at the end of the 1990s. Slowly, the legal framework has incorporated more organizations, more technologies, and more details when it comes to digital accessibility. The years 1998 and 1999 were watershed times in digital accessibility, with the release of the first WCAG, and Section 508 being amended to more fully incorporate all types of technologies. Similarly, 25 years later, 2023 was a watershed year, when the legal and policy activity in digital accessibility incrementally increased in the legislative, judicial, and executive branches at the U.S. federal level, as well as the creation of new leadership roles in digital accessibility by the states. It is important for all interested in digital accessibility to become involved and knowledgeable in this fast-moving area of the law, which involves and impacts so much design and development in HCI.

4

Privacy

4.1 INTRODUCTION

Ideally, privacy would be a protective shield for your personal information and space. It means having control over what you want to keep to yourself and what you're comfortable sharing with others. However, privacy is a much-contested concept that has been disputed and transformed throughout its history in response to wave after wave of new technological capabilities and social configurations.[1] Privacy is enshrined as a fundamental human right, as it is an important part of preserving individual autonomy, dignity, and personal freedom and is enshrined in the United Nations Declaration of Human Rights.[2] Nearly every country in the world recognizes a right of privacy explicitly or implicitly in their Constitution. Recently created Constitutions, such as South Africa's, include specific rights to access[3] and control[4] one's personal information, while in older Constitutions such as the United States[5] or Ireland,[6] national courts have inferred it. For instance, the United States Supreme Court held that privacy is a "fundamental right" protected by the many amendments to the Constitution, including the Fourteenth Amendment, which reads in part, "nor shall any State deprive any person of life, liberty, or property, without due process of law; nor deny to any person within its jurisdiction the equal protection of the laws."[7]

In an increasingly interconnected and digital world, maintaining privacy has become a complex balancing act. Advances in technology and the widespread use of the Internet have led to new privacy concerns, such as data breaches, online

---

[1] Mulligan, D. K., Koopman, C., & Doty, N. (2016). A Multi-dimensional Analytic for Mapping Privacy. *Philosophical Transactions of the Royal Society A: Mathematical, Physical and Engineering Sciences*, 374(2083), p. 20160118.
[2] Universal Declaration of Human Rights, G.A. Res. 217A (III) (U.N. 1948).
[3] Constitution of the Republic of South Africa, 1996, § 14.
[4] Constitution of the Republic of South Africa, 1996, § 32.
[5] U.S. Constitution, 1787.
[6] Constitution of Ireland, 1937.
[7] Griswold v. Connecticut, 381 U.S. 479 (1965).

surveillance, and the collection of personal information for commercial purposes. Efforts to protect privacy involve a combination of legal measures, technological safeguards, individual awareness, and responsible data practices by organizations and governments, and balancing privacy rights with other societal interests, such as security and public welfare, remains an ongoing debate and challenge.

One way to balance these complex balancing priorities is through privacy by design,[8] which calls for privacy to be considered throughout the whole system implementation process. For example, under EU's General Data Protection Regulation (GDPR),[9] website providers must receive users' consent before they can use any cookies except strictly necessary cookies; and provide accurate and specific information about the data each cookie tracks and its purpose in plain language before consent is received, and make it as easy for users to withdraw their consent as it was for them to give their consent in the first place, among other requirements.[10] Some researchers believe that while these processes attempt to comply with the laws, many implementations don't help protect anyone's privacy, and arguably don't comply with the law.[11] A major challenge for human–computer interaction (HCI) researchers, developers, and practitioners is finding the right balance between usability and privacy. For instance, users often have diverse needs and expectations, leading to varied levels of understanding and concern about privacy. A second challenge is for HCI researchers and practitioners to understand the legal requirements. And a third challenge is having lawyers and legal scholars understand the HCI aspects of privacy. Designing systems that cater to this wide range of user expectations, from those who are indifferent to privacy to those who are highly concerned, is challenging. HCI practitioners need to create flexible privacy settings and options to accommodate these diverse needs. Similarly, users' privacy norms and legal requirements are constantly evolving. This can make it difficult to design systems that remain compliant over time. HCI practitioners need to design systems that are adaptable to changes in the concept of privacy and associated privacy laws and norms, such as the General Data Protection Regulation (GDPR) in Europe, which, even though they are not binding law in the U.S., have a massive impact on U.S. privacy in practice. Lawyers and legal scholars need to consider these changing technological and social conditions and adapt to the changes in the societal and individual changes in privacy conceptions.

---

[8] Cavoukian, A. (2011). Privacy by Design: The 7 Foundational Principles. Information and Privacy Commissioner of Ontario, Canada. Retrieved from https://iapp.org/media/pdf/resource_center/pbd_implement_7found_principles.pdf.

[9] Regulation (EU) 2016/679 of the European Parliament and of the Council of 27 April 2016 on the Protection of Natural Persons with Regard to the Processing of Personal Data and on the Free Movement of Such Data (General Data Protection Regulation), 2016 O.J. (L 119) 1 (EU).

[10] Regulation (EU) 2016/679 of the European Parliament and of the Council of 27 April 2016 on the Protection of Natural Persons with Regard to the Processing of Personal Data and on the Free Movement of Such Data (General Data Protection Regulation), art. 7(3), 2016 O.J. (L 119) 1, 38 (EU).

[11] Bouma-Sims, E. R., Li, M., Lin, Y., Sakura-Lemessy, A., Nisenoff, A., Young, E., Birrell, E., Cranor, L. F. & Habib, H. (2023, April). A US-UK usability evaluation of consent management platform cookie consent interface design on desktop and mobile. In *Proceedings of the 2023 CHI Conference on Human Factors in Computing Systems*, pp. 1–36.

Another challenge for HCI designers is to hide technical complexity. Making these technologies understandable and manageable for the average user is a significant challenge. They must develop innovative ways to abstract this complexity in user interfaces. Similarly, many users may not be fully aware of privacy issues or how their data is used and shared, and it can be hard to develop content that assists users through design, making privacy policies and practices transparent and understandable.

HCI practitioners, especially those focused on user experience, also need to navigate ethical considerations, ensuring that privacy designs do not inadvertently manipulate user choices (refer to Chapter 9 on Dark Patterns) or diminish user autonomy in providing effective and meaningful control of their personal information and protecting their privacy. For example, they could consider the design and presentation of widgets that correspond with user priorities[12] through appropriate interface notifications related to privacy. For HCI practitioners to understand privacy through a legal lens requires an expansion of their field of view from traditional HCI domains such as social psychology and cognitive science, to a broader picture which includes community values,[13] ethics,[14] and economics.[15]

In summary, as strong privacy measures can sometimes make systems more complex and harder to use, HCI practitioners need to design interfaces and interactions that make privacy features easy to understand and manage without overwhelming the users. Addressing these challenges requires HCI practitioners to be innovative, empathetic, and forward-thinking, ensuring that privacy design is both human-centered and effective in protecting users' personal information. Effective collaboration and integrating diverse perspectives into design processes can be challenging between HCI practitioners, legal experts, data protection officers, and technologists.

Similarly, legal scholars can conduct in-depth research to understand the implications of new technologies on privacy and work with HCI professionals and other stakeholders to develop new privacy regulations that are flexible enough to adapt to technological advancements while still protecting individual rights. More intentional collaboration with other stakeholders, such as ethicists, sociologists, and other experts, can provide a multidisciplinary approach and lead to a more holistic understanding of privacy issues and more effective legal responses.

---

[12] Amft, S., Höltervennhoff, S., Huaman, N., Acar, Y., & Fahl, S. (2023). Would you give the same priority to the bank and a game? I do {not!}: Exploring credential management strategies and obstacles during password manager setup. In *Nineteenth Symposium on Usable Privacy and Security* (SOUPS 2023), pp. 171–190.

[13] Vitak, J., Shilton, K., & Ashktorab, Z. (2016, February). Beyond the Belmont principles: Ethical challenges, practices, and beliefs in the online data research community. In *Proceedings of the 19th ACM Conference on Computer-Supported Cooperative Work & Social Computing*, pp. 941–953.

[14] Shilton, K. (2013). Values Levers: Building Ethics into Design. *Science, Technology, & Human Values*, 38(3), pp. 374–397.

[15] McDonald, A. M. & Cranor, L. F. (2008). The Cost of Reading Privacy Policies. *Isjlp*, 4, p. 543.

4.2 EVOLUTION

The evolution of privacy is a complex and ongoing process that evolved along with societies in ancient times, when people began to value their personal space and the ability to control who had access to information about them. In common law jurisdictions, the law of privacy can be traced as far back as 1361, when the English Statute of Peace Act[16] shifted the justice system from a centralized, royal-controlled judicial system to a localized judicial system to address community and personal violations, such as the arrest of peeping toms and eavesdroppers. While the act did not explicitly address privacy rights or personal privacy, it aimed to provide a framework for maintaining public order and safety.

In 1890, Samuel Warren and Louis Brandeis published a seminal article, "The Right to Privacy,"[17] which was one of the first U.S. law articles on privacy law. It discussed the foundational concepts for legal protections against invasions of personal life, especially in the context of emerging technologies such as photography and the telegraph. The deployment of mainframes for mass data processing of personal information posed new challenges to privacy in the 1960s. In 1967, Alan Westin introduced a seminal definition of privacy as the claim of individuals, groups, or institutions to determine for themselves when, how, and to what extent information about them is communicated to others.[18] It framed the interaction between individuals, corporations, and government as a continuing engagement in which they must balance the desire for privacy with disclosure and communication.

From the 1960s onward, the Supreme Court of the United States established that while the constitutional language does not explicitly mention privacy, it established the right to privacy as a constitutional principle implicitly based on the various guarantees within the Bill of Rights that create zones of privacy into which the government may not intrude, including the First, Third, Fourth, Fifth, Ninth, and Fourteenth Amendments. Through a series of landmark cases, the Supreme Court progressively established the right to privacy as a fundamental constitutional principle. These cases included *Griswold v. Connecticut* (1965),[19] which struck down a state law banning the use of contraceptives and *Katz v. U.S.* (1967)[20], which expanded protection against unreasonable searches and seizures to all areas where an individual has a "reasonable expectation of privacy," and not just to physical intrusions into private spaces. In the 1970s, this was further extended by Supreme Court cases, such as *Eisenstadt v. Baird* (1972),[21] which struck down a Massachusetts law that prohibited the distribution of contraceptives to unmarried individuals, and

---

[16] 34 Edw. 3. c. 1, 1361, English Parliament.
[17] Warren, S. & Brandeis, L. D. (1890). The Right to Privacy. *Harvard Law Review*, 4(5), pp. 193–220.
[18] Westin, A. (1967). Privacy and Freedom. Atheneum.
[19] Griswold v. Connecticut, 381 U.S. 479 (1965).
[20] Katz v. U.S., 389 U.S. 347 (1967).
[21] Eisenstadt v. Baird, 405 U.S. 438 (1972).

Lawrence v. Texas (2003),[22] which invalidated sodomy laws in Texas, further expanding the privacy rights to include the freedom of adults to engage in private consensual sexual acts. Recent court cases, such as *Dobbs v. Jackson Women's Health Org*[23] may reverse privacy holdings from the now-overturned *Roe v. Wade*,[24] by permitting states to track and prosecute women who seek abortions, for example, through online activity, phone calls, and text messages.[25] States may also sue to compel businesses to provide medical data to law enforcement. Furthermore, people may self-censor their online activity or avoid seeking medical care for fear of being tracked or prosecuted[26].

The ubiquity of personal technologies and information-producing applications has greatly increased the amount of personal information and benefits of sharing it with third parties in personal or commercial transactions,[27] which requires navigation among state, national, and international privacy paradigms and regulations. Much information about individuals is public, available to anyone to see and use, while other information about individuals, though not public in the sense that anyone may see or use them, can become public through inference. For example, for individuals with disabilities, genetic data posted by relatives on public sites such as ancestry.com can reveal information about their condition and make them vulnerable to discrimination in areas such as employment, housing, and health care.[28] This can limit their opportunities and negatively impact their quality of life. To mitigate this risk, it's important for individuals to be aware of the potential uses of their personal data and to consider the potential long-term consequences before sharing their data.

Additionally, it's important to carefully review the privacy policies of companies and organizations that collect personal data and to understand how they plan to use and protect that data. However, this places quite a bit of burden on individuals. The burden should be on companies to limit their uses of user data, perhaps enforced by regulators, as in the EU, and then to make their uses of data transparent to users, but perhaps more realistically, to the watchdog groups who work on behalf of consumer privacy. Privacy policies aren't really meant for your average user, but they can be important documents for advocates and watchdog groups.

---

[22] Lawrence v. Texas, 539 U.S. 558 (2003).
[23] Dobbs v. Jackson Women's Health Org., 597 U.S. 215 (2022).
[24] Roe v. Wade, 410 U.S. 113 (1973).
[25] Texas SB 14, 88th Leg., R.S. (2023). Available at: https://capitol.texas.gov/tlodocs/88R/billtext/pdf/SB00014F.pdf.
[26] Cao, J., Laabadli, H., Mathis, C., Stern, R., & Emami-Naeini, P. (2024). "I Deleted It After the Overturn of Roe v. Wade": Understanding Women's Privacy Concerns Toward Period-Tracking Apps in the Post Roe v. Wade Era. In *Proceedings of the 2024 CHI Conference on Human Factors in Computing Systems (CHI '24)*. Association for Computing Machinery, New York, NY, USA, Article 813, 1–22.
[27] Kang, J. (1998). Information Privacy in Cyberspace Transactions. *Stanford Law Review*, 50(1), pp. 1193–1294.
[28] Clayton, E. W., Evans, B. J., Hazel, J. W., & Rothstein, M. A. (2019). The Law of Genetic Privacy: Applications, Implications, and Limitations. *Journal of Law and the Biosciences*, 6(1), pp. 1–36.

In the European Union, the regulator views information privacy as a human right that must be protected,[29] while the United States at the federal level does not have statutorily defined general information privacy rights, though it has sector-specific rights in education,[30] health,[31] and others. In this viewpoint, privacy is not a right in par with liberty or freedom, and is a byproduct of protecting personal security,[32] in varying social contexts and norms around who can share what information about whom and with whom and under what circumstances – that is, when, where, how, and for what purpose. Privacy is not usually considered to be a right on par with human rights, which is regarded as a fundamental right that is not subject to regulatory considerations such as cost-benefit analyses. By contrast, the most common approach in privacy laws and regulations is to weigh costs and benefits for individuals versus society due to variations in legal frameworks across countries and the subjective nature of privacy itself.

Information and social networking growth has resulted in a variety of benefits, including access to more information, communication, increased economic growth and new products and services that people and businesses want, and enhanced innovation and economic growth by fostering creativity, consumer trust, and clarity on what practices are permitted. For instance, more than a billion people worldwide have joined information and social networks to consume information they are interested in, in exchange for giving up personal information. Another example is supermarket club memberships. These work by collecting information about what you purchase and then providing discounts in return. Given that privacy has both individual and social benefits and risks, citizens and society must balance between satisfying the desires of an individual versus the needs of groups or societies.

4.3 PRIVACY FROM HCI POINT OF VIEW

From an HCI point of view, privacy refers to the protection of personal information and the control over how that information is collected, used, and shared. As the use of technology for personal information or communication has become ubiquitous, individuals have started to center their lives around it. Advances in technology have facilitated use of personal information in daily activities such as interaction, communication, or services. Consequently, the stakes for its use have increased for individuals, groups, or institutions on how it is shared or communicated with others. However, people are uncertain about their privacy and often become blasé about privacy except when

---

[29] Regulation (EU) 2016/679 of the European Parliament and of the Council of 27 April 2016 on the Protection of Natural Persons with Regard to the Processing of Personal Data and on the Free Movement of Such Data (General Data Protection Regulation), 2016 O.J. (L 119) 1 (EU).

[30] Family Educational Rights and Privacy Act of 1974, Pub. L. No. 93-380, 88 Stat. 571 (1974) (codified as amended in 20 U.S.C. § 1232g).

[31] Health Insurance Portability and Accountability Act of 1996, Pub. L. No. 104-191, 110 Stat. 1936 (1996) (codified as amended in 42 U.S.C. § 1320d et seq).

[32] Moor, J. H. (1997). Towards a Theory of Privacy in the Information Age. ACM Sigcas Computers and Society, 27(3), pp. 27–32.

concerns are raised, either by commercial or governmental interests. Given that personal information has both individual and social benefits and risks, technology designers and developers must satisfy tensions between satisfying the desires of an individual versus the needs of groups,[33] and to support individuals and groups' use of personal information, and on how it is communicated to others.[34] They also have an obligation to be aware of, and avoid, dark patterns[35] (see Chapter 9 on Dark Patterns), which can mislead users and lead to unwanted outcomes related to personal data. HCI practitioners can and should also help facilitate contextual privacy, for they are experts in context and can bring knowledge of contextual appropriateness to design teams.

Privacy concerns often arise when designing interactive systems, such as websites and mobile apps, that collect and use personal information. To address these concerns, HCI practitioners often employ a number of different design strategies such as providing clear and transparent information about how personal information will be used and shared; allowing users to control the collection and use of their personal information through settings and preferences; designing interfaces that make it easy for users to understand and manage their privacy settings; and considering the ethical implications of personal information collection and use.[36]

HCI professionals face a fundamental tension between the inherent risks of collecting personal information versus using it to build and evaluate it for a more personalized experience. One way to improve privacy is to involve users in cocreating privacy requirements.[37] This can be done by engaging users in workshops or focus groups where they can share their privacy concerns and suggest solutions for addressing those concerns. This approach allows designers to understand the specific privacy needs of the users and to design solutions that are tailored to those needs.

Another way to improve privacy is to involve users in usability testing of privacy-enhancing features.[38] This can be done by having users test prototypes of the system and provide feedback on the effectiveness and usability of privacy features such as controls for managing personal information. This approach allows designers to evaluate the effectiveness of privacy features and to adjust as needed. Additionally, by involving users in the design process and educating them about the potential risks and benefits of the system and the importance of protecting their personal

---

[33] Boyd, D., & Crawford, K. (2012). Critical Questions for Big Data in Information, Communication & Society. *Communication and Society*, 15(5), pp. 662–679.
[34] California Consumer Privacy Act, 2018 California Legis. Serv. Ch. 55 (A.B. 375).
[35] Gray, C., Chivukula, S. S., & Lee, A. (July 1, 2020). What Kind of Work Do "Asshole Designers" Create? Describing Properties of Ethical Concern on Reddit. *Proceedings of the Designing Interactive Systems Conference 2020*. Designing Interactive Systems Conference 2020, Eindhoven, Netherlands.
[36] Lederer, S., Hong, J. I., Dey, A. K., & Landay, J. A. (2004). Personal Privacy through Understanding and Action: Five Pitfalls for Designers. *Personal and Ubiquitous Computing*, 8, pp. 440–454.
[37] Vicini, S., Alberti, F., Notario, N., Crespo, A., Pastoriza, J. R. T., & Sanna, A. (2016, August). Co-Creating Security-and-Privacy-by-Design Systems. In *2016 11th International Conference on Availability, Reliability and Security* (ARES), pp. 768–775.
[38] Habib, H., & Cranor, L. F. (2022). Evaluating the Usability of Privacy Choice Mechanisms. In *Eighteenth Symposium on Usable Privacy and Security* (SOUPS 2022), pp. 273–289.

information, developers can identify the most effective ways to create awareness of privacy concerns among users.[39] Furthermore, it can be difficult to tease cause and effect apart: whether social practices and expectations drive the development of technology or vice versa. The relationship between social constructs and technology is better described as coevolution, which requires a commitment to involving users throughout the design process and to consider ethical and cultural issues related to privacy and to include marginalized groups.[40]

As new technologies emerge, HCI professionals will need to continue to adapt their understanding of privacy and find new ways to protect it. They should consider privacy laws through being aware of the relevant privacy laws in the jurisdictions where their products or services will be used. This includes understanding the different types of personal information that are protected by law, the purposes for which personal information can be collected and used, and the rights that individuals have over their personal information. HCI designers should also offer to codesign their products or services in a way that complies with the relevant privacy laws. This includes ensuring that users are informed about how their personal information will be collected, used, and shared, and that they can control their personal information. Additionally, designers should involve privacy experts in the design process. Privacy experts can help to identify privacy risks and ensure that the design complies with the relevant privacy laws through privacy-by-design principles.

Privacy by design[41] is an approach to product development that takes privacy into account from the very beginning of the design process, by getting user feedback on privacy practices to identify privacy concerns and ensure that the design meets the needs of users. Privacy design can be combined with a closely related but distinct concept, such as security. In contrast to the high-level definition of privacy being the right of individuals to control information about themselves, the high-level definition of security is about protecting information – both personal and organizational – from unauthorized access, use, disclosure, disruption, modification, or destruction. The aim of security is to safeguard data integrity, confidentiality, and availability, regardless of whether the information is personal or not. So, designers can also consider using privacy-enhancing technologies to protect the security of their own data. For example, designers could require the use of multifactor authentication (MFA) to add an extra layer of security to online accounts, making it harder for unauthorized users to gain access, even if they have the password. Similarly, they could encourage the use of anonymous payments, such as Bitcoin, to allow for pseudonymous

---

[39] Scacchi, W. (2004). Socio-Technical Design. *The Encyclopedia of Human-Computer Interaction*, 1, pp. 656–659.
[40] McDonald, N. & Forte, A. (2020). The Politics of Privacy Theories: Moving from Norms to Vulnerabilities. *Proceedings of the 2020 CHI Conference on Human Factors in Computing Systems*, pp. 1–14.
[41] Hustinx, P. (2010). Privacy by Design: Delivering the Promises. *Identity in the Information Society*, 3(2), pp. 253–255.

transactions, making it challenging to trace financial activities back to individual users. In other words, effective security measures are essential to maintain privacy. Without adequate security, personal information could be accessed, stolen, or misused, thus violating privacy, and the need to maintain privacy dictates the level and types of security measures that should be implemented. For example, data that is more sensitive requires higher levels of security. Understanding this relationship helps in implementing strategies that both protect data (through security) and ensure that individuals' rights to privacy are respected. Mismanagement of either can lead to risks like identity theft, financial fraud, and unauthorized surveillance, among others.

Designers can also consider conducting systematic privacy impact assessments to identify and mitigate privacy risks. A privacy impact assessment[42] is a process for systematically identifying, assessing, and mitigating the privacy risks associated with a new product or service and being transparent about their privacy practices. This includes providing clear and concise information about how personal information is collected, used, and shared. For example, designers could consider giving users the ability to opt out of data collection and tracking and to delete their personal information. In summary, by considering privacy laws in the design process, HCI designers can help to protect user privacy and build trust with users.[43]

There have been many cases where technologies that affect privacy are developed without much public debate. For example, the introduction of digital cameras and GPS sensing in phones coevolved with new applications and regulations that emerged with early, less mature apps, and evolved to larger, more mature apps. Digital cameras and GPS technology can collect and store personal photographs with location identifiers. In many jurisdictions, individuals have a reasonable expectation of privacy in certain contexts, such as in their homes or other private spaces. Taking photos without consent in these contexts can violate privacy laws. Legal frameworks like the GDPR in the EU also stipulate that personal data, which can include photographs, must be collected and processed lawfully and transparently. The legality of taking photographs without consent often hinges on whether the subject is in a public or private space. Generally, there is a lesser expectation of privacy in public areas, so photography without explicit consent may not always be illegal. However, even in public settings, the use of such photos, especially if they are deemed invasive or are used for commercial gain, can still raise privacy concerns.[44]

---

[42] Clarke, R. (2009). Privacy Impact Assessment: Its Origins and Development. *Computer Law & Security Review*, 25(2), pp. 123–135.

[43] Hadar, I., Hasson, T., Ayalon, O., Toch, E., Birnhack, M., Sherman, S., & Balissa, A. (2018). Privacy by Designers: Software Developers' Privacy Mindset. *Empirical Software Engineering*, 23, pp. 259–289; Li, T., Louie, E., Dabbish, L., & Hong, J. I. (2021). How Developers Talk about Personal Data and What It Means for User Privacy: A Case Study of a Developer Forum on Reddit. *Proceedings of the ACM on Human-Computer Interaction*, 4(CSCW3), pp. 1–28.

[44] Stangl, A., Shiroma, K., Davis, N., Xie, B., Fleischmann, K. R., Findlater, L., & Gurari, D. (2022). Privacy Concerns for Visual Assistance Technologies. *ACM Transactions on Accessible Computing (TACCESS)*, 15(2), pp. 1–43.

This combination of photos and GPS information can raise privacy concerns when photos are taken and shared without the knowledge or consent of the individuals captured in the photos.[45] To address this concern, developers have started to implement features such as a "privacy mode" that allows users to control when and how their photos are shared. As an example, Google Street View automatically blurs the faces of individuals captured in the photos to protect their identity.[46] In terms of location data information through GPS, privacy concerns can arise when location data is collected and shared without the knowledge or consent of the individual. To address this concern, designers have started to include features such as a "privacy mode" that allows users to control when and how their location data is shared, or to automatically anonymize location data to protect the identity of the individual, consistent with local laws and regulations for personal privacy.[47] Similar design choices have led to the support of hiding sensitive photos on phones in Android.[48]

Similarly, submitting your genetic information to companies that analyze and interpret genetic data, like Ancestry.com can have both benefits and potential drawbacks. Benefits of submitting your genetic information to Ancestry.com can include learning about your ancestry and family history, including the regions of the world where your ancestors likely came from, and connecting with relatives who have also taken the genetic test, which can help people to learn more about their family history and build relationships with relatives they may not have known existed.[49] Customers can also glean personalized health insights, which can help people to make more informed decisions about their health. However, there are also potential drawbacks to submitting your genetic information to Ancestry.com, including privacy concerns – genetic data is personal information that can be used for various purposes, such as targeted marketing or research. While companies like Ancestry.com claim to take privacy and security of user's data seriously, there is always a risk of data breaches or unauthorized access of your data, for example, your interaction with it on social media.[50] Similarly, the data and interpretations, if breached, may potentially be used to discriminate against individuals in areas such as employment, insurance, and lending. The Genetic Information Nondiscrimination Act of 2008[51] (GINA), a federal statute in the United States, was passed to protect individuals from discrimination based on their genetic information in both health insurance and

[45] Gupta, R., Crane, M., & Gurrin, C. (2021). Considerations on Privacy in the Era of Digitally Logged Lives. *Online Information Review*, 45(2), pp. 278–296.
[46] www.google.com/streetview/policy/.
[47] www.facebook.com/help/166181076782926.
[48] https://support.google.com/photos/answer/10694388.
[49] Garner, S. A., & Kim, J. (2018). The Privacy Risks of Direct-To-Consumer Genetic Testing: A Case Study of 23andMe and Ancestry. *Washington University Law Review*, 96(6), pp. 1219–1265.
[50] Your Privacy. www.ancestry.com/c/legal/privacystatement
[51] Genetic Information Nondiscrimination Act of 2008, Pub. L. No. 110-233, 122 Stat. 881 (2008) ((codified as amended in 42 U.S.C. §§ 2000ff et seq).

employment. For instance, Sections 101–103 amended the Employee Retirement Income Security Act, the Public Health Service Act, and the Internal Revenue Code to prohibit health insurers from discriminating based on genetic information. They specifically bar health insurers from using genetic information to deny coverage, adjust premiums, or impose preexisting condition exclusions. Even though it prohibits discrimination based on genetic information, some employers and insurance companies may find ways around it, as it primarily addresses discrimination in health insurance and employment. It does not cover areas such as life insurance, long-term-care insurance, or disability insurance, leaving individuals vulnerable to genetic discrimination in these domains. Similarly, employers or insurers could potentially obtain genetic information through other sources, such as social media, and use that information to make decisions, as GINA does not explicitly address these indirect sources of genetic information.

Additionally, genetic data is complex and can be subject to interpretation, which means that the results may not be entirely accurate.[52] Finally, there are ethical concerns about who owns and controls genetic data, and how that data is used. Even though GINA extends its protective provisions to cover not only the individual but also their family members, it does not cover voluntary disclosure outside of these contexts. For example, if an individual uploads their genetic data, it impacts the privacy of their relatives, even if they have not uploaded their data – and they have no ability to weigh in on this.[53] Some people may also have concerns about the commercialization of genetic testing and the use of genetic data for research. As a result, designers and developers need to carefully consider the potential benefits and drawbacks and to understand local laws or corporate policies for private data that is sensitive and permanent that can also introduce risks at both the individual and community levels.

As a multidisciplinary field that analyzes the interaction between humans and computers, HCI has expanded from analyzing individual and generic user behavior with technologies, to include social and organizational computing, accessibility for people with disabilities, for all people, and for the widest possible spectrum of human experiences and activities. It expanded from desktop office applications to include games, learning and education, commerce, health and medical applications, emergency planning and response, and systems to support collaboration and community. It expanded from early graphical user interfaces to include myriad interaction techniques and devices, multimodal interactions, tool support for model-based user interface specification, and a host of emerging ubiquitous, handheld,

---

[52] Clayton, E. W., Halverson, C. M., Sathe, N. A., & Malin, B. A. (2018). A Systematic Literature Review of Individuals' Perspectives on Privacy and Genetic Information in the United States. *PloS One*, 13(10), e0204417.

[53] Woodage, T. (2010). Relative Futility: Limits to Genetic Privacy Protection Because of the Inability to Prevent Disclosure of Genetic Information by Relatives. *Minnesota Law Review* 95(2), pp. 682–713; Barocas, S. & Levy, K. (2020). Privacy Dependencies. *Washington Law Review*, 95(2), pp. 555–616.

and context-aware interactions.[54] As such, practitioners possess a holistic view of the interaction of the user with the technology for personal information and privacy and are ideally positioned to optimally work through and solve these tradeoffs.

Different countries have developed paradigms that reflect their historical priorities and precedents. For instance, China's Personal Information Protection Law,[55] prioritizes broader societal interests and government priorities over individual privacy rights, such as privacy exceptions for news reporting, public opinion supervision, or other such activities for the public interest, versus the United States' Health Insurance Portability and Accountability Act (HIPAA),[56] which has no exception for news reporting or public opinion supervision. Yet these paradigms continue to evolve, reflecting a complex interplay between technological advancements, legal frameworks, cultural shifts, and individual values. As new technologies continue to be developed to use more personal information about people, HCI professionals need a solid understanding of existing privacy frameworks to ensure that their products or services are compliant in countries that use these technologies.

4.4 PRIVACY FROM A LEGAL POINT OF VIEW

From a legal perspective, privacy encompasses a variety of rights and principles that protect individuals from unwarranted interference in their personal lives. This concept of privacy has evolved over time, influenced by legal precedents, statutory laws, and societal values. Its scope is shaped by history, culture, and personal experience and differs by country. In ancient times, personal information about others was stored among small, isolated communities or tribes. As they grew into larger and more organized states, the amount of personal information and the benefits and risks of sharing it grew proportionately and the concept of informational privacy was developed to provide individuals with the ability to determine when others may collect and how they may use personal information.[57]

In the United States, early privacy laws focused on protecting individuals from government intrusion, such as the Fourth Amendment to the U.S. Constitution,[58] which states: *"The right of the people to be secure in their persons, houses, papers, and effects, against unreasonable searches and seizures, shall not be violated, and no Warrants shall issue, but upon probable cause, supported by Oath or affirmation, and particularly describing the place to be searched, and the persons or things to be seized."* Prior to the digital era, it was interpreted to protect physical areas such as homes, offices, and personal belongings. Over time, court interpretations have

---

[54] Carroll, J. M. (Ed.). (2003). *HCI Models, Theories, and Frameworks: Toward a Multidisciplinary Science*. Elsevier.
[55] Personal Information Protection Law of the People's Republic of China (2021).
[56] Health Insurance Portability and Accountability Act of 1996, Pub. L. No. 104–191, 110 Stat. 1936.
[57] Westin, A. F. (1967). *Privacy and Freedom*. New York: Atheneum.
[58] U.S. Const. amend. IV.

expanded its protections to include certain forms of digital data, such as phone call metadata and internet communications, under specific conditions. With the advent of digital information sharing through mainframes in the 1960s and 1970s, the Fair Credit Reporting Act[59] (FCRA) of 1970 was signed into law, which regulated the collection, dissemination, and use of consumer information, including consumer credit. This was followed up by the Privacy Act of 1974[60] respectively, which protected individuals' personal information from private sector intrusion and federal agencies from disclosing an individual's personal information without their consent. Collectively, these provided consumers with the right to access their own credit report, to dispute incomplete or inaccurate information, to know who has accessed their credit report and so on.

Subsequent laws protected personal information in specific sectors, such as the HIPAA[61] of 1996, which regulates the use and disclosure of protected health information. It was a large act divided into many titles, each focused on a particular aspect. For instance, Title I focused on Health Care Access, Portability, and Renewability, by protecting workers and families through provisions that gave workers the option of maintaining health insurance coverage when they change or lose their jobs. Other sections of Title I also focused on limiting exclusions for preexisting conditions, and to provide special enrollment rights for individuals in certain circumstances, such as loss of other health coverage or life events like marriage or birth of a child.

The rise of the Internet and digital technology in the 1980s and 1990s led to a renewed focus on privacy, with laws such as the Electronic Communications Privacy Act[62] (ECPA) of 1986, which regulates the interception of electronic communications. It was a large act divided into many titles; each focused on a particular aspect. For example, the first title, the Wiretap Act, is further divided into sections such as 2511 that prohibits the intentional interception, use, or disclosure of wire, oral, or electronic communications unless authorized by law or by the parties involved. This section protects consumers from unauthorized eavesdropping and surveillance.

In the twenty-first century, privacy laws have continued to evolve to address new concerns worldwide, including the GDPR.[63] While the GDPR is a European regulation, its impact on the United States is significant, affecting legal compliance, business operations, and data transfer practices. It governs the collection, use, and storage of personal data, and it is a comprehensive data protection law enacted by the European Union (EU). The GDPR attempts to protect the privacy and personal

---

[59] Fair Credit Reporting Act, 5 U.S.C. § 552a; 15 U.S.C. §§ 1681 (1970).
[60] Privacy Act of 1974, Pub. L. No. 93-579, 88 Stat. 1896 (1974).
[61] Health Insurance Portability and Accountability Act of 1996, Pub. L. No. 104-191, 110 Stat. 1936 (1996) (codified as amended in 42 U.S.C. § 1320d et seq).
[62] Electronic Communications Privacy Act of 1986, Pub. L. No. 99-508, 100 Stat. 1848 (1986) (codified as amended in 18 U.S.C. §§ 2510–2522).
[63] Regulation (EU) 2016/679 of the European Parliament and of the Council of 27 April 2016 on the Protection of Natural Persons with Regard to the Processing of Personal Data and on the Free Movement of Such Data (General Data Protection Regulation), 2016 O.J. (L 119) 1 (EU).

data of individuals within the EU and to harmonize data protection laws across all member states. It was very broadly written: The GDPR applies to all organizations that process the personal data of individuals residing in the EU, regardless of where the organization is located. This includes U.S. companies outside the EU that offer goods or services to, or monitor the behavior of, EU residents. Similarly, it covers all information relating to an identified or identifiable natural person (data subject), such as names, addresses, email addresses, identification numbers, and online identifiers, and requires organizations to demonstrate compliance with the GDPR principles, maintain records of processing activities, and implement appropriate technical and organizational measures to ensure data protection. It provides rights to consumers, by setting a high standard for consent, requiring that it be freely given, specific, informed, and unambiguous. Consent must be given by a clear affirmative action and individuals have the right to withdraw consent at any time.

There are no broad national laws in the U.S. like the GDPR. The closest are state laws passed by influential states such as California and copied by other states. For example, after the GDPR was passed, several years later, California passed its California Consumer Privacy Act[64] (CCPA) in 2020, which provides California residents with certain rights regarding their personal information. It is a state statute intended to enhance privacy rights and consumer protection for residents of California, and it applies to for-profit businesses that do business in California and meet criteria such as having gross revenues over $25M. Similar to the GDPR, it provides broad, high-level requirementsthat businesses disclose the categories and specific pieces of personal information collected about individuals, the sources of the information, the purposes for collecting it, and the third parties with whom the information is shared, such as other companies, codified in the California Civil Code sections 1798.100 to 1798.199. Consumers have the right to request that businesses disclose the categories and specific pieces of personal information collected about them, the sources of the information, the purposes for collecting it, and the third parties with whom the information is shared. The CCPA grants California residents significant control over their personal information and imposes stringent requirements on businesses regarding data privacy and protection.

Following California's lead, states like Virginia,[65] Colorado,[66] and Utah[67] have enacted their own consumer privacy laws. These laws, while similar to the CCPA, have their nuances but generally reflect the growing trend toward enhancing consumer privacy protections. Providers have been reassessing their privacy practices to ensure compliance not only with California's regulations but also to prepare for potential future state or federal laws and has served as a catalyst for change across

---

[64] California Consumer Privacy Act of 2018, Cal. Civ. Code §§ 1798.100–.199.100 (2024).
[65] Virginia Consumer Data Protection Act, Va. Code Ann. §§ 59.1–575 to 59.1–585 (2023).
[66] Colorado Privacy Act, Colo. Rev. Stat. §§ 6–1-1301 to 6–1-1313 (2022).
[67] Utah Consumer Privacy Act, Utah Code Ann. §§ 13–61-101 to 404 (2023).

the U.S., influencing how states consider and enact data privacy laws and the way businesses approach consumer data nationwide.

Where are most legal rules for privacy found? At the federal level, there are no broad privacy laws, only sector-specific privacy laws that relate to specific sectors such as health data – the HIPAA of 1996,[68] and educational data – Family Educational Rights and Privacy Act – FERPA.[69] However, there are some narrow constitutional bases and substantial case law for privacy protections. In terms of constitutional bases, the U.S. Supreme court has held that some constitutional amendments implicitly protect privacy (details on case law are in the next paragraph). The First Amendment,[70] while it is primarily known for protecting freedom of speech and religion, has been interpreted to protect the freedom of association and the belief that private thoughts and expressions should be free from government scrutiny. The Third Amendment[71] prohibits the quartering of soldiers in private homes without the owner's consent and has been interpreted to protect the sanctity of the home and private life. The Fourth Amendment,[72] which protects citizens from unreasonable searches and seizures by the government, has often been cited in privacy rights cases, especially those involving law enforcement and issues of surveillance. The Fifth Amendment,[73] which protects against self-incrimination, has been interpreted to protect the privacy of personal information. The Ninth Amendment,[74] which states that the enumeration of certain rights in the Constitution does not mean other rights do not exist, has been interpreted to support the existence of a right to privacy. Finally, the Fourteenth Amendment[75] has substantive due process language, which has been interpreted to protect privacy rights, particularly in cases involving family life, procreation,[76] and child rearing,[77] which collectively protects a broad range of personal autonomy and privacy issues. Courts have construed these protections of the Bill of Rights to uphold the individual's right not to be coerced into revealing political,[78] social, or philosophical beliefs, or private associations, unless national security or public order are at stake. Prior to the mass media distribution era, information was primarily shared through news and publications, and direct relationships

---

[68] Health Insurance Portability and Accountability Act of 1996, Pub. L. No. 104–191, 110 Stat. 1936. 42 U.S. Code § 201 note.
[69] Family Educational Rights and Privacy Act of 1974, Pub. L. No. 93–380, 88 Stat. 571 (codified as amended at 20 U.S.C. §§ 1232g–1232h).
[70] U.S. Const. amend. I.
[71] U.S. Const. amend. III.
[72] U.S. Const. amend. IV.
[73] U.S. Const. amend. V.
[74] U.S. Const. amend. IX.
[75] U.S. Const. amend. XV.
[76] Griswold v. Connecticut 381 U.S. 479 (1965).
[77] Meyer v. Nebraska 262 U.S. 390 (1923); Pierce v. Society of Sisters 268 U.S. 510 (1925); Troxel v. Granville 530 U.S. 57 (2000).
[78] United States v. Rumely, 345 U.S. 41, 47 (1953) and United States v. Harriss, 347 U.S. 612 (1954)

and was reflected in the U.S. constitution's Fourth Amendment,[79] which protects personal properties, including their personal information, from unwarranted search and seizure.

In response to the rise of cheap, mass-distributed tabloids, new legal understandings on privacy arose, as the object of privacy (e.g., personal writings) could not be characterized as intellectual property nor as a property granting future profits, buttressed by case law such as *Katz v. U.S.*[80] (1967) and *Roe v. Wade*[81] (1973), which established the concept of a "reasonable expectation of privacy." *Katz v. U.S.* (1967) transformed the understanding of the right to privacy under the Fourth Amendment of the U.S. Constitution. Charles Katz was convicted for illegal gambling activities based on evidence obtained by the FBI through an eavesdropping device attached to the outside of a public phone booth he used. The Supreme Court ruled in favor of Katz, holding that he had a reasonable expectation of privacy in the phone booth and that the FBI's eavesdropping without a warrant constituted a violation of the Fourth Amendment. The judicial opinion famously stated that the Fourth Amendment protects people, not places, and what a person "seeks to preserve as private, even in an area accessible to the public, may be constitutionally protected." These culminated in *Katz v. U.S.*[82] establishing the "reasonable expectation of privacy" test, which has become a cornerstone in Fourth Amendment jurisprudence. According to this test, for a search to be considered to violate privacy under the Fourth Amendment, two criteria must be met: (1) the individual must have exhibited an actual (subjective) expectation of privacy, and (2) the expectation must be one that society is prepared to recognize as "reasonable."

While the Fourth Amendment itself doesn't explicitly mention "privacy," *Griswold v. Connecticut*[83] held that through the concept of "penumbra," privacy can be derived from the broader principles and values of the Fourth Amendment. The term "penumbra" is often used to describe the shadowy or indistinct areas surrounding explicit constitutional rights, where broader rights are implied by the text and the structure of the Constitution. *Griswold* held that the Fourth Amendment protection against unreasonable searches and seizures extends to protect individuals in areas where they have a reasonable expectation of privacy, even if those areas are not physically private.[84]

With the advent of personal devices, *Riley v. CA*[85] (2014) established that law enforcement generally requires a warrant to search the digital contents of a cell

---

[79] U.S. Const. amend. IV.
[80] Katz v. United States, 389 U.S. 347 (1967).
[81] Roe v. Wade, 410 U.S. 113 (1973), overturned by Dobbs v. Jackson Women's Health Org., 597 U.S. 715 (2022).
[82] Katz v. United States, 389 U.S. 347 (1967).
[83] Griswold v. Connecticut 381 U.S. 479 (1965).
[84] Griswold v. Connecticut 381 U.S. 479 (1965).
[85] Riley v. California, 573 U.S. 373 (2014).

phone seized from an individual during an arrest. The court stated that cell phones differ in both a quantitative and a qualitative sense from other objects that might be kept on an arrestee's person and are typically examined as part of a search incident to arrest. However, the legal foundation for a general federal right to privacy under the "penumbra" right has become shakier, after *Dobbs v. Jackson*[86] (2022), which overturned *Roe v. Wade* and significantly impacted privacy laws in the United States, particularly in the context of reproductive rights and the concept of privacy as it relates to personal medical decisions.

4.5 SOURCES OF LEGAL RULES

Before we start describing statutory sources of legal rules, we want to acknowledge that some of these are from before the time of personal computers and therefore, the relationship to HCI is inferred; other statutes are more recent and the relationship to HCI is expressly described in the statutory text.

4.5.1 *Privacy Act, 1974*

In 1973, a federal advisory committee to the U.S. Department of Health, Education, and Welfare (HEW) published a comprehensive study addressing privacy risks associated with electronic information technologies and proposed a "code of fair information practices," which laid the groundwork for the Privacy Act of 1974.[87] This was a response to the realization of the potential for arbitrary or abusive recordkeeping practices in the wake of Watergate and the Surveillance Programs that targeted domestic groups as disparate as the KKK, the Communist Party, and the Black Panthers, and illegal surveillance on opposition political parties and individuals deemed to be subversive.[88] Until then, privacy had, at that point in time, been understood as a narrow, property-based concept of individual control.

The Fair Information Practice Principles (FIPPs) are a set of internationally recognized guidelines and principles that serve as a framework for data protection and privacy. They include concepts like Notice/Awareness, where individuals are informed about data collection practices; Choice/Consent, allowing individuals to opt in or out of data collection; Access/Participation, enabling individuals to view and correct their information; Integrity/Security, ensuring data is accurate and protected; and Enforcement/Redress, providing mechanisms to enforce these principles and address violations. They were developed to provide a foundation for establishing responsible and ethical data practices, ensuring that individuals' personal information is collected, used, and managed in a fair and transparent manner.

---

[86] Dobbs v. Jackson Women's Health Org., 597 U.S. 715 (2022).
[87] Privacy Act of 1974, Pub. L. No. 93–579, 88 Stat. 1896 (codified as amended at 5 U.S.C. § 552a).
[88] Privacy Act of 1974, Pub. L. No. 93–579, 88 Stat. 1896 (codified as amended at 5 U.S.C. § 552a).

The legal theories underlying FIPPs replaced the narrow, property-based individual control with a governance framework to mediate control of the information between individuals and organizations. As implemented in the Privacy Act, the multi-stakeholder governance idea underlying the FIPPs can be seen in the fact that each of the individual rights that Congress created also serves the interests of any reasonable agency and is consistent with the need for other legitimate secondary users, such as public health authorities, financial oversight agencies, law enforcement, and national security agencies – indeed any stakeholder with a legitimate need to use the information in the public interest – to access and appropriately use the information.

Just as loss of trust in the governance framework would harm the interests of all, so proper and appropriate use of personal information within a secure governance framework would maintain trust and benefit the interests of all. The FIPPs allow individuals to determine what records pertaining to them are collected, maintained, used, or disseminated by an agency; require agencies to procure consent before records pertaining to an individual collected for one purpose could be used for other incompatible purposes; afford individuals a right of access to records pertaining to them and to have them corrected if inaccurate; and require agencies to collect such records only for lawful and authorized purposes and safeguard them appropriately. Exceptions from some of these principles are permitted only for important reasons of public policy. Judicial redress is afforded to individuals when an agency fails to comply with access and amendment rights, but only after an internal appeals process fails to correct the problem. Otherwise, liability for damages is afforded in the event of a willful or intentional violation of these rights. For example, the FIPP transparency requirement is detailed in Section 552a(e)(4) of the Act, which requires each agency that maintains a system of records to publish in the Federal Register upon establishment or revision a notice of the existence and character of the system of records, which includes the name and location of the system and the categories of individuals on whom records are maintained in the system, among other requirements.

The FIPPs are not only central to the framework of the Privacy Act but they also have also been the basis of many subsequent privacy laws worldwide, including the GDPR[89] in the European Union, the CCPA[90] and the Children's Internet Protection Act[91] (CIPA) in the United States. By considering these general or sectoral-specific requirements and principles, HCI practitioners can contribute to the development of safe and user-friendly digital experiences in these sectors.

---

[89] Regulation (EU) 2016/679 of the European Parliament and of the Council of 27 April 2016 on the protection of natural persons with regard to the processing of personal data and on the free movement of such data, and repealing Directive 95/46/EC (General Data Protection Regulation), 2016 O.J. (L 119) 1.

[90] California Consumer Privacy Act of 2018, Cal. Civ. Code §§ 1798.100–.198 (2024).

[91] Children's Internet Protection Act, 20 U.S.C. § 9134(f), codified as amended in 47 U.S.C. § 254(h)(5)–(6) (2022).

4.5.2 Health Insurance Portability and Accountability Act (HIPAA)

Data privacy becomes even more concerning when it concerns personally identifiable information (PII) or protected health information (PHI). As medical records began being transmitted in electronic form, two major issues arose – there was a demand to keep data private to reduce the stigma and insurance coverage issues that arose when information about a person's HIV status became public. There was also a recognition that the theft of health care data had become a serious issue, as it was often used for committing identity theft. This not only had financial implications for patients whose data was stolen but also enabled criminals to obtain health care under false pretenses or sell the data on the black market to uninsured persons who could receive expensive health care treatments. This resulted in increased insurance costs which were passed down to individuals in the form of increased insurance premiums. Information privacy is concerned with the proper handling, processing, and protection of personal data, while personal privacy concerns the individual's right to keep their personal life and personal space free from intrusion or visibility to others unless consent is provided.

Congress passed the HIPAA[92] law to protect private health information. In general, HIPAA's portability requirements were intended to promote greater continuity of health plan coverage, while its privacy and security rules govern how individuals' health information, that is, protected health information (PHI), is used and disclosed. Personal medical information is to be kept strictly confidential.

The Standards for Privacy of Individually Identifiable Health Information[93] ("Privacy Rule") establishes a set of national standards for the protection of certain health information. The Privacy Rule standards address the use and disclosure of individuals' health information – called "protected health information" by organizations subject to the Privacy Rule – called "covered entities," as well as standards for individuals' privacy rights so they may understand and control how their health information is used. The Privacy Rule applies to health plans, health care clearinghouses, and any health care provider who transmits health information in electronic form in connection with transactions for which the Secretary of HHS has adopted standards under HIPAA (the "covered entities"). The Privacy Rule protects all "individually identifiable health information" held or transmitted by a covered entity or its business associate, in any form or media, whether electronic, paper, or oral. The Privacy Rule calls this information PHI.[94] Individually identifiable health information is information, including demographic data, that relates to the individual's past, present, or future physical or mental health or

---

[92] Health Insurance Portability and Accountability Act of 1996, Pub. L. No. 104–191, 110 Stat. 1936 (codified as amended in 42 U.S.C. §§ 1320d–1320d-9 and 29 U.S.C. § 1181).
[93] HIPAA Privacy Rule, 45 C.F.R. §§ 164.500–.534 (2023).
[94] Protected Health Information, 45 C.F.R. § 160.103 (2023).

condition, the provision of health care to the individual, or the past, present, or future payment for the provision of health care to the individual and that identifies the individual or for which there is a reasonable basis to believe it can be used to identify the individual. Individually identifiable health information includes many common identifiers (e.g., name, address, birth date, and Social Security Number). The Privacy Rule excludes from PHI employment records that a covered entity maintains in its capacity as an employer and education and certain other records subject to, or defined in, the Family Educational Rights and Privacy Act, 20 U.S.C. §1232g.

There are no restrictions on the use or disclosure of de-identified health information. De-identified health information neither identifies nor provides a reasonable basis to identify an individual. Under HIPAA, there are two recognized methods for de-identifying PHI to ensure that it no longer constitutes PHI and thus is not subject to HIPAA's use and disclosure restrictions. The Expert Determination[95] section for instance states: "A qualified expert applies generally accepted statistical and scientific principles to evaluate the risk that the information could be used, alone or in combination with other reasonably available information, by an anticipated recipient to identify an individual who is a subject of the information."

Similarly, the Safe Harbor test in the same section[96] specifies the removal of eighteen specific identifiers of the individual and of the individual's relatives, household members, and employers. These identifiers include names, geographic subdivisions smaller than a state, all elements of dates (except year) directly related to an individual, telephone numbers, Social Security numbers, and more. The entity must also have no actual knowledge that the remaining information could be used alone or in combination with other information to identify the individual.

4.5.3 Family Educational Rights and Privacy Act (FERPA)

The Family Educational Rights and Privacy Act (FERPA)[97] is a federal law that protects the privacy of student education records. It applies to all schools that receive federal funding, including public schools, private schools, and colleges and universities. It balances rights and responsibilities for three groups – parents, children, and schools. Parents have the right to inspect and review their child's education records, or to request that schools correct any inaccuracies in their child's education records, or to consent to the disclosure of their child's education records to third parties, or to file a complaint with the U.S. Department of Education if they believe that their child's privacy rights have been violated.

---

[95] Expert Determination for De-identification, 45 C.F.R. § 164.514(b) (2023).
[96] Ibid.
[97] Family Educational Rights and Privacy Act of 1974, Pub. L. No. 93-380, 88 Stat. 571 (1974) (codified as amended in 20 U.S.C. § 1232g).

Once students reach the age of 18, they have the same rights as parents under FERPA. In addition, students have the right to restrict the disclosure of their education records to certain parties, such as prospective employers, or file a complaint with the U.S. Department of Education if they believe that their privacy rights have been violated. There are some exceptions to FERPA's privacy protections. For example, schools may disclose student education records without parental consent in certain circumstances, such as when the disclosure is necessary to protect the health or safety of the student or others; respond to a lawful subpoena or court order, or enforce a school policy, or transfer a student's records to another school. FERPA plays a crucial role in safeguarding the privacy of students' educational records, ensuring that schools and educational institutions handle sensitive information responsibly. It aims to strike a balance between providing access to educational records for legitimate purposes while also protecting students' rights and maintaining their privacy.

4.5.4 Children's Internet Protection Act (CIPA)

The CIPA[98] is a federal law in the United States that addresses concerns about children's access to explicit and inappropriate content on the Internet, particularly in schools and libraries. Enacted in 2000, CIPA aims to promote internet safety and ensure that children have a safe online experience when using computers and accessing the Internet in educational settings. It requires schools and libraries to have an internet safety policy that includes the following elements: a statement of the library's or school's commitment to safety and security; a description of the library's or school's internet safety practices; and a procedure for reporting child pornography. It also requires institutions to implement technology protection measures that block or filter internet access to pictures that are obscene, child pornography, or harmful to minors. It should also allow adults to disable filters for computers that are used by adults only. It attempts to strike a balance between protecting children from harmful online content and ensuring their access to valuable educational resources.

While it has been effective in enhancing online safety for minors, it has also been controversial for the potential to over-block legitimate content and the challenges of implementing effective filtering technologies.[99] For instance, even though the Supreme Court upheld CIPA in *United States v. American Library Association*,[100]

---

[98] Children's Internet Protection Act, Pub. L. No. 106-554, 114 Stat. 2763A-335 (2000), codified as amended in 20 U.S.C. § 9134(f) and 47 U.S.C. § 254(h)(5)-(6). Jaeger, P. T., Lazar, J., Gorham, U., & Taylor, N. G. (2023). *Foundations of Information Law*. American Library Association.

[99] Jaeger, P. & McClur, C. (2004). Potential Legal Challenges to the Application of the Children's Internet Protection Act (CIPA) in Public Libraries: Strategies and issues. *First Monday*, 9(2).

[100] U.S. v. American Library Association, 539 U.S. 194 (2003).

the Court also noted that adults must have the ability to request the unblocking of incorrectly filtered content.

4.5.5 Electronic Communications Privacy Act of 1986

The ECPA[101] is a federal law in the United States that was designed to update and extend the protections of the Fourth Amendment to cover modern forms of communication and electronic data. It extended government restrictions on wiretaps from telephone calls to include transmissions of electronic data by computer. It was an amendment to the Federal Wiretap Act of 1968 and addressed the growing use of electronic communications and the need for privacy protections surrounding such communications. It protected communications through provisions to protect wire, oral, and electronic communications while those communications are being made, are in transit, and when they are stored on computers. It acknowledged the importance of electronic data and sought to protect it from unauthorized surveillance and interception. It also aimed to protect stored communications through the Stored Communications Act (SCA),[102] which provided a set of procedural safeguards to protect the privacy of stored electronic communications with service providers. The ECPA also had provisions to balance privacy against recording or decoding users' dialing, routing, addressing, and signaling information. For example, it includes a general prohibition on Pen Register and Trap and Trace Device Use:

> Except as provided in this section, no person may install or use a pen register or a trap and trace device without first obtaining a court order under §3123 of this title or under the Foreign Intelligence Surveillance Act of 1978 (50 U.S.C. 1801 et seq.) or an order from a foreign government that is subject to an executive agreement that the Attorney General has determined and certified to Congress satisfies §2523.[103]

The act imposed statutory requirements for their use, providing a layer of privacy protection for individuals against wide-ranging surveillance. It also established a legal framework for law enforcement agencies to follow when attempting to obtain access to electronic communications. This included requirements for search warrants, subpoenas, and court orders, depending on the nature of the information being sought and its age. This framework aimed to balance the needs of law enforcement with the privacy rights of individuals and acknowledged the need for privacy protections beyond the traditional scope of wiretapping laws that were designed for telephone communications.[104]

---

[101] Electronic Communications Privacy Act, Pub. L. No. 99–508, 18 USC §§ 2510–2523 (1986).
[102] Electronic Communications Privacy Act, Pub. L. No. 99–508, 18 USC §§ 2701–2712 (1986).
[103] Electronic Communications Privacy Act, Pub. L. No. 99–508, 18 U.S.C. §§ 2523 (1986).
[104] Johnson, E. (2017). Lost in the Cloud: Cloud Storage, Privacy, and Suggestions for Protecting Users' Data. *Stanford Law Review*, 69(3), pp. 867–909.

4.5.6 Privacy Protection Act of 1980

The Privacy Protection Act of 1980[105] (PPA) is a United States federal law that aims to protect the First Amendment rights of journalists and other individuals engaged in news-gathering activities. It restricts the government's ability to search and seize materials related to journalistic work, particularly when it comes to unpublished information or materials used for news reporting.

This act was passed in response to a 1978 Supreme Court case, *Zurcher v. Stanford Daily*,[106] in which the Court held that a newsroom could be searched if it was believed to contain evidence of a crime, which balances the need for effective law enforcement and the protection of constitutional rights, particularly the freedom of the press. The ruling raised concerns about the potential for abuse and the chilling effect such actions could have on the freedom of the press and the ability to report on sensitive or controversial issues. It provides protections to journalists and newsrooms from searches and seizures by generally prohibiting law enforcement officers from searching for or seizing work product or documentary materials possessed by a person reasonably believed to have a purpose to disseminate to the public a newspaper, book, broadcast, or other similar form of public communication. The Privacy Protection Act of 1980 was Congress's legislative response to the *Zurcher* decision to strengthen press protections. The act aimed to statutorily curb overly broad, unannounced third-party newsroom searches, by imposing federal statutory limits on searches and seizures of journalists' materials.[107] It aims to strike a balance between law enforcement's need to investigate criminal activities and the need to protect the constitutionally guaranteed rights of journalists. However, like many legal protections, the act's effectiveness and scope have been subjects of legal debate and interpretation, especially in the context of changing technology and dissemination practices.[108]

4.5.7 Computer Matching and Privacy Protection Act of 1988

The Computer Matching and Privacy Protection Act of 1988[109] amends the Privacy Act of 1974. It was enacted to regulate the use of computer matching by federal agencies. Computer matching is a method used by federal agencies to verify eligibility

---

[105] Privacy Protection Act of 1980, Pub. L. No. 96–440, 94 Stat. 1879 (codified as amended in 42 U.S.C. §§ 2000aa et seq).
[106] Zurcher v. Stanford Daily, 436 U.S. 547 (1978).
[107] Sariego, J. M. (1980). The Privacy Protection Act of 1980: Curbing Unrestricted Third-Party Searches in the Wake of Zurcher v. *Stanford Daily*. *University of Michigan Journal of Law Reform*, 14(3), pp. 519–561.
[108] Teeter Jr, D. L., & Singer, S. G. (1978). Search Warrants in Newsrooms: Some Aspects of the Impact of Zurcher v. The Stanford Daily. *Kentucky Law Journal*, 67(4), pp. 847–865.
[109] Computer Matching and Privacy Protection Act of 1988, Pub. L. No. 100–503, 102 Stat. 2507, codified as amended at 5 U.S.C. § 552a.

for certain benefits or programs and reduce fraud in the process. For example, to verify an individual's social security benefits eligibility, records may be accessed and compared if that same individual is registered with another government agency, such as the IRS. It provided additional safeguards when federal agencies performed automated matching of individual's personal records, particularly for the purpose of verifying eligibility for government benefits and for uncovering fraud, particularly when it comes to the exchange of personal information between agencies for the purpose of verifying eligibility for federal benefit programs or for recouping payments or delinquent debts under these programs. Its main goal is to safeguard individuals' privacy rights by imposing strict controls on computer matching activities involving personal information. By doing so, the act aims to prevent erroneous deprivation of federal benefits and to ensure that individuals are treated fairly and with respect to their privacy when agencies use computer systems to match data.

The act requires federal agencies to enter into written agreements with other agencies or nonfederal entities before they can engage in computer matching activities. These agreements must specify the purpose and legal authority for the matching program, describe the records that will be matched, and ensure the security and confidentiality of the data.[110]

The act has had a significant impact on how federal agencies manage and share personal information for administrative purposes. It has led to greater transparency, accountability, and protection of individuals' rights in the context of computer matching activities. This is an example of the ongoing evolution of privacy laws in response to technological advancements, highlighting the need for continuous updates to privacy regulations as data processing technologies develop and become more integrated into government operations.

4.5.8 Federal Trade Commission Act of 1914

The Federal Trade Commission (FTC) Act[111] is a foundational piece of legislation in the United States that established the FTC in 1914. It was passed to prevent unfair or deceptive practices in the marketplace and to promote consumer protection and competition. The act grants the FTC the authority to investigate and prevent deceptive, unfair, or anticompetitive business practices through various means, including administrative and judicial processes and is responsible for enforcing privacy and consumer protection laws in the United States to ensure fair business practices.

Section 5 of the FTC Act empowers the FTC to take action against companies that engage in "unfair or deceptive acts or practices," which can include privacy-related

---

[110] Strong, D. R. (1987). The Computer Matching and Privacy Protection Act of 1988: Necessary Relief from the Erosion of the Privacy Act of 1974. *Software Law Journal*, 2.
[111] Federal Trade Commission Act of 1914, Pub. L. No. 63-203, 38 Stat. 717, codified as amended at 15 U.S.C. §§ 41-58.

concerns such as misleading data collection practices, hidden tracking, and inadequate security. The FTC also relies on related acts such as the Children's Online Privacy Protection Act (COPPA), as the FTC was granted rulemaking authority under Section 6502(b) of COPPA to issue and update rules as necessary to keep up with technological changes and evolving business practices.[112] This has resulted in various updates to the COPPA Rule, which outline the requirements for operators of websites or online services directed to children and operators who knowingly collect personal information from children. Similarly, in the Gramm-Leach-Bliley Act (GLBA), the FTC derives its jurisdiction to enforce the GLBA, particularly its privacy provisions, from the act itself, specifically in Title V.[113] These laws grant the FTC jurisdiction over aspects of privacy and consumer protection in industries.

The act prohibits unfair or deceptive acts or practices in or affecting commerce. This broad mandate allows the FTC to address a wide range of practices that may harm consumers or competition. It also aims to promote competition by preventing anticompetitive business practices, such as monopolies, mergers that substantially lessen competition, and other practices that can harm consumers by reducing choice or increasing prices.

The FTC uses the act to protect consumers from unfair or deceptive practices in the marketplace. This includes false advertising, scams, and other misleading business practices, and provides FTC with the authority to issue regulations (known as Trade Regulation Rules)[114] to define unfair or deceptive acts in particular industries or practices. It also enables the agency to investigate companies and practices, issue cease and desist orders, impose penalties, and take legal action against violators, and to conduct studies and research related to its mandate. Furthermore, the FTC has the authority to issue rules and regulations related to privacy and consumer protection. For example, the FTC has promulgated rules under COPPA[115] to protect children's online privacy and has issued various guidelines for businesses to follow in handling consumer data. Furthermore, the FTC can initiate investigations into companies and individuals suspected of engaging in unfair or deceptive practices related to privacy. It can also respond to consumer complaints regarding privacy violations. Individuals and organizations can file complaints with the FTC, which the agency then investigates. If the FTC finds that a company has violated privacy or consumer protection laws, it can negotiate settlements or consent orders with the offending party. These agreements often include requirements for the company to change its practices, pay fines or restitution to affected consumers, and adhere to specific privacy safeguards in the future. For example, in 2019, FTC determined that Facebook had violated a 2012 FTC order by deceiving users about their ability

---

[112] 15 U.S.C. § 6502(b).
[113] 15 U.S.C. §§ 6801–6827.
[114] 16 CFR Part 400 to 499.
[115] 16 CFR Part 312.

to control the privacy of their personal information. The FTC found that Facebook had misled users with deceptive practices related to personal data privacy, including the misuse of phone numbers collected under the guise of enhancing security (for two-factor authentication) and providing user data to third-party apps accessed by friends without the users' informed consent. The FTC fined Facebook $5 billion for this violation.[116] When a company fails to comply with a consent order or refuses to settle, the FTC can initiate enforcement actions in federal court. This may involve seeking injunctions, civil penalties, or other legal remedies to address privacy violations. In summary, the FTC enforces privacy under its jurisdiction by investigating complaints, issuing rules and regulations, negotiating settlements, taking enforcement actions, educating the public and businesses, and advocating for stronger privacy protections. Its primary goal is to promote fair business practices and protect consumers' privacy rights in various industries.

However, in the absence of a comprehensive federal privacy law, the enforcement is ad hoc and sector specific. Additionally, enforcement actions can be time-consuming and complex, meaning companies may find loopholes or delay corrective actions. Given these limitations, states have started to take on the privacy mantle, as discussed below.

The FTC enforces several federal privacy laws, including the Children's Online Privacy Protection Act (COPPA), the Gramm-Leach-Bliley Act (GLBA), and the Fair Credit Reporting Act (FCRA). These laws set specific requirements for how companies must handle personal information, especially in sensitive areas like children's data, financial information, and credit reporting. Furthermore, under Section 5 of the FTC act, the FTC can take action against companies that engage in deceptive or unfair practices. This includes misleading consumers about how their personal data is collected, used, or shared. If a company makes promises about privacy or data security that it does not keep, the FTC can intervene. The FTC maintains a privacy and security website[117] that informs businesses to create robust privacy practices that protect consumer data and comply with federal regulations. By following these guidelines, companies can build consumer trust and avoid potential enforcement actions by the FTC. Its best practices include privacy by design, in which businesses are encouraged to integrate privacy protections into their products and services from the outset. This involves limiting data collection, implementing robust security measures, and ensuring data is only retained for as long as necessary. These practices also include simplified consumer choice by providing customers with clear options regarding how their personal data is collected, used, and shared.

---

[116] FTC (July 24, 2019), *FTC Imposes $5 Billion Penalty and Sweeping New Privacy Restrictions on Facebook*. Available at: www.ftc.gov/news-events/news/press-releases/2019/07/ftc-imposes-5-billion-penalty-sweeping-new-privacy-restrictions-facebook.

[117] FTC. *Privacy and Security*. Retrieved January 2, 2025, from www.ftc.gov/business-guidance/privacy-security.

This includes making it easy for consumers to opt out of data processing for purposes like targeted advertising, and to provide transparency, in which businesses must clearly disclose their data practices, including what information is collected, how it is used, and with whom it is shared. Clear and accessible privacy notices are essential.

The FTC website also provides corporate advertising guidelines.[118] These guidelines refer to a set of principles designed to provide a framework for companies that engage in the collection and use of data related to consumers' online activities for advertising purposes. The FTC guidelines also aim to protect consumer privacy while also enabling advertisers to continue using behavioral advertising practices. For instance, the guidelines emphasize the need for websites and advertisers to provide clear and prominent notice regarding the behavioral advertising techniques they use and to provide consumers with choices about whether and how their information is collected and used. These guidelines also emphasize the need for companies to provide reasonable security for any data they collect for behavioral advertising and to retain data only as long as necessary to fulfill a legitimate business or law enforcement need, or, if the company makes a material change to its privacy policy, it must obtain affirmative express consent from the consumer before that change can be applied retroactively to data previously collected under an old policy. Finally, these guidelines advise that companies should only collect sensitive data for behavioral advertising if they obtain affirmative express consent from the consumer to receive such advertising.

4.6 STATE LAWS

At the federal level, in the absence of an explicit provision for a right of privacy, federal law regulates personal data regulations and privacy in specific domains of economic activity, based on the specific risks to citizens concerning their status as consumers. At the state level, several state constitutions have explicit articles on the right of privacy, for example, Alaska,[119] California,[120] Florida,[121] Montana,[122] and South Carolina.[123] These state constitutions provide more expansive rights than those recognized at the federal level. For instance, the constitutional right to privacy in Alaska is stated in Article I, Section 22 of its State Constitution, which reads: *"The right of the people to privacy is recognized and shall not be infringed. The legislature shall implement this section. The laws and governmental actions that might infringe upon personal privacy are subject to strict scrutiny."*

---

[118] Leonard, B. (Ed.). (2011). *Self-Regulatory Principles for Online Behavioral Advertising*. DIANE Publishing.
[119] Alaska Const. Art. 1, §. 22.
[120] California Const. Art. 1, §. 1.
[121] Florida Const. Art. 1, §. 23.
[122] Montana Const. Art. 2, §. 10.
[123] South Carolina Const. Art. 1, §. 10.

This means that for such a law to be upheld, the state must show that it has a compelling interest in enacting the law and that the law is narrowly tailored to meet that interest. Other states have general, sector-neutral privacy laws, including California,[124] Colorado,[125] Connecticut,[126] Iowa,[127] Virginia,[128] and Utah.[129] California's economy is nearly 15 percent of the United States economy, and many companies dealing with personal data are headquartered there, so its privacy laws are followed by nearly all national and international companies seeking to do business in the United States.

4.6.1 California Consumer Privacy Act (CCPA) and California Privacy Rights Act (CPRA)

The CCPA[130] CCPA and California Privacy Rights Act (CPRA)[131] mutually reinforce each other to protect their residents' privacy. CCPA is a comprehensive data privacy law that went into effect on January 1, 2020. It grants California residents certain rights regarding the collection, use, and sharing of their personal information by businesses. California residents have the right to know what personal information is being collected about them, the sources of that information, the purpose of the collection, and the categories of third parties with whom the data is shared. Consumers also have the right to request the deletion of their personal information, opt out of the sale of their data, and opt in for children under the age of 16. Businesses are required to disclose their data collection and usage practices to consumers in a clear and accessible manner, such as through a privacy policy. They must also implement mechanisms to honor consumers' rights, provide at least two methods for consumers to make data-related requests, and respond to such requests within specific timeframes.

The California Attorney General has the authority to enforce the CCPA and can impose fines and penalties on businesses found in violation of the law. The CCPA grants specific authorities and responsibilities to the California Attorney General (AG) in relation to the enforcement and implementation of the act. These powers are crucial for ensuring compliance with the CCPA's provisions and for protecting consumer privacy rights within the state. Key aspects of the

---

[124] California Consumer Privacy Act of 2018, as amended by the California Privacy Rights Act of 2020. Cal. Civ. Code §§ 1798.100 to 1798.199.100.
[125] Colorado Privacy Act – Effective July 1, 2023. Colo. Rev. Stat. Ann. §§ 6–1–1301 to 6-1-1313
[126] Connecticut Data Privacy Act – Effective July 1, 2023 (Codified as the "Connecticut Personal Data Privacy and Online Monitoring Act"). Conn. Gen. Stat. Ann. §§ 42–515 to 42–52.
[127] Iowa Consumer Data Protection Act – Effective January 1, 2025. Iowa Code Ann. §§ 715D.1–9.
[128] Virginia Consumer Data Protection Act of 2021 – Effective January 1, 2023. Va. Code Ann. §§ 59.1–575 to 59.1–584.
[129] Utah Consumer Privacy Act – Effective December 31, 2023. Utah Code §§ 13–61–101 to 13–61–404.
[130] California Consumer Privacy Act of 2018, Cal. Civ. Code §§ 1798.100–1798.199 (2020).
[131] California Civil Code §§ 1798.100–1798.199.100.

authority given to the Attorney General under the CCPA include investigating violations of the CCPA, bringing actions against violators, and seeking remedies and penalties for noncompliance. It also includes responsibility for drafting and adopting regulations, and to draft guidelines and interpretations. This helps businesses and consumers understand their rights and obligations under the law. The AG also handles consumer complaints related to the CCPA and engages in educational outreach to raise awareness about consumer privacy rights and business responsibilities under the CCPA. Additionally, the CCPA allows consumers to take legal action against businesses if their personal information is subject to unauthorized access or disclosure due to the business's failure to implement reasonable security measures.

The CPRA[132] is a data privacy law that builds upon and amends the CCPA. The CPRA aims to strengthen and enhance consumer privacy rights by introducing additional provisions and requirements for businesses that collect and process personal information of California residents. The CPRA created a new independent regulatory agency responsible for enforcing and implementing the CPRA's provisions, the California Privacy Protection Agency (CPPA). It has the authority to issue regulations, conduct investigations, and enforce penalties for violations of the CPRA. The CPRA introduces a new category of personal information called "sensitive personal information," which includes data such as social security numbers, religious beliefs, and more. Consumers have increased rights and control over the processing of this sensitive data. For example, consumers have the right to limit the use and disclosure of their sensitive personal information, the right to correct inaccurate personal information, and the right to access information about automated decision-making processes that significantly affect them. Businesses that are larger than specified thresholds (such as revenues over $25 million, or transact with over 100,000 California consumers) or have over 50 percent annual revenue in California must limit the retention of personal information to only what is necessary for the purposes for which it was collected, and when contracting with service providers, requiring written agreements that include specific provisions related to data processing and protection. Several other states in the United States have moved toward creating similar agencies or enhancing existing frameworks to oversee the enforcement of privacy laws. These agencies are designed to implement and enforce state privacy regulations, handle complaints, and provide guidance on privacy matters to consumers and businesses. As one example, the Colorado Privacy Act (CPA)[133] established a Division of Privacy within the Department of Law to enforce the CPA. While it was not set up to be an independent agency like the CPPA, this division is tasked with similar responsibilities concerning privacy regulation and enforcement.

---

[132] Cal. Civ. Code §§ 1798.100 to 1798.199.
[133] Colo. Rev. Stat. §§ 6–1–1301 to 6–1–1313.

4.6.2 Virginia Consumer Data Protection Act

The Virginia Consumer Data Protection Act[134] (VCDPA) is a privacy law that was enacted in Virginia in 2021. It protects the consumer, which is defined as a natural person who is a Virginia resident, and protects personal information, which is defined as any information that is linked or reasonably linkable to an identified or identifiable natural person. It applies to businesses that control or process personal data of at least 100,000 consumers or derive over 50 percent of gross revenue from the sale of personal data and control or process personal data of at least 25,000 consumers. The VCDPA is modeled after the CCPA but strengthens it in some ways and weakens it in other ways. For instance, Virginia does not allow businesses to sell data when consumers opt out. Conversely, Virginia doesn't include drivers' license numbers and financial account numbers as sensitive data.

4.6.3 Colorado Privacy Act

The Colorado Privacy Act[135] (CPA) protects the consumer, which is defined as an individual who is a Colorado resident. It went into effect on July 1, 2023, and applies to businesses that control or process personal data of at least 100,000 consumers or derive over 50 percent of gross revenue from the sale of personal data and control or process personal data of at least 25,000 consumers. It provides several rights, including consumer rights, which grant Colorado residents certain rights regarding their personal data, including the right to access, correct, delete, and obtain a copy of their personal data held by businesses; opt out rights, which allow consumers to opt out of the processing of their personal data for targeted advertising, sale of personal data, or profiling. It also imposes corporate requirements, including requiring businesses to conduct data protection assessments for certain processing activities that present a heightened risk of harm to consumers, such as processing sensitive data or engaging in large-scale data processing; to minimize data collection and storage by limiting the collection of personal data to what is necessary for the purposes for which it is processed, and to establish data retention schedules to ensure that personal data is not kept longer than necessary. It also gives enforcement authority to the Colorado Attorney General. Finally, it exempts specific kinds of data already covered by federal privacy laws (like HIPAA or GLBA) and data collected for employment purposes.

4.6.4 Connecticut

The Connecticut Data Privacy Act[136] (CTDPA) is a state law that gives Connecticut consumers certain rights over their personal data. It went into effect on July 1, 2023 and

---

[134] Virginia Consumer Data Protection Act, Va. Code Ann. §§59.1–530 et seq.
[135] Colorado Privacy Act, Colo. Rev. Stat. §§18–6–1001 to 18–6–1010.
[136] Connecticut Privacy Act, Conn. Gen. Stat. §§ 36a-880 et seq.

applies to businesses that control or process personal data of at least 100,000 consumers or derive over 50 percent of gross revenue from the sale of personal data and control or process personal data of at least 25,000 consumers. While it is modeled on the CCPA, there are some differences: The CTDPA provides more specific requirements for businesses to protect the confidentiality, integrity, and security of personal data and gives consumers more rights to access and correct their personal data. Businesses that violate the CTDPA may be subject to civil penalties of up to $10,000 per violation. The CTDPA grants consumers several rights regarding their personal data, including the right to access personal data; to correct inaccuracies in their personal data; to delete personal data; to data portability (i.e., to obtain a copy of their personal data in a portable and, to the extent technically feasible, readily usable format), and to opt out of the processing of their personal data for purposes of targeted advertising, sale, or profiling in furtherance of decisions that produce legal or similarly significant effects. It also requires businesses to provide consumers with a clear and accessible privacy notice; to collect data only for specified, explicit, and legitimate purposes and not further process it in a manner that is incompatible with those purposes; and to limit data collection to adequate, relevant, and limited to what is necessary in relation to the purposes for which they are processed should be collected. It also imposes requirements to ensure the implementation of appropriate technical and organizational measures to ensure a level of security appropriate to the risk. The Connecticut Attorney General has the authority to enforce the CTDPA. There is no private right of action under the CTDPA, meaning consumers cannot sue businesses directly for violations. Instead, they must report violations to the Attorney General's office.

4.6.5 Iowa

The Iowa Privacy Act (IPA),[137] officially known as the "Iowa Consumer Data Protection Act" (ICDPA), is a state-level legislation aimed at protecting the personal data of Iowa residents. It applies to businesses that control or process personal data of at least 100,000 consumers or derive over 50 percent of gross revenue from the sale of personal data and control or process personal data of at least 25,000 consumers. It also requires businesses to take reasonable steps to protect the confidentiality, integrity, and security of personal data. Businesses must also conduct data protection assessments for certain types of processing activities. The ICDPA grants Iowa residents several rights concerning their personal data, including the right to access personal data; correct inaccuracies in their personal data; delete personal data; data portability, allowing consumers to obtain a copy of their personal data in a usable format; and to opt out of the processing of their personal data for purposes of targeted advertising, sale, or profiling in furtherance of decisions that produce legal or similarly significant effects. While it is modeled after the CCPA, there are some

---

[137] Iowa Privacy Act, Iowa Code Ann. §§ 507A.1 et seq.

differences: The ICDPA does not provide a separate requirement that consumers must opt in for the processing of "sensitive data," and does not explicitly provide any right to correct inaccurate information or to opt out of profiling. The Iowa Attorney General has the authority to enforce the ICDPA. There is no private right of action, meaning consumers cannot directly sue businesses for violations. Instead, they must report violations to the Attorney General's office. Businesses that violate the ICDPA may be subject to civil penalties of up to $10,000 per violation.

4.6.6 Utah

The Utah Consumer Privacy Act[138] (UCPA) is a state-level legislation designed to protect the personal data of Utah residents. It applies to businesses that control or process personal data of at least 100,000 consumers or derive over 50 percent of gross revenue from the sale of personal data and control or process personal data of at least 25,000 consumers. It is modeled after the CCPA but has some differences. For example, it does not provide a separate requirement that consumers must opt in for the processing of "sensitive data," and does not explicitly provide any right to correct inaccurate information or to opt out of profiling. Specifically, the UCPA places additional requirements on the processing of sensitive data, such as data revealing racial or ethnic origin, religious beliefs, sexual orientation, citizenship or immigration status, medical or health information, genetic or biometric data, and specific geolocation data. Controllers must obtain consumer consent before processing sensitive data. The Utah Attorney General has the authority to enforce the UCPA. There is no private right of action, meaning consumers cannot sue businesses directly for violations. Instead, they must report violations to the Attorney General's office. Businesses that violate the UCPA may be subject to civil penalties of up to $7,500 per violation.

4.7 INTERNATIONAL LAWS

Most countries differ in terms of their privacy norms and laws. For instance, the European Union (EU) frames information privacy as a human right that must be protected, while the United States at the federal level does not have general information privacy rights, though it has sector-specific rights in education, health, and others. However, for multinationals and online commerce that crosses borders, U.S. companies must consider and comply with international law.

The GDPR[139] regulates personal data and in the European Union (EU). Its primary focus is on safeguarding individuals' privacy rights and controlling how their

---

[138] Utah Consumer Privacy Act, Utah Code Ann. §§ 13–61–101 et seq.
[139] EU General Data Protection Regulation (GDPR): Regulation (EU) 2016/679 of the European Parliament and of the Council of 27 April 2016.

personal data is collected, used, and shared and applies to all EU companies and organizations that hold or process personal data in the EU. It also applies to companies in third countries that provide goods or services to people in the EU or monitor their behavior there. It translates the right to be informed, the right to access, and the right to be forgotten, in the context of electronic platforms operating within the EU. It has therefore conferred greater autonomy on users in making informed decisions and easier control over access to their data.

In contrast with the privacy frameworks in the United States, in Europe there is no data ownership, and personal data cannot be commercialized as material goods. The GDPR outlines the requirements for obtaining informed and explicit consent from users before processing their personal data in Article 7.[140] The article specifies the conditions under which consent is considered valid, including the need for a clear affirmative act establishing a freely given, specific, informed, and unambiguous indication of the data subject's agreement to the processing of personal data relating to them. It further mandates that the data subject has the right to withdraw their consent at any time, and it must be as easy to withdraw consent as to give it. This could include ticking a box when visiting a website, choosing technical settings for information society services, or another statement or conduct which clearly indicates in this context the data subject's acceptance of the proposed processing of their personal data. Therefore, HCI professionals should consider how to incorporate consent mechanisms into their designs and ensure that users understand the purposes of information processing and make informed decisions about sharing their information. It also encourages HCI professionals to incorporate the "privacy by design" concept, to collaborate with privacy experts and legal teams to provide privacy-enhancing features and create interfaces and experiences that prioritize user consent, transparency, and control over their personal data, which may lead to more ethical and user-friendly systems. Refer to Chapter 11 for additional discussion on international laws and treaties.

4.8 PRIVACY LAWS FROM AN HCI PERSPECTIVE

From an HCI perspective, privacy laws significantly influence how digital products and services are designed and developed. HCI professionals focus on creating user-centered designs that are not only intuitive and engaging but also compliant with relevant privacy regulations. These laws shape various aspects of the user experience, including user consent mechanisms, data handling practices, transparency, and user control over personal information.

Here's how privacy laws impact HCI and what designers and developers need to consider: For instance, privacy laws often require clear and informed consent for data collection and processing. From an HCI standpoint, this necessitates

---

[140] GDPR, Article 7 – Conditions for consent.

designing consent forms and opt in mechanisms that are easily understandable by users, avoiding dark patterns that might trick users into giving consent unwittingly. In the United States, absent a general federal law, HCI designers can rely on published guidelines from regulators such as the FTC. For instance, the FTC maintains guidelines to encourage organizations to incorporate a "privacy by design" philosophy in all phases, including design, process, and procedures. For instance, the guidelines call for a proactive approach by incorporating security and privacy as early in the design cycle as possible and to set privacy as a default setting. These were further developed in settlements with Facebook[141] and Google,[142] to be used as roadmaps to implement and maintain a "comprehensive security program" or to "identify commonly known and foreseeable risks," and distilled in their publication "Start with Security: A Guide for Business," which provides a list of recommendations and lessons for ensuring that the privacy by design guidelines are followed.

HCI professionals must ensure that privacy policies and data practices are communicated to users in a clear, concise, and accessible manner. This might involve innovative design solutions that present information in digestible formats, avoiding legal jargon that could confuse users. Privacy regulations often emphasize collecting only the data that is necessary for a specified purpose. HCI designers must consider this when creating user interfaces, ensuring that data collection is justified and aligns with user expectations and the context of use.

In the EU, GDPR implemented the concept of privacy by design through Article 25 (GDPR).[143] This regulation requires organizations to focus on data protection by design and default, which requires organizations to implement appropriate technical and organizational measures to implement the data protection measures and integrate safeguards, such as requiring designers to use only personal data which is necessary for each specific purpose of the processing. For instance, GDPR encourages organizations to adopt a user-centric approach to data processing, and HCI professionals should align their design principles and practices with GDPR requirements to create interfaces and experiences that prioritize user consent, transparency, and control over their personal data. Similarly, GDPR requirements emphasize obtaining informed and explicit consent from users before processing their personal data. HCI professionals can integrate clear and concise consent mechanisms into their designs, ensuring users understand the purposes of data processing and can make informed decisions about sharing their information. GDPR requires organizations to design for data minimization, which involves collecting only the necessary data for specific purposes.

---

[141] Federal Trade Commission v. Facebook, Inc., Case No. 1:19-cv-02184 (D.D.C. 2019).
[142] Federal Trade Commission and People of the State of New York, by Letitia James, Attorney General v. Google LLC and YouTube, LLC, Case No. 1:19-cv-02642 (D.D.C. 2019).
[143] Regulation (EU) 2016/679 of the European Parliament and of the Council of 27 April 2016 on the protection of natural persons with regard to the processing of personal data and on the free movement of such data, and repealing Directive 95/46/EC.

Many countries around the world have implemented data protection regulations that are similar to the GDPR. These laws typically aim to protect individuals' personal data, regulate its processing, and enhance privacy rights. For example, Brazil's Lei Geral de Proteção de Dados (LGPD)[144] shares many similarities with the GDPR, including strict requirements for data processing and substantial rights for data subjects. Similarly, South Africa's Protection of Personal Information Act (POPIA)[145] regulates the processing of personal information, requires responsible parties to safeguard the integrity of personal data, and provides data subjects with rights of access and correction.

HCI professionals can support this principle by designing interfaces that request minimal personal information and guide users through the process of providing relevant data without unnecessary information gathering. Consider the challenge in designing appropriate user interfaces for EULAs, or End-User License Agreements. These are lengthy legal contracts that users must consent to using the service. EULAs can be valuable tools for protecting both users and providers. They outline the terms of service, define acceptable use, and limit liability. In an ideal world, they would also provide clear and concise explanations of how our data is collected, used, and shared. However, reality often falls short of this ideal. EULAs are frequently written in opaque language, making it difficult for users to understand the true extent of the privacy concessions they're making. Furthermore, they often grant companies broad rights to collect users' data, sometimes for purposes beyond what they might reasonably expect, and are context dependent.[146]

For instance, consider a social media platform's EULA. It might state that the platform can collect and use our data to personalize the users' experience, show targeted advertising, and even share it with third-party partners. While some of these practices might be acceptable to users, others might find them intrusive and a violation of their privacy.[147] The lack of transparency and user control surrounding data collection in EULAs is a major concern. It can lead to issues such as surveillance creep, data misuse, or erosion of trust. Surveillance creep occurs when data collection starts small and gradually expands over time, without users' knowledge or consent; data misuse occurs when companies use consumer data in ways that were not disclosed in the EULA, potentially harming the consumer's privacy and security; and erosion of trust occurs when users feel their privacy is not respected and lose

---

[144] Lei nº 13.709, de 14 de agosto de 2018.
[145] Protection of Personal Information Act 4 of 2013.
[146] Sailaja, N., Jones, R., & McAuley, D. (2021, May). Designing for Human Data Interaction in Data-Driven Media Experiences. In *Extended Abstracts of the 2021 CHI Conference on Human Factors in Computing Systems*, pp. 1–7.
[147] Acquisti, A., Adjerid, I., Balebako, R., Brandimarte, L., Cranor, L. F., Komanduri, S., Leon, P. G., Sadeh, N., Schaub, F., Sleeper, M., Wang, Y., & Wilson, S. (2017). Nudges for Privacy and Security: Understanding and Assisting Users' Choices Online. *ACM Computing Surveys (CSUR)*, 50(3), pp. 1–41.

trust in the companies they interact with online. To mitigate these issues, designers can incorporate privacy-focused tools and settings such as ad blockers, privacy browsers, and strong password managers.

4.9 LEGAL PROCEDURES OR REMEDIES UNIQUE TO PRIVACY

In the United States, there is no general federal law on privacy; instead, most privacy laws are either domain specific, for example, health, education, or finance, or state-level laws. In response to the growth of online commerce, in the past few years, states have started to pass online privacy laws that govern the collection, processing, and sharing of personal information. However, some state privacy laws, such as California's CCPA, do not have a private right of action for data breaches and instead authorize the state Attorney General to enforce the state laws.[148] This approach has benefits and drawbacks. The benefits are that the Attorney General's office has legal expertise and resources dedicated to understanding complex privacy issues, making it well equipped to enforce privacy laws effectively. This specialization ensures that enforcement is consistent and grounded in a deep understanding of the law. This promotes consistency in enforcement; centralizing enforcement authority within the AG's office can lead to more consistent application and interpretation of the CCPA across the state. This helps avoid a patchwork of enforcement standards that could arise if local authorities had concurrent jurisdiction, compared with other states that permit a private right of action, for example, Illinois's Biometric Information Privacy Act (BIPA),[149] which includes a private right of action. It allows individuals to sue businesses that unlawfully collect or use their biometric information (like fingerprints or face scans) without proper consent. It also promotes consumer trust – having a centralized and authoritative body like the AG's office enforcing the CCPA can increase consumer trust in the digital economy. Consumers may feel more confident knowing there is a state-level authority protecting their privacy rights. However, the AG's office may face resource constraints, limiting its ability to investigate and prosecute all potential CCPA violations. This could lead to enforcement gaps, where some violations go unchecked due to limited manpower or financial resources. HCI designers can face a similar tradeoff – in having to decide whether to centralize privacy-focused user interaction, or to decentralize and adapt to privacy at various levels. For instance, centralizing privacy settings in one easily accessible location can simplify the user interface, making it easier for users to understand and manage their privacy settings. This can be particularly effective for general users who may not be very tech-savvy. However, centralized settings might not provide the flexibility needed for different contexts within the application. Users may find it

---

[148] California Civil Code, Section 1798.155.
[149] 740 ILCS 14/ (Illinois Compiled Statutes, Chapter 740, Act 14).

cumbersome to navigate back to a central location to adjust settings that are relevant to specific features or tasks. The alternative is to decentralize, which allows privacy controls to be embedded directly where they are relevant. For instance, a social media app might offer privacy settings directly on the post interface, making it intuitive for users to select who can see a post as they are creating it. But the disadvantage is that multiple privacy settings can confuse users, especially if the interface does not clearly indicate where to find these controls.

In practice, many HCI designers opt for a hybrid approach that combines centralized and decentralized elements, with a main privacy center that provides control over global privacy settings and information about data collection and usage policies, and contextual privacy settings are available at the point of interaction, such as within specific features or modules, allowing users to make immediate decisions based on the context. This hybrid model aims to balance ease of use with contextual appropriateness, striving to empower users with both comprehensive oversight and specific control where it matters most. It is crucial for designers to continuously test and iterate on these designs with real users to ensure that privacy controls are intuitive, effective, and truly meet user needs without compromising their experience or security.

Legally speaking, what's clear, what's still ambiguous, and what often causes confusion? Due to the evolving interaction between the evolution of information and communication technologies and societal norms, privacy laws often struggle to keep pace with rapid advancements in society and technology. In terms of technology evolution, new online platforms, data collection methods, and communication channels regularly emerge, lead to challenges in interpreting privacy laws in the new ways of transmitting or exchanging information. For instance, existing privacy laws might not be able to cover or regulate emerging types of customer data, such as geospatial or biometric information. Geospatial data can often be de-identified or anonymized, but there is a risk of reidentification, especially with the increasing sophistication of data analysis techniques. Laws like the GDPR consider the potential for reidentification when determining what constitutes personal data. Similarly, for biometric information, the global nature of data flows means that biometric information collected in one jurisdiction may be processed or stored in another, raising challenges in compliance with multiple and potentially conflicting privacy regimes.

In terms of societal evolution, changing cultural norms and societal expectations can lead to confusing legal interpretations. For instance, before the advent of ride sharing, hailing a stranger's car could be considered rude and a privacy violation, unlike now, and this evolving landscape can be confusing to navigate legally. Furthermore, privacy laws often need to strike a balance between an individual's right to privacy and other societal interests, such as freedom of expression, public safety, and national security. Determining the appropriate balance can be complex and lead to legal ambiguities.

4.10 WHAT ARE THE LEGAL QUESTIONS THAT MAY BE DECIDED IN THE FUTURE?

Most privacy laws agree on basic principles like the need for consent to collect personal data, the right to access and correct personal data, and the requirement for data security. There is a clear consensus on the necessity for organizations to notify individuals and authorities in the event of a data breach that compromises personal information.[150] Likewise, privacy laws generally agree on heightened protection for sector-specific personal data, such as health information, financial data, and information related to minors. However, different countries' laws differ on their requirements and scopes, and even within countries, especially in those that do not have a national general privacy law, their states or provinces have individual privacy laws that do not always align. As a result, determining the jurisdiction and applicability of certain laws to international or intra-state entities can be complex. For instance, non-EU companies often struggle with determining whether and how GDPR applies to them.[151]

The rapid emergence and deployment of artificial intelligence (AI) and machine learning (ML) technologies (refer to Chapter 8 on artificial intelligence) outpace the development of specific legal frameworks, leading to ambiguity in how existing privacy laws apply, and raise the risk for automated decision-making processes to infringe upon individual privacy rights. Privacy laws might need to adapt to address issues such as algorithmic bias, explainability, and the collection and processing of sensitive personal data for AI training. For instance, the GDPR mandates that data processing be fair and transparent. This can be interpreted to require that algorithms, particularly those that make decisions affecting individuals, operate in a manner that is fair and understandable to data subjects. The European Union has formally adopted the Artificial Intelligence Act[152]. It defines a risk-based regulatory model (unacceptable, high-risk, limited or minimal/no risk) to ensure that AI systems placed on the EU market are safe, transparent, traceable, and non-discriminatory. The Act entered into force on 1 August 2024 and will become fully applicable in 2026. The regulation also has extraterritorial reach, applying to providers and deployers of AI systems that affect individuals within the EU, regardless of establishment location.

---

[150] Vitak, J., Shilton, K., & Ashktorab, Z. (2016, February). Beyond the Belmont principles: Ethical Challenges, Practices, and Beliefs in the Online Data Research Community. In *Proceedings of the 19th ACM Conference on Computer-Supported Cooperative Work & Social Computing*, pp. 941–953.

[151] Bouma-Sims, E. R., Li, M., Lin, Y., Sakura-Lemessy, A., Nisenoff, A., Young, E., Birrell, E., Cranor, L. F. & Habib, H. (2023, April). A US-UK Usability Evaluation of Consent Management Platform Cookie Consent Interface Design on Desktop and Mobile. In *Proceedings of the 2023 CHI Conference on Human Factors in Computing Systems*, pp. 1–36.

[152] Regulation (EU) 2024/1689 of the European Parliament and of the Council of 13 June 2024 laying down harmonised rules on artificial intelligence and amending Regulations (EC) No 300/2008, (EU) No 167/2013, (EU) No 168/2013, (EU) 2018/858, (EU) 2018/1139 and (EU) 2019/2144 and Directives 2014/90/EU, (EU) 2016/797 and (EU) 2020/1828 (Artificial Intelligence Act), O.J. L 2024/1689.

Noncompliance penalties range up to 35 million euros or 7 percent of global annual turnover for unacceptable risk, and up to 15 million euros or 3 percent for high-risk.

Designers also must be mindful of presenting consumers with information about their privacy rights without overwhelming them while also appropriately handling business obligations, especially for small and medium-sized businesses that lack dedicated legal resources. Similarly, they must be mindful of navigating the interplay between different privacy laws, which can be confusing and resource intensive. While laws are often written to be technologically neutral, the emergence of unforeseen technologies can lead to confusion on how to apply these laws across jurisdictions.

4.11 WHAT ARE THE HCI WORK AREAS THAT COULD HELP SUPPORT THE LEGAL SIDE, AND VICE VERSA?

Since much technology spans state or national borders, HCI professionals need to be familiar with principles that follow jurisdictional requirements, such as enabling a user to access, correct, or delete data, pursuant to the principles of "privacy by design" and "privacy by default," which are legal requirements in some jurisdictions, like under the GDPR, Article 25:[153]

> Taking into account the state of the art, the cost of implementation and the nature, scope, context and purposes of processing as well as the risks of varying likelihood and severity for rights and freedoms of natural persons posed by the processing, the controller shall, both at the time of the determination of the means for processing and at the time of the processing itself, implement appropriate technical and organisational measures, such as pseudonymisation, which are designed to implement data-protection principles, such as data minimisation, in an effective way and to integrate the necessary safeguards into the processing in order to meet the requirements of this Regulation and protect the rights of data subjects.

Similarly, HCI professionals can consider how to disclose and enforce more understandable and accessible privacy or informed consent that is consistent with legal requirements across different states and countries. Similarly, HCI professionals should ensure that privacy settings and controls are not only user-friendly and effective but also comply with legal requirements. This involves designing systems and services in a way that minimizes data collection and maximizes data protection. Finally, they could also consider contributing to developing educational tools and materials that help users understand their privacy rights and how to protect their personal data, in compliance with legal requirements for transparency and accountability. HCI professionals can also use legal mandates for inclusivity and nondiscrimination to guide privacy practices and tools that are accessible to all users, including those with disabilities.

---

[153] General Data Protection Regulation, Article 25, 2016 O.J. (L 119) 1.

HCI research can inform legal debates on privacy, especially in understanding how people interact with technology and perceive privacy, and set up design constraints in HCI, shaping the development of technologies in a way that respects and upholds privacy rights. HCI professionals can contribute to the development of privacy policies by providing insights into user behavior and technology design. They can also advocate for user-centered privacy laws. Finally, HCI professionals can strive to collaborate with legal experts to develop technologies and systems that are both user-friendly and legally compliant.

5

Human Subjects Research Regulation

5.1 INTRODUCTION

Law and ethics are two very different concepts that at times overlap. Law consists of rules that are enforced by an authority, whereas ethics are a set of moral principles that may or may not be enforced. When speaking of *research ethics*, we typically mean standards of conduct for researchers, and these may or may not be enforced by regulatory authorities. However, in the United States, some research conducted with or on people ("human subjects") is legally regulated by a law known as "The Common Rule."[1] Given the importance of *humans* in HCI, the law that governs research involving them is also highly relevant to the field.

This chapter provides (1) an overview of human subjects research in HCI; (2) a brief history of legal regulation for human subjects research in the United States; (3) an overview of applicable laws and how these are operationalized for academic research via university Institutional Review Boards (IRBs); (4) challenges for HCI research specifically under this regulatory regime; and (5) regulatory mechanisms for research beyond formal law, including professional responsibility and social norms. Though this chapter focuses on law, there will be coverage of many familiar topics in research ethics.

5.2 WHAT IS HUMAN SUBJECTS RESEARCH IN HCI?

HCI as a field has strong roots in psychology, and unlike many other subfields of computer science, it heavily involves people in the scientific research process.[2] As the book *Ways of Knowing in HCI* describes: "We study not only the design of the interface but also the setting in which computing is embedded, the needs of people in various contexts, and the activities they engage in while using various forms of

---

[1] 45 CFR §46.
[2] Olson, J. S. & Kellogg, W. A. (Eds.). (2014). *Ways of Knowing in HCI* (Vol. 2). New York: Springer; Lazar, J., Feng, J. H., & Hochheiser, H. (2017). *Research Methods in Human-Computer Interaction*. Morgan Kaufmann.

computing."³ Studying the needs and activities of people necessitates direct interaction with people and/or the data that people create, which is not true for all types of computer science research. Common data collection methods employed in the field of HCI include ethnography, interviews, surveys, experiments, and research through design, all methods that involve direct interaction with humans.

It is important to keep in mind that "ethics" in terms of the standards or norms that we should have for research practices (e.g., endeavoring to not do harm to either individuals or society) goes far beyond what is *legal*. Within HCI, research ethics is an important and complicated topic that has gained increasing attention in recent years, in part because of the expansion of our field into new methods that might go beyond the scope of traditional human subjects research (e.g., data science).⁴ One challenge is that research practices outside of the domain of human subjects are for the most part not directly regulated – even those that might have significant implications or have the potential for doing harm, such as the creation and deployment of artificial intelligence using data created by humans. For example, predictive machine learning research has prompted widespread discussion of research ethics, including issues of consent, privacy, and limitations of regulatory review.⁵ As explained in more detail in Section 5.3.1, the legal definition of human subjects research involves direct interaction or intervention with a human or collection of identifiable, private information.⁶ A great deal of HCI research, even when involving data that comes from humans, falls outside this scope.

In addition to some applications of data science or machine learning, there are other examples of computing-related research that may involve humans without falling easily into this legal definition. For example, in 2022 researchers installed sensors into student lab space without their knowledge or consent, stating that they were tracking "heat" rather than humans.⁷ Similarly, in 2021 a group of researchers sent thousands of automated deceptive emails to websites asking for information about their privacy practices, resulting in labor and worry from many people running those websites; following backlash, the researchers stated that their university IRB

---

[3] Olson, J. S. & Kellogg, W. A. (Eds.). (2014). *Ways of Knowing in HCI* (Vol. 2). New York: Springer, p. ix.

[4] Froomkin, A. M. (2019). Big Data: Destroyer of Informed Consent. *Yale Journal of Law and Technology*, 21, pp. 27–54; Metcalf, J. & Crawford, K. (2016). Where Are Human Subjects in Big Data Research? The Emerging Ethics Divide. *Big Data & Society*, 3(1), 2053951716650211.

[5] Metcalf, J. (November 30, 2017). The Study Has Been Approved by the IRB: Gayface AI, Research Hype and the Pervasive Data Ethics Gap. *Medium*. Available at: https://medium.com/pervade-team/the-study-has-been-approved-by-the-irb-gayface-ai-research-hype-and-the-pervasive-data-ethics-ed76171b882c; Froomkin, A. M. (2019). Big Data: Destroyer of Informed Consent. *Yale Journal of Law and Technology*, 21, pp. 27–54.

[6] 45 CFR §46.

[7] Ongweso, E. (December 2, 2022). NO: Grad students analyze, hack, and remove under-desk surveillance devices designed to track them. *Vice*. Available at: www.vice.com/en/article/m7gwy3/no-grad-students-analyze-hack-and-remove-under-desk-surveillance-devices-designed-to-track-them.

determined that the project was not human subjects research because the focus of the study was on understanding website practices rather than humans.[8] Therefore, it is important to remember that though research ethics is a much broader topic, in terms of *legal* regulation, this chapter focuses on this specific subset of human subjects research within HCI.

As Amy Bruckman articulated in an overview of research ethics in *Ways of Knowing in HCI*: "What is codified in institutional policies and procedures is typically a higher standard than merely legal, and what is ethical is a higher standard than what is allowed by policy or law. Laws shift at political boundaries, policies shift at institutional boundaries, and ethics shift at cultural boundaries."[9] She also laid out three primary risks associated with HCI research: (1) the risk of harming their subjects; (2) the risk of disturbing the environments being studied; and (3) the risk of serious consequences for their institution if ethical violations occur.[10] As we will see from the history of human subjects research guidelines, the regulatory regime in the United States as well as other countries was largely inspired by cases of individual harm to research subjects, particularly medical and psychological experiments that resulted in extreme physical and/or psychological harm.

However, though downstream effects such as widespread societal harm are not part of U.S. research regulations,[11] Bruckman's second risk of disturbing environments is an important one to consider from an ethical perspective. She gave the example of disturbing online communities through research solicitation,[12] though a more societal-level example of this risk might be the potential damage that unethical research can do to public trust in science. As Metcalf and Crawford noted in their discussion of research ethics for data science, regulatory gaps can undermine public trust, and it is therefore critical that researchers model practices and norms that can build and sustain that trust.[13] Within HCI, the 2014 Facebook emotional contagion study, in which academic researchers partnered with Facebook researchers to experimentally test whether exposure to emotional content influences a user's subsequent content, resulted in expansive media attention that had a significant effect on public trust for both the platform and for social media research.[14] Regardless of whether there was a violation of the Common Rule in the Facebook study (which is a complex analysis that spawned several

---

[8] Princeton-Radboud Study on Privacy Law Implementation. https://web.archive.org/web/20250620104202/https://privacystudy.cs.princeton.edu/.
[9] Bruckman, A. (2014). Research Ethics and HCI. *Ways of Knowing in HCI*, pp. 449–468.
[10] Ibid.
[11] See Section 5.4.3 for a discussion of the limitations of the Common Rule and IRBs.
[12] Bruckman, A. (2014). Research Ethics and HCI. *Ways of Knowing in HCI*, pp. 449–468.
[13] Metcalf, J., & Crawford, K. (2016). Where Are Human Subjects in Big Data Research? The Emerging Ethics Divide. *Big Data & Society*, 3(1), 2053951716650211.
[14] Hallinan, B., Brubaker, J. R., & Fiesler, C. (2020). Unexpected Expectations: Public Reaction to the Facebook Emotional Contagion Study. *New Media & Society*, 22(6), pp. 1076–1094.

law review articles),[15] the research had negative consequences not necessarily in the form of individual harm but to a platform and public trust. However, currently these types of consequences are by and large not relevant to legal analyses, only ethical ones.

The third risk that Bruckman raised is that of consequences to the researcher's institution.[16] These may be reputational (e.g., the bad press that both Facebook and the university involved received in the wake of the emotional contagion study), or even more concrete – for example, when a university was banned from the Linux kernel due to an experiment perceived to be unethical.[17] It is also worth noting that this sort of institutional harm might also extend to HCI as a field when research is conducted poorly. Finally, there may also be legal consequences, as discussed in Section 5.3.2 regarding violations of the Common Rule, as well as possible tort claims for injuries.

Though our hope is that HCI researchers are thinking about research ethics beyond personal consequences, these institutional and regulatory consequences are important to understand as well. However, the legal regulations themselves have their roots in negative consequences to research subjects – particularly the long history of ethical controversies and subsequent guidelines for human experimentation.

5.3 BACKGROUND AND SOURCES OF LEGAL RULES

Though some countries had guidelines for human experimentation prior to World War II (e.g., the 1931 Reichsgesundheitsamt Guidelines for Human Experimentation in Germany, which of course were not well applied or enforced during the war),[18] the first major set of guidelines created in the U.S. was the Nuremberg Code. The Nuremberg War Trials uncovered atrocities of Nazi human experimentation in World War II, and the Code was drafted as part of a military tribunal.[19] It includes principles such as informed consent, absence of coercion, properly formulated scientific experimentation, and beneficence toward human participants.[20] It also

---

[15] Grimmelmann, J. (2015). The Law and Ethics of Experiments on Social Media Users. *Colorado Technology Law Journal*, 13, pp. 219–271; Meyer, M. N. (2015). Two Cheers for Corporate Experimentation: The A/B Illusion and the Virtues of Data-Driven Innovation. *Colorado Technology Law Journal*, 13, pp. 273–331; Bambauer, J. R. (2015). All Life Is an Experiment: (Sometimes It Is a Controlled Experiment). *Loyola University Chicago Law Journal*, 47, pp. 487–513.
[16] Bruckman, A. (2014). Research Ethics and HCI. *Ways of Knowing in HCI*, pp. 449–468.
[17] Monica Chin. (2021, April 30). How a university got itself banned from the Linux kernel. *The Verge*. Available at: www.theverge.com/ 2021/4/30/22410164/linux-kernel-university-of-minnesota-banned-open-source. (Also see Section 5.4.2 for a discussion of this example.)
[18] Sass, H. M. (1983). Reichsrundschreiben 1931: Pre-Nuremberg German Regulations Concerning New Therapy and Human Experimentation. *The Journal of Medicine and Philosophy*, 8(2), pp. 99–112.
[19] Weindling, P. (2001). The Origins of Informed Consent: The International Scientific Commission on Medical War Crimes, and the Nuremberg Code. *Bulletin of the History of Medicine*, 75(1), pp. 37–71.
[20] Ibid.

specifies that experimentation must yield results for the benefit of society and that unnecessary risk should be avoided.

A large reason that the Nuremberg Trials, held in a court tasked with prosecuting war crimes, also resulted in a set of ethical and moral principles governing clinical research was that it was critical at the time to differentiate between war atrocities and legitimate scientific research. Some of these basic principles had already been outlined before the trial began – for example, U.S. physiologist Andrew Conway Ivy recommended what would become the principle of informed consent without coercion.[21] His report to the court described the principle thus: "Consent of the human subject must be obtained. All subjects have been volunteers in the absence of coercion in any form. Before volunteering, subjects have been informed of the hazards, if any."[22] The Nuremberg Code itself further provided that voluntary consent must have legal capacity, free will, and sufficient comprehension.[23]

In addition to informed consent, the Code also established guidelines for proper experimentation, including that experiments should be designed with sufficient knowledge of the underlying problem and only by scientifically qualified persons. It also established the importance of beneficence – having the welfare of the participant as the goal – by emphasizing the minimization of harm and the duty of the scientist to terminate an experiment if harm will occur. Also related to beneficence, the weighing of risk versus benefit also appears in the Code: "The degree of risk to be taken should never exceed that determined by the humanitarian importance of the problem to be solved by the experiment."[24]

However, despite the existence of these guidelines, ethical problems in human research continued in the U.S. well past World War II. One well-known, horrific example is the Tuskegee syphilis experiments, in which 400 African-American men with syphilis were monitored for 40 years (1932–1972) without being told of their disease, continuing for decades after the discovery in 1947 that penicillin cures the disease.[25] In fact, many examples of research-related harm in the U.S. in the twentieth century impacted the Black community, which has resulted in lingering mistrust steeped in a long history of medical and institutional racism.[26]

However, not all unethical experiments during this time were medical in nature or involved physical harm. Closer to the type of research conducted in HCI, a number of famous psychology experiments illustrated the ability for such experimentation

---

[21] Ibid.
[22] Shuster, E. (1997). Fifty Years Later: The Significance of the Nuremberg Code. *New England Journal of Medicine*, 337(20), pp. 1436–1440.
[23] Weindling, P. (2001). The Origins of Informed Consent: The International Scientific Commission on Medical War Crimes, and the Nuremberg Code. *Bulletin of the History of Medicine*, 75(1), pp. 37–71.
[24] Van Ness, P. H. (2001). The Concept of Risk in Biomedical Research Involving Human Subjects. *Bioethics*, 15(4), pp. 364–370.
[25] Bruckman, A. (2014). Research Ethics and HCI. *Ways of Knowing in HCI*, pp. 449–468.
[26] Klassen, S., & Fiesler, C. (2022). This Isn't Your Data, Friend: Black Twitter as a Case Study on Research Ethics for Public Data. *Social Media+ Society*, 8(4), 20563051221144317.

to result in significant emotional distress for human subjects.[27] For example, in Stanley Milgram's obedience experiment, participants were led to believe that they were actively causing harm to other human beings. These participants experienced extreme psychological distress, raising questions about whether it is possible to conduct this kind of research ethically. The Stanford prison experiment of 1971, in which participants role-played guards and prisoners, similarly caused such extreme reactions from participants that the study was terminated early.[28] Moreover, this research was conducted under Stanford's ethical guidance and review at the time, including informed consent.

Prompted by cases such as these, particularly the atrocity of the Tuskegee study, in 1974 the National Research Act was signed into law, creating the National Commission for the Protection of Human Subjects of Biomedical and Behavioral Research in the United States.[29] One of the charges to the Commission was to identify the basic ethical principles that should underlie the conduct of biomedical and behavioral research involving human subjects and to develop guidelines, which should be followed to assure that such research is conducted in accordance with those principles. In 1978 the commission released the Belmont Report ("*Ethical Principles and Guidelines for the Protection of Human Subjects of Research*") which created the basis for human subjects research regulation in the United States.[30] The report lays out three main principles:

(1) Respect for persons: Treat people as ends in themselves, not means to an end;
(2) Beneficence: Do not harm, and maximize possible benefits and minimize possible harms; and
(3) Justice: Distribute the burdens and benefits of research equally across society.

These three pillars have also been adopted as part of research ethics regulation in other countries; for example, the Canadian Tri-Council Policy Statement on research ethics defines respect for persons, concern for welfare, and justice as their core principles.[31] The National Research Act also created the foundation for further research ethics regulation in the United States,[32] and next we lay out how these regulations evolved and are operationalized.

---

[27] Lazar, J., Feng, J. H., & Hochheiser, H. (2010). Working with Human Subjects. *Research Methods in Human-Computer Interaction (Second Edition)*, pp. 455–491.
[28] Ibid.
[29] Hohmann, A. R. (2024). History of Bioethics: Crimes against Humanity in Human-Subject Research. *Journal of Contemporary Pharmacy Practice*, 71(2), pp. 41–42.
[30] National Commission for the Protection of Human Subjects of Biomedical, & Behavioral Research. (1978). *The Belmont report: Ethical principles and guidelines for the protection of human subjects of research* (Vol. 2). Department of Health, Education, and Welfare, National Commission for the Protection of Human Subjects of Biomedical and Behavioral Research.
[31] Government of Canada Panel on Research Ethics. Tri-Council Policy Statement 2 (2018). Available at: https://ethics.gc.ca/eng/policy-politique_tcps2-eptc2_2018.html.
[32] National Research Act. Pub. L. No. 93–348, 88 Stat. 342 (1974).

5.3.1 The Common Rule and Institutional Review Boards

Originally the National Research Act applied only to medical research, but in 1991, a number of U.S. federal departments and agencies also adopted a uniform set of rules for the protection of human subjects, identical to similar Health and Human Services (HHS) regulations. This uniform set of regulations is the Federal Policy for the Protection of Human Subjects,[33] informally known as the "Common Rule." The Office of Human Research Protections (OHRP) was later established within HHS.

The Common Rule as the major source of regulation for human subjects research in the U.S. has a narrower purview than many people realize. It only applies to research conducted or funded by the federal government, and it only applies to narrowly defined "human subjects" research, which may exclude even some types of interactions or interventions with humans. According to §46.101: "[T]his policy applies to all research involving human subjects conducted, supported, or otherwise subject to regulation by any federal department or agency that takes appropriate administrative action to make the policy applicable to such research ... and institutional review boards (IRBs) reviewing research that is subject to this policy must comply with this policy."[34]

Definitions provided in 45 CFR §46.102 (quoted here verbatim) further clarify the meaning of this rule:[35]

- *Research* means a systematic investigation, including research development, testing, and evaluation, designed to develop or contribute to generalizable knowledge.
- *Human subject* means a living individual about whom an investigator (whether professional or student) conducting research: (1) obtains information or biospecimens through intervention or interaction with the individual and uses, studies, or analyzes the information or biospecimens; or (2) obtains, uses, studies, analyzes, or generates identifiable private information or identifiable biospecimens.
- *Private information* includes information about behavior that occurs in a context in which an individual can reasonably expect that no observation or recording is taking place and information that has been provided for specific purposes by an individual and that the individual can reasonably expect will not be made public (e.g., a medical record).
- *Identifiable private information* is private information for which the identity of the subject is or may readily be ascertained by the investigator or associated with the information.

---

[33] 45 CFR §46.
[34] 45 CFR §46.101.
[35] 45 CFR §46.102.

The Common Rule also lays out rules and responsibilities for institutional review, empowering institutional review boards (IRBs) to approve, require modifications to, or disapprove research. 45 CFR §46.111 describes basic criteria for IRB approval, which include four major components: (1) minimizing risks and weighing risks against benefits (beneficence); (2) ensuring equitable selection of research subjects (justice); (3) adequate informed consent (respect for persons); and (4) maintaining confidentiality of data. In their study of IRB perspectives toward sensing technologies, Nebeker et al. also mapped concerns over data protection to the concept of beneficence, in the sense that privacy is a type of risk management and also integral to the welfare of participants.[36] IRBs typically call for data management plans that include plans for storage and access, particularly while data includes identifiable information. However, the Common Rule does not include details about what such plans should entail, but rather specifies that when appropriate, the research plan must include "adequate provision" for protecting subject privacy and the confidentiality of their data.[37]

The Common Rule also does not provide guidance for *how* IRBs might evaluate risk, only that they are tasked with determining whether "risks to subjects are reasonable in relation to anticipated benefits."[38] However, as Huh-Yoo and Rader point out in their study of how IRBs evaluate risk for digital data, "risk" implies both harm that results from research and the likelihood that that harm will occur.[39] The Belmont Report lays out categories of harm – "psychological harm, physical harm, legal harm, social harm and economic harm, loss of autonomy, and any forms of injustice perpetuated through the research as forms of harm" – but not how to determine how likely those harms might be.[40] However, a critical component of IRB review is the determination of whether a protocol is *exempt* from further review due to being "minimal risk," defined as when "the probability and magnitude of harm or discomfort anticipated in the research are not greater in and of themselves than those ordinarily encountered in daily life or during the performance of routine physical or psychological examinations or tests."[41] Highly relevant to how we think about the role of IRBs in HCI research, Huh-Yoo and Rader found that IRB

---

[36] Nebeker, C., Harlow, J., Espinoza Giacinto, R., Orozco-Linares, R., Bloss, C. S., & Weibel, N. (2017). Ethical and Regulatory Challenges of Research Using Pervasive Sensing and Other Emerging Technologies: IRB Perspectives. *AJOB Empirical Bioethics*, 8(4), pp. 266–276.
[37] 45 CFR §46.111.
[38] Ibid.
[39] Huh-Yoo, J. & Rader, E. (2020). It's the Wild, Wild West: Lessons Learned from IRB Members' Risk Perceptions Toward Digital Research Data. *Proceedings of the ACM on Human-Computer Interaction*, 4(CSCW1), pp. 1–22.
[40] National Commission for the Protection of Human Subjects of Biomedical, & Behavioral Research. (1978). *The Belmont Report: Ethical Principles and Guidelines for the Protection of Human Subjects of Research* (Vol. 2). Department of Health, Education, and Welfare, National Commission for the Protection of Human Subjects of Biomedical and Behavioral Research.
[41] §45 CFR 46.102(j).

members perceived data or research "being digital" increased their perception of risk while also acknowledging that it was difficult to pinpoint harms, making this type of research more challenging to evaluate.[42] Their findings follow previous work that has pointed to the challenges that IRBs can have in dealing with computing research, particularly as it relates to emerging technology and research practices.[43]

Additionally, local IRBs have a great deal of power in terms of internal guidelines around some aspects of research compliance, and several research studies over the past several decades have revealed inconsistency across IRBs.[44] It is also not surprising that an IRB would function very differently at a primarily undergraduate institution versus at a medical school. The role of IRBs has been widely debated over time and a few common critiques of IRBs have arisen, including around goals misalignment of researchers and IRBs, concerns about overreach, and inability to handle emerging research paradigms.[45] However, as it stands, local IRBs are the regulatory force behind enforcing the Common Rule.

The first major changes to the Common Rule did not appear until 2017, signed into law after a six-year period of comment and revision and intended to enhance protections while reducing administrative burden. The change that likely impacted much HCI research is that more categories of minimal risk research now fall more clearly into the category of "exempt" research. These include surveys, interviews, educational tests, public observations, and benign behavioral interventions. "Exempt" research must go through IRB review, but following a determination of this status, they do not require any continuing review submission unless there are any changes to procedures or risks to participants.[46]

Finally, it is worth noting that though typically Common Rule jurisdictions (and thus IRBs) are thought of as primarily associated with universities or hospitals, this requirement applies to *any* institution that receives federal funding. So, for example, an NGO that conducts research and has received a federal grant might have its own IRB, or it might use a private IRB. Private or "for-profit" IRBs provide the same

---

[42] Huh-Yoo, J. & Rader, E. (2020). It's the Wild, Wild West: Lessons Learned from IRB Members' Risk Perceptions Toward Digital Research Data. *Proceedings of the ACM on Human-Computer Interaction*, 4(CSCW1), pp. 1–22.

[43] Vitak, J., Proferes, N., Shilton, K., & Ashktorab, Z. (2017). Ethics Regulation in Social Computing Research: Examining the Role of Institutional Review Boards. *Journal of Empirical Research on Human Research Ethics*, 12(5), pp. 372–382.

[44] Ibid.; Lidz, C. W., Pivovarova, E., Appelbaum, P., Stiles, D. F., Murray, A., & Klitzman, R. L. (2018). Reliance Agreements and Single IRB Review of Multisite Research: Concerns of IRB Members and Staff. *AJOB Empirical Bioethics*, 9(3), pp. 164–172; Klitzman, R. (2011). The Myth of Community Differences as the Cause of Variations among IRBs. *AJOB Primary Research*, 2(2), pp. 24–33.

[45] Vitak, J., Proferes, N., Shilton, K., & Ashktorab, Z. (2017). Ethics Regulation in Social Computing Research: Examining the Role of Institutional Review Boards. *Journal of Empirical Research on Human Research Ethics*, 12(5), pp. 372–382.

[46] Walch-Patterson, A. (2020). Exemptions and Limited Institutional Review Board Review: A Practical Look at the 2018 Common Rule Requirements for Exempt Research. *Ochsner Journal*, 20(1), pp. 87–94.

services as any other IRB but without affiliation to a medical or academic institution. Private IRBs also provide services to individuals or institutions who are not required by law to follow the Common Rule but want to have safeguards in place to ensure that they are conducting research responsibly.

5.3.2 Remedies and Case Law

With respect to remedies, the Common Rule does not afford private rights of action (where individuals or organizations can file civil lawsuits) for human subjects who might suffer any form of research-related injury, even when it directly applies. In part due to this lack of a private right of action, there is limited case law related to the Common Rule, or research ethics more generally, and what does exist overwhelmingly involves medical research – perhaps because medical injuries are more likely to be severe enough to justify a lawsuit.

This lack of a right to private action also seems to be a somewhat commonly misunderstood issue, as 45 CFR § 46 appears as an add-on in a number of similar lawsuits, including for example, a 2022 pro se case against the CDC and Anthony Fauci for "conduct[ing] research on United States citizens without their consent."[47] As noted in a case in which a patient at a university medical center attempted to sue both the university and a pharmaceutical company with a number of claims, including violations of the Common Rule, this law "does not create a cause of action for a private party against private actors or a state organization."[48] In another case, a participant in an adoption court proceeding claimed that an employee of Youth and Family Services was collecting data for his thesis without consent; this claim was dismissed on these same grounds of a lack of right to private action, with the court noting that protections for human subjects in the Common Rule "were not phrased in terms of persons benefitted" but rather "designed to control aggregate behavior of research facilities, and enforcement sections of the regulations provided for regulatory action."[49] In other words, though the Common Rule benefits human subjects in the abstract, it was not designed to do so directly.

It is worth noting, however, that despite the lack of direct remedy for potential violations of the Common Rule, research ethics standards and guidelines may be referenced by courts in considering other causes of action. For example, when a participant in a medical experiment sued in part for negligence in conjunction with alleged injuries, the court referred to the Nuremberg Code in analyzing appropriate standards of informed consent.[50]

---

[47] Reinoehl v. Ctrs. for Disease Control & Prevention, No. 22–1401 (7th Cir. October 25, 2022).
[48] Touma v. Gen. Counsel of the Regents, Case No. SA CV 17–01132-VBF-KS (C.D. Cal. July 6, 2018).
[49] McClure v. Youth and Family Services of Solano County, No. C 14–5629 MMC (N.D. Cal. April 24, 2015).
[50] Whitlock v. Duke University, 637 F. Supp. 1463 (M.D.N.C. 1986).

Additionally, although research participants may not have standing to sue based on the Common Rule, there are forms of research-related compensation that depend on where the study is conducted, what entities are sponsoring the study, and whether and by whom the participant is insured.[51] Though the Common Rule does not require research institutions or pharmaceutical sponsors to provide medical care or compensation for injured research subjects, it does specify that consent forms should include "an explanation as to whether any compensation and an explanation as to whether any medical treatments are available if injury occurs, and if so, what they consist of, or where further information may be obtained."[52] Institutions handle this differently, but many have voluntary systems set up for this; for example, the University of Washington (UW) established a system for human subjects who experience a "medical problem that is more likely than not caused by UW-conducted research," where they could receive medical care up to $250,000 funded directly by the UW health care system.[53]

Beyond these systems that may be in place, research participants' other option is to rely on tort law – suing for the actual injury (e.g., infliction of emotional distress) rather than for research ethics violations. Due to both the lack of standardization of voluntary systems and the lack of equal access to legal assistance or health insurance, some legal scholars have argued for a formal system for research injury compensation in the U.S.[54] Such a system might also, appropriately, cover institutions that fall outside of research ethics regulations, such as industry and private researchers. Currently, if a research participant were harmed due to a study conducted at a corporation (e.g., Google or Meta), they would similarly likely have to rely on tort law to sue for the actual injury, unless covered under state law (discussed in Section 5.3.3).

However, with respect to institutions that do fall under the jurisdiction of the Common Rule, enforcement of compliance rests with the federal Office of Human Research Protections, which has a statutory responsibility for "taking appropriate action" regarding allegations of noncompliance.[55] A finding of noncompliance might trigger a corrective action plan (e.g., additional training for IRB staff or researchers), restrictions on or suspension of the institution's Federal Wide Assurance (FWA) that constitutes the institution's promise to abide by the Common Rule (which might result in requirements for OHRP approval for research), suspension or restrictions

---

[51] Chapman, C. R., Sukumaran, S., Tsegaye, G. T., Shevchenko, Y., & Caplan, A. L. (2019). The Quest for Compensation for Research-Related Injury in the United States: A New Proposal. *The Journal of Law, Medicine & Ethics*, 47(4), pp. 732–747.

[52] 49 CFR §11.116.

[53] Chapman, C. R., Sukumaran, S., Tsegaye, G. T., Shevchenko, Y., & Caplan, A. L. (2019). The Quest for Compensation for Research-Related Injury in the United States: A New Proposal. *The Journal of Law, Medicine & Ethics*, 47(4), pp. 732–747.

[54] Ibid.

[55] Meyer, M. N. (2020). There Oughta Be a Law: When Does (n't) the US Common Rule Apply? *Journal of Law, Medicine & Ethics*, 48(S1), pp. 60–73.

of individual investigators from conducting research, or, in the most severe scenario, a government-wide debarment where an institution or individual is debarred from receiving any federal research funds.[56]

Such consequences, particularly debarment, appear to be rare but not unheard of. For example, in 2018 a University of Pittsburgh professor agreed to pay the government $132,000 and be excluded from applying for or participating in any federal grants for one year, following revelations that over the course of a decade he created false IRB approvals in connection with proposals for National Science Foundation funding.[57]

It is also worth noting that despite the limited direct application of these regulations, there are some ways in which the Common Rule is applied indirectly. For example, academic institutions commonly require adherence to the Common Rule as part of employment contracts, making this adherence then a matter of employment law.[58] In other words, if a contract lays out a duty to abide by these guidelines, and the employee does not do so, this might be grounds for terminating their employment. For example, a National Institutes of Health (NIH) researcher was terminated from his position after an audit revealed that the vast majority of his human subjects records were incomplete; he sued for wrongful termination, and the court affirmed that the research ethics violations constituted cause.[59]

An application of the Common Rule might also be more roundabout. For example, in one case where a graduate student sued his university for dismissing him from his academic program without due process, the student claimed that he was unable to make progress on his research due to the university IRB failing to review his protocol.[60] The question came to the court as to whether his research constituted human subjects research; they determined that it did, but also that the IRB was not involved in the student's dismissal, and the case was dismissed.[61] In another wrongful termination case, the court had to determine whether the Common Rule justified a claim that the plaintiff acted in the interest of public policy when blowing the whistle on alleged data mishandling.[62] The court ultimately dismissed the plaintiff's claims, ruling that the actions taken by her employer did not violate any specific public policy protections related to the Common Rule.[63]

---

[56] Ibid.
[57] United States District Attorney's Office, Western District of Pennsylvania. (2018, March 21). University of Pittsburgh Professor Pays $132,000 and Agrees to Exclusion to Resolve Allegations of False Claims for Federal Research Grants. Available at: www.justice.gov/usao-wdpa/pr/university-pittsburgh-professor-pays-132000-and-agrees-exclusion-resolve-allegations.
[58] Meyer, M. N. (2020). There Oughta Be a Law: When Does (n't) the US Common Rule Apply? *Journal of Law, Medicine & Ethics*, 48(S1), pp. 60–73.
[59] Braun v. Department of Health and Human Services, No. 19-1949 (Fed. Cir. 2020).
[60] Missert v. Trustees of Boston Univ., 73 F. Supp. 2d 68 (D. Mass. 1999).
[61] Ibid.
[62] Hidalgo-Semlek v. Hansa Med., Inc., 498 F. Supp. 3d 236 (D.N.H. 2020).
[63] Ibid.

5.3.3 *State Law*

Though the basic protections that U.S. federal regulations offer cannot be diminished by state law (due to the supremacy clause of the U.S. Constitution), states may choose to have additional protections beyond federal law. The Common Rule explicitly states that it does not impact any state or local laws or regulations that may be otherwise applicable or provide additional protections for informed consent,[64] with further specification that such local regulations may require additional information to be disclosed in order for informed consent to be legally effective.[65] However, state-specific regulation of general human subjects research is rare, likely due to the inefficiency and increased compliance costs that arise from rules that differ from state to state given the prevalence of multisite research collaborations.[66]

However, as of 2020, at least three states (Maryland, Virginia, and New York) have laws that impose some or all of the Common Rule on *all* human subjects research conducted in their jurisdiction, regardless of the funding source.[67] For example, the Maryland law enacted in 2002 requires "a person conducting human subject research to comply with federal regulations on the protection of human subjects" regardless of whether that research is federally funded or who is conducting the research.[68] Virginia's law, enacted in 1979, requires that "every person engaged in the conduct of human research" must be affiliated with "an institution or agency having a research review committee."[69]

New York's relevant law defines human subjects research as:

> Any medical experiments, research, or scientific or psychological investigation, which utilizes human subjects and which involves physical or psychological intervention by the researcher upon the body of the subject and which is not required for the purposes of obtaining information for the diagnosis, prevention, or treatment of disease or the assessment of medical condition for the direct benefit of the subject.[70]

It is worth noting that even laws specific to medical research might still apply to HCI research, especially in industry – for example, if Apple were conducting an experiment about the health applications of the Apple watch in New York State's jurisdiction.

---

[64] 45 CFR § 46.101(f).
[65] 45 CFR § 46.116(e).
[66] Schwartz, J. (2001). Oversight of Human Subject Research: The Role of the States. *National Bioethics Advisory Commission.*
[67] Tovino, S. A. (2020). Mobile Research Applications and State Research Laws. *The Journal of Law, Medicine & Ethics,* 48(1_suppl), pp. 82–86.
[68] Maryland Attorney General. Maryland Law on Human Subjects Research. Available at www.marylandattorneygeneral.gov/Pages/HealthPolicy/humansubject.aspx; Md. Code Ann., Health-Gen. § 13–2002(b).
[69] Virginia Acts 1979, ch. 38, § 37.1–234.
[70] N.Y. CLS Public Health § 2441 (2014).

These state laws also have some specific penalties and remedies associated with them. In New York, the liability for violating public health laws is generally a fine.[71] A violation of Virginia health law is a Class 1 misdemeanor.[72] In Maryland, the Attorney General can seek injunctive and other relief to prevent human subjects research from being conducted in violation of the Common Rule.[73]

Other states, including New Jersey (pertaining to a bill of rights for patients),[74] Oklahoma (covering research related to stem cells),[75] California (via the Protection of Human Subjects in Medical Experimentation Act),[76] Illinois (prohibiting experimentation on patients without consent),[77] and Wisconsin (governing experimentation on patients),[78] have state-specific research laws that pertain explicitly to medical research, which may apply to health-related HCI human subjects research.

Other laws are even more specific, such as Massachusetts', which is part of the Controlled Substances Act, so it only pertains to research studies regarding drugs.[79] New Hampshire's state law establishes an institutional review board that oversees state-funded research related to mental health or substance abuse.[80] With respect to licensing, in Florida psychologists will receive disciplinary action for experimenting on human subjects without informed consent.[81] Louisiana also explicitly criminalizes human experimentation on "any infant who is born alive" except to protect or preserve life, with a potential penalty of imprisonment for five to twenty years.[82]

These laws do not cover every state in the U.S., and many of the laws enumerated here are even narrower in scope than the Common Rule. As a result, when research is conducted without federal funds, in a jurisdiction with no statutory provision related to human subjects research, legal oversight may be practically nonexistent.

Finally, it is also important to note that the Common Rule's statement that it does not preempt local regulations also applies to "tribal laws passed by the official governing body of an American Indian or Alaska Native tribe."[83] Indeed, a number of tribes in the U.S. have established their own processes for oversight of research activities that take place on their lands and/or with their citizens,

---

[71] N.Y. CLS Public Health § 12-b (2014).
[72] Va. Code Ann. § 32.1–27.
[73] Md. Code Ann., Health-Gen. § 13–2004a.
[74] NJ Stat. 26:2H-12.8.
[75] OK Sat. 63 § 1–270.2.
[76] CA Health & Safety Code §§ 24170–24179.5.
[77] 410 ILCS 50/3.1.
[78] Wis. Stat. § 51.61(1)(j).
[79] Mass. General Laws c. 94C § 8.
[80] N.H. Rev. Stat. § 171-A:19-a.
[81] FL Stat. § 490.009.
[82] LA Rev Stat § 14:87.2 (2022).
[83] 45 CFR § 46.101(f).

including tribal IRBs.[84] Building upon discussion of research harm in the start of Section 5.3, indigenous communities in the U.S. have good reason to mistrust researchers, given a long history of abuse and unethical practices.[85] In addition to additional requirements and context around informed consent, tribal IRBs may also have requirements around data management and data sovereignty.[86]

5.3.4 International Sources of Regulation

Though this chapter focuses on U.S. law, it is also important to remember that international standards for human subjects research regulation differ and, indeed, are missing entirely in many parts of the world. Given the global scope of the field of HCI, this lack of standardization sometimes creates challenges in contexts such as research collaborations and paper reviewing.

As previously noted with respect to the historical roots of human subjects regulation, though there were a small number of countries with national policies, the Nuremberg Code in the United States following World War II created the first broadly accepted set of research ethics principles. These principles also subsequently influenced the World Medical Association (WMA)'s 1964 Declaration of Helsinki, which expanded statements of medical ethics such as the Hippocratic Oath to include the duties of physician-researchers. Internationally, it is considered a critical cornerstone for human subjects research in medical contexts, and though not a legally binding instrument itself, it draws legal authority through substantial influence on national and regional legislation.[87]

The international influence of documents of general principles such as Helsinki, the Nuremberg Code, and the Belmont Report has therefore created some amount of consistency in human subjects regulations globally with the necessity of legally binding international treaties. However, international human rights law also speaks to the protection of human research subjects. For example, the Universal Declaration of Human Rights (UDHR), adopted in 1948, laid the groundwork for the 1966 multilateral treaty the International Covenant on

---

[84] Him, D. A., Aguilar, T. A., Frederick, A., Larsen, H., Seiber, M., & Angal, J. (2019). Tribal IRBs: A Framework for Understanding Research Oversight in American Indian and Alaska Native Communities. *American Indian and Alaska Native Mental Health Research*, 26(2), pp. 71–95.

[85] Marley, T. L. (2019). Indigenous Data Sovereignty: University Institutional Review Board Policies and Guidelines and Research with American Indian and Alaska Native Communities. *American Behavioral Scientist*, 63(6), pp. 722–742.

[86] Ibid.; Kuhn, N. S., Parker, M., & Lefthand-Begay, C. (2020). Indigenous Research Ethics Requirements: An Examination of Six Tribal Institutional Review Board Applications and Processes in the United States. *Journal of Empirical Research on Human Research Ethics*, 15(4), pp. 279–291.

[87] Dhai, A. (2014). The Research Ethics Evolution: From Nuremberg to Helsinki. *SAMJ: South African Medical Journal*, 104(3), 178–180; Sprumont, D., Girardin, S., & Lemmens, T. (2007). The Helsinki Declaration and the Law: An International and Comparative Analysis. *History and Theory of Human Experimentation–The Declaration of Helsinki and Modern Medical Ethics*, pp. 223–252.

Civil and Political Rights (ICCPR), which as of June 2024 had 174 ratified country signatories.[88] Also influenced strongly by the atrocities of Nazi concentration camps, ICCPR provides that "no one shall be subjected without his free consent to medical or scientific experimentation."[89] The requirements of this treaty are then implemented within each country, but human rights law is one means of promoting state accountability for adopting positive measures that ensure the protection of research participants.[90]

In part because the Declaration of Helsinki has such a strong influence globally, and it established that "[t]he research protocol must be submitted for consideration, comment, guidance and approval to the concerned research ethics committee before the study begins," ethics review mechanisms are widely accepted as the norm in many countries.[91] In most countries it is legally associated with clinical drug trials, but a number of countries beyond the United States also have more comprehensive research ethics regulations similar to the Common Rule.

For example, perhaps most like the U.S., the most significant human subjects research regulations in Canada apply specifically to the context of federally funded research. Established in 1996, the Tri-Council Policy Statement: Ethical Conduct for Research Involving Humans (TCPS) covers all federally funded research as well as, through memoranda of understanding, research taking place at federally funded institutions. In Canada, Research Ethics Boards (REBs) function similarly to U.S. IRBs, and HCI research faces challenges similar to those we will discuss in the U.S. context in the Section 5.4.[92]

Other countries have also enacted statutes that regulate an extensive range of human subjects research, but still often focus (as does the Declaration of Helsinki) on medical research. For example, in Norway, the Act on Medical and Health Research applies to "medical and health research on human beings, human biological material or personal health data."[93] However, in Taiwan, the Human Subjects Research Act regulates research that involves "investigating, analyzing, or using human specimens or an individual person's biological behavior, physiological,

---

[88] U.N. Treaty Collection. International Covenant on Civil and Political Rights. Retrieved July 20, 2024 from https://treaties.un.org/Pages/ViewDetails.aspx?src=TREATY&mtdsg_no=IV-4&chapter=4&clang=_en.
[89] International Covenant on Civil and Political Rights (ICCPR), G.A. Res. 2200A (XXI) (1966), Art. 7.
[90] Constantin, A. (2018). Human Subject Research: International and Regional Human Rights Standards. *Health and Human Rights*, 20(2), p. 137.
[91] Chen, C. L. (2014). Constitutional Analysis of Research Ethics Review Laws: The United States and Beyond. *Columbia. Science & Technology Law Review*, 16, pp. 248–273.
[92] Munteanu, C., Molyneaux, H., Moncur, W., Romero, M., O'Donnell, S., & Vines, J. (2015). Situational Ethics: Re-thinking Approaches to Formal Ethics Requirements for Human-Computer Interaction. In *Proceedings of the ACM CHI Conference on Human Factors in Computing Systems*, pp. 105–114.
[93] Chen, C. L. (2014). Constitutional Analysis of Research Ethics Review Laws: The United States and Beyond. *Columbia Science & Technology Law Review*, 16, pp. 248–273.

psychological, genetic or medical information" and the Ministry of Science and Technology requires ethics review when funding all types of research, including social science.[94]

It is also worth noting that the countries such as the United States that enact research ethics review requirements have traditionally tended to be wealthy ones, and in many low-income countries, there were no laws that required such oversight, or the laws that existed were under-enforced. As a result, low- and middle-income countries have been frequently selected as locations for international clinical trials, a practice that many have considered to be exploitative.[95] Over the past two decades, however, more low- and middle-income countries have strengthened ethics review processes, in part due to research sponsors conducting more research in these countries.[96]

When researchers at U.S. institutions that require IRB review conduct research in other countries, researchers are required to comply with all sets of standards. Typically, this means that the research must undergo both IRB review at their home institution and the local equivalent. When there is not an IRB equivalent in that location, some IRBs require that the researchers work with local researchers or community leaders to ensure that the research is consistent with the cultural and legal expectations and requirements of that community.[97] And when multiple standards might conflict with each other, the researcher must comply with the higher standard.[98]

Within the international field of computer science, the ACM Publications Policy on Research Involving Human Subjects and Participants (established in 2021) largely defers to these same types of local regulation, with additional nods to principles established by the Declaration of Helsinki and the Belmont Report.[99] The first statement of the policy is: "All authors conducting research involving human participants and subjects must meet appropriate ethical and legal standards guiding such research."[100] However, it goes on to note both that not all research falls under local regulation, and that research may be legal but not ethical, and subsequently

---

[94] Ibid.
[95] Rake, B. (2022). Controversies with Clinical Trial Regulations in Low-and Middle-Income Countries. *Integrity of Scientific Research: Fraud, Misconduct and Fake News in the Academic, Medical and Social Environment*, 235–242; Jalali, R., Nogueira-Rodrigues, A., Das, A., Sirohi, B., & Panda, P. K. (2022, April). Drug Development in Low- and Middle-Income Countries: Opportunity or Exploitation? In *American Society of Clinical Oncology Educational book. American Society of Clinical Oncology. Annual Meeting*, 42, pp. 1–8.
[96] Alahmad, G., Al-Jumah, M., & Dierickx, K. (2012). Review of National Research Ethics Regulations and Guidelines in Middle Eastern Arab Countries. *BMC Medical Ethics*, 13, pp. 1–10.
[97] IRB Considerations for International Research. Cornell. (February 1, 2023). Available at: https://researchservices.cornell.edu/resources/irb-considerations-international-research
[98] Ibid.
[99] ACM Publications Board. (August 15, 2021). ACM Publications Policy on Research Involving Human Participants and Subjects. Available at: www.acm.org/publications/policies/research-involving-human-participants-and-subjects.
[100] Ibid.

lays out a familiar set of principles: minimization of harm; privacy and right to self-determination; informed consent; and justice. Refer to Chapter 11 for more on international laws and treaties.

5.4 REGULATORY CHALLENGES FOR HCI RESEARCH

Changes in both technology and research paradigms have impacted human subjects research in HCI as well as a variety of other fields, particularly with respect to conventional definitions of researchers, participants, and research settings. As a result, many have asked whether it makes sense to apply a single set of regulations or even norms to research ethics within such a diverse field, and discussion of this topic has been on the rise within HCI in recent years.

5.4.1 Participatory Methods

The HCI research community has a strong emphasis on participatory research methods and including participants as stakeholders in the research process, practices which sometimes struggle to fit into traditional human subjects regulatory requirements. In these paradigms, in which the line between researcher and participant are blurred, who are the human subjects and what specific protections do they have? For example, in action research, the focus is to create research efforts "with" people experiencing real problems in their everyday lives rather than "for," "about," or "focused on" them.[101] Despite some early discussion where this was in question, typically U.S. IRBs treat action research as human subjects research falling under the Common Rule; however, the research paradigm sometimes has trouble fitting into rigid requirements of preplanning as well as traditional notions of research participants.[102] As Gillian Hayes explains in her explanation of action research in the context of HCI: "Not only must participants understand the research, they must be allowed to be in positions of greater power than those afforded the 'subjects' of a controlled study or even the participants in a design project."[103]

Similarly, the HCI community has a rich history of supporting citizen science, in which members of the public participate in scientific research to achieve real-world goals.[104] Due to the participatory nature of the research and the type of data collected, citizen science sometimes creates unique privacy challenges that researchers must solve with careful co-creation of procedures with the volunteer participant-scientists. However, like the similar problem described for action

---

[101] Hayes, G. R. (2011). The Relationship of Action Research to Human-Computer Interaction. *ACM Transactions on Computer-Human Interaction (TOCHI)*, 18(3), pp. 1–20.
[102] Ibid.
[103] Ibid.
[104] Preece, J. (2016). Citizen Science: New Research Challenges for Human–Computer Interaction. *International Journal of Human-Computer Interaction*, 32(8), pp. 585–612.

research, IRB approval prior to volunteers being recruited has made it difficult for some citizen science practitioners to determine ethical best practices in coordination with volunteers.[105] However, there have been some movements recently to recognize some of these challenges. For example, the potential value of new participatory research methods was recognized by Congress when it enacted the Crowdsourcing and Citizen Science Act of 2017 that grants federal agencies (from the National Park Service to NASA) the authority to use crowdsourcing and citizen science in their research and makes such research fall under the regulatory power of the Common Rule.[106]

Another shared concern with these research paradigms can be the necessity for participants to be able to fluidly join and leave the research, which presents challenges for informed consent. One possible solution for this challenge is to obtain a full IRB waiver of informed consent. The Common Rule provides guidance for such waivers, notably that an IRB must determine that the research involves "no more than minimal risk" to subjects and that the research "could not be practicably carried out" without such a waiver.[107]

Finally, it is worth remembering with respect to participatory methods that, as noted in Section 5.3.4, under some circumstances IRBs may require that researchers work with community leaders to understand the cultural context for the research. Tribal IRBs (as discussed in Section 5.3.3) also often have extensive relevant requirements. Within the context of research ethics for HCI, many researchers also suggest going beyond regulatory requirements and making it standard practice to work *with* communities in making decisions about how to conduct research.[108]

5.4.2 *Online Research and Big Data*

As our computing capabilities change, and so does the nature of research we can conduct, these changes are leaving significant gaps in both ethical norms and oversight. The HCI community, like others, continues to struggle to form ethical norms, standards, and even best practices around work that does not fit traditional

---

[105] Bowser, A., Shilton, K., Preece, J., & Warrick, E. (2017, February). Accounting for Privacy in Citizen Science: Ethical Research in a Context of Openness. In *Proceedings of the ACM CSCW Conference on Computer Supported Cooperative Work and Social Computing*, pp. 2124–2136.

[106] 15 U.S.C. § 3724; Citizenscience.gov. (June 18, 2019). Report to Congress describes the breadth and scope of Federal crowdsourcing and citizen science. Available at: www.citizenscience.gov/2019/06/18/report-to-congress-2019/; Rothstein, M. A., Wilbanks, J. T., Beskow, L. M., Brelsford, K. M., Brothers, K. B., Doerr, M., ... & Tovino, S. A. (2020). Unregulated Health Research Using Mobile Devices: Ethical Considerations and Policy Recommendations. *Journal of Law, Medicine & Ethics*, 48(S1), pp. 196–226.

[107] 45 CFR 46.116(f).

[108] Fiesler, C., Zimmer, M., Proferes, N., Gilbert, S., & Jones, N. (2024). Remember the Human: A Systematic Review of Ethical Considerations in Reddit Research. *Proceedings of the ACM on Human-Computer Interaction*, 8(GROUP), pp. 1–33.

paradigms of human subjects research. Examples of these include the collection and use of public data, sharing and combining datasets, identifying harms beyond the individual subject, and consideration for potential downstream effects.

For example, since the early 2000s there has been discussion in the HCI community about the ethical implications of conducting research online.[109] Online research spans geographic and disciplinary boundaries, and introduces novel challenges around anonymity and privacy in the context of these differing norms.[110] For example, in 2002, Bruckman pointed to the growing practice of studying online content and the confusion at the time over whether Internet users should be considered "human subjects" (with standards for anonymization) or "amateur artists" (with standards for creative credit), particularly when it came to protecting their privacy.[111] Two decades later, we still do not have a clear answer to this question, but it has become even more complicated by big data – and the exponential growth in research conducted using online content (typically without consent), much of which is happening in subfields of computer science that do not have as much experience with human subjects research as HCI.

In 2016, Metcalf and Crawford asked, "Where are the human subjects in big data research?" and noted that the discontinuities between data science practice and research ethics regulation have led many data science practitioners and researchers to move toward rejecting ethics regulations outright.[112] Meanwhile, online communities like those on Reddit are treasure troves of data for researchers, often collecting content on very sensitive topics,[113] and with the majority of users having no idea that their content is being used in this way.[114] As a result, when research like this comes to light, the humans behind the data are often unsettled by discovering that their content is in a dataset or their face is in a scientific paper.[115] A particularly troubling example of this challenge was when a researcher created a dataset of YouTube videos of people going through gender transition, in order to train a facial recognition system; one of the YouTubers who discovered that her face was in a scientific paper

---

[109] Bos, N., Karahalios, K., Musgrove-Chávez, M., Poole, E. S., Thomas, J. C., & Yardi, S. (2009). Research Ethics in the Facebook Era: Privacy, Anonymity, and Oversight. *CHI'09 Extended Abstracts on Human Factors in Computing Systems*, pp. 2767–2770.

[110] Ibid.

[111] Bruckman, A. (2002). Studying the Amateur Artist: A Perspective on Disguising Data Collected in Human Subjects Research on the Internet. *Ethics and Information Technology*, 4, pp. 217–231.

[112] Metcalf, J., & Crawford, K. (2016). Where Are Human Subjects in Big Data Research? The Emerging Ethics Divide. *Big Data & Society*, 3(1), 2053951716650211.

[113] Fiesler, C., Zimmer, M., Proferes, N., Gilbert, S., & Jones, N. (2024). Remember the Human: A Systematic Review of Ethical Considerations in Reddit Research. *Proceedings of the ACM on Human-Computer Interaction*, 8(GROUP), pp. 1–33.

[114] Fiesler, C. & Proferes, N. (2018). "Participant" Perceptions of Twitter Research Ethics. *Social Media+ Society*, 4(1), 2056305118763366.

[115] Chu, Jane C. Should Researchers Be Allowed to Use YouTube Videos and Tweets? (June 3, 2019). *Slate*. Available at: https://slate.com/technology/2019/06/youtube-twitter-irb-human-subjects-research-social-media-mining.html.

said that she shared her videos because she wanted to help other trans people, and that it felt like a violation to be included in this dataset without her consent.[116] This case illustrates the complex gap between ethics and law; though raising clear ethical concerns, this practice was likely legal, both with respect to YouTube's Terms of Service and human subjects research regulations.

Despite the growing awareness of these kinds of ethical issues within HCI and related fields and the potential limitations of IRBs to address them,[117] both researchers and reviewers still often pass responsibility onto IRBs and the regulatory compliance described in this chapter. However, given their limitation to oversight of "human subjects research" as narrowly defined by government regulations, researchers might over-rely on this convenient external review process that might determine that a project is "not human subjects research" or "exempt" – and inappropriately conclude that the project therefore must not have ethical concerns. Though IRBs can be inconsistent in this judgment, this is the case much of the time for research like the YouTube gender transition video project described above; use of "public" data in research is often interpreted as not falling into the definition of "human subjects research."[118]

Moreover, it is not uncommon for researchers to make this call themselves rather than going to their IRB at all. For example, in 2021 the entire University of Minnesota was banned from contributing to the Linux kernel due to a research study conducted by researchers there.[119] As a piece of security research, they tested their ability to introduce vulnerabilities into the Linux kernel by submitting patches that appeared to fix real bugs but also introduced subtle flaws. Though the researchers stated that

---

[116] Vincent, J. (August 22, 2017). Transgender YouTubers Had their videos grabbed to train facial recognition software. *The Verge*. Available at: www.theverge.com/2017/8/22/16180080/transgender-youtubers-ai-facial-recognition-dataset.

[117] Friesen, P., Douglas-Jones, R., Marks, M., Pierce, R., Fletcher, K., Mishra, A., … & Sallamuddin, T. (2021). Governing AI-driven Health Research: Are IRBs up to the Task? *Ethics & Human Research*, 43(2), pp. 35–42; Munteanu, C., Molyneaux, H., Moncur, W., Romero, M., O'Donnell, S., & Vines, J. (2015, April). Situational Ethics: Re-thinking Approaches to Formal Ethics Requirements for Human-Computer Interaction. In *Proceedings of the ACM CHI Conference on Human Factors in Computing Systems*, pp. 105–114; Pater, J., Fiesler, C., & Zimmer, M. (2022). No Humans Here: Ethical Speculation on Public Data, Unintended Consequences, and the Limits of Institutional Review. *Proceedings of the ACM on Human-Computer Interaction*, 6(GROUP), pp. 1–13; Vitak, J., Shilton, K., & Ashktorab, Z. (2016). Beyond the Belmont Principles: Ethical Challenges, Practices, and Beliefs in the Online Data Research Community. In *Proceedings of the 19th ACM Conference on Computer-Supported Cooperative Work & Social Computing*, pp. 941–953.

[118] Pater, J., Fiesler, C., & Zimmer, M. (2022). No Humans Here: Ethical Speculation on Public Data, Unintended Consequences, and the Limits of Institutional Review. *Proceedings of the ACM on Human-Computer Interaction*, 6(GROUP), pp. 1–13; Vitak, J., Shilton, K., & Ashktorab, Z. (2016). Beyond the Belmont Principles: Ethical Challenges, Practices, and Beliefs in the Online Data Research Community. In *Proceedings of the 19th ACM Conference on Computer-Supported Cooperative Work & Social Computing*, pp. 941–953.

[119] Chin, M. (April 30, 2021). How a university got itself banned from the Linux kernel. *The Verge*. Available at: www.theverge.com/2021/4/30/22410164/linux-kernel-university-of-minnesota-banned-open-source.

these patches were never merged into the mainline kernel, when the paper was published, it caused an outcry in large part due to the perception that the research wasted the time of real people and could have caused harm. The researchers subsequently applied for a post-hoc IRB determination – and though they did receive a formal letter of exemption, many members of both the Linux and research communities thought that this project should have undergone ethics review.[120] Other research ethics controversies, such as the Facebook emotional contagion study and the privacy policy audit described earlier in this chapter, received similar reactions: concern over how an IRB could have approved the research, when in both cases, an IRB determined that it did not fit the legal criteria for their oversight.

5.4.3 Beyond the IRB

As a result of concerns about the limitations of IRBs, there are calls to expand the scope of research ethics regulation, or at least for norms to greatly expand. However, at the same time, there are also concerns about IRB "mission creep" that focus largely on its role for compliance, for example, "focusing more on procedures and documentation than difficult ethical questions" and "efforts to protect against lawsuits."[121] As noted previously, though there is not a direct cause of action for research subjects for violations of the Common Rule, institutions might still be held vicariously liable under tort law for research-related injuries, which might lead to risk-averse research vetting. However, it is worth noting there is nearly no litigation in social science or humanities research involving human subjects; the vast majority of HCI research will not involve the kind of medical research that has traditionally led to lawsuits.[122] Though there has been a rise in litigation related to human experimentation, it is nearly entirely limited to medical research.[123]

Therefore, there is some concern about the expansion of IRBs in terms of misdirecting their energies and drawing resources from intervening in riskier research. It is therefore important to keep in mind that, according to the U.S. Code of Federal Regulations, an "IRB should not consider possible long-range effects of applying knowledge gained in the research (for example, the possible effects of the research on public policy) as among those research risks that fall within the purview of its responsibility." The further assessment of long-term, potentially speculative harms to populations could not only put additional strain on this limited resource, but also

---

[120] Ibid; Wu, Q. & Lu, K. (2020). Clarifications on the "hypocrite commit" work (FAQ). www-users.cse.umn.edu/~kjlu/papers/clarifications-hc.pdf.
[121] Gunsalus, C. K., Bruner, E. M., Burbules, N. C., Dash, L., Finkin, M., Goldberg, J. P., ... & Aronson, D. (2007). The Illinois White Paper: Improving the System for Protecting Human Subjects: Counteracting IRB "Mission Creep". *Qualitative Inquiry*, 13(5), pp. 617–649.
[122] Ibid.
[123] Mello, M. M., Studdert, D. M., & Brennan, T. A. (2003). The Rise of Litigation in Human Subjects Research. *Annals of Internal Medicine*, 139(1), pp. 40–45.

could have a chilling effect on research "while simultaneously distracting an IRB from the important oversight issues that do fall under its purview."[124]

For example, in the AI research community, the NeurIPS conference instituted a requirement in 2020 that all papers include a statement of the "potential broader impact of their work, including its ethical aspects and future societal consequences" and provided guidance for authors on how to do so, including highlighting uncertainties.[125] This call for explicit speculative reflection on impact mirrors similar ideas for technology design, such as "social impact statements" that acknowledge concerns during the development process.[126] They also necessitate a broader view of research than considering individual harms.

Similarly, there have been calls in the HCI community to more directly discuss negative unintended consequences of our research in published papers.[127] This trend toward research ethics regulation occurring within research communities, outside the context of legal regulation, has been recognized by the ACM with their Publications Policy on Research Involving Human Subjects[128] (though as noted, this policy still relies in part on local regulation) and by the HCI community specifically with the instantiation of the SIGCHI Research Ethics Committee in 2016, tasked with assisting program committees in evaluating research ethics concerns that arise during the paper review process.[129] However, the interdisciplinary and international nature of the research community has made it difficult to create more explicit guidelines than the general principles (e.g., informed consent, justice) that we see across a wide range of disciplines and countries.

5.5 CRITIQUES AND OPPORTUNITIES

Both within and beyond computing, criticisms of human subjects regulation in the U.S., and specifically IRBs, is common. These criticisms often focus on

---

[124] Havard, M. & Magnus, D. (2011). Beyond the IRB: Local Service Versus Global Oversight. *The American Journal of Bioethics*, 11(5), pp. 1–2.

[125] Nanayakkara, P., Hullman, J., & Diakopoulos, N. (2021, July). Unpacking the Expressed Consequences of AI Research in Broader Impact Statements. In *Proceedings of the AAAI/ACM AIES Conference on AI, Ethics, and Society*, pp. 795–806.

[126] Shneiderman, B. & Rose, A. (1996). Social Impact Statements: Engaging Public Participation in Information Technology Design. In *Proceedings of the Symposium on Computers and the Quality of Life*, pp. 90–96.

[127] Hecht, B. (March 29, 2018). It's Time to Do Something: Mitigating the Negative Impacts of Computing Through a Change to the Peer Review Process. *ACM Future of Computing Academy*. Available at: https://perma.cc/K22T-5DFU.

[128] ACM Publications Board. (August 15, 2021). ACM Publications Policy on Research Involving Human Participants and Subjects. Available at: www.acm.org/publications/policies/research-involving-human-participants-and-subjects.

[129] Fiesler, C., Frauenberger, C., Muller, M., Vitak, J., & Zimmer, M. (2022). Research Ethics in HCI: A SIGCHI Community Discussion. *CHI Conference on Human Factors in Computing Systems Extended Abstracts*.

inconsistency, narrow focus, and bureaucracy. In addition to the overarching issues described earlier in terms of a narrow definition of human subjects research and lack of consideration for downstream effects, this issue of narrow focus comes out in terms of the limitation to federally funded research and an abundance of red tape over nuance. As one legal scholar put it: "The Common Rule has imposed a narrow, rule-following approach to ethics, while neglecting, perhaps even obscuring, the powerful social and economic forces that drive researchers to exploit research participants."[130]

An interesting component of these critiques is that they often simultaneously argue for both more IRB oversight and less. For example, one legal scholar, noting that the U.S. Supreme Court established in *Keyishian v. Board of Regents* that the country is "deeply committed to safeguarding academic freedom," argues that research ethics review raises first amendment concerns because it constitutes content-based prior restraint of a type of expression.[131] He argues both for expanding the IRB requirement to encompass equal application regardless of funding source (therefore not limiting it to largely academia) and for further limiting the power of IRBs by providing remedies for individual researchers for "undue intervention" from IRBs.[132]

Similarly, we know that individual IRBs can be inconsistent in their judgments, in part due to the lack of explicit guidelines.[133] And beyond the Common Rule, state law on human subjects regulation also creates inconsistencies across the U.S., particularly with respect to what types of research fall under these regulations. As a result of both things, collaborations across institutions can sometimes be complicated. However, recent updates to the Common Rule added a provision for multisite studies to have a single IRB of record.[134] It has also been proposed that *more* states should pass laws that extend the Common Rule or other research regulation to cover more types of research, and that this is a case where a model law could be very helpful.[135]

---

[130] Burris, S. (2008). Regulatory Innovation in the Governance of Human Subjects Research: A Cautionary Tale and Some Modest Proposals. *Regulation & Governance*, 2(1), pp. 65–84.

[131] Chen, C. L. (2014). Constitutional Analysis of Research Ethics Review Laws: The United States and Beyond. *Columbia Science & Technology Law Review*, 16, pp. 248–273.

[132] Ibid.

[133] Vitak, J., Proferes, N., Shilton, K., & Ashktorab, Z. (2017). Ethics Regulation in Social Computing Research: Examining the Role of Institutional Review Boards. *Journal of Empirical Research on Human Research Ethics*, 12(5), pp. 372–382; Lidz, C. W., Pivovarova, E., Appelbaum, P., Stiles, D. F., Murray, A., & Klitzman, R. L. (2018). Reliance Agreements and Single IRB Review of Multisite Research: Concerns of IRB members and Staff. *AJOB Empirical Bioethics*, 9(3), pp. 164–172; Klitzman, R. (2011). The Myth of Community Differences as the Cause of Variations among IRBs. *AJOB Primary Research*, 2(2), pp. 24–33.

[134] Association of American Medical Colleges. Common Rule Resource and Updates. Retrieved July 20, 2024, from www.aamc.org/what-we-do/mission-areas/medical-research/common-rule.

[135] Woltjen, Maria. (1986). Regulation of Informed Consent to Human Experimentation. *Loyola University Chicago Law Journal*, 17, pp. 507–532.

However, there is also growing recognition that research *ethics* as a critical component of HCI, computer science, and beyond involves far more consideration than regulatory requirements. In addition to encouraging ethical considerations beyond the formal definition of human subjects research, there have also been discussions of how we can more explicitly account for ethics in publication review processes, as well as how we might evaluate the real-world impacts for research, for example, similarly to how we conduct environmental or algorithmic impact assessments.[136]

Finally, it is critical that as a research community we have open discussions about the ethical challenges we face so that we can learn from each other and move toward shared understandings. In addition to writing more about both ethical considerations and regulatory compliance in reporting research, we should also continue to push for more research ethics education – both professionally (e.g., workshops) and formal (e.g., graduate school courses).

5.6 CONCLUSION

As noted at the start of this chapter, *ethics* and *law*, though they frequently intersect, are two different things. Research ethics as a whole is a complex and nuanced topic that continues to receive thoughtful and important attention within the field of HCI. As the ACM publications policy reminds us, something may not be ethical even though it is permissible under the law. It is therefore critical that researchers both comply with human subjects regulations and think about ethical obligations beyond them.

An important critique of human subjects regulation in the U.S. is that the most sweeping and clear regulation (the Common Rule) is limited in scope regarding what research falls under its purview, and additional regulations, for example, at the state level, are inconsistent and scattered. It may therefore not always be obvious to individual researchers which regulations a particular project might fall under. However, nearly all such regulations in the U.S. and beyond (including local to our research community) map broadly to the general principles of the Belmont Report involving consent, beneficence, and justice. Carefully considering these aspects of any research project is the best start for both ensuring legal compliance and thinking through ethical issues beyond regulation.

---

[136] Metcalf, J., Moss, E., Watkins, E. A., Singh, R., & Elish, M. C. (2021). Algorithmic Impact Assessments and Accountability: The Co-Construction of Impacts. In *Proceedings of the ACM FAccT Conference on Fairness, Accountability, and Transparency*, pp. 735–746.

6

Intellectual Property

6.1 INTRODUCTION

Intellectual property (IP) emerges as a relevant and often critical factor for any subfield of computer science that involves innovation. This is certainly true for human–computer interaction (HCI), where innovative technologies and user experiences converge, since IP law can influence how we interact with technology. This chapter will delve into the relationship between IP and HCI, examining how intellectual property rights and limitations influence the design process, drive technological progress, and shape user experiences.

According to the World Intellectual Property Organization (WIPO), intellectual property refers to "creations of the mind, such as inventions; literary and artistic works; designs; and symbols, names and images used in commerce."[1] One way to think about IP is the importance of striking a balance between the interests of creators and innovators with the wider public – to both incentivize creativity and to contribute to the public domain. There are three major types of IP protection, each of which protects a different type of creation by providing recognition and/or financial benefit for what people invent or create: patent, copyright, and trademark.

Though we will go into each of these in more detail, briefly, the distinction between these types of IP is that patents protect inventions, processes, or scientific creations; trademark protects brands, logos, and slogans; and copyrights protect original works of authorship. There are also two major types of patents: a "utility patent" protects the way an invention is used and works[2] and a "design patent" protects the way an invention looks.[3] Each form of IP serves a distinct purpose and offers different types of exclusive rights and protections to their respective creators or owners.

---

[1] The World Intellectual Property Organization. What is intellectual property? Retrieved February 20, 2024, from www.wipo.int/about-ip/en/.
[2] 35 U.S.C. § 101.
[3] 35 U.S.C. § 171.

Beyond these three primary types, trade secrets and publicity rights are also considered forms of intellectual property, though this chapter will not delve into these in detail. Right of publicity is a legal concept that grants individuals control over the commercial use of their identity, such as their name, image, voice, or other distinctive aspects of their persona. It is separate from trademark law, which focuses on brand identifiers, in that it protects personal identity from unauthorized exploitation. Relevant laws exist largely at the state level, but particularly given complications arising from generative AI (e.g., voice cloning), there has been discussion of the potential for federal laws that could create legal avenues for artists to combat AI-based exploitations of personas.[4] Trade secrets, by contrast, are a form of intellectual property that protects confidential business information that provides a competitive advantage, including, for example, algorithms. Trade secrets do not require registration but instead must be actively kept secret through measures like nondisclosure agreements and restricted access. This is an area in which artificial intelligence also creates some complications, as there can be tensions between trade secret protection and goals toward or even requirements for AI transparency.[5]

In the sense that IP rights can provide incentives and protections for innovators and creators, IP is relevant to both researchers and practitioners who invest time, effort, and resources into advancing HCI technologies and methodologies. IP protection also has the potential to foster collaboration, knowledge sharing, and fair competition, as it provides mechanisms for researchers and practitioners to share and build upon each other's work, which may lead to accelerated progress. However, at the same time, strict IP enforcement has the potential to impede collaboration, limit knowledge sharing, and hinder progress in the field. One significant challenge with respect to IP law is striking the right balance between protection and openness.

As a specific example of how IP laws of different types apply in practice, consider the case of software (or "computer programs") – these are generally protected by copyright, though some aspects of software as an invention can also be protected by patents. The underlying social policy goals of patent and copyright are similar. Both seek to draw a balance between, on the one hand, providing an incentive for the creation of works desired by society and recognizing in some fair and just way the efforts of their creators and, on the other hand, ensuring a broad public domain that permits later inventors and authors to build on the existing foundation to advance technology and culture for the overall benefit of society. Both patents and copyright also protect the fruits of intellectual creativity, and neither demands nor protects, in general, more creativity than the other. Some copyright-protected works are mundane,

---

[4] Jones, F. (2024). Tune In or Tune Out: AI Developments Urges Federal Proposal for Voice Protection in Right of Publicity. *University of Denver Sports & Entertainment Law Journal*, 28, pp. 31–65.
[5] Mylly, U. M. (2023). Transparent AI? Navigating Between Rules on Trade Secrets and Access to Information. *IIC-International Review of Intellectual Property and Competition Law*, 54(7), pp. 1013–1043.

and some patents reflect creative genius. But computer programs are functional in a way that law has traditionally reserved to patent subject matter, so the decision to bring them under copyright was a radical break from intellectual property tradition.[6] However, patent and copyright constitute two different means of legal protection.

Meanwhile, graphical user interfaces, the visual display through which users interact with software, fall into something of a gap in IP protection. Since, unlike software, it is not exactly written code, copyright law offers little protection, mostly protecting exact knockoffs of a design. Under trademark law, trade dress, which protects against confusingly similar designs, takes a large amount of time to establish. Design patents provide the most potential protection, protecting an interface as a whole from substantially similar copies, but these are expensive to obtain.[7] Along similar lines, legal scholars have suggested that with respect to web design, the underlying thematic differences between copyright and trade dress law – that is, the difference between protecting a website owner's expression and protecting consumer impression – suggests that trade dress is the more appropriate basis for look and feel protection.[8]

Software and user interface protection, with respect to all three major types of intellectual property, are examples of how HCI practitioners and researchers might engage directly with IP law in the course of their work. As we dig into sources of rules, major court cases will also highlight more specific examples.

6.2 SOURCES OF LEGAL RULES

The first and primary source of law for intellectual property in the U.S. is the Constitution. Effective in 1789, the U.S. Constitution states: *"The Congress shall have power ... To promote the progress of science and useful arts, by securing for limited times to authors and inventors the exclusive right to their respective writings and discoveries."*[9] Commonly known as the Intellectual Property Clause, this component of the country's founding document can be attributed to the framers' attempt to strike a balance between rewarding creators and inventors and ensuring that society as a whole benefits from their contributions.

While the specific origins of IP protection in the Constitution cannot be attributed to a single foreign influence, it is widely recognized that they were influenced by the legal and philosophical traditions of other nations, especially the British system of IP law. The British Statute of Monopolies of 1623, for example, limited the

---

[6] Karjala, D. S. (1998). The Relative Roles of Patent and Copyright in the Protection of Computer Programs. *The John Marshall Journal of Computer and Information Law*, 17, pp. 41–74.
[7] Stigler, R. (2014). Ooey GUI: The Messy Protection of Graphical User Interfaces. *Northwestern Journal of Technology and Intellectual Property*, 12(3), pp. 215–251.
[8] Brown, L. (2013). Bridging the Gap: Improving Intellectual Property Protection for the Look and Feel of Websites. *NYU Journal of Intellectual Property & Entertainment Law*, 3, pp. 310–357.
[9] U.S. Constitution, Article 1, Section 8.

grant of monopolies and emphasized the public interest in promoting innovation and encouraging trade,[10] and the Statute of Anne established authors rather than publishers as the primary beneficiaries of copyright.[11] Philosopher John Locke's writings on property rights, specifically his notion that individuals have a natural right to the fruits of their labor, were also likely influential in discussions surrounding IP protection. His ideas on property rights and the connection between labor and ownership provided a philosophical basis for recognizing the importance of protecting intellectual creations.[12]

Beyond the Constitution, primary sources of IP law also include federal statutes and administrative regulations. Congress has enacted various statutes that govern IP law, including the Patent Act,[13] Copyright Act,[14] and the Lanham Act (for trademarks).[15] These statutes establish frameworks for IP protection, define scope of rights, and outline procedures for registration, enforcement, and remedies. Government agencies, such as the United States Patent and Trademark Office (USPTO) and the United States Copyright Office, also issue regulations to provide guidance and procedures for IP-related matters. These regulations supplement the statutes and govern the practical aspects of obtaining and managing IP rights. With some exceptions, notably related to trademarks and right of publicity, in the U.S. IP law is governed almost entirely at the federal level.

With respect to case law, court decisions, particularly those from the U.S. Supreme Court and appellate courts, have also critically shaped and interpreted IP law. Precedents established by the judiciary provide guidance on issues such as patentability, copyright infringement, fair use, and trademark disputes. Further, the U.S. is a signatory to several international treaties and agreements related to IP, such as the Berne Convention for the Protection of Literary and Artistic Works,[16] the Paris Convention for the Protection of Industrial Property,[17] the Agreement on Trade-Related Aspects of Intellectual Property Rights (TRIPS),[18] and the Marrakesh Treaty to Facilitate Access to Published Works for Persons who are Blind, Visually Impaired or Otherwise Print Disabled.[19] These treaties help harmonize IP laws

---

[10] 21 Jas. 1. c. 3.
[11] 8 Ann. c. 19 / c. 21.
[12] Fisher, W. (2001). Theories of Intellectual Property. In Munzer, S. (Ed.), *New Essays in the Legal and Political Theory of Property*. Cambridge University Press.
[13] 35 USC.
[14] 17 USC.
[15] 15 U.S.C. § 1051.
[16] Berne Convention for the Protection of Literary and Artistic Works, September 9, 1886, as revised at Stockholm on July 14, 1967, 828; U.N.T.S. 221.
[17] Paris Convention for the Protection of Industrial Property, as last revised at the Stockholm Revision Conference, March 20, 1883; 21 U.S.T. 1583; 828 U.N.T.S. 305.
[18] TRIPS: Agreement on Trade-Related Aspects of Intellectual Property Rights, April 15, 1994, Marrakesh Agreement Establishing the World Trade Organization, Annex 1C, 1869 U.N.T.S. 299, 33 I.L.M. 1197.
[19] Marrakesh Treaty to Facilitate Access to Published Works for Persons Who Are Blind, Visually Impaired or Otherwise Print Disabled, adopted June 27, 2013, in Marrakesh, Morocco.

globally and influence domestic legislation. (See Chapter 11 for more detail on international law and treaties.) In the following sections, we will go into more detail about the history, U.S. laws, case law, and remedies for each of the three major types of intellectual property.

6.3 PATENT

Patents as a form of IP protect new and useful inventions, whether they are processes, machines, compositions of matter (such as chemical compounds), designs, or improvements of any of those. The underlying stated purpose of this protection is to incentivize innovation by rewarding inventors for their creations, while also encouraging the dissemination of technical knowledge by ensuring that patents do not last indefinitely.

Patent rights are territorial, which means that they are granted on a country-by-country basis – inventors must file patent applications in each jurisdiction where they seek protection. The U.S. grants three types of patents:

(1) *Utility patents.* The most common type of patent, utility patents protect the functional and utilitarian aspects of an invention. Focused on how the invention works, they provide broad protection for the underlying concept, functionality, and practical application of that invention.
(2) *Design patents.* In contrast to utility patents, design patents protect the ornamental or aesthetic aspects of an invention. Focused on the visual appearance of an invention (e.g., shape, configuration, surface ornamentation, and overall design elements), they are directed toward the visual appeal and overall aesthetic impression that the design creates.
(3) *Plant patents.* Though rarely relevant in HCI, plant patents are the last type of patent granted in the U.S. They cover new and distinct varieties of asexually reproducible plants, allowing inventors to exclusively control the propagation and distribution of a plant variety.

Patents in the U.S. are governed by federal law and administered by the USPTO. Next, we will describe the basics of relevant laws, as well as some major case precedents that have shaped relevant patent law in the context of HCI.

6.3.1 *Federal Law*

Various versions of the Patent Act in federal law in the U.S. have resulted in significant overhauls to patent law. Shortly following the formalization of intellectual property in the U.S. Constitution, the Patent Act was first enacted in 1790 and established the foundation for the country's patent system, granting inventors with exclusive rights to their inventions. Compared to today's patent system, the original system had a shorter patent duration (no more than fourteen years, with no mechanism for extension), a narrower subject matter scope, and patents were granted without thorough examination. Decisions were made by a small group on a Patent Board, who determined if the invention was "sufficiently useful and important."[20]

The 1836 Patent Act[21] brought about significant changes by establishing the USPTO as the governing body responsible for examining and granting patents and introduced a formal examination process for patent applications and professional patent examiners. Over the next century, the Patent Act continued to undergo reforms, leading up to another major overhaul with the Patent Act of 1952.[22] Major changes included the requirement for inventors to disclose the best mode of their invention, as well as the concept of "nonobviousness" as a criterion for patentability and definitions of the modern categories of patentable subject matter.

Based on these Acts and various amendments over time, patent law in the U.S. is encompassed by United States Code 35.[23]

6.3.1.1 U.S.C. Title 35

Title 35 lays out the major legal framework for patent law in the U.S., including requirements for patentability and requirements for patent applications. Critically, Title 35 establishes some important requirements an invention must meet to be patentable:

(1) *Patentable subject matter.*[24] This includes processes, machines, manufactures, compositions of matter, and certain improvements of those. Abstract ideas, laws of nature, and natural phenomena are generally not eligible.
(2) *Novel and timely.*[25] The invention must be new, which means it wasn't previously known or disclosed to the public before the filing date of the patent application.
(3) *Nonobvious.*[26] The invention must be nonobvious to a person skilled in the relevant field. That is, it involves an inventive step beyond what would be considered obvious to an ordinary skilled practitioner.

Title 35 also specifies patent terms: "beginning on the date on which the patent issues and ending 20 years from the date on which the application for the patent was filed."[27]

---

[20] Federico, P. J. (1990). Operation for the Patent Act of 1790. *Journal of the Patent and Trademark Office Society*, 72, p. 373.
[21] Ch. 357, 5 Stat. 117 (July 4, 1836).
[22] Ch. 950, §1, 66 Stat. 792 (July 19, 1952).
[23] 35 U.S.C.
[24] 35 U.S.C. § 101.
[25] 35 U.S.C. § 102.
[26] 35 U.S.C. § 103.
[27] 35 U.S.C. § 154.

In 2012, significant changes to Title 35 went into effect following the passage of the Leahy-Smith America Invents Act (AIA).[28] Major changes included, first, a switch from a "first-to-invent" to a "first-to-file" system, meaning that the right to a patent is granted to the first inventor who files a patent application, rather than the first inventor to conceive of the invention. This change is especially important to fast-moving technology fields, as it emphasizes the importance of promptly filing patent applications, though it also presents challenges – for example, to universities where discoveries are often disclosed at a very early stage.[29]

Second, the AIA introduced new post-grant proceedings that provide mechanisms for challenging the validity of granted patents after they have been issued (e.g., a way for a third party to assert prior art against granted patents in a more streamlined way). Third, the AIA expanded the definition of prior art, considering more types of publicly available information that can be used to assess the novelty of inventions, including prior research and publications. It also enhanced patent examination procedures to expand opportunities for third-party submissions of prior art during patent examination. Finally, the AIA modified the patent fee structure, introducing new fees and incentives, with the intention of promoting innovation by reducing costs for smaller entities such as independent inventors and startups.

As with many codified laws in the U.S., the language of Title 35 often does not provide sufficient explanatory power for all cases. As such, the specifics of many of these requirements and terms have been established through case law.

6.3.1.2 Major Case Law

Due to the importance of common law and precedent in establishing and evolving the specifics of IP protection in the U.S., a number of the most relevant aspects of patent law for HCI have been established through litigation – for example, patentability of computer programs and interfaces. Next, as examples, we will briefly describe some of the court cases that have established important legal rules around patents.

Diamond v. Diehr (1981)[30]

- The dispute was over a patent for a computer-controlled rubber molding process. The court held that the use of a computer to control the process was not merely a mathematical algorithm and was therefore eligible for patent protection.
- The case established the principle that software can be eligible for patent protection under certain circumstances.

---

[28] 125 Stat. 284.
[29] Dahl, C. L. (2021). Did the America Invents Act Change University Technology Transfer? *Texas Intellectual Property Law Journal*, 29, pp. 1–38.
[30] 450 U.S. 175 (1981).

Bilski v. Kappos (2010)[31]

- The dispute was over the patent office rejecting a patent application for a method of hedging risk in commodities trading via mathematical calculation. The patent claims were directed toward a series of steps that involved performing mathematical calculations to identify and mitigate the risks associated with commodities trading. The court held that Bilski's method was an abstract idea and did not meet the requirements for patent eligibility.
- The case narrowed the scope of patentability for abstract claims without excluding business models entirely, leaving the door open for some computer-implemented and financial-services inventions.

Alice Corp. v. CLS Bank International (2014)[32]

- The dispute was over patents that Alice Corp. owned related to a computerized trading platform that used a method for mitigating "settlement risk" in financial transactions. CLS Bank International, a provider of foreign exchange settlement services, sued, saying that the patents were invalid because they claimed an abstract idea, which is not eligible for patent protection under U.S. patent law. The court held that the patents were invalid because they claimed an abstract idea and that the computerized implementation of the idea was not enough to make it eligible for patent protection.
- The case established a test for determining whether computer-implemented inventions (i.e., software patents) are eligible for patent protection via the Alice/Mayo test, which looks at whether the invention involves an abstract idea and whether the implementation of the idea is "significantly more" than just a generic computer.

DDR Holdings, LLC v. Hotels.com, L.P. (2014)[33]

- The dispute was over a patent owned by DDR Holdings related to an e-commerce system. The court held that DDR's patent for a system that "lured" users to websites was eligible for patent protection in part because it was an inventive concept "necessarily rooted in computer technology."
- The case established that software inventions that provide a unique technological solution to a problem in a specific context may be eligible for patent protection.

Ultramercial, LLC v. Hulu, LLC (2014)[34]

- The dispute was over a patent owned by Ultramercial that covered a method for monetizing copyrighted digital content through displaying ads before the

---

[31] 561 U.S. 593 (2010).
[32] 573 U.S. 208 (2014).
[33] 773 F.3d 1245 (Fed. Cir. 2014).
[34] 772 F.3d 709 (Fed. Cir. 2014).

content is accessed. The court found that the idea of offering free access to copyrighted content in exchange for viewing ads was abstract and not eligible for patent protection on its own. Though the patent described a series of steps as computer functions, they did not add an "inventive concept" sufficient to make that abstract idea patentable.
- The case established that the "inventive concept" required to render an otherwise abstract idea patent eligible must go beyond generic computer functions.

Enfish LLC v. Microsoft Corp. (2016)[35]

- The dispute was over whether some of Microsoft's software products infringed on the patents for Enfish's self-referential database system. Microsoft claimed the original patent was invalid. The appeals court, despite affirming non-infringement, found that Enfish's patent was eligible for protection because it improved the functioning of computers rather than simply being an abstract idea.
- The case established the principle that software inventions that are directed to a specific improvement in computer technology can be patent eligible, even if they do not involve a physical component or operate in a networked environment.

Apple Inc. v. Samsung Electronics Co. (2015)[36]

- One of the most well-known cases in design patents, this drawn-out legal dispute was over Apple's claims that Samsung had infringed upon its design patents and trade dress elements related to the iPhone. Apple argued that Samsung's smartphones, particularly their physical design and user interface, copied key elements of Apple's iPhone and iPad.
- The Federal Circuit decision emphasized that both design and utility patents can be enforced in the context of consumer electronics. Later, the Supreme Court held that with respect to design patent damages, the "article of manufacture" to which a patented design is applied can be only a component of a product.[37]

6.3.2 *Enforcement and Remedies*

In the U.S., patent law is primarily enforced through legal proceedings in federal courts. When a patent holder believes that their rights have been infringed, they can file a lawsuit against the alleged infringer to seek enforcement of their patent rights. A court will assess whether the accused product, process, or invention infringes upon the patent holder's claims. This determination involves analyzing

---

[35] 822 F.3d 1327 (Fed. Cir. 2016).
[36] 786 F.3d 983 (Fed. Cir. 2015).
[37] 580 U.S. 53 (2016).

the elements of the patent claims and comparing them to the accused product or process and may also consider the determination of the validity of the patent in the first place.

If a court finds that a patent is both valid and has been infringed, there are a variety of potential remedies for the patent holder, including injunctive relief (preventing the infringing party from further acts of infringement), damages (monetary compensation for actual damages, e.g., lost profits or reasonable royalties), attorney's fees and costs (typically reserved for situations where the offending party's conduct was exceptional), or corrective actions such as recall or destruction of infringing products. Of course, not all patent disputes go to court, and they might also be resolved through alternative means such as negotiation, mediation, or arbitration.

One challenge with patent enforcement is that there may be motivations beyond a good faith belief of infringement to challenge a patent. For example, inventors may go to court to attempt to invalidate the patent of a competitor. With software patents in particular, overly broad patents have been granted in the past, resulting in future litigation or "patent trolling." This term refers to a practice where nonpracticing entities (NPEs) acquire patents with the primary purpose of using them as leverage for extracting monetary settlements or licensing fees from alleged infringers. These entities often do not produce or manufacture any products themselves but rather focus on aggressively asserting their patent rights against others. Whereas these "patent trolls" are typically operating within the bounds of the legal system, in many cases their tactics and outcomes are contrary to the goals of intellectual property in the U.S. and have a negative impact on innovation.[38] This activity can also lead to unnecessary litigation; for example, Tim Berners-Lee, inventor of the World Wide Web, had to testify on behalf of a group of defendants who were being sued by patent owners claiming that anyone using interactive web features was infringing upon their intellectual property; the plaintiffs eventually lost.[39]

6.3.3 Patents and HCI

Overall, patents have a potentially significant role in the field of computing in general and, by extension, HCI, by incentivizing innovation in relevant technologies. Patents provide inventors and organizations with exclusive rights to their inventions, which might encourage investment of time and resources into the development of new technologies, software, hardware, and user interfaces. Patent law also provides mechanisms for legal protection against unauthorized use, reproduction, or

---

[38] Cohen, L., Gurun, U. G., & Kominers, S. D. (2016). The Growing Problem of Patent Trolling. *Science*, 352(6285), pp. 521–522.

[39] Krakovsky, M. (2012). Patently Inadequate: The Biggest Change to US Patent Law in Nearly 60 Years Brings Many Changes, but Fails to Solve the Software Industry's Most Vexing Problems. *Communications of the ACM*, 55(7), pp. 18–20.

commercial exploitation of inventions, which allows researchers and companies to disclose their innovations to the public while ensuring they retain the right to control and benefit from them.

Of course, despite the intended goals of patent law for innovation, it is important to keep in mind the challenges it may present for HCI practitioners and researchers as well. Some argue that the patent system can stifle innovation by limiting others from building upon or improving existing technologies, leading to a slowdown in progress.[40] It can also create barriers to entry, especially in cases of unintentional or even inappropriately alleged infringement; even outside the context of patent trolling, litigation is costly, and fear of infringement can lead to chilling effects.[41]

The patent system can also just be difficult for researchers and practitioners to navigate. Even outside the context of litigation, the quality of patents granted can vary greatly, leading to overly broad or low-quality patents. This can result in "patent thickets," where a large number of overlapping or conflicting patents exist, making it difficult to navigate and assess how new inventions might fit in.[42]

Finally, patents have the potential to raise ethical concerns in the HCI field, particularly when they involve technologies that impact accessibility, inclusion, or essential human rights. Though this issue tends to come up more commonly in the context of the pharmaceutical industry,[43] patents may restrict the availability of affordable and accessible technological solutions, limiting adoption and potentially hindering progress in addressing societal challenges that HCI may be well suited to tackle.

Also related to the relationship between HCI and patent law, it is worth noting the impact on HCI basic research. For instance, searching for prior art is one of the most critical, time-intensive aspects of patent examination.[44] Therefore, patent law is also a domain area in which HCI has been commonly applied to assist practitioners – for example, with interface design to aid with information retrieval tasks for patent searches.[45] At the same time, patents are also potentially a valuable source of data for HCI research questions. For example, one HCI study analyzed 86 patent applications for emotion recognition technology to understand how this emerging

---

[40] Jaffe, A. B. & Lerner, J. (2011). *Innovation and Its Discontents: How Our Broken Patent System is Endangering Innovation and Progress, and What to Do About It.* Princeton University Press.

[41] Chen, F., Hou, Y., Qiu, J., & Richardson, G. (2023). Chilling Effects of Patent Trolls. *Research Policy,* 52(3), Article 104702, pp. 1–13.

[42] Shapiro, C. (2000). Navigating the Patent Thicket: Cross Licenses, Patent Pools, and Standard Setting. *Innovation Policy and the Economy,* 1, pp. 119–150.

[43] Bonadio, E. & Baldini, A. (2020). COVID-19, Patents and the Never-Ending Tension Between Proprietary Rights and the Protection of Public Health. *European Journal of Risk Regulation,* 11(2), pp. 390–395.

[44] Krishna, A. M., Feldman, B., Wolf, J., Gabel, G., Beliveau, S., & Beach, T. (2016). User Interface for Customizing Patents Search: An Exploratory Study. In *HCI International 2016 Posters' Extended Abstracts.* Springer International Publishing.

[45] Becks, D., Görtz, M., & Womser-Hacker, C. (2010). Understanding Information Seeking in the Patent Domain and Its Impact on the Interface Design of IR Systems. In *Proceedings of the HCIR Human-Computer Information Retrieval Conference,* pp. 87–90.

technology is being developed and speculatively applied.[46] Therefore, patent law has the potential to help HCI researchers both address research questions and pose brand new ones.

6.4 COPYRIGHT

Copyright law is the legal framework that grants exclusive rights to creators and authors of original creative works, providing them with the right to control and protect a wide range of expressions, including books, songs, movies, paintings, software code, and architectural designs.

Under U.S. copyright law, creators are granted a bundle of exclusive rights, including the rights to reproduce, distribute, publicly display, publicly perform, and create derivative works based on their original creations. Though copyright protection is automatic upon the creation of an original work fixed in a tangible medium (e.g., writing it down, recording it, and saving it digitally), registration with the U.S. Copyright Office provides certain benefits and advantages, such as the ability to sue for infringement. Copyright in the U.S. is primarily governed by federal law, notably the U.S. Copyright Act.

The Copyright Act, which appears in Title 17 of the United States Code not only enumerates these exclusive rights but also includes, for example, the critical copyright exception of the Fair Use Doctrine in Section 107, as well as the Digital Millennium Copyright Act (DMCA). These laws are administered by the U.S. Copyright Office, a department of the Library of Congress, though their authority is somewhat limited beyond formalities such as registration. For the most part, state laws do not govern copyright, though contracts governed by state law can be very relevant to copyright, for example, works for hire and licensing.

Next, we will describe the basics of these laws, as well as some major case precedent that has shaped relevant copyright law in the context of HCI.

6.4.1 *Federal Law*

Introduced by the Parliament of Great Britain in 1710, the Statute of Anne[47] was a pivotal piece of legislation that laid the foundation for modern copyright law. While not directly applicable to the United States, the Statute of Anne still directly influenced the development of copyright principles and provided a framework for subsequent copyright laws, including those in the United States. For example, one of the significant contributions of the Statute of Anne was its recognition of the public interest, aiming to balance authors' exclusive rights with the public's need for access

---

[46] Boyd, K. L. & Andalibi, N. (2023). Automated Emotion Recognition in the Workplace: How Proposed Technologies Reveal Potential Futures of Work. *Proceedings of the ACM on Human-Computer Interaction*, 7(CSCW1), Article 95, pp. 1–37.

[47] 8 Ann. c. 19 / c. 21.

to information and creative works.[48] It also limited the duration of copyright protection to ensure that works would eventually enter the public domain.

Initially, because the American colonies had a largely agrarian economy, copyright protection was not a priority. Prior to the ratification of the U.S. Constitution, a few states enacted their own copyright statutes, but following the Constitutional power given to Congress to grant copyrights "for limited times," the Copyright Act of 1790[49] was the first federal copyright act instituted in the U.S. This law granted copyright protection to "maps, charts, and books" for a term of only fourteen years, with the possibility of renewal for another fourteen years if the author was still alive. Subsequent copyright laws, including the Copyright Act of 1831[50] and Copyright Act of 1909,[51] expanded and refined copyright protections, including the recognition of more categories of creative works and extending copyright terms.

6.4.1.1 The Copyright Act of 1976

In the latter half of the twentieth century, the need for copyright reform became evident as technological advancements such as photocopiers and audio recordings posed new challenges. Aimed at addressing these challenges and bringing U.S. law in line with international standards, the Copyright Act of 1976 became the law that is still in effect today.[52]

This law introduced several important changes and principles to copyright law. Unlike the previous laws that required formalities like registration, this Act established automatic copyright protection as soon as a work is created and fixed in a tangible form.

This Act defined copyrightable subject matter (or "works of authorship") as any of the following: literary works; musical works, including accompanying words; dramatic works, including accompanying music; pantomimes and choreographic works; pictorial, graphic, and sculptural works; motion pictures and other audio-visual works; sound recordings; and (added in 1990) architectural works.[53] This section of the Act also codified the "idea-expression distinction," a doctrine that originated in the 1879 Supreme Court case *Baker v. Selden*,[54] which limits the scope of copyright protection by differentiating an idea from the expression of that idea.

The Act also importantly defined the exclusive rights granted to a copyright holder in the work: to reproduce in copies; to prepare derivative works; to distribute

---

[48] Zimmerman, D. L. (1994). Copyright in Cyberspace: Don't Throw Out the Public Interest with the Bath Water. *Annual Survey of American Law*, 3, pp. 403–413.
[49] 1 Stat. 124 (1790).
[50] 4 Stat. 436 (1831).
[51] 35 Stat. 1075 (1909).
[52] U.S.C. 17.
[53] 17 U.S.C. 102.
[54] 101 U.S. 99 (1879).

copies to the public; to perform publicly; to display publicly; and (added in 1995) to perform publicly by means of a digital audio transmission.

One of the purposes of the overhaul of U.S. copyright law that occurred with the Copyright Act of 1976 was also to modernize and harmonize copyright protection with international standards, notably those set forth by the Berne Convention for the Protection of Literary and Artistic Works. The Berne Convention is an international treaty that establishes minimum standards for copyright protection among its member countries.[55] These standards include automatic protection, national treatment (that authors in member countries are granted the same rights and protections in other countries), lack of formalities (such as mandatory registration), and limitations and exceptions to copyright. As part of the last requirement, the Copyright Act of 1976 also codified the important principle of fair use. The Act has also been amended several times since then, sometimes in response to changing technologies. Next, we will delve into further developments in the law.

6.4.1.2 Fair Use

The doctrine of fair use, which permits limited use of copyrighted material without permission from the copyright holder, also has its roots in English common law and the Statute of Anne, which allowed for some uses of copyrighted material, for example, for critical commentary. Outside the U.S., this principle exists primarily in the form of "fair dealing" rights, which in most countries are more specific in scope and application than fair use.[56]

Though early U.S. copyright law laid the groundwork for the importance of balancing copyright against public interest, the principle of fair use as we know it today began to be recognized by U.S. courts in the nineteenth century.[57] Notably in the 1841 case *Folsom v. Marsh*, Justice Joseph Story's opinion articulated a set of factors to take into account in deciding whether a use was fair: "the nature and objects of selections made, the quantity and value of the materials used, and the degree in which the use may prejudice the sale, or diminish the profits, or supersede the objects, of the original work."[58]

Following over a century of case law that drew from Story's opinion, the fair use doctrine was officially codified in the Copyright Act of 1976, which outlines the four factors that determine whether any particular use qualifies as fair use:[59]

---

[55] Berne Convention for the Protection of Literary and Artistic Works, September 9, 1886, revised at Paris July 24, 19711161 U.N.T.S. 3.

[56] D'Agostino, G. (2008). Healing Fair Dealing-A Comparative Copyright Analysis of Canada's Fair Dealing to UK Fair Dealing and US Fair Use. *McGill Law Journal*, 53, pp. 309–363.

[57] Bunker, M. D. (2002). Eroding Fair Use: The "Transformative" Use Doctrine After Campbell. *Communication Law & Policy*, 7(1), pp. 1–24.

[58] 9 F. Cas. 342 (C.C.D. Mass. 1841).

[59] 17 U.S.C. 107.

1. The purpose and character of the use (e.g., whether it is for commercial or nonprofit purposes, and whether it is transformative or derivative).
2. The nature of the copyrighted work (e.g., whether it is factual or creative).
3. The amount and substantiality of the portion used in relation to the whole work.
4. The effect of the use on the potential market for or value of the copyrighted work.

Because fair use is determined on a case-by-case basis by courts, the doctrine has the benefit of being flexible and adaptable, for example, to new technology. Fair use was the primary instrument for clearing the way for or drawing boundaries around technologies like the Betamax machine (*Sony v. Universal*),[60] peer-to-peer file sharing (*A&M Records v. Napster*),[61] and Google image search (*Perfect 10 v. Google*).[62] The recent *Google v. Oracle* decision also had significant implications for the technology industry, as it clarified the boundaries of fair use in determining copyright infringement in the context of software development.[63]

However, the subjectivity and case-by-case nature of fair use can make it challenging for end users to rely on. Fair use is also famously confusing; in *Folsom v. Marsh*, Justice Story referred to the problem of carving out copyright exceptions as the "metaphysics of law."[64] HCI research has shown that one of the side effects of the lack of bright-line rules in fair use is that uncertainty can result in chilling effects, for example, in online creative communities where creators might be remixing or making other uses of existing content.[65]

In recent years, fair use has also received a great deal of attention in the context of artificial intelligence and training data. Many of the copyright lawsuits that are ongoing as of 2025 – brought by a range of plaintiffs including large companies such as Getty Images,[66] well-resourced authors such as George R. R. Martin and John Grisham,[67] and smaller content creators and artists[68] – may end up turning in

---

[60] 464 U.S. 417 (1984).
[61] 239 F.3d 1004 (2001).
[62] 508 F.3d 1146 (2007).
[63] 593 U.S. 1 (2021).
[64] 9 F. Cas. 342 (C.C.D. Mass. 1841).
[65] Fiesler, C. & Bruckman, A. S. (2014, February). Remixers' Understandings of Fair Use Online. In *Proceedings of the ACM CSCW Conference on Computer Supported Cooperative Work & Social Computing*, pp. 1023–1032; Fiesler, C., Paup, J., & Zacher, C. (2023). Chilling Tales: Understanding the Impact of Copyright Takedowns on Transformative Content Creators. *Proceedings of the ACM on Human-Computer Interaction*, 7(CSCW2), Article 304, pp. 1–21.
[66] Getty Images (US), Inc. v. Stability AI, Inc., 1:23-cv-00135 (D. Del.); Brittain, B. (February 7, 2023). Getty Images lawsuit says Stability AI misused photos to train AI. *Reuters*. Available at: www.reuters.com/legal/getty-images-lawsuit-says-stability-ai-misused-photos-train-ai-2023-02-06/.
[67] Authors Guild v. OpenAI Inc., 1:23-cv-08292, (S.D.N.Y.); David, E. (September 21, 2023). George R. R. Martin and other authors sue OpenAI for copyright infringement. *The Verge*. Available at: www.theverge.com/2023/9/20/23882140/george-r-r-martin-lawsuit-openai-copyright-infringement.
[68] Andersen v. Stability AI Ltd., 3:23-cv-00201 (N.D. Cal.); Brittain, B. (December 1, 2023). Artists take new shot at Stability, Midjourney in updated copyright lawsuit. *Reuters*. Available at: www.reuters.com/legal/litigation/artists-take-new-shot-stability-midjourney-updated-copyright-lawsuit-2023-11-30/.

part on whether the use of these plaintiff's copyrighted content as part of very large training datasets constitutes fair use. In June 2025, a district court judge ruled that Anthropic's use of lawfully purchased and digitized books for training its Claude AI model constituted fair use, finding the use "exceedingly transformative," though also that the same may not apply to storage of pirated books, leaving that issue for trial.[69] This early decision suggests that training AI models has a plausible fair use defense under some circumstances, but with many pending fact-specific cases, this is likely to be an evolving legal landscape. (For more on copyright issues in the context of AI, refer to Chapter 8.)

6.4.1.3 Copyright Terms

The U.S. Constitution specifies that exclusive rights granted to authors are for "limited times," with the expectation (again, with the public interest in mind) that when copyright expires, that work will go into the public domain. However, the amount of time in the context of copyright has expanded significantly over the centuries from when the 1790 Copyright Act began with a maximum of 28 years total.

As of the 1976 Copyright Act, the term for works created on or after January 1, 1978 was life of the author plus 50 years, or for works made for hire, to 75 years from publication or 100 years from creation, whichever was shorter. In 1998, Congress passed the Copyright Term Extension Act (also known as the Sonny Bono Copyright Term Extension Act) which added another 20 years to these terms – extending protection to the life of the author plus 70 years, or for corporate authorship, 95 years from publication or 120 years from creation, whichever was shorter.[70]

The Copyright Term Extension Act was challenged in the lawsuit *Eldred v. Ashcroft*, which eventually reached the Supreme Court.[71] The argument was that the act exceeded the power granted to Congress by the Copyright Clause in the Constitution, because it violated the principle of "limited times." The Court determined that copyright term extensions are within the scope of Congress' authority, though it did recognize that extensions should not be unlimited and would undergo constitutional scrutiny in the future.

The Copyright Term Extension Act is also sometimes (derisively) called the "Mickey Mouse Protection Act." Disney initially successfully lobbied for longer copyright terms in 1976, which at the time extended the copyright protection for Mickey Mouse (who first appeared in the Steamboat Willy cartoon in 1928) from 1984 to 2003.[72] Then in the late 90s, with 2003 looming ahead, they lobbied

---

[69] Bartz v. Anthropic PBC, No. 3:24-cv-05417 (N.D. Cal. 2025).
[70] 17 U.S.C. 302.
[71] 537 U.S. 186 (2003).
[72] Hennessey, K. (2020). Intellectual Property-Mickey Mouse's Intellectual Property Adventure: What Disney's War on Copyrights Has to Do with Trademarks and Patents. *Western New England Law Review*, 42, pp. 25–41.

Congress and were once again successful. With no further copyright term extensions on the horizon, Steamboat Willy officially entered the public domain on January 1, 2024.

6.4.1.4 The Digital Millennium Copyright Act

With the rapid growth of the Internet and digital technologies in the 1990s, including the ease of copying and distributing digital content, there was a desire to update copyright laws to address issues such as online piracy and digital distribution. The U.S. was also under pressure at the time to update its laws to comply with international standards under the Berne Convention and the WIPO Copyright Treaty, which had introduced new provisions related to digital rights management (DRM) and protection of digital copyrighted works.[73]

The development of the DMCA involved significant negotiations among various stakeholders, including copyright holders, tech companies, online service providers, consumer advocates, and legal experts, in an attempt to find common ground on issues around DRM, safe harbors, and fair use. It was signed into law by President Bill Clinton in 1998 and brought about significant changes to the landscape of copyright enforcement in the internet age. In addition to some lesser-known provisions (e.g., protecting the design of boat hulls), the two major components of the DMCA are Section 1201, which covers circumvention of technological copyright protection measures (e.g., DRM), and Section 512, which established rules around copyright infringement liability.

Section 1201 of the DMCA criminalizes circumventing technological copyright protection: "no person shall circumvent a technological measure that effectively controls access to a work protected under [copyright law]."[74] It further defines circumvention as an attempt to "descramble a scrambled work, to decrypt an encrypted work, or otherwise to avoid, bypass, remove, deactivate, or impair a technological measure" – for example, ripping a DVD. It is also illegal to create and distribute a technology that accomplishes this, such as the software that can be used for ripping that DVD. This provision was also part of international harmonization efforts since the WIPO Copyright Treaty of 1996 requires adequate legal protection against copyright circumvention.

This provision in the DMCA is also somewhat unique in that the law has a mechanism to change itself; every three years, the U.S. Copyright Office holds rulemaking proceedings, in which they consider new possible exemptions to the law. A 2020 HCI paper makes the case that this mechanism is a rare way for ordinary technology

---

[73] Okediji, R. L. (2008). Regulation of Creativity under the WIPO Internet Treaties. *Fordham Law Review*, 77, pp. 2379–2410.

[74] 17 U.S.C. § 1201.

users to have their voices heard when it comes to ways that policy might limit their interactions with technology.[75]

Scholars working at the intersection of law and technology have written extensively about the possible negative impacts of DMCA 1201 absent appropriate exemptions. For example, law professor Pamela Samuelson expands on computer scientist Edward Felten's articulation of the importance of the "freedom to tinker," calling on policymakers to protect the activities that are integral to creativity and innovation yet substantially constrained by copyright law.[76] Others have pointed to the power of technology manufacturers to, for example, monopolize markets by requiring users to repeatedly purchase copies of the same software,[77] the inability of cybersecurity researchers to find glitches and reasonable alternatives,[78] and challenges for creating technologies accessible for people with disabilities.[79] Researchers have also shown that DRM can result in poor user experiences due to mismatches between models of ownership or norms for technology use.[80] However, exemption proceedings in recent years have been friendlier to non-infringing uses, particularly around issues of reverse engineering.[81]

In writing about the relevance of DMCA 1201 and DRM in general to HCI practitioners, Casey Fiesler describes it as an example of when the answer to "can I do this?" technology might be one of legal constraints rather than technological affordances, adding: "It is important for technology designers to be aware of these potential constraints on desirable use, and the patterns of rights that impact user [mental] models for what they *should* be able to do."[82]

---

[75] Fiesler, C. (2020, April). Lawful Users: Copyright Circumvention and Legal Constraints on Technology Use. In *Proceedings of the 2020 CHI Conference on Human Factors in Computing Systems*, pp. 1–11.

[76] Samuelson, P. (2016). Freedom to Tinker. *Theoretical Inquiries in Law*, 17(2), pp. 562–600.

[77] Adelmann, T. C. (2010). Are Your Bits Worn Out? The DMCA, Replacement Parts, and Forced Repeat Software Purchases. *Journal on Telecomm. & High Technology Law*, 8, pp. 185–215.

[78] Weigle, K. (2018). How the Digital Millennium Copyright Act Affects Cybersecurity. *American University Intellectual Property Law Brief*, 9(1), pp. 1–24.

[79] Giannoumis, G. A., Land, M., Beyene, W., & Blanck, P. (2017). Web Accessibility and Technology Protection Measures: Harmonizing the Rights of Persons with Cognitive Disabilities and Copyright Protections on the Web. *Cyberpsychology: Journal of Psychological Research on Cyberspace* 11(1), pp. 1–19.

[80] Bebenek, K. (2011). Strong Wills, Weak Locks: Consumer Expectations and the DMCA Anticircumvention Regime. *Berkeley Technology Law Journal*, 26, pp. 1457–1487; Fiesler, C. (2020). Lawful Users: Copyright Circumvention and Legal Constraints on Technology Use. In *Proceedings of the ACM CHI Conference on Human Factors in Computing Systems*, pp. 1–11; Miller, C. L. (2007). The Video Game Industry and Video Game Culture Dichotomy: Reconciling Gaming Culture Norms with the Anti-Circumvention Measures of the DMCA. *Texas Intellectual Property Law Journal*, 16, pp. 453–481.

[81] Samuelson, P. (2016). New Exemptions to Anti-Circumvention Rules. *Communications of the ACM*, 59(3), pp. 24–26.

[82] Fiesler, C. (2020). Lawful Users: Copyright Circumvention and Legal Constraints on Technology Use. In *Proceedings of the ACM CHI Conference on Human Factors in Computing Systems*, pp. 1–11.

Additionally, despite some of the challenges previously noted, DMCA 1201 exemptions granted over the past two decades of rulemaking allow for specific activities relevant to HCI research and practice that might otherwise have been prohibited under anti-circumvention provisions. For example, exemptions permit bypassing DRM on e-books in order to enable screen readers for visually impaired users, studying and testing software and devices to identify and address security vulnerabilities, bypassing technological protection measures for certain types of repairs, and reverse engineering for the purposes of interoperability.

Section 512 of the DMCA addresses the liability of online service providers for copyright infringement committed by their users. This section establishes a framework for copyright holders and online platforms to handle instances of copyright infringement in the digital environment, known as "notice and takedown." Its purpose was to strike a balance between protecting copyright holders' rights and fostering the growth of online services and platforms.

A central element of 512 is the notice-and-takedown system. Copyright holders can send a formal notice (DMCA takedown notice) to online service providers (OSPs), requesting the removal of infringing content. OSPs are then obligated to expeditiously remove or disable access to the material. If the user disputes the takedown, they can submit a counter-notification, and the OSP may restore the content unless the copyright holder files a legal action.

This provision has had a significant impact on the functioning of online platforms and services. It provides a legal framework that enables OSPs to respond to copyright infringement but has also faced significant criticisms. For example, some copyright holders argue that the notice-and-takedown system is cumbersome and that OSPs may not always adequately address repeat infringers.

In 2020, the U.S. Copyright Office released a report documenting the results of a five-year study to evaluate the current effectiveness of DMCA 512; one obvious conclusion of the study was that "no potential solution(s) will please everybody."[83] However, the "everybody" in this report included two categories of stakeholders: online service providers (e.g., YouTube) and large-scale copyright owners like movie studios and record companies. Even in concluding that "the notice-and-takedown system as experienced by parties today is unbalanced," the report noticeably omitted everyday users and content creators as stakeholders. Multiple research studies of content creators such as YouTubers and remixers have concluded that takedown procedures as laid out by DMCA 512 and related automated systems such as YouTube's ContentID can be burdensome and result in chilling effects for non-infringing users.[84]

---

[83] United States Copyright Office. 2020. Section 512 of Title 17: A Report of the Register of Copyrights. Available at: www.copyright.gov/policy/section512/section-512-full-report.pdf.

[84] Fiesler, C., Paup, J., & Zacher, C. (2023). Chilling Tales: Understanding the Impact of Copyright Takedowns on Transformative Content Creators. *Proceedings of the ACM on Human-Computer Interaction*, 7(CSCW2), Article 304, pp. 1–21; Kaye, D. B. V., & Gray, J. E. (2021). Copyright Gossip: Exploring Copyright Opinions, Theories, and Strategies on YouTube. *Social Media+ Society*, 7(3),

6.4.2 Licensing

Though copyright law grants exclusive rights to a copyright holder by default, and fair use allows for some limited uses by others without permission, the mechanism by which copyright holders grant that permission is typically licensing. Licensing allows individuals or organizations to legally use, reproduce, distribute, display, perform, or create derivative works based on the original copyrighted material, with the scope of use, duration, geographical area, and any other conditions or limitations set as part of the licensing agreements. For example, academics or others who publish scholarly articles own the copyright in that work. Therefore, in order for a journal or other publication venue to reproduce and distribute that article, the author(s) must grant the venue a license.

For instance, the Association for Computing Machinery (ACM) is a nonprofit professional society that publishes a great deal of computer science scholarship, including major HCI venues. After decades of requiring a copyright *transfer* rather than a license, ACM began providing authors with the option to grant an exclusive or nonexclusive license to ACM to publish their work.[85] An exclusive license means that *only* ACM can use the rights granted; that includes the author, who cannot share the work with anyone else. In practice, the outcome of an exclusive license is much the same as a full transfer of ownership.[86] A nonexclusive license, however, means that the author maintains all those rights which they can choose to use themselves or to grant to others. Yet even with a nonexclusive license, most parties, to access material, must pay a fee or for a license, unless content is posted as open access. ACM also encourages open access publications to include Creative Commons licenses and has announced a plan to transition to 100 percent open access by 2026.[87]

6.4.2.1 Creative Commons

The plaintiff in *Eldred v. Ashcroft,* the case that (unsuccessfully) challenged the Copyright Term Extension Act, was Eric Eldred, a web publisher who was making a career out of making works available as copyright expired and they passed into the public domain. He was represented by a team led by legal scholar Lawrence Lessig, well known at that point for his work on cyberlaw that culminated in the 1999 book

---

20563051211036940; Brøvig-Hanssen, R., & Jones, E. (2023). Remix's Retreat? Content Moderation, Copyright Law and Mashup Music. *New Media & Society,* 25(6), pp. 1271–1289.

[85] ACM Publication Rights & Licensing Policy. (January 1, 2023). Retrieved January 5, 2024, from www.acm.org/publications/policies/publication-rights-and-licensing-policy.

[86] Fiesler, C. (2018). ACM Copyright Licenses: Which should you choose, and how should you handle third-party material? *Medium.* Available at: https://cfiesler.medium.com/acm-copyright-licenses-which-should-you-choose-and-how-do-you-handle-third-party-material-dbe87be8b57c.

[87] Open Access Publication & ACM. Retrieved August 9, 2025, from https://www.acm.org/publications/openaccess.

Code and Other Laws of Cyberspace.[88] Further inspired by Eldred's goal to make more creative work freely available on the Internet, in addition to the growing internet community of people creating, remixing, and sharing content, Lessig and others came up with the idea for Creative Commons (CC), and the first licenses launched in 2002.[89]

Again, copyright is automatic, and by default a copyright owner has "all rights reserved." They might choose to give up their copyright entirely and donate the work to the public domain, but the concept behind Creative Commons is a middle ground: what if the copyright owner wants *some* rights reserved?

CC licenses are a set of standardized copyright licenses that allow the author to specify the permissions and conditions under which their work can be used, shared, or adapted by others. They are modular, meaning that the user can pick and choose which components to use. The four types of (mix-and-match) licenses are:

1. **Attribution (BY):** This license allows others to use, share, and adapt the work as long as they give appropriate credit to the original creator.
2. **Non-Commercial (NC):** This license allows others to use the work for non-commercial purposes only. Commercial use is restricted without additional permission.
3. **No Derivatives (ND):** This license allows others to use the work as long as it is not changed or adapted in any way.
4. **Share Alike (SA):** This license allows others to use, share, and adapt the work, but any derivative works must be released under the same license.

CC licenses are machine-readable, which means they can be easily understood and interpreted by both humans and computers. The idea is to simplify the process of sharing and using creative content while respecting the rights of the original creators. CC licensing and other mechanisms toward open access publishing and sharing of information have been huge boons for the open science movement, and research has shown that open research is associated with increases in citations, media attention, potential collaborators, job opportunities, and funding opportunities for researchers and academics.[90] Technically a CC license can apply to any work that is governed by copyright law, which includes software and code. However, Creative Commons recommends against using their licenses in software due to backward-compatibility limitations with existing commonly used open-source

---

[88] Levy, S. (2002, October) Lawrence Lessig's Supreme Showdown. WIRED. Available at: www.wired.com/2002/10/lessig-3/.

[89] The Story of Creative Commons. Creative Commons Certificate for Educators, Academic Librarians, and GLAM. Retrieved July 20, 2024, from https://certificates.creativecommons.org/cccertedu/chapter/1-1-the-story-of-creative-commons/.

[90] McKiernan, E. C., Bourne, P. E., Brown, C. T., Buck, S., Kenall, A., Lin, J., McDougall, D., Nosek, B. A., Ram, K., Soderberg, C. K., Spies, J. R., Thaney, K., Updegrove, A., Woo, K. H., & Yarkoni, T. (2016). How Open Science Helps Researchers Succeed. *elife*, 5, e16800.

software licenses and because their licenses do not contain specific terms about the distribution of source code.[91]

6.4.2.2 Open Source

Under U.S. copyright law, computer programs fall into the category of literary works, which makes them protected by copyright (though as noted earlier, some elements can also be patented). The Copyright Act defines "literary works" as "works, other than audiovisual works, expressed in words, numbers, or other verbal or numerical symbols or indicia, regardless of the nature of the material objects, such as books, periodicals, manuscripts, phonorecords, film, tapes, disks, or cards, in which they are embodied."[92] The Copyright Office also specifies that protection in the context of "computer programs" extends to "all of the copyrightable expression embodied in the program" but not to functional aspects such as algorithms, logic, or system design.[93]

However, there are times when it is desirable for software to be more open than copyright law would allow by default. Open-source software refers to software with source code that is made available to the public, typically via licensing. Unlike proprietary or closed-source software, where the source code is kept hidden and controlled by the software's developer, open-source software is often developed collaboratively and transparently by a community of contributors.

Free and Open Source Software (FOSS) licenses are legal agreements that govern the terms under which software can be used, modified, distributed, and shared. These licenses are designed to promote the principles of open-source software, which include transparency, collaboration, and the freedom to use and modify software for various purposes. There are various types of FOSS licenses, each with its own terms and conditions. Two of the more well-known FOSS licenses include the GNU General Public License (GPL), which requires that any software using GPL-licensed code is also released under GPL to ensure it remains open source, and the MIT License, which allows use even in proprietary projects as long as the original copyright notice is retained.

Open-source software has been used in a wide range of applications, from operating systems (e.g., Linux) and web servers (e.g., Apache) to productivity tools (e.g., LibreOffice) and content management systems (e.g., WordPress). The open-source movement has also played a significant role in fostering innovation and democratizing access to software tools and solutions. The HCI research community has examined a number of elements related to FOSS projects and communities, including

---

[91] Creative Commons Frequently Asked Questions. Retrieved July 24, 2024, from https://creativecommons.org/faq/.

[92] 17 U.S.C. § 101.

[93] U.S. Copyright Office. Copyright Registration of Computer Programs. Revised 2021. Retrieved November 20, 2024, from www.copyright.gov/circs/circ61.pdf.

usability issues,[94] teamwork and coordination,[95] and the impact of a lack of demographic diversity among contributors.[96]

6.4.2.3 Terms of Service

Another context in which HCI researchers or practitioners might encounter copyright licenses is in terms of service (TOS), for example, for user-generated content platforms. If a piece of content meets the bar for copyrightability (which may or may not be the case for small pieces of content such as social media posts),[97] the creator owns a copyright in that content automatically – which means that in order for LinkedIn or YouTube or Medium to publish and display that content, the platform must be granted a copyright license. For example, in their TOS effective November 2024, LinkedIn requires that users grant "a worldwide, transferable and sublicensable right to use, copy, modify, distribute, publicly perform and display, host, and process your content and other information without any further consent, notice and/or compensation to you or others."[98]

This license is fairly standard for what is commonly seen across online platforms. Similar to publishing open access with ACM, users will almost always be granting nonexclusive licenses in their content, which means that LinkedIn has the right to display your blog post, but there is nothing to keep you from posting it on Medium as well. Though this is a common misconception, it is almost never the case that a platform such as Facebook "owns" your content. However, platforms do sometimes grab more rights in content than may seem necessary, and it is unlikely that users have a good grasp on what rights they are providing. A 2017 study that analyzed the copyright terms on a set of user-generated content site and then surveyed users about their understandings of them revealed (unsurprisingly) that few users read copyright licenses in TOS and that, though they do have some intuitions on some copyright terms, would find others to be unexpected and unwelcome.[99] In this sense,

---

[94] Terry, M., Kay, M., & Lafreniere, B. (2010). Perceptions and Practices of Usability in the Free/Open Source Software (FoSS) Community. In *Proceedings of the ACM CHI Conference on Human Factors in Computing Systems*, pp. 999–1008.

[95] Hergueux, J., & Kessler, S. (2022). Follow the Leader: Technical and Inspirational Leadership in Open Source Software. In *Proceedings of the ACM CHI Conference on Human Factors in Computing Systems*, pp. 1–15.

[96] Vasilescu, B., Posnett, D., Ray, B., van den Brand, M. G., Serebrenik, A., Devanbu, P., & Filkov, V. (2015). Gender and Tenure Diversity in GitHub Teams. In *Proceedings of the ACM CHI Conference on Human Factors in Computing Systems*, pp. 3789–3798.

[97] Haas, R. (2010). Twitter: New Challenges to Copyright Law in the Internet Age. *John Marshall Review of Intellectual Property Law*, 10(1), pp. 231–254.

[98] LinkedIn. User Agreement. Retrieved November 20, 2024, from www.linkedin.com/legal/user-agreement.

[99] Fiesler, C., Lampe, C., & Bruckman, A. S. (2016). Reality and Perception of Copyright Terms of Service for Online Content Creation. In *Proceedings of the ACM CSCW Conference on Computer-Supported Cooperative Work & Social Computing*, pp. 1450–1461.

copyright licenses and terms of service in general, similar to privacy policies and other legal documents that are typically written at a reading level far above average, present a usability problem.[100]

6.4.3 Major Case Law

Due to the importance of common law and precedent in establishing and evolving the specifics of IP protection in the U.S., similar to patent law, some aspects of copyright relevant to HCI and especially software have been established through litigation. Next, we will briefly describe some of the major court cases that have established important legal precedent for copyright.

Nintendo of America Inc. v. Lewis Galoob Toys, Inc. (1992)[101]

- The dispute was over whether the Game Genie, a device that allowed users to alter features of Nintendo games during gameplay, infringed on Nintendo's copyrights. The court held the Game Genie did not infringe on copyrights as it merely allowed users to modify the game experience but did not create a new game or copy the original game's code, thus not constituting derivative works.
- Established the principle that creating a device or product that works with a copyrighted work, without copying or modifying the underlying software, does not necessarily constitute copyright infringement.

Sega Enterprises Ltd. v. Accolade, Inc. (1992)[102]

- The dispute was over whether Accolade's reverse engineering of Sega's video game console in order to create its own games was copyright infringement. The court held that intermediate copying during reverse engineering can be protected under fair use as long as the resulting product does not incorporate protected expression.
- Established that reverse engineering of software for the purpose of achieving interoperability can be a fair use of copyrighted material.

Apple Computer, Inc. v. Microsoft Corporation (1994)[103]

- The dispute was over whether Microsoft's Windows operating system infringed on Apple's copyrights for the Macintosh user interface. The court held that many of the features Apple claimed as unique were actually functional elements that weren't necessarily copyrightable.

---

[100] Ibid; Jensen, C. & Potts, C. (2004). Privacy Policies as Decision-Making Tools: An Evaluation of Online Privacy Notices. In *Proceedings of the ACM CHI Conference on Human Factors in Computing Systems*, pp. 471–478.
[101] 964 F.2d 965 (9th Cir. 1992).
[102] 977 F.2d 1510 (9th Cir. 1992).
[103] 35 F.3d 1435 (9th Cir. 1994).

- Reinforced that functional aspects of computer programs cannot be protected by copyright, only creative expression.

Lotus Development Corp. v. Borland International, Inc. (1996)[104]

- The dispute was over whether Borland's Quattro Pro spreadsheet program infringed on Lotus's copyrights for its 1-2-3 program. The Supreme Court was split, thus maintaining a lower court ruling that the program's "menu hierarchy" was a "method of operation" and therefore not copyrightable.
- Reinforced a distinction in copyright law between the interface of a software product and its implementation, and that simply the set of available operations is not copyrightable.

A&M Records, Inc. v. Napster, Inc. (2001)[105]

- The dispute focused on whether Napster, a peer-to-peer file-sharing service, was liable for copyright infringement for allowing its users to share copyrighted music without permission. The court held that Napster may not be protected by the DMCA safe harbor provisions, and that it was liable for contributory and vicarious infringement for allowing the sharing of copyrighted music on its platform.
- Established the principle that companies that facilitate the sharing of copyrighted material may be held liable for copyright infringement if they have knowledge of the infringing activity and fail to take reasonable steps to prevent it.

6.4.4 Enforcement and Remedies

Copyright law in the United States is enforced through a combination of legal remedies, civil actions, and practical measures that are primarily aimed at protecting the rights of copyright holders. With respect to legal enforcement and remedies, the most common mechanism is infringement lawsuits. Copyright holders can file civil lawsuits against individuals or entities that have allegedly infringed upon their copyrighted work; these lawsuits seek remedies like injunctive relief (to stop the infringement), monetary damages, and/or legal fees.

In private civil causes of action, which is how most copyright disputes are settled, remedies include: injunctive relief, where the infringing party must cease using the copyrighted work; monetary damages as compensation for harm that may include actual damages (financial losses) and statutory damages (predefined amounts set by law); profits derived from the unauthorized use in the case of willful infringement; attorney's fees and costs for litigation; impoundment and destruction of unauthorized copies; and even nonmonetary remedies such as corrective measures.

---

[104] 516 U.S. 233 (1996).
[105] 239 F.3d 1004 (9th Cir., 2001).

As one technology-based example of enforcement and remedies for copyright infringement, consider a string of cases in the early 2000s related to file sharing. The Recording Industry Association of America (RIAA), representing major record labels, pursued civil legal action to enforce copyrights. High-profile cases included the lawsuits that shut down Napster in 2001[106] and Grokster in 2005,[107] in addition to legal action against individuals.[108] The association filed lawsuits against thousands of individuals who were identified as sharing copyrighted music files on peer-to-peer networks; many of these cases resulted in out-of-court settlements, with defendants agreeing to pay damages to copyright holders.

Criminal copyright infringement cases were also pursued against individuals and entities engaged in "large-scale and willful" distribution of copyrighted content through file sharing. For example, the operators of the file-sharing website The Pirate Bay were charged with criminal copyright infringement and faced legal action in multiple countries. Though outside the U.S. in 2009, they were found guilty in a Swedish court of aiding copyright infringement, which led to prison sentences and substantial fines for the individuals involved.[109]

Though these legal actions by the RIAA and criminal cases may have had an impact as well on a shift toward legal music distribution, changing consumer preferences and the rise of legal digital music platforms like iTunes and later streaming services were significant contributors to subsequent changes in how music is distributed and consumed online.

It is worth noting, however, that criminal penalties for copyright infringement are rare. As noted previously, Section 1201 of the DMCA also includes criminal enforcement measures related to the act of circumventing digital rights management (DRM) measures used to protect copyrighted works or distributing those tools or services. 18 U.S.C. § 2318 also criminalizes the trafficking of counterfeit labels or counterfeit copies of copyrighted works, including unauthorized reproductions or imitations. Criminal copyright enforcement focuses on deterring and punishing intentional and willful acts of copyright infringement that are considered serious offenses and most often involve large-scale or commercial activities rather than individuals.

Typically, copyright is adjudicated in civil cases between specific parties, however. As an alternative to often complex and expensive litigation, the Copyright Alternative in Small Claims Enforcement (CASE) Act of 2020 established a small claims court-like system within the U.S. Copyright Office.[110] The Copyright Claims

---

[106] Ibid.
[107] MGM Studios v. Grokster, 545 U.S. 913 (2005).
[108] Reynolds, D. (2008). The RIAA Litigation War on File Sharing and Alternatives More Compatible with Public Morality. *Minnesota Law Journal of Science and Technology*, 9, pp. 977–1008.
[109] Larsson, S. (2013). Metaphors, Law and Digital Phenomena: The Swedish Pirate Bay Court Case. *International Journal of Law and Information Technology*, 21(4), pp. 354–379.
[110] 17 U.S. 1501–1511.

Board handles cases with claims for damages of no more than $30,000. This new system has had mixed support: Proponents see it as a low-cost alternative to litigation that could allow small creators to defend their rights more effectively, but opponents worry that it could be abused and encourage frivolous lawsuits while still not doing enough to protect individuals from sophisticated actors in the legal system.[111]

6.4.5 Copyright and HCI

There is an interesting relationship between copyright law and HCI research and practice, with each being quite relevant to the other. Copyright law provides a framework that protects the outputs of HCI research and innovation, but also HCI research informs and shapes the practical application and evolution of copyright law, especially in the digital realm where user interaction with copyrighted material is a constant and evolving challenge.

With respect to the application of copyright law, HCI research and practice often involve creating original content such as software interfaces, user experience (UX) designs, interactive technologies, and academic research papers. Copyright law protects these creations, ensuring that the intellectual efforts of researchers are safeguarded. Though at the same time, HCI researchers frequently build upon existing digital works, and IP law dictates how and to what extent existing copyrighted materials can be used.

Copyright also presents interesting usability challenges and research questions for HCI researchers. By studying how people interact with digital content and technology, HCI researchers provide insights into how copyright laws are perceived and followed, potentially even impacting the evolution of copyright policy.[112] HCI expertise also has the potential to contribute to the development of user-friendly copyright management tools, for example, creating interfaces that help users understand their rights and responsibilities under copyright law, thereby aiding compliance and education. One example of this is how HCI might play a role in exploring and improving the user experience of DRM systems, ensuring that DRM does not overly hinder the legitimate use of digital content. As HCI research has previously suggested, copyright is an area where user understandings (or misunderstandings) of the law can have a significant impact on user experiences with technology, and so it is an important area for researchers to be aware of and to consider.[113]

---

[111] Fortney, K. & Hansen, D. (2024). Assessing the Copyright Claims Board After Two Years. *Journal of the Copyright Society*, 70(3), pp. 452–472.

[112] Fiesler, C. (2020). Lawful Users: Copyright Circumvention and Legal Constraints on Technology Use. In *Proceedings of the ACM CHI Conference on Human Factors in Computing Systems*, pp. 1–11.

[113] Ibid.; Fiesler, C. & Bruckman, A. S. (2014). Remixers' Understandings of Fair Use Online. In *Proceedings of the ACM CSCW Conference on Computer-Supported Cooperative Work & Social Computing*, pp. 1023–1032.

6.5 TRADEMARK

Trademarks are the form of intellectual property that protect words, phrases, symbols, designs, or a combination of these elements that distinguish and identify the source of goods or services. In the U.S., trademark law provides exclusive rights to the owner, and trademarks can be registered with the USPTO to further strengthen legal protection. The major sources of trademark law in the U.S. are federal statutes (most notably the Lanham Act), as well as state common law principles and international treaties. As with patent law, the USPTO is responsible for administering and enforcing federal trademark law in the U.S.

Trademarks are critical in various industries and sectors, helping businesses establish brand identity, protect their reputation, and distinguish themselves from competitors. In the context of HCI, trademarks might play a role in branding user interfaces, software products, and technology-related services.

Next, we will describe the basics of laws relevant to trademark, as well as some major case precedent that has shaped trademark law in the context of HCI.

6.5.1 *Federal Law*

Unlike patents and copyright, trademark is not explicitly covered by the U.S. Constitution in Article I as part of the goal to "promote science and the useful arts" by securing rights "for limited times."[114] While patents and copyrights are designed to encourage innovation by offering inventors and creators a temporary and exclusive privilege to produce their unique inventions or original creative works, trademarks, on the other hand, do not necessarily serve as incentives for generating new products. Instead, trademark law in the U.S. relies on the Commerce Clause, which grants Congress the authority to regulate commerce among the states.[115] This commerce-related power is used to regulate trademarks, as they often involve the identification of goods and services in interstate commerce. Trademarks exist to protect both consumers and the brands that are used to create associations with goods and services in commerce, and so, unlike patents and copyright, they do not last for a specific amount of time but instead only last so long as they are used in commerce.

Before the establishment of explicit federal trademark laws in the U.S., merchants and craftsmen used distinctive marks to identify goods and services and had some common law protection as well as limited remedies available in state courts to address unfair competition. These cases could be complex and resulted in varying interpretations of relevant law from one state to another. Therefore, the federal government was strongly urged by manufacturers to handle trademarks at the federal

---

[114] U.S. Constitution, Article I, Section 8, Clause 8.
[115] U.S. Constitution, Article I, Section 8, Clause 3.

level since the inconsistency across states was a trade issue. The first federal trademark law, passed in 1870, had severe limitations and was eventually replaced and superseded by later trademark legislation, including the Trademark Act of 1905 and, most notably, the Lanham Act of 1946.[116]

There are also multiple international agreements that collectively facilitate the protection of U.S. trademarks abroad, streamline international trademark registration processes for U.S. businesses, and ensure that trademark laws meet international standards. Notably, the Paris Convention for the Protection of Industrial Property[117] and the TRIPS[118] require member countries to offer minimum standards of protection to foreign trademarks, which helps to create basic trademark principles across countries and a more uniform and predictable international trademark system.

6.5.1.1 The Lanham Act

The Lanham Act[119] governs trademark registration, protection, and enforcement and provides a legal basis for trademark infringement lawsuits. It also provided authority to the USPTO to handle trademark registration and administration.

The Lanham Act established the basics of trademark protection that still exist today. Under the Lanham Act, a trademark is defined as any word, name, symbol, device, or combination thereof that is used by a person or entity to identify and distinguish their goods (products) from those manufactured or sold by others. This definition encompasses a wide range of elements that can serve as trademarks, including word marks (e.g., brand names like "Apple" or slogans like "Think Different"), design marks (e.g., logos such as the Twitter bird icon), or combinations (e.g., a logo that includes a name, such as the multicolored window pane combined with the word "Microsoft"). Additionally, while the term "trademark" is used broadly, the Lanham Act also covers service marks that identify services rather than goods; for example, Apple uses the service mark "App Store" for its digital distribution platform for mobile apps. Another type of mark relevant to technology is a certification mark, used to indicate that a product or service meets certain established standards or specifications; for example, "Wi-Fi CERTIFIED" is used by the Wi-Fi Alliance to identify wireless networking products that comply with industry standards.

---

[116] Gorman, C. (2017). The Role of Trademark Law in the History of US Visual Identity Design, c. 1860–1960. *Journal of Design History*, 30(4), pp. 371–388.

[117] Paris Convention for the Protection of Industrial Property, as last revised at the Stockholm Revision Conference, Mar. 20, 1883, 21 U.S.T. 1583; 828 U.N.T.S. 305.

[118] TRIPS: Agreement on Trade-Related Aspects of Intellectual Property Rights, Apr. 15, 1994, Marrakesh Agreement Establishing the World Trade Organization, Annex 1C, 1869 U.N.T.S. 299, 33 I.L.M. 1197 (1994).

[119] 15 U.S.C. 1051.

A mark must be distinctive, meaning it must have the capacity to uniquely identify the source of goods or services. The degree of distinctiveness can vary, but there are some major ways that a mark may or may not be considered distinctive. Marks are often "fanciful," as in a made-up word (e.g., Google), or "arbitrary," as in used in an unrelated context (e.g., Apple). "Suggestive" marks hint at a characteristic of something without directly describing it (e.g., Netflix, which suggests the idea of a movie network).

However, if a mark is too descriptive, it is not eligible for trademark registration. For example, the USPTO refused to register the mark "Veterinary Technician Specialist" for being a mere description of the identified services.[120] These cases can be quite nuanced, however. On appeal, a company was granted a trademark for MagnetNotes after a judge's lengthy explanation of how "notes" is not equivalent to the term "paper."[121] Similarly, generic terms that describe the actual product or service are not eligible for trademark protection, for example, "computer" could not be trademarked for a type of computer.

In order to be granted a trademark, there also must be no "likelihood of confusion" with existing trademarks. This means it should not be so similar to another registered mark that consumers could be confused regarding the source of the goods or services. For example, in 2001 Microsoft sued Lindows Inc., claiming that "Lindows" was too similar to its trademark "Windows"; the case settled out of court, and Lindows changed their name to Linspire.[122]

Finally, again, trademarks have to be used in commerce. "Use in commerce" refers to the use of a trademark in connection with the sale or advertising of goods or services. For example, the use of a computer's brand name on its packaging when it is sold would qualify as use in commerce. This is a critical requirement for trademark registration with the USPTO and for enforcing trademark rights, since it demonstrates that the trademark is not merely an idea but is actively being used to identify something in the marketplace.

6.5.1.2 Trademark Application Procedures

Though not technically required prior to applying for registration, it is highly advisable to conduct a trademark search to ensure that there are no existing trademarks that would result in application rejection due to a conflict. The USPTO has had a computerized trademark search system since the 1980s, a key advancement considering how important comprehensive, systematic searches are to the trademark process.[123]

---

[120] In re National Association of Veterinary Technicians in America, Inc. (T.T.A.B. July 9, 2019).
[121] In re MagnetNotes Ltd. (T.T.A.B. September 14, 2007).
[122] Chaudri, A. & Patja, V. (2004). Windows v Lindows–Have Microsoft Won the Battle Only to Lose the War? *Computer Law & Security Review*, 20(4), pp. 321–323.
[123] Bryant, J. H. (1987). USPTO's Automated Trademark Search System. *World Patent Information*, 9(1), pp. 5–9.

More recently, advancements in natural language processing and computer vision have improved the performance of automated trademark similarity searches, in part due to resolving the complexity of trademarks with respect to their visual, aural, and conceptual features.[124]

Trademark applications are filed with the USPTO, where an examining attorney reviews the application to ensure compliance with relevant regulations and that there are no conflicts with existing trademarks. Once the application passes review, it is published in the Official Gazette, a weekly publication of the USPTO that provides the public an opportunity to oppose the registration if they believe they will be harmed by it, for example, if the mark might be confusingly similar to an existing mark. Following that process, the trademark is registered and the owner gains exclusive rights in its use.

6.5.1.3 Trademark Loss

Once a trademark has been granted, though it does not expire like copyrights and patents, there are ways that it can be lost. First, if a trademark is not actively used in commerce for a certain period, typically three years, it can be considered abandoned. It is also possible to lose a trademark through failure to enforce it against infringers (since the mark can lose distinctiveness). Trademarks also have to be renewed at regular intervals, so that failure to renew, or a fraudulent registration, can result in cancellation.

Finally, a trademark can be lost through "genericide" – where a trademark or brand name becomes so commonly used to refer to a type of product or service in general, rather than the specific product or service, that it loses its ability to reduce consumer confusion. This typically happens over time as people start using the brand name as a generic term, leading to the trademark becoming a victim of its own success. Famous examples include terms like "Aspirin" and "Escalator." Sometimes trademark owners even attempt to prevent genericide with ad campaigns (e.g., "When you use 'xerox' the way you use 'aspirin' we get a headache").[125] A number of technology companies have faced the possibility of genericide – notably Google, who successfully fought against genericide in court when domain names including "google" were registered by other parties.[126] Adobe also includes a statement on their website that "trademarks are not verbs" (e.g., "the image was photoshopped").[127]

---

[124] Kim, J., Jeong, B., Kim, D., Kim, J., Jeong, B., & Kim, D. (2021). Is Trademark the First Sparring Partner of AI? *Patent Analytics: Transforming IP Strategy into Intelligence*, pp. 175–186. Springer.

[125] Hughes, E. C. (2018). A Search by Any Other Name: Google, Genericism, and Primary Significance. *American University Business Law Review*, 7, pp. 269–295.

[126] Elliott v. Google (9th Cir. 2017).

[127] Adobe. General Trademark Guidelines. Retrieved February 10, 2024, from www.adobe.com/legal/permissions/trademarks.html.

6.5.1.4 Trade Dress

Trade dress is a type of protection that refers to the visual appearance of a product or its packaging. It serves the same purpose as a trademark, in that it signifies the source of the product to consumers. It might encompass the design, shape, color, and texture of a product, as well as the graphics or packaging. Trade dress can also apply to computer interfaces, including the visual appearance and design aspects of software, websites, or UX designs. For example, Apple has been involved in litigation asserting trade dress rights over various aspects of its iOS interface.[128] In order for trade dress protection to apply, it must be distinctive and nonfunctional, and it must be associated in consumers' minds with a particular source or brand.

6.5.1.5 Unfair Competition Laws

Unfair competition laws in the United States are designed to protect businesses against deceitful or unfair business practices by competitors. These laws have been intertwined with trademark law since the late nineteenth century. Historically, courts have used unfair competition principles to address cases beyond the scope of trademark infringement and to justify expanded trademark rules. Although some have argued for merging trademark law and unfair competition into a single theory focused on protecting source-identifying marks, the distinction still persists.[129]

Unfair competition also covers trademark-adjacent issues such as false representation (which might include intentionally confusing consumers about a product's origins), false advertising (making misleading statements, including suggesting connections to another trademarked product), or passing off (when a business intentionally tries to pass off its goods as those of other business, e.g., through imitation of a trademark).

Outside of the Lanham Act, which covers some specific aspects of unfair competition such as "false designation of origin," additional unfair competition laws tend to be at the state law level. However, the FTC Act, as the federal law that established the Federal Trade Commission (FTC), also gives it the authority to protect consumers and promote competition in the marketplace, including prohibitions on unfair or deceptive acts or practices that affect commerce, such as false advertising, fraud, or antitrust violations.[130]

6.5.2 Domain Names

The popularization of the Internet presented a tricky problem for trademark law: domain names. A particular difficulty was that while domain names (or internet

---

[128] Apple Inc. v. Samsung Electronics Co., Ltd., 786 F.3d 983 (Fed. Cir. 2015).
[129] Bone, R. G. (2019). Rights and Remedies in Trademark Law: The Curious Distinction Between Trademark Infringement and Unfair Competition. *Texas Law Review*, 98, pp. 1187–1217.
[130] 15 U.S.C. § 41.

addresses) are handed out on a first-come-first-serve basis, trademark rights come from using the trademark and from federal registration. However, in the early days of the Internet, established companies were not always among the first to realize the importance of being online – so they were not always the first to register domain names associated with their business. Of course, that isn't the case today; as James Grimmelman points out in his Internet law casebook, any company or entrepreneur contemplating a new business name or trademark today knows to register the appropriate domain name as soon as possible, just in case.[131] However, this state of affairs led to the common problem of cybersquatting, where individuals or entities register domain names mirroring well-known trademarks, often intending to sell them to the trademark owner at a high price or to misuse the trademark's reputation. Such situations can lead to consumer confusion, as customers might mistakenly believe that the website is officially connected to or endorsed by the trademark owner.

Of course, using a trademark in a domain name without authorization may constitute trademark infringement, particularly when used to offer similar or competing goods or services. To address these challenges, in 1999 the Internet Corporation for Assigned Names and Numbers (ICANN) established the Uniform Domain-Name Dispute-Resolution Policy (UDRP), a mechanism allowing trademark owners to challenge domain names that are identical or confusingly similar to their trademarks.[132]

In cases of infringement or cybersquatting, trademark owners can seek legal remedies, including litigation, and courts have the authority to order the transfer or cancellation of such domain names. The Anti-Cybersquatting Consumer Protection Act (ACPA) in the U.S. was also enacted in 1999 to address the problem of cybersquatting.[133] The ACPA allows trademark owners to sue alleged cybersquatters in federal court and obtain court orders to transfer the domain name back to the trademark owner. In addition to providing a remedy for trademark owners, the act includes a provision for civil liability where a person registers a domain name that is identical or confusingly similar to a distinctive mark or dilutive of a famous mark, with the intention of selling the domain name to the trademark owner for financial gain. Overall, the intersection of trademarks and domain names represents an example of the difficulty in balancing the protection of intellectual property against the dynamics of emerging technology.

6.5.3 *Major Case Law*

Major trademark case law in the domain of HCI addresses a multitude of challenges that arise as users engage with software interfaces, online platforms, and

---

[131] Grimmelmann, J. (2017). *Internet Law: Cases and Problems.* Semaphore Press.
[132] World Intellectual Property Organization. WIPO Guide to the Uniform Domain Name Dispute Resolution Policy (UDRP). Retrieved July 24, 2024, from www.wipo.int/amc/en/domains/guide/.
[133] 15 U.S.C. § 1125(d).

various digital services. This section delves into court decisions that have shaped the understanding and enforcement of trademark rights in this area, from disputes over domain names to the contentious issues surrounding the look and feel of software.

Panavision International L.P. v. Toeppen (1998)[134]

- The dispute was over the registration of domain names containing the trademark "Panavision" by a cybersquatter. The court ruled in favor of Panavision, recognizing that Toeppen's actions constituted trademark dilution.
- This case established that the registration and use of domain names that infringe on existing trademarks can be prohibited.

Digital Equipment Corp. v. Alta Vista (1997)[135]

- Similar to the Panavision case, the dispute was over the use of a domain name: altavista.com as used by Alta Vista Technology, registered after the launch of Digital Equipment Corp's AltaVista search engine. The court ruled in favor of Digital Equipment Corp. and granted an injunction due to the fact that the search engine had gained significant public recognition and therefore its use by another company would create consumer confusion.
- This case demonstrated that even the use of a domain name for a legitimate business can infringe on an established trademark.

Microsoft Corp. v. Lindows.com, Inc. (2004)[136]

- This dispute was over the use of the term "Lindows" by Lindows.com for its operating system, which Microsoft claimed infringed upon its trademark "Windows." Following denial of a preliminary injunction due to questions about whether "Windows" was generic, the case ended up settling with Microsoft purchasing the trademark.
- This case highlighted the potential for a famous mark to be challenged as generic.

Multi Time Machine, Inc. v. Amazon.com, Inc. (2015)[137]

- This dispute was over whether Amazon's online search results created consumer confusion. MTM, a watch manufacturer, claimed that Amazon infringed their trademark by displaying alternative products in response to specific searches for their products, creating a situation where consumers would be confused about the source of a product. The court ruled in favor of Amazon and held that the use of MTM's trademark in the search query was not misleading.

---

[134] 141 F.3d 1316 (9th Cir. 1998).
[135] 960 F. Supp. 456 (D. Mass. 1997).
[136] 319 F. Supp. 2d 1219 (W. D. Wash. 2004).
[137] 804 F.3d 930 (9th Cir. 2015).

- This case established that clear labeling can protect online retailers from claims of trademark infringement and that descriptive use of trademarks in search functionality is not inherently infringing.

6.5.4 Enforcement and Remedies

Trademark law in the United States is enforced through legal frameworks that grant trademark owners the right to protect their marks against unauthorized use, similar to copyright enforcement. Trademark owners can bring legal action in federal court for infringement, where they can seek damages, injunctions, and orders compelling the destruction or forfeiture of infringing goods.

When a trademark owner believes their rights have been violated, they can initiate a lawsuit in either federal or state court, depending on the circumstances, such as the geographical scope of the infringement and whether the trademark is federally registered. Remedies in a civil trademark lawsuit can include injunctive relief (a court order to stop the infringing action), monetary damages (including the infringer's profits, any damages sustained by the plaintiff, and the costs of the action), and sometimes the recovery of attorney's fees. However, the entire process can be lengthy and costly, often encouraging parties to consider settlement or alternative dispute resolution methods such as mediation or arbitration before reaching trial.

Big tech companies are particularly known for aggressive trademark enforcement through both litigation and pre-litigation tactics – tactics that some have characterized as aggressive or anticompetitive.[138] For example, a 2020 hearing before the House antitrust committee included testimony from executives of smaller companies described by *Politico* as illustrating how "Apple, Amazon and Google wield their market dominance to bully smaller tech players with relative impunity."[139] One issue with trademark enforcement is that very large companies have the resources and money to file potentially meritless lawsuits, which then smaller companies (e.g., startups) do not have the resources to defend against them and may result in them simply leaving the market.[140]

State laws also offer protection and means of enforcement through unfair competition laws, often mirroring the principles of the Lanham Act. Common law rights are also recognized, allowing trademark owners to take action based on the actual use of a mark in commerce, even without registration.

---

[138] Pritchard, D. (2022). Big Tech Trademarks: Trademark Law Empowers Big Tech to Maintain Market Dominance. *Hastings Science & Technology Law Journal*, 13, pp. 101–126.

[139] Lylen, L. & Lima, C. (2020). Big Tech's "bully" tactics stifle competition, smaller rivals tell Congress. *Politico*. Available at: www.politico.com/news/2020/01/17/big-tech-competition-investigation-100701.

[140] Pritchard, D. (2022). Big Tech Trademarks: Trademark Law Empowers Big Tech to Maintain Market Dominance. *Hastings Sci. & Tech. LJ*, 13, pp. 101–126.

U.S. Customs and Border Protection (CBP) also plays a role in enforcing trademark laws by regulating the importation of goods into the United States to prevent the entry of counterfeit and potentially infringing merchandise. Trademark owners can record their registered trademarks with the CBP, which then actively monitors and inspects incoming shipments for counterfeit items. When CBP officers suspect that goods infringe on recorded trademarks, they can detain the shipment, notify the trademark owner, and ultimately seize the goods if infringement is confirmed.

6.5.5 Trademark and HCI

While trademark law provides a legal framework to protect the unique elements emerging from HCI research and practice that are associated with a brand, HCI research also offers insights and tools that can aid in the effective management and understanding of trademarks in the rapidly evolving digital landscape.

For example, HCI research often involves the creation of unique user interfaces, designs, or interaction experiences. When there is a desire to commercialize or brand these elements, trademark becomes relevant in their protection. HCI research can also influence how users perceive and interact with trademarks, especially in digital environments. For example, the way a trademark is integrated into a software interface might impact its effectiveness and the overall user experience.

HCI also has the potential to contribute to understanding of how trademarks function in the digital space – for example, how users recognize and respond to trademarks in various online contexts. This type of research might even help inform legal decisions about trademark distinctiveness and infringement. And of course, HCI expertise might really help in developing user-friendly tools for managing and researching trademarks. This includes interfaces for trademark registration, search databases, and tools for monitoring potential trademark infringements.

6.6 CONCLUSION

As noted at the start of this chapter, intellectual property becomes relevant for HCI both with respect to the potential creation of innovative technologies, and with respect to user experience, since IP law can influence how we interact with technology. IP law can provide incentive for inventors and creators and has the potential to foster collaboration and cooperation by enabling sharing between researchers, users, and technologists. Additionally, IP law has some ability to adapt and evolve to respond to the challenges and opportunities of new technologies.

However, there are also a number of common critiques of IP law that relate to technology, many of which are contradictory. It may be too restrictive in ways that stifle innovation and creativity rather than encouraging it, by granting excessive exclusive rights to IP owners who might limit use of their works, especially in digital environments. On the other hand, others think that it is too lenient, failing to protect the rights and interests of IP owners, especially given the difficulty of enforcing and monitoring IP in digital environments. There are also overarching concerns that IP law is outdated, not reflecting the realities of new technologies such as artificial intelligence. It is entirely possible that in the coming years, there will be reforms to intellectual property law largely driven by technological advancements.

7

Telecommunications

7.1 INTRODUCTION

Telecommunications technologies play a vital role in connecting people and supporting both social and business interactions through services like voice or video calls and internet-based platforms. These technologies enable access to information and promote learning, crucial for individual and societal progress, by enhancing human relationships. For example, the telephone revolutionized communication, and the Internet has further transformed it with instant messaging, video calls, and social networking. Given its impact on individuals and society, governments strive to balance the interests of telecommunications companies, consumers, and governments through telecommunication laws, regulations, and policies. The goal is to ensure that services are provided to individuals and communities fairly, safely, and equitably while fostering innovation and growth in the industry. Human–computer interaction (HCI) and telecommunications laws, regulations, and policies intersect in ways that shape both the design of technologies and the regulatory landscape. By aligning their design processes with legal mandates for telecommunication accessibility, privacy, security, and fair competition, HCI designers can not only comply with regulations but also improve the overall user experience. The rise of new telecommunication technologies, such as satellite phones, ubiquitous Internet of Things (IoT) devices, has raised new regulatory challenges, particularly around security, privacy, and interoperability. HCI designers can help regulators to ensure these devices provide privacy, security, and accessibility for all. By considering how people interact with technology, laws and regulations can be more effective in promoting usability, accessibility, privacy, security, and ethical standards. This interconnection between HCI, laws, and regulations is crucial for creating a technology landscape that serves the needs and rights of users while fostering innovation and compliance with laws and regulations.

HCI research often includes detailed studies on user needs, behaviors, and challenges. This data can inform policymakers about how users interact with telecommunication technologies, leading to policies that better address real-world issues. As laws evolve, HCI professionals can stay informed of regulatory changes by designing flexible, modular interfaces that can be easily updated to meet new legal standards. This proactive approach can save time and resources in the long run. HCI designers can leverage this evolution in the development of interfaces that comply with evolving legal and regulatory standards and be accessible for diverse users in terms of location, ability, or status. By involving HCI designers in policy development, user testing, accessibility initiatives, and new technologies, regulators can ensure that their policies lead to better outcomes for users, while promoting fairness, security, and inclusivity.

7.2 THE INTERSECTION OF HCI WITH TELECOMMUNICATIONS LAW

HCI professionals can leverage their understanding of telecommunication laws and regulations to design products that comply with legal requirements. This includes ensuring that interfaces adhere to standards for accessibility, data protection, and content regulation. For instance, indirect telecommunication services, called over-the-top (OTT), such as WhatsApp, operate over telecommunication networks, but are independent from telecommunications carrier services. While most countries provide emergency services over direct telecommunication services, some countries opted to provide indirect, OTT, text- and icon-based emergency apps for visitors and deaf and hard-of-hearing people. Investigations that included HCI professionals[1] showed that, while these OTT services were promising in terms of accessibility, few people downloaded these apps; and even if they did, these apps failed to connect with emergency services due to reliance on an internet connection for users to send emergency messages instead of voice or SMS. In emergency situations, lack of availability or failure in communication can have serious, even life-threatening, consequences. Given that telecommunications laws have traditionally regulated voice and SMS services, not internet-based messaging platforms, this creates an unequal and fragmented user experience for emergency OTT apps.

An example of the intersection of HCI and telecommunications is how understanding common user difficulties with accessing broadband services can play a crucial role in shaping policies aimed at increasing accessibility and affordability. Users in rural and remote locations often face significant challenges in accessing broadband services due to the high costs of infrastructure deployment and maintenance, and even in urban areas, there can be pockets where broadband service is unreliable or unavailable.[2] By understanding these challenges, designers can create more inclusive and user-friendly digital interfaces and experiences, for example,

---

[1] Haunschild, J., Kaufhold, M. A., & Reuter, C. (2022). Perceptions and Use of Warning Apps–Did Recent Crises Lead to Changes in Germany? In *Proceedings of Mensch und Computer*, pp. 25–40.
[2] Federal Communications Commission. (2021). 2021 Broadband Deployment Report. Retrieved December 15, 2024, from www.fcc.gov/reports-research/reports/broadband-progress-reports/fourteenth-broadband-deployment-report.

through designing for mobile devices with low bandwidth and high latency[3] through approaches such as supporting offline functionality, which lets users continue working even without an active internet connection, and then updating online when connectivity is restored. This can work in conjunction with designing interfaces that adapt based on the user's environment and device capabilities, for example, to simplify the interface when a user is on a low-bandwidth connection.

HCI research can provide evidence-based recommendations for user-friendly privacy and security features, which can influence regulatory frameworks for secure application-level telecommunications. For instance, research on the usability of security features like two-factor authentication (2FA)[4] has uncovered challenges that users face when setting up and using multiple security factors, such as complexity, inconvenience, or lack of understanding.[5] These findings have led to laws that encourage or require these features to be implemented in a user-friendly manner. Additionally, HCI professionals are critical in assuring that communication technologies meet regulatory standards and norms. For example, for 2FA, HCI professionals can help ensure that using the additional security factors can be completed with minimal steps and clear instructions. Similarly, to address convenience, professionals could incorporate security methods that balance security with convenience, such as biometric authentication (e.g., fingerprint or facial recognition) that is quick and easy to use.

To address diverse populations, including those from different cultural, socioeconomic, and geographic backgrounds, HCI practitioners can create applications that are not only more accessible and user-friendly but also better suited to the diverse needs of users and comply with local laws. For example, by using the user's location, telecommunication services can provide personalized content that is more relevant to the user's current context. For example, local news, weather updates, and event information can be tailored to the user's specific area. However, this requires professionals to be familiar and comply with local laws, regulations, and expectations. Compliance with local laws can minimize digital discrimination based on location (sometimes known as digital redlining) and ensure more inclusive products that do not disadvantage any user group based on geographic location, economic status, or other factors. Another way HCI professionals can assist with telecommunication services is to ensure that these services provide clear, standardized information about the services, such as transparent pricing or straightforward

---

[3] Wobbrock, J. O. (2006, April). The Future of Mobile Device Research in HCI. In *CHI 2006 Workshop Proceedings: What is the Next Generation of Human-Computer Interaction*, pp. 131–134.

[4] Reese, K., Smith, T., Dutson, J., Armknecht, J., Cameron, J., & Seamons, K. (2019). A Usability Study of Five {Two-Factor} Authentication Methods. In *Fifteenth Symposium on Usable Privacy and Security (SOUPS 2019)*, pp. 357–370.

[5] Marky, K., Ragozin, K., Chernyshov, G., Matviienko, A., Schmitz, M., Mühlhäuser, M., Eghtebas, C., & Kunze, K. (2022). "Nah, It's Just Annoying!" A Deep Dive into User Perceptions of Two-Factor Authentication. *ACM Transactions on Computer-Human Interaction*, 29(5), pp. 1–32.

pathways to cancel services or opt-out of data sharing, for example, FCC's nutrition labels,[6] which are modeled after nutrition labels found on food packaging. The goal is to make it easier for consumers to compare internet service plans and make informed decisions. Similarly, from a billing viewpoint, the Telecommunications Act of 1996,[7] Title VII promotes consumer choice and control over telecommunications services. Designers can leverage this prioritization of consumer choice and control over telecommunications services to create interfaces that give users greater control over payment.

7.3 TELECOMMUNICATIONS LAW IS NATIONAL, BUT HCI IS GLOBAL

Telecommunications technology has evolved from the early telegraph to today's complex global networks, enabling instant communication and data exchange. Samuel Morse's development of the telegraph and Morse code in the early 1800s marked the start of long-distance, electronic communication, drastically improving the speed of information transfer for business and government. As technology advanced, telecommunications policies and regulations also developed to address new challenges. Initially focused on standardizing telegraph and telephone services, regulations now encompass issues like data privacy, with bodies like the FCC guiding the regulatory framework. The development of telecommunication infrastructure, such as telegraph and telephone networks, led to the Communications Act of 1934,[8] which established the Federal Communications Commission (FCC) to regulate these industries. As the telecommunications networks became a tool for electronic communication, new laws were introduced, including the Computer Fraud and Abuse Act[9] (CFAA) and the Electronic Communications Privacy Act[10] (ECPA) in 1986. These laws addressed issues like unauthorized access to computer systems and protected electronic communications such as emails. For more information, please refer to the discussion of these laws in Chapter 4 (Privacy). The National Information Infrastructure Protection Act[11] (NIIPA), passed in 1996, updated the CFAA to include computers connected to the Internet and aimed to strengthen cybersecurity protections as the Internet became vital to national security and global commerce.

---

[6] Federal Communications Commission. (2022). Broadband Consumer Labels [Nutrition labels for broadband service]. Retrieved December 15, 2024, from www.fcc.gov/broadband-consumer-labels.
[7] Telecommunications Act of 1996, Pub. L. No. 104–104, 110 Stat. 56 (1996) (codified at 47 U.S.C. § 151 et seq.).
[8] Communications Act of 1934, ch. 652, 48 Stat. 1064 (codified as amended at 47 U.S.C. §§ 151–623).
[9] Computer Fraud and Abuse Act, 18 U.S.C. § 1030.
[10] Electronic Communications Privacy Act of 1986, Pub. L. No. 99–508, 100 Stat. 1848 (codified as amended in 18 U.S.C. §§ 2510–2523, 2701–2712, 3121–3127).
[11] National Information Infrastructure Protection Act of 1996, Title II of Pub. L. No. 104–294, §§ 201–203, 110 Stat. 3491 (codified as amended in 18 U.S.C. § 1030).

Yet telecommunications technologies, such as the Internet and mobile networks, transcend national borders, allowing users and businesses to interact on a global scale. So, understanding just U.S. law for telecommunications is insufficient. This borderless nature poses unique challenges for telecommunications laws and regulations, as data can be transmitted and stored in multiple countries, making it difficult to determine which jurisdiction's laws apply. Another factor is that businesses often serve customers from various countries, each with its own set of telecommunication regulations that typically need to be harmonized to comply with the most restrictive laws to ensure they are not violating any country's regulations.

For instance, if a designer works on a product to be available in both the United States and the European Union, they would need to comply with both the Telecommunications Act of 1996[12] and the European Electronic Communications Code[13] by incorporating all relevant requirements. One way would be to implement geo-location features to customize interfaces according to the user's location, ensuring compliance with local laws while providing a consistent user experience. The interfaces would likely need to provide localized content, language options, and region-specific features to cater to users in different jurisdictions, ensuring that interfaces meet local regulatory standards.

One example of an HCI lens would be to employ ethnographic methods[14] to immerse in the community and observe how people interact with technology in their daily lives. For example, research has shown that mobile phone technology can impact migration at the individual level, but at the expense of their home communities.[15] Similarly, research has shown that a digital divide exists for people from rural and regional areas, where they are less likely and confident to engage in digital health technologies.[16]

As global data flows increase, HCI professionals should be aware about laws that govern cross-border data transfers, like the 2023 EU-US Data Privacy Framework[17] (DPF), which is a framework designed to facilitate the transfer of personal data from

---

[12] Telecommunications Act of 1996, Pub. L. No. 104–104, 110 Stat. 56 (1996) (codified at 47 U.S.C. § 151 et seq.).

[13] European Parliament and Council of the European Union. (2018). Directive (EU) 2018/1972 of the European Parliament.

[14] Blomberg, J., Burrell, M., & Guest, G. (2003). An Ethnographic Approach to Design. In Jacko, J. A. & Sears, A. (Eds.), *The Human-Computer Interaction Handbook*, pp. 964–986. Lawrence Erlbaum Associates.

[15] Mikal, J., Grace, K., DeWaard, J., Brown, M., & Sangli, G. (2020). Domestic Migration and Mobile Phones: A Qualitative Case Study Focused on Recent Migrants to Ouagadougou, Burkina Faso. *PLOS ONE*, 15(8), p. e0236248.

[16] Jongebloed, H., Anderson, K., Winter, N., Nguyen, L., Huggins, C. E., Savira, F. Cooper, P., Yuen, E., Peeters, A., Rasmussen, B., Reddy, S., Crowe, S., Bhoyroo, R., Muhammad, I., & Ugalde, A. (2024). The Digital Divide in Rural and Regional Communities: A Survey on the Use of Digital Health Technology and Implications for Supporting Technology Use. *BMC Research Notes*, 17(1), p. 90.

[17] European Commission. (2023). *EU-U.S. Data Privacy Framework*. Retrieved August 12, 2025, from www.dataprivacyframework.gov/Program-Overview.

the European Union to the United States while ensuring adequate data protection standards, after the invalidation of the 2016 EU-US Privacy Shield.[18] HCI professionals would need to design interfaces that give users control over their data, in line with the DPF's emphasis on user rights. For example, they can design features that allow users to easily access, modify, or delete their data, and provide transparency about how and why data is collected. This helps identify barriers to technology adoption and usage.

By balancing the global nature of telecommunication use, and local laws and regulations, professionals will ensure that technology serves users effectively and equitably while complying with legal and ethical standards. For example, professionals need to be aware of how user data can be collected, stored, and used by services in one country and used by users in another country in order to comply with regulations that aim to protect user privacy and secure personal information.

7.4 U.S. TELECOMMUNICATIONS STATUTES AND REGULATIONS

The foundation of the U.S. national legislation is the U.S. Constitution, which provides a basis for telecommunications law primarily through the Commerce Clause[19] and the Necessary and Proper Clause,[20] which collectively empower the federal government to regulate interstate and international commerce, as well as ensure the protection of certain individual rights.

The Commerce Clause grants Congress the power *"to regulate Commerce with foreign Nations, and among the several States, and with the Indian Tribes."* This clause forms the constitutional foundation for federal regulation of telecommunications, as it allows Congress to legislate on matters that affect interstate and international communications. This clause has been the basis for a wide range of federal legislation affecting economic activity and has been interpreted broadly by the U.S. Supreme Court to encompass various aspects of interstate and international commerce, including telecommunications. The Commerce Clause justifies the FCC's power to regulate communications that cross state borders. For instance, radio and television broadcasts, telephone calls, and internet traffic typically do not remain confined within a single state; they cross state and national borders, thereby falling under the category of interstate commerce. The FCC's authority is grounded in its mandate to oversee and regulate these interstate communications to ensure fair and efficient service across the country, and its federal regulations on interstate commerce generally preempt conflicting state laws. For instance, in *Federal Radio Commission v. Nelson Brothers Bond & Mortgage Co.* (1933),[21] the Supreme Court

---

[18] U.S. Department of Commerce. (2016). *EU-U.S. Privacy Shield Framework Principles*. Retrieved December 10, 2024, from www.privacyshield.gov/EU-US-Framework.
[19] U.S. Const. art. I, § 8, cl. 3.
[20] U.S. Const. art. I, § 8, cl. 18.
[21] Federal Radio Commission v. Nelson Brothers Bond & Mortgage Co., 289 U.S. 266 (1933).

recognized the federal government's authority to regulate radio frequencies as part of interstate commerce, laying the groundwork for the FCC's later jurisdiction. The Internet inherently involves interstate and international communication, and this supports the FCC's role in regulating broadband internet access, managing spectrum allocation for wireless services, and overseeing digital communication.

The Necessary and Proper Clause grants Congress the power to make all laws which shall be necessary and proper for carrying into execution its enumerated powers, including those under the Commerce Clause:[22] *"The Congress shall have Power [...] To make all Laws which shall be necessary and proper for carrying into Execution the foregoing Powers, and all other Powers vested by this Constitution in the Government of the United States, or in any Department or Officer thereof."* This clause provides flexibility in the U.S. constitutional system by allowing Congress to pass laws needed to effectively execute its constitutional powers and to empower regulatory agencies and their actions based on the authority granted by Congress. For instance, in *United States v. Southwestern Cable Co.* (1968)[23] and *National Broadcasting Co. v. United States* (1943),[24] the Supreme Court upheld the FCC's authority to regulate broadcasting and cable through its grant of power to regulate areas not explicitly contemplated by the organic statute, as long as the regulations are within the scope of the purpose of the original statute. Where agency action is necessary to fulfill the agency's ultimate goal, the Court may not prohibit such action.

These two clauses, the Commerce Clause and Necessary and Proper Clause, provide a broad mandate for telecommunication regulatory powers.

The First Amendment is also a significant consideration in telecommunications law. The text of the First Amendment[25] reads: *"Congress shall make no law respecting an establishment of religion, or prohibiting the free exercise thereof; or abridging the freedom of speech, or of the press; or the right of the people peaceably to assemble, and to petition the Government for a redress of grievances."*

This restriction provides crucial protections for telecommunications services by safeguarding the free flow of information and preventing government censorship. It ensures that service providers can distribute content without undue interference, to protect users' rights to speak freely online, or to balance commercial speech with regulatory interests. The First Amendment requires the FCC to balance commercial speech with regulatory interests by ensuring that its regulations align with its protections for free speech while also serving substantial government interests, such as consumer protection, public safety, and the efficient use of communication resources, and to regulate broadcast TV,[26] cable TV,[27] or broadcast

---

[22] U.S. Const. art. I, § 8, cl. 18.
[23] United States v. Southwestern Cable Co., 392 U.S. 157 (1968).
[24] National Broadcasting Co. v. United States, 319 U.S. 190 (1943).
[25] U.S. Const. amend. I.
[26] National Broadcasting Co. v. United States, 319 U.S. 190 (1943).
[27] Turner Broadcasting System, Inc. v. FCC, 512 U.S. 622 (1994).

TV content.[28] As technology evolves, the application of the First Amendment to telecommunications continues to be a vital area of legal interpretation and policy development. However, this right is not absolute, as there are regulations regarding obscene, indecent, and profane content, especially on public airwaves.

Similarly, First Amendment protections extend to online platforms, protecting individuals' rights to express opinions, share information, and engage in public discourse, for example, on social media, blogs, forums, and other digital communication channels. While private companies that operate social media and other platforms have the right to set their own content guidelines, the First Amendment informs debates over how these companies manage and moderate content. Issues around censorship, misinformation, and hate speech are often discussed in the context of free speech rights. It also supports legal protections for journalists, including the right to protect confidential sources, which is vital for investigative reporting. It also protects commercial speech, including advertising. However, this protection is subject to greater regulation than other forms of speech, particularly to prevent false advertising and protect consumer interests. Overall, the First Amendment significantly influences telecommunications by protecting various forms of speech and expression, shaping the legal landscape for broadcasting and digital media, and guiding regulatory approaches to content and communication technologies.

The Fourth Amendment[29] protects against unreasonable searches and seizures, requiring any government search or seizure to be conducted with a warrant supported by probable cause. The text of the Fourth Amendment is: *"The right of the people to be secure in their persons, houses, papers, and effects, against unreasonable searches and seizures, shall not be violated, and no Warrants shall issue, but upon probable cause, supported by Oath or affirmation, and particularly describing the place to be searched, and the persons or things to be seized."*

It is a cornerstone for privacy laws that impact telecommunications by limiting the government's ability to access data, especially in the context of digital communications and stored electronic information. These limits include regulations on wiretapping, data retention, and surveillance by government agencies. Please refer to Chapter 4 (Privacy) for more information. To access private digital data, such as emails or files stored on personal devices or cloud servers, the government generally needs to obtain a warrant. The warrant must be based on probable cause and must describe the specific data to be searched or seized. Warrants for accessing data must be specific, detailing the scope of the search, including the type of data sought and the place where it is stored. Broad or overly general warrants that do not specify the exact data to be searched or seized may be challenged as unconstitutional. There are three main exceptions to the warrant requirement. The first

---

[28] Red Lion Broadcasting Co. v. FCC, 395 U.S. 367 (1969).
[29] U.S. Const. amend. IV.

one is consent, in which an individual consents to a search, freely and voluntarily. The second one is exigent circumstances, primarily emergencies with immediate threat to life, serious injury, or destruction of evidence. The third one is plain view doctrine, in which if the government lawfully accesses data and finds evidence of a crime in plain view, they may seize it without a warrant. However, this has limited application in telecommunications due to the vast amounts of data stored electronically.

The third-party doctrine is a legal principle in telecommunications law that emerged in the 1970s based on Supreme Court cases: *United States v. Miller* (1976),[30] which held that a person does not have a legitimate expectation of privacy in financial records held by a bank because those records are voluntarily conveyed to the bank as a third party, and *Smith v. Maryland* (1979),[31] which held that individuals do not have a reasonable expectation of privacy in the phone numbers they dial, which are conveyed to the telephone company for routing and billing purposes. These cases and subsequent cases held that individuals do not have a reasonable expectation of privacy for information voluntarily shared with third parties, such as banks, phone companies, or internet service providers. As a result, the government can often access this information without a warrant under the Fourth Amendment.

The courts have limited the application of the third-party doctrine in cases such as *United States v. Warshak* (2010)[32] and *Carpenter v. United States* (2018),[33] in part due to the finding that individuals often have little choice but to share their data with third parties to participate in society, due to ubiquitous third-party information storage. In the latter case, the Supreme Court ruled that accessing personal data requires a warrant, acknowledging that the ubiquity of stored personal data in telecommunications requires more robust privacy protections. These cases are triggering a broader reevaluation of how privacy is protected when data is shared with third parties in the context of modern telecommunications.

7.4.1 *Telecommunications Act of 1996*

The antecedent for the Telecommunications Act of 1996 was the FCC's trio of interrelated Computer Inquiries (Computer I,[34] II,[35] and III[36]) from the 1960s through 1980s, which analyzed problems posed by the convergence of regulated telephony

---

[30] United States v. Miller, 425 U.S. 435 (1976).
[31] Smith v. Maryland, 442 U.S. 735 (1979).
[32] United States v. Warshak, 631 F.3d 266 (6th Cir. 2010).
[33] Carpenter v. United States, 585 U.S. 296 (2018).
[34] Regulatory and Policy Problems Presented by the Interdependence of Computer and Communication Services and Facilities, 28 F.C.C.2d 267 (1971).
[35] Amendment of Section 64.702 (Computer II), 77 F.C.C.2d 384 (1980).
[36] Amendment of Sections 64.702 (Computer III), 104 F.C.C.2d 958 (1986).

with unregulated computing services and created rules and requirements designed to prevent cross subsidization, discrimination, and anticompetitive behavior.

The culmination was the breakup of AT&T's (American Telephone and Telegraph Company) near-monopoly over telephone services in 1982 to promote competition by preventing it from leveraging network control to stifle competition. These definitions became crucial in determining how different types of services would be regulated. The separation between basic telecommunications services and enhanced or information services compelled Congress to revise the Communications Act of 1934, with the Telecommunications Act of 1996.[37] The goal of the act was to promote competition and reduce regulation and barriers to telecommunications by providers by easing requirements for telecommunication platforms to promote competition, reduce regulation, and encourage the rapid deployment of new telecommunications technologies. It aimed to overhaul and modernize the regulation of the telecommunications industry. The Act sought to encourage competition, reduce regulation, and promote innovation in the telecommunications sector, which includes telephone, broadcasting, and cable industries. Furthermore, it updated the definition of telecommunications as follows: *"The term, 'telecommunications' means the transmission, between or among points specified by the user, of information of the user's choosing, without change in the form or content of the information as sent and received."*[38]

The Act also updated various aspects of telecommunications, including local and long-distance telephone services, broadcasting, cable television, and the internet sector. It has had profound and far-reaching effects on the industry and its regulation. It also established the Universal Service Fund[39] (USF) to ensure that all Americans, regardless of their geographic location or income, have access to essential telecommunications services at reasonable and affordable rates. It includes those in rural and high-cost areas, as well as low-income consumers or those with disabilities. The USF is funded through contributions from telecommunications companies, which typically pass the cost on to consumers as a universal service fee on their phone bills. The USF has played a vital role in expanding telecommunications infrastructure in rural and underserved regions, in supporting digital inclusion by improving access to broadband, and enhancing educational opportunities, health care delivery, and economic development through improved connectivity. The USF is a key cornerstone in making essential communication services universally accessible and affordable. It supports several programs, including the Lifeline program, which provides discounted telephone services to low-income households, and the E-rate program, which helps schools and libraries obtain affordable telecommunications and internet access.

---

[37] Telecommunications Act of 1996, Pub. L. No. 104–104, 110 Stat. 56 (1996) (codified at 47 U.S.C. § 151 et seq.).
[38] Ibid.
[39] 47 U.S.C. § 254 (1996).

The E-rate program[40] (formally known as the Schools and Libraries Program) is a federal initiative established under the Telecommunications Act of 1996[41] to provide discounted telecommunications and internet access to eligible schools and libraries in the United States, thereby helping to ensure that these institutions have affordable access to modern communication technologies. By offering discounts on telecommunications services, the E-Rate program helps to bridge the digital divide, particularly in underserved and rural areas where such services might otherwise be prohibitively expensive. While this funding helped bridge the digital divide by improving infrastructure, it did not cover user training.

7.4.2 Communications Decency Act of 1996 and Section 230

The Communications Decency Act of 1996[42] (CDA) was enacted as part of the broader Telecommunications Act of 1996.[43] It was designed to regulate and manage online content and communications in the rapidly growing internet environment of the mid-1990s. The CDA aimed to shield children from obscene or indecent material on the Internet. It sought to criminalize the transmission of obscene or indecent communications to individuals under eighteen years. To support this, it encouraged internet service providers (ISPs) and online platforms to monitor and moderate content without fear of being held liable for user-generated content. Parts of the CDA, particularly those attempting to regulate indecent content, were struck down by the Supreme Court in *Reno v. American Civil Liberties Union* (1997) for violating the First Amendment. The court ruled that the law's restrictions on indecent speech were overly broad and infringed on free speech rights.

The law has had a profound impact on internet regulation, particularly due to its famous Section 230.[44] Sometimes called "the 26 words that created the Internet,"[45] Section 230(c)(1) states: *"No provider or user of an interactive computer service shall be treated as the publisher or speaker of any information provided by another information content provider."*

Section 230 provides two main protections – provider liability protection, and content moderation protection. Providers are not considered the publisher or speaker of third-party content. This means they generally cannot be held liable for what users post on their platforms. For example, social media platforms like Facebook

---

[40] 47 U.S.C. § 254(h)(1)(B) (1996).
[41] Telecommunications Act of 1996, Pub. L. No. 104–104, 110 Stat. 56 (1996) (codified at 47 U.S.C. § 151 et seq.).
[42] Communications Decency Act of 1996 (CDA), Title V of the Telecommunications Act of 1996, Pub. L. No. 104–104, §§ 501–561, 110 Stat. 56, 133–137, 47 U.S.C. §§ 223, 230.
[43] Ibid.
[44] Communications Decency Act of 1996 (CDA), Title V of the Telecommunications Act of 1996, Pub. L. No. 104–104, §§ 501–561, 110 Stat. 56, 133–137, 47 U.S.C. §§ 223, 230.
[45] Kosseff, J. (2019). *The Twenty-Six Words That Created the Internet.* Cornell University Press.

or Twitter are not legally responsible for defamatory posts made by users. Similarly, providers may remove or restrict content they consider objectionable, as long as it is done in good faith, even if the content is constitutionally protected. This means that platforms are not considered publishers of user-generated content and are therefore not legally responsible for what users post, with certain exceptions.

Section 230(c)(2) of the Communications Decency Act (part of the Telecommunications Act of 1996) provides immunity for online platforms in their efforts to moderate or restrict content they deem inappropriate. It states that:

> No provider or user of an interactive computer service shall be held liable on account of (A) any action voluntarily taken in good faith to restrict access to or availability of material that the provider or user considers to be obscene, lewd, lascivious, filthy, excessively violent, harassing, or otherwise objectionable, whether or not such material is constitutionally protected; or (B) any action taken to enable or make available to information content providers or others the technical means to restrict access to material described in paragraph (1).

This clause provides platforms with protection from liability for moderating or removing content that they believe to be harmful or objectionable, even if the content would otherwise be protected by the First Amendment.

Section 230 has frequently been interpreted and applied by the courts in the context of lawsuits involving internet platforms, service providers, and users. This interpretation often involves determining whether a platform or service provider is protected by the immunity provisions of Section 230. It does not cover content that violates federal criminal laws, state or federal sex trafficking laws, or intellectual property laws. *Zeran v. America Online*[46] was the first major case applying Section 230. In that case, AOL was sued by an individual falsely accused of selling t-shirts mocking the Oklahoma City bombing, but AOL invoked Section 230. The court held that Section 230 protects AOL from liability as a publisher of third-party content and was found not liable.

The Fourth Circuit interpreted Section 230 immunity broadly, and the decision continues to shape how courts view Section 230. It has been the subject of significant debate and controversy. Critics argue that it allows platforms to evade responsibility for harmful content, including misinformation, hate speech, and illegal activities. Calls for reforming or repealing Section 230 of the Communications Decency Act have come from various political figures, organizations, and advocacy groups across the political spectrum. The Supreme Court in *Zeran v. America Online, Inc.* (1997)[47] noted that Section 230 is crucial for protecting free speech online by providing immunity to platforms for third-party content, thus enabling the diversity of content and innovation that characterizes the Internet. The ongoing

---

[46] Zeran v. America Online, Inc. 129 F.3d 327 (4th Cir. 1997).
[47] Ibid.

debate around Section 230 revolves around balancing the need for free expression with the need for accountability and responsible content management on the Internet. Section 230 immunity generally applies even if the platform is aware of or has actual knowledge of unlawful content posted by users, provided that it removes the content as soon as possible. This means that an online platform is not automatically liable for hosting illegal content simply because it knows about it. However, if a platform is involved in the creation or development of the unlawful content, it can lose Section 230 immunity. In this case, the platform is treated as an "information content provider" and may be held liable for the content, regardless of its awareness or knowledge.

Section 230 distinguishes between a "provider" of an interactive computer service (like a platform) and an "information content provider." If a platform itself acts as an "information content provider" by contributing to the development of unlawful content, it is not protected by Section 230 for that content. In the *Fair Housing Council of San Fernando Valley v. Roommates.com, LLC* (2008),[48] the platform required users to submit information about their gender, sexual orientation, and familial status and used this information to match potential roommates. Because Roommates.com actively developed the discriminatory content, the court ruled that it was an active participant as an "information content provider," and therefore it was not protected by Section 230. The distinction between being a passive and active intermediary is crucial in determining whether an online platform is protected by Section 230. Passive intermediaries, which simply host or transmit third-party content without contributing to it, are generally shielded from liability. By contrast, active intermediaries that participate in failing to act, or in creating or developing unlawful content may lose this protection and be held liable for the content.

In *Doe v. Internet Brands, Inc.* (2016),[49] Section 230 did not bar a negligence claim against a website operator who allegedly knew about a specific threat to a user but failed to warn them. However, this was based on the website's failure to warn, not on the content itself.

Courts have interpreted Section 230 immunity broadly to foreclose a wide variety of lawsuits and to preempt laws that would make providers and users liable for third-party content, starting with *Zeran v. America*.[50] For example, platforms have been allowed to invoke Section 230 to be held not liable even when they knew their services were being used for criminal activity. However, courts have interpreted the language providing that Section 230 will not "limit" or "impair the enforcement of" other laws as creating "exceptions" to Section 230.[51]

---

[48] Fair Housing Council of San Fernando Valley v. Roommates.com, LLC, 521 F.3d 1157 (9th Cir. 2008).
[49] Doe v. Internet Brands, Inc., 824 F.3d 846 (9th Cir. 2016).
[50] Zeran v. America Online, Inc., 129 F.3d 327 (4th Cir. 1997).
[51] See, for example, Universal Commc'n Sys., Inc., 478 F.3d at 418.

For example, if intellectual property laws would impose liability on a provider, then applying Section 230 to bar that lawsuit "would 'limit' the laws pertaining to intellectual property in contravention of § 230(e)(2)."[52] Accordingly, Section 230 immunity generally will not apply to suits brought under federal criminal law,[53] intellectual property law,[54] any state law "consistent" with Section 230,[55] certain electronic communications privacy laws,[56] or certain federal and state laws relating to sex trafficking.[57]

7.4.3 Digital Millennium Copyright Act (DMCA)

The Digital Millennium Copyright Act (DMCA)[58] introduced new protections for copyright holders while also providing safe harbors for providers. The DMCA is covered in Chapter 6 (Intellectual Property), but specific to Telecommunications, Section 512[59] provides safe harbor protections to service providers, shielding them from liability for copyright infringement committed by users, provided that the service providers meet certain conditions. The provider loses safe harbor protection if it has actual knowledge of specific instances of infringement on its platform and fails to act to remove or disable access to the infringing content. Likewise, it can lose its protection if it is "aware of facts or circumstances from which infringing activity is apparent" – often referred to as "red flag" knowledge. Courts have also recognized the concept of "willful blindness," where a provider cannot avoid liability by deliberately avoiding knowledge of infringement. If a provider intentionally ignores obvious signs of infringement, it may be deemed to have knowledge and thus lose safe harbor protection. In *Viacom International Inc. v. YouTube, Inc.* (2012),[60] actual knowledge and red flag knowledge were crucial in determining whether a provider can claim safe harbor protection, the standards are nuanced and context dependent. The case also reinforced that while providers are not required to monitor their platforms proactively, they must act when they become aware of specific instances of infringement. Willful blindness to infringement can also result in the loss of safe harbor protection, making it a complex and fact-intensive area of law. However, there are exceptions, such as for copyright infringement under the Digital Millennium Copyright Act (DMCA), where a notice-and-takedown procedure is used. It is a legal process that allows copyright holders to request the removal

---

[52] Gucci Am., Inc. v. Hall & Assocs., 135 F. Supp. 2d 409, 413 (S.D.N.Y. 2001).
[53] 47 U.S.C. § 230(e)(1).
[54] Id. § 230(e)(2).
[55] Id. § 230(e)(3).
[56] Id. § 230(e)(4).
[57] Id. § 230(e)(5).
[58] Digital Millennium Copyright Act, 17 U.S.C. § 512 (1998).
[59] 17 U.S.C. § 512 (1998).
[60] Viacom International Inc. v. YouTube, Inc., 676 F.3d 19 (2d Cir. 2012).

of infringing content from the Internet. It can also put an administrative burden on service providers to handle takedown requests, which can be significant, especially for smaller platforms. Overall, the notice and takedown system aims to balance the protection of intellectual property and other rights with content creators' rights and the public's access to information.

7.4.4 Twenty-First Century Communications and Video Accessibility Act

The Twenty-First Century Communications and Video Accessibility Act (CVAA),[61] enacted in 2010, was designed to ensure that individuals with disabilities have access to modern communication technologies, including advanced communication services (ACS)[62] such as email, text messaging, and video communications. While it is often discussed in the context of disability rights, its implications as a telecommunications law are equally important, particularly for HCI professionals. One of its most critical contributions is its application to hardware manufacturers. This includes any company that produces telecommunications devices capable of ACS, such as smartphones, tablets, computers, and other connected devices.

The CVAA requires that hardware used for advanced communication services (ACS), such as smartphones, tablets, and video conferencing equipment, must be designed to be accessible to individuals with disabilities. This means HCI designers must consider a range of disabilities, including visual, auditory, motor, and cognitive impairments, when creating these devices. For instance, hardware must include user interfaces that are usable by people with disabilities, such as the inclusion of screen readers for the visually impaired, tactile feedback for users with limited vision, or simplified navigation for those with cognitive disabilities on their phones. The design of physical buttons, ports, and other controls also needs to be accessible, such as including raised symbols or voice control options.[63] These questions reflect the evolution of telecommunications and tracking of legal developments and design and development legal implications.

The CVAA helps create a unified standard for accessibility across telecommunications hardware. This uniformity benefits users by providing consistent experiences across devices, which is particularly important as users transition between different platforms. HCI professionals can help ensure that all aspects of a device's interaction are accessible and user-friendly by working closely with hardware engineers, software developers, and accessibility experts. Designers can also leverage this

---

[61] Twenty-First Century Communications and Video Accessibility Act of 2010, Pub. L. No. 111–260, 124 Stat. 2751 (2010).

[62] Twenty-First Century Communications and Video Accessibility Act of 2010, Pub. L. No. 111–260, § 716, 124 Stat. 2751, pp. 2774–2778 (2010).

[63] Twenty-First Century Communications and Video Accessibility Act of 2010, Pub. L. No. 111–260, § 716, 124 Stat. 2751, pp. 2774–2778 (2010), 47 U.S. Code § 613 et. seq.

to do continuous research and user testing for iterative improvements and to ensure that devices continuously improve to meet the needs of all users.

7.5 THE FEDERAL COMMUNICATIONS COMMISSION

Beyond the constitution, foundational, enabling laws are required. The U.S. Congress passed the Communications Act of 1934,[64] which established the FCC, an independent agency of the United States government that regulates communications by radio, television, wire, satellite, and cable. The act established the FCC as a federally established independent agency directed by five commissioners who are appointed by the U.S. president and confirmed by the Senate. It has broad authority to regulate the telecommunications marketplaces to ensure that the "public interest, convenience, and necessity" is served. For example, the FCC strives to increase the deployment of broadband facilities, such as regulatory streamlining and grants and financing. Similarly, they require companies to provide telecommunications services on a nondiscriminatory basis at just and reasonable rates and terms. As telecommunications technologies evolved to touch many personal and commercial spheres of life, the other agencies have gained a role in telecommunications regulations. For example, the National Telecommunications and Information Administration (NTIA) advises the President on telecommunications and information policy, managing the federal spectrum, and promoting the development of telecommunications services through an enabling NTIA Organization Act.[65] The Federal Trade Commission (FTC)[66] regulates telecommunications primarily through its consumer protection and antitrust enforcement roles, and the Department of Justice's Antitrust Division[67] regulates telecommunications by enforcing antitrust laws to ensure competition. At the state level, each state regulates intrastate telecommunications services.

7.6 NET NEUTRALITY

The underlying principles surrounding net neutrality have been a topic of debate since the early days of the Internet, though legal scholar Tim Wu coined the term "network neutrality" in a 2004 law review article to describe the concept that ISPs should treat internet data equally – that is, to not slow down or speed up data based on preferences such as paid prioritization.[68]

---

[64] U.S. Congress. (1934). *Communications Act of 1934.* Pub. L. No. 73–416, 48 Stat. 1064.
[65] U.S. Congress. (1978). National Telecommunications and Information Administration Organization Act, Pub. L. No. 95–567, 92 Stat. 2402.
[66] The Federal Trade Commission. Retrieved January 3, 2025, from www.ftc.gov/.
[67] The Department of Justice's Antitrust Division. Retrieved January 3, 2025, from www.justice.gov/atr.
[68] Wu, T. (2003). Network Neutrality, Broadband Discrimination. *Journal on Telecommunications & High Technology Law,* 2, 141–178.

7.6 Net Neutrality

The FCC has used its authority under Title II of the Communications Act of 1934[69] (which includes provisions on common carrier regulation and covers issues like nondiscrimination, rate regulation, interconnection, and universal service obligation) to attempt to create and regulate net neutrality. Under Title II, Section 202[70] prohibits unreasonable discrimination by common carriers:

> It shall be unlawful for any common carrier to make any unjust or unreasonable discrimination in charges, practices, classifications, regulations, facilities, or services for or in connection with like communication service, directly or indirectly, by any means or device, or to make or give any undue or unreasonable preference or advantage to any particular person, class of persons, or locality, or to subject any particular person, class of persons, or locality to any undue or unreasonable prejudice or disadvantage.

Net neutrality has become a partisan issue, with Democrats generally supporting strong net neutrality protections and Republicans typically opposing them, advocating for less regulation.[71] The debate often centers around the role of the government in regulating the Internet. Proponents of net neutrality view regulation as necessary to protect consumers and ensure fair access, while opponents see it as government overreach that hinders free market dynamics.[72] The status of net neutrality remains a contentious issue in U.S. policy and law due to its significant implications for consumers, ISPs, technology companies, and broader societal values. Since 2004, the legal status of net neutrality has changed multiple times. As of early 2025, there is no legal requirement for net neutrality in the United States.

The two most recent actions related to net neutrality came in 2024 and 2025. In May 2024, the FCC adopted a new order to reclassify broadband as a "telecommunications service," thus making broadband providers subject to net neutrality regulations.[73] Industry groups challenged the order as unlawful, particularly in light of the Supreme Court decision in *Loper Bright v. Raimondo*[74] that overruled the concept of Chevron deference that had previously directed courts to defer to agency interpretations of laws. Refer to Chapter 1 for more details about Chevron deference. Within the first days of 2025, the 6th Circuit issued an opinion that rejected FCC arguments to uphold its statutory authority to impose net neutrality policies. As part of this decision, the Court classified broadband providers as offering an "information service" rather than "telecommunications service," which escapes common

---

[69] Communications Act of 1934, Title II, 47 U.S.C. §§ 201–276.
[70] 47 U.S.C. § 202 (1934).
[71] Net Neutrality: Both Sides of a Heated Debate. Retrieved January 3, 2025, from www.govtech.com/network/net-neutrality-both-sides-of-a-heated-debate.html.
[72] The Federal Net Neutrality Debate: Access to Broadband Networks. Retrieved January 3, 2025, from https://crsreports.congress.gov/product/pdf/R/R40616.
[73] Federal Communications Commission. Safeguarding and Securing the Open Internet. Adopted April 25, 2024. Available at https://docs.fcc.gov/public/attachments/FCC-24–52A1.pdf.
[74] 603 U.S. 369 (2024).

carrier regulations.[75] The *Loper Bright* decision allowed the court to reject long-standing deference to the FCC's technical and policy expertise.

Without net neutrality, HCI designers face the challenge of ensuring that applications and services remain accessible, efficient, and user-friendly in a landscape where traffic can be prioritized (and deprioritized) without notice. For example, users may face inconsistent experiences across different ISPs.[76] HCI designers may need to educate users about these discrepancies and provide transparency about how their app behaves under different network conditions. Designers could strive to inform users when their ISP is affecting the app's performance, potentially offering them the option to switch to a lower-data mode or alternative method of using the service, or to provide users with clear and helpful error messages that explain the situation and guide them through possible solutions. Others might consider partnerships with ISPs to ensure that their applications receive favorable treatment, though this could raise ethical concerns about inequality. In these cases, ethical considerations should guide the design process to ensure that all users have fair access to digital services. For instance, HCI designers would need to ensure that their interfaces and applications perform well across a range of network conditions. This includes optimizing load times, reducing the size of assets (such as images and videos), and implementing adaptive content delivery that adjusts based on the user's current bandwidth. If traffic prioritization becomes common, designers may need to account for tiers of service, where certain features or levels of performance are only available to users with higher-tier subscriptions or in prioritized traffic scenarios, as outlined in guidelines such as Android's Connectivity for Billions[77] or W3C Accessibility, Usability, and Inclusion Guidelines.[78] Designers should incorporate features that ensure equitable access to essential services, regardless of traffic prioritization, for example, during emergencies when timely access to information is critical, such as in wildfires. Alternatively, designers could implement fallback options for when network conditions are poor. For example, if a video call cannot be maintained, the application could switch to an audio-only call or text messaging.

The future of net neutrality in the U.S. will likely continue to be a subject of public debate and potential legislative action. The outcome of this debate has significant implications for HCI professionals in how they design interfaces and interactions to comply with the ever-evolving regulatory changes.

---

[75] Ohio Telecom Ass'n v. FCC, No. 24-3449 (6th Cir. 2025).
[76] Hildebrandt, C. & Wiewiorra, L. (2024). The Past, Present, and Future of (Net) Neutrality: A State of Knowledge Review and Research Agenda. *Journal of Information Technology*, 39(1), pp. 167–193; Easley, R. F., Guo, H., & Kraemer, J. (2016). From Network Neutrality to Data Neutrality: A Techno-Economic Framework and Research Agenda. Information Systems: Behavioral & Social Methods eJournal.
[77] Connectivity for Billions. Retrieved January 3, 2025, from https://developer.android.com/docs/quality-guidelines/build-for-billions/connectivity.
[78] Accessibility, Usability and Inclusion. Retrieved January 3, 2025, from www.w3.org/WAI/fundamentals/accessibility-usability-inclusion/.

7.7 INTERNATIONAL TELECOMMUNICATIONS POLICY AND STANDARDS

HCI designers rely on standards and guidelines developed by international agencies, such as the International Telecommunication Union (ITU) or World Wide Web Consortium (WWW) standards and guidelines to create accessible, interoperable, and secure telecommunication experiences. By incorporating global standards and internationalization best practices, designers can ensure that their interfaces are inclusive and compliant across jurisdictions. These standards not only help in creating universally compliant designs but also promote consistency, reliability, and trust across countries and jurisdictions.

The ITU's mission is to facilitate international connectivity in communications networks, and improve access to ICTs to underserved communities worldwide, among other responsibilities. Designers can ensure that their designs comply with ITU-T Recommendations to guarantee consistency and interoperability across different platforms and devices. For example, following ITU standards related to user interfaces, such as those for video and audio quality (e.g., ITU-T P.910[79] for video quality assessment), can help ensure high-quality and consistent user experiences. Similarly, ITU-T F.790[80] ensures ICT products and services are accessible to people with disabilities. Designers can use these standards to design interfaces that are inclusive and usable by a wider audience. Following these ITU standards can help HCI professionals ensure that their products comply with international regulations and are suitable for global markets. Furthermore, by designing products that meet ITU standards, designers can facilitate easier entry into international markets, where compliance with these standards might be required or expected. Designers would benefit from following relevant ITU-T Recommendations for their designs and incorporating these into the design and development processes.

For instance, the FCC uses ITU standards to ensure that its spectrum allocations, technical definitions, and coordination efforts for international telecommunications services align with global practices. This international alignment is essential to prevent interference and ensure smooth operation of telecommunications systems across borders. ITU Human Factors standards play a critical role in the design and usability of telecommunications systems, ensuring they are accessible and user-friendly, particularly for people with disabilities. While ITU Human Factors standards are not directly incorporated into U.S. law in the same way as technical standards related to spectrum or satellite communications, some of their principles

---

[79] International Telecommunication Union. (2008). Subjective Video Quality Assessment Methods for Multimedia Applications (ITU-T Recommendation P.910). Retrieved December 10, 2024, from www.itu.int/rec/T-REC-P.910.

[80] International Telecommunication Union. (2007). Telecommunication Accessibility Guidelines for Older Persons and Persons with Disabilities (ITU-T Recommendation F.790). Retrieved December 10, 2024, from www.itu.int/rec/T-REC-F.790.

have influenced U.S. accessibility regulations, such as ITU-T's Human Factors Recommendations related to the accessibility of telecommunications equipment and services (e.g., ITU-T F.790).[81] These discuss the importance of user-centered design, assistive technologies, and usability testing for diverse populations. These ideas are reflected in U.S. regulations requiring accessibility in telecommunications under the CVAA and FCC rules (such as the requirement for accessible telecommunications equipment and services).

7.8 WORLD WIDE WEB CONSORTIUM

A substantial part of all telecommunication technologies and regulations are now conducted over the web. Given the ubiquity of web technologies in telecommunications use, it is important for designers to refer to the World Wide Web Consortium (W3C)[82] standards and guidelines. W3C plays a vital role in harmonizing web standards with telecommunications networks and services. By developing standards that promote interoperability, accessibility, security, and performance, W3C ensures that web services can function seamlessly across different telecommunications infrastructures. HCI designers, developers, and telecommunications providers can leverage W3C standards to create products and services that are not only compliant with international regulations but also optimized for a wide range of devices and networks.

W3C standards provide the building blocks for robust and secure web platforms. By adhering to these standards, HCI designers can ensure that their designs are consistent and compatible across different telecommunication service stacks. Similarly, W3C has developed recommendations for issues related to telecommunication technologies and regulation issues, such as content security L3,[83] web authentication L2,[84] or federated credential management.[85] For example, designers can incorporate W3C recommendations for secure web development, such as using secure web connections (https), implementing content security policies (CSPs), and preventing cross-site scripting (XSS) attacks. These practices help protect user data and build trust in the telecommunication technology application stack level.

Similarly, designers can use W3C guidelines for internationalization[86] (often abbreviated as i18n, where the "18" represents the 18 letters between the "i" and the "n" in the word). It is the process of designing and developing software

---

[81] ITU-T F.790, Telecommunication Accessibility Guidelines for older persons and persons with disabilities, International Telecommunication Union, Telecommunication Standardization Sector, February 2007. Retrieved January 3, 2025, from www.itu.int/rec/T-REC-F.790.
[82] World Wide Web Consortium. Retrieved January 3, 2025, from www.w3.org/.
[83] Available at: www.w3.org/TR/CSP3/.
[84] Available at: www.w3.org/TR/webauthn-3/.
[85] Available at: www.w3.org/TR/fedcm-1/.
[86] Available at: www.w3.org/TR/international-specs/.

applications in a way that makes them easy to adapt to various languages, regions, and cultures without requiring extensive engineering changes. Designers should consider how the user interface can accommodate different languages, especially those with varying text lengths, reading directions, and character sets, through flexible layouts that can expand or contract depending on the length of text, especially since some languages (e.g., German) tend to have longer words, while others (e.g., Chinese) may use fewer characters to convey the same meaning, or that can be mirrored to adapt to both left-to-right (LTR) and right-to-left (RTL) languages. For example, Arabic and Hebrew are read from right to left, which requires mirroring the entire interface for proper readability. International standards agencies play a crucial role in harmonizing standards, leveraging their expertise to address the complexity of interfaces and interactions that easily adapt to various languages, regions, and cultures.

7.9 LEGAL ASPECTS UNIQUE TO U.S. TELECOMMUNICATIONS LAW

Telecommunications law has been and continues to be a rapidly evolving field in response to technological advancements, societal needs, and regulatory priorities. In the United States, telecommunication laws and regulations have developed as a combination of federal and state laws, industry self-regulation, and enforcement actions. HCI designers should be aware of the differences in reach and enforcement of these laws and regulations, but be able to provide a unified and simplified view for end users to understand their rights and to be transparent. In terms of laws and regulations, the telecommunications legal framework is usually split between statutes that set mandatory expectations and regulations that provide the detailed instructions necessary to implement and enforce those laws. Understanding the difference between them is crucial for comprehending how the legal and regulatory systems function together to govern behavior and ensure compliance. In essence, legislation sets out the "what" and "why" of telecommunications policy, while regulation deals with the "how." Both are essential components of the governance framework for the telecommunications industry.

Regulation translates broad telecommunication laws to narrow, actionable regulations.[87] To be more responsive and to address the complexity and possible conflicts, regulatory bodies are usually set up to quickly set up regulations for adaptation to changing circumstances and emerging challenges and narrow enough to minimize conflicts between potentially contradictory imperatives. Regulatory

---

[87] Crandall, R. W. (2001). The Role of Regulation in the Telecommunications Sector. *Brookings Institution*; Hazlett, T. W. (2003). Telecommunications Regulation: Regulatory Myopia or Rational Choices? *Journal of Legal Studies*, 31(S2), S521–S588; Hausman, J. A. (1997). Regulatory Reform in Telecommunications: The Case of the United States. *Journal of Economic Perspectives*, 11(4), pp. 119–136.

bodies often have specialized knowledge and expertise in their respective fields, enabling them to craft more precise and effective regulations. They can implement pilot programs or temporary measures to test new approaches before making permanent changes, or issue guidelines, advisories, and directives that provide immediate responses to emerging technologies and issues. They can also take enforcement actions, such as fines or sanctions, to ensure compliance with regulations.

Telecommunication technologies and policies vary widely across different domains due to the specific needs, technologies, laws, and regulatory environments unique to each. For example, in education, the biggest use of telecommunications is to access online resources, provide virtual classrooms, or promote collaboration among students. Telecommunication policies in education focus on improving access to technology, ensuring equity, protecting data privacy, and fostering digital literacy. They are typically shaped by governments, educational institutions, and international organizations. For example, many communities aim to bridge the digital divide to ensure all students, regardless of their language, location, or socioeconomic background, have access to technology and the Internet. HCI designers can help by designing interfaces that are available in multiple languages and culturally relevant by ensuring interfaces are easy to translate and can support multiple languages and that icons, symbols, and metaphors used in the interface are culturally appropriate for the intended audience. For example, certain colors, symbols, or design elements may carry different meanings in different cultural contexts.

There is very much a tug-of-war between the federal and state governments when it comes to Telecom. The Federal government, through the enabling Communications Act of 1934, established the FCC to regulate interstate and international communications by radio, television, wire, satellite, and cable. This Act gives the FCC broad authority over telecommunications, including the power to preempt state and local regulations that conflict with federal policy. The Telecommunications Act of 1996 further expanded federal control by promoting competition and reducing regulatory barriers in the telecommunications industry. The Act sought to create a national framework for telecommunications regulation, emphasizing the role of the federal government in overseeing and facilitating the development of new telecommunications technologies and services. The FCC has the authority to preempt state and local laws that it determines are barriers to telecommunications development. This preemption power is intended to create uniformity in telecommunications regulation and prevent a patchwork of local rules that could hinder the deployment of services like broadband internet that is inherently interstate.

States traditionally have the authority to regulate intrastate communications, such as local telephone service and cable television. However, the line between federal and state jurisdiction can be blurred, particularly with the advent of the Internet and broadband services that cross state boundaries. States have also enacted laws regulating the deployment of telecommunications infrastructure, such as cell towers and broadband networks, sometimes in ways that conflict with federal policies. Local governments have significant control over land use and zoning, which directly impacts the deployment of telecommunications infrastructure, such as cell towers, fiber optic cables, and small cell networks for 5G. Municipalities also play a critical role in managing public rights-of-way, which are essential for the installation and maintenance of telecommunications infrastructure. In response to inadequate service from private providers, some local governments have sought to create their own municipal broadband networks to ensure affordable, high-speed internet access for their residents. However, these initiatives often face legal challenges from state governments and telecommunications companies, leading to a complex legal landscape where local control is pitted against state and federal regulations.

Many cities have limited or expensive services by private providers. Many cities and towns have sought to develop their own networks to ensure that all residents have access to affordable, high-speed internet. Municipal broadband refers to internet services provided by local governments, and local governments feel they can fill gaps left by private companies, particularly in underserved rural or low-income urban areas. Many states, such as Missouri,[88] Nebraska,[89] or Texas,[90] have passed laws that restrict or outright prohibit local governments from building or operating their own broadband networks. These laws often reflect the influence of private telecommunications companies, which argue that municipal networks represent unfair competition because they are subsidized by taxpayers.

The courts have played a central role in adjudicating these conflicts. For example, in *Tennessee v. FCC* (2016),[91] the court ruled that the FCC did not have the authority to preempt state laws that restricted municipal broadband, highlighting the limits of federal power in this area. Going forward, a key challenge will be finding a balance between the need for a coherent national telecommunications policy and the desire of local governments to have a say in how infrastructure is deployed in their communities. This balance will require ongoing negotiation and, likely, continued litigation as courts seek to define the boundaries of federal, state, and local authority.

There can be opportunities for HCI professionals to build collaborative approaches that involve federal, state, and local governments working together to achieve shared goals. For instance, professionals could engage with the community to understand their specific needs, preferences, and pain points through surveys, focus groups, and public forums and use this feedback to tailor services that meet the unique needs of municipalities and their communities. Professionals could also consider implementing mechanisms for feedback from users, such as in-app surveys, user testing sessions, and customer support interactions, and use this feedback to make iterative improvements to the service, ensuring it remains responsive to community needs.

---

[88] Mo. Rev. Stat. § 392.410(7).
[89] Neb. Rev. Stat. Ann. § 86–575, § 86–594.
[90] Tex. Utilities Code, § 54.201 et seq.
[91] Tennessee v. FCC, 832 F.3d 597 (6th Cir. 2016).

As telecommunications is often an interstate activity, it is regulated primarily at the federal level, with an overlay of some state-level laws. Enforcement depends upon the specifics of the law or regulation. For example, Section 255 of the Communications Act of 1934 ensures that accessibility standards for telecommunications services and equipment are consistent across the United States, as administered by the FCC. This preemption prevents states from imposing conflicting requirements, promoting a uniform approach to telecommunications. For example, if the FCC requires certain features on phones to be accessible, a state law requiring different or fewer features could be challenged and possibly overturned.

7.10 FUTURE LEGAL QUESTIONS

Telecommunications is a broad field in which communications technology intersects with many other fields, including privacy, accessibility, education, and ethics. In terms of complying with telecommunication privacy laws and regulations, HCI professionals should consider laws and guidelines from these fields in designing user interfaces and interactions that comply with privacy, accessibility, educational or ethics laws and regulations.

HCI professionals need to be aware of how regulations will evolve to protect privacy and personal data in an increasingly digital and connected world. As more devices become internet-enabled, data privacy concerns will grow, potentially leading to new laws or amendments to existing ones. The balance between national security, corporate interests, and individual privacy rights will continue to be a contentious issue. HCI designers can leverage emerging technologies such as AI and high-bandwidth interfaces to shape the future of privacy in telecommunications through new types of natural interfaces and context-sensitive privacy interaction paradigms.

Similarly, with the increasing availability of 5G networks, how can HCI professionals ensure the accessibility and usability of telecommunication systems? The FCC has and continues to auction more bandwidth to support high-speed 5G cellular networks.[92] 5G offers high-speed data transfer, low latency, and the ability to connect many devices simultaneously. Professionals should work closely with network engineers, software developers, and cybersecurity experts to ensure that the design of 5G systems is cohesive and user-centered. They should design applications and services that take full advantage of these capabilities, ensuring that users experience the benefits of 5G, such as seamless video streaming, real-time gaming, and responsive smart home systems. This collaboration ensures that the technological advancements of 5G are matched by intuitive, accessible, and secure user interfaces. They should also involve stakeholders from different areas, including accessibility advocates, privacy experts, and end users, in the design process to ensure that the final

---

[92] Available at: www.fcc.gov/5G.

product meets diverse needs and adheres to best practices. For instance, professionals could leverage the low latency of 5G to provide real-time feedback in user interactions and instantly respond to user inputs, improving the overall user experience, particularly in applications where immediate feedback is crucial, such as health care or smart home systems.

When HCI professionals work on telecommunication systems that span states and countries, they should consider the impact of international laws on telecommunications design and operation that support users' navigation of complex legal requirements related to data sovereignty and international data transfer. As telecommunication services increase their reach and ubiquity across all people in a state or country, HCI professionals would benefit from tracking their legal responsibilities to ensure that telecommunications services are accessible to all users, including those with disabilities.

In terms of incorporating legal requirements, HCI professionals can ensure that the design of telecommunications products and services comply with regulations related to privacy, security, accessibility, and consumer protection. They can also select appropriate HCI strategies, particularly in the design of systems that collect and utilize user data to comply with legal frameworks regarding data collection, processing, and sharing, and influencing aspects like user consent, data portability, and the right to be forgotten. As telecommunications platforms manage user-generated content, legal standards can guide the design of content moderation tools and systems, balancing freedom of expression with responsibilities to control harmful content. For international telecommunications, HCI professionals who are familiar with international laws and regulations can effectively address the challenge of designing systems that comply with these international laws and regulations.

Finally, HCI professionals can contribute insights into user behavior and technology design in the development of telecommunications policies and regulations, especially through collaborative efforts between legal experts and HCI researchers that can lead to more effective telecommunications technologies that respect legal norms and address user needs.

8

Artificial Intelligence

8.1 INTRODUCTION

Artificial intelligence (AI) has been an important component of research and practice in HCI and beyond for many years, but particularly since the widespread release of new generative AI tools in 2022 and 2023, there has been a significant increase in public awareness and conversation around the integration of AI into our lives. Unsurprisingly, given the speed of advancements in this space, legal frameworks for AI are still in early stages. As with many new technologies, legal rules are often reactive (and based on adverse events) rather than proactive. Particularly in the context of fast-moving technical situations, initial legal rules are often those that can be implemented quickly such as executive orders (see Chapter 1) or those resulting from case law, rather than a substantial body of statutes and regulations that take more time to develop.

AI broadly refers to any computer system that performs tasks typically associated with human intelligence;[1] this definition covers a lot of ground and includes contexts that have been studied within HCI for many years, such as mental health prediction and support[2] or recommender systems,[3] to currently hot topics such as chatbots[4] and image generation.[5] A 2023 special issue on AI for the *International Journal of Human-Computer Interaction* included research papers on topics such

---

[1] Russell, S. J. & Norvig, P. (2016). *Artificial Intelligence: A Modern Approach*. Pearson.
[2] Thieme, A., Belgrave, D., & Doherty, G. (2020). Machine Learning in Mental Health: A Systematic Review of the HCI Literature to Support the Development of Effective and Implementable ML Systems. *ACM Transactions on Computer-Human Interaction (TOCHI)*, 27(5), pp. 1–53.
[3] Calero Valdez, A., Ziefle, M., & Verbert, K. (2016). HCI for Recommender Systems: The Past, the Present and the Future. In *Proceedings of the ACM Conference on Recommender Systems*, pp. 123–126.
[4] Rapp, A., Boldi, A., Curti, L., Perrucci, A., & Simeoni, R. (2024). How Do People Ascribe Humanness to Chatbots? An Analysis of Real-World Human-Agent Interactions and a Theoretical Model of Humanness. *International Journal of Human–Computer Interaction*, 40(19), pp. 6027–6050.
[5] Mack, K. A., Qadri, R., Denton, R., Kane, S. K., & Bennett, C. L. (2024). "They Only Care to Show Us the Wheelchair": Disability Representation in Text-to-Image AI Models. In *Proceedings of the ACM CHI Conference on Human Factors in Computing Systems*, pp. 1–23.

as trust, transparency, explainability, responsible AI, human–AI interaction and teaming, chatbots, and health and well-being applications.[6] There is also already an international community of researchers working on what is known as human-centered AI,[7] and major research centers at universities including Stanford and the University of Maryland.[8]

With respect to the quickly shifting legal landscape, HCI as a field is important to AI regulation due to how much of that regulation is based on how humans use and/ or are impacted by AI. This includes understanding those impacts for the purpose of crafting regulation and responding to the sociotechnical requirements of those regulations. For example, there is a need for interfaces that make AI-driven decisions transparent and understandable to users, to help identify biases and unintended consequences of AI, to guide more responsible AI development, and to promote trust and help users feel in control.

You may notice that this is the only chapter in this book focused on a specific technology rather than on a legal concept. In the context of emerging technology, there is a longstanding debate about whether such technological contexts require new specialized legal frameworks or whether existing laws can be applied as-is. This debate largely originated in the early days of internet regulation, culminating in Judge Frank Easterbrook's essay "Cyberspace and the Law of the Horse," with the general argument that legal scholars do not develop knowledge by studying "horse law," but instead how concepts such as torts and property law apply to horses.[9] Lawrence Lessig (author of *Code: And Other Laws of Cyberspace*) famously responded that the horse analogy overlooked how cyberspace created unique regulatory challenges and that specialized doctrines and tools are sometimes needed.[10] Technology law scholar Ryan Calo later drew parallels between cyberspace and robotics in this context, ultimately arguing that regulation for emerging technologies such as AI and robotics requires an understanding of when that technology's novel features matter legally and when they do not.[11]

Given the evolving and fast-moving nature of AI and its regulation in this present moment, there is still much debate about when new legal frameworks are required and when existing laws and precedent suffice.[12] Some court rulings have already

---

[6] Antona, M., Margetis, G., Ntoa, S., & Degen, H. (2023). Special Issue on AI in HCI. *International Journal of Human–Computer Interaction*, 39(9), pp. 1723–1726.
[7] Human-Centered AI. Available at: https://hcai.site/.
[8] Human-Centered Artificial Intelligence. Available at: hai.stanford.edu/; Values-Centered Artificial Intelligence. Available at: vcai.umd.edu/.
[9] Easterbrook, F. H. (1996). Cyberspace and the Law of the Horse. *The University of Chicago Legal Forum 1996*, pp. 207–216.
[10] Lessig, L. (1999). The Law of the Horse: What Cyberlaw Might Teach. *Harvard Law Review*, 113, pp. 501–546.
[11] Calo, R. (2015). Robotics and the Lessons of Cyberlaw. *California Law Review*, 103, pp. 513–563.
[12] In Chapter 3, there is a similar argument about whether the nexus rule, which originates from before the days of the web, is an appropriate and relevant rule for website accessibility.

applied longstanding rules to AI contexts; for example, both *Thaler v. Hirshfeld*[13] and *Thaler v. Vidal*[14] held that under U.S. patent law, only humans can be recognized as inventors.

In other cases, such as autonomous-vehicle (AV) technology, which is still in its relative infancy, there are not many foundational court decisions in the way we might see for more established areas of law. California has been a pioneer in regulating the testing[15] and deployment of AVs, setting comprehensive standards through its Department of Motor Vehicles (DMV), with regular updates since then. Several other states have either adopted similar regulations inspired by California's framework or incorporated elements of California's approach into their own autonomous vehicle policies,[16] to ensure public safety, promote innovation, and create a standardized approach to AV integration across different jurisdictions. Most disputes so far have involved, for example, (1) trade secret and intellectual property issues, (2) product liability lawsuits after crashes, or (3) regulatory or criminal investigations, rather than high-level judicial precedent.[17] As a result, user-interface (UI) designers for self-driving cars operate in something of a legal gray area. The lack of legal precedent in autonomous-vehicle litigation may therefore result in cautious, often overly conservative user-interface design. Without clear mandates, professionals rely on best practices, internal risk assessments, and regulatory signals to guide how they alert and inform drivers.[18]

For other AI contexts such as privacy, bias, or deepfakes, there has been more pending or enacted legislation, especially at the state level to govern specifics of AI-enabled tools. In the 2025 legislative session, all 50 states, Puerto Rico, the Virgin Islands, and Washington, D.C. introduced or enacted legislation related to AI, from Montana's "Right to Compute" law that sets requirements for critical infrastructure controlled by an AI system, to Oregon's law that specifies that AI agents cannot use licensed medical professionals' titles, to multiple new state laws around deceptive deepfakes in the context of elections.[19]

There are a number of categories of law, many of which have already been discussed in this book, that are highly relevant in the context of AI. For example, Paul Ohm, Margot Kaminski, and Andrew Selbst's forthcoming casebook on AI law covers topics such as product liability, bias and discrimination, data privacy,

---

[13] Thaler v. Hirshfeld, 559 F. Supp. 3d 238 (E.D. Va. 2021).
[14] Thaler v. Vidal, 42 F.4th 597 (Fed. Cir. 2022).
[15] Cal. Code Regs. Tit. 13, § 227.00 et. seq.
[16] National Council of State Legislatures. Autonomous Vehicles Legislation Database. Retrieved January 2, 2025, from www.ncsl.org/transportation/autonomous-vehicles-legislation-database.
[17] Smith, B. W. (2017). Automated Driving and Product Liability. *Michigan State Law Review 1*, pp. 1–74.
[18] Ibid.
[19] National Council of State Legislatures. (July 10, 2025). Artificial Intelligence 2025 Legislation. Retrieved August 12, 2025, from www.ncsl.org/technology-and-communication/artificial-intelligence-2025-legislation.

generative AI and copyright, speech harms, and medical malpractice.[20] Based on a rights-based framework, the White House's 2022 Blueprint for an AI Bill of Rights (which provided principles that could guide future regulation) focused on the topics of safety, algorithmic discrimination, data privacy, notice and explanation, and human fallbacks.[21] President Biden's Executive Order on Safe, Secure, and Trustworthy Artificial Intelligence, signed in October 2023 and drafted with the intention to "ensure that America leads the way in seizing the promise and managing the risks of artificial intelligence," directed various actions around safety and security standards, privacy protections, equity and civil rights, consumer protection, and worker support.[22] After President Trump revoked this Executive Order in January 2025, he issued a new Order titled "Removing Barriers to American Leadership in Artificial Intelligence" that shifted the federal approach toward reducing regulatory constraints.[23]

In this chapter, rather than focusing on specific relevant legal frameworks or proposed regulations, we will describe a few areas of interest at the intersection of AI and HCI that are likely to be legally significant in the coming years. We will note existing regulatory actions where relevant. However, it is important to know that much of what is discussed here may be quickly outdated.[24] The following topics are also not comprehensive, and were chosen as interesting, important, and human-centered examples.

8.2 DEEPFAKES

Though there is not a single universally accepted definition of "deepfake," the term typically refers to hyper-realistic but fabricated video, audio, or visual content, most commonly generated by AI.[25] Sometimes legal definitions will be more specific; for example, a Colorado law enacted in 2024 defines deepfake as "*an image,*

---

[20] Ohm, P., Kaminski, M., Selbst, A. Artificial Intelligence and Law Casebook 1.0: Table of Contents. Retrieved January 2, 2025, from https://aila.ws/docs/ailaw.ToC.fall2023.pdf.

[21] Office of Science and Technology Policy. (2022, October). Blueprint for an AI Bill of Rights: Making automated systems work for the American people. The White House. Available at: https://bidenwhitehouse.archives.gov/ostp/ai-bill-of-rights/.

[22] The White House. (October 30, 2023). Executive Order on Safe, Secure, and Trustworthy Development and Use of Artificial Intelligence. Available at: bidenwhitehouse.archives.gov/briefing-room/presidential-actions/2025/01/14/executive-order-on-advancing-united-states-leadership-in-artificial-intelligence-infrastructure/.

[23] The White House. (January 23, 2025). Removing Barriers to American Leadership in Artificial Intelligence. Available at: www.whitehouse.gov/presidential-actions/2025/01/removing-barriers-to-american-leadership-in-artificial-intelligence/.

[24] For example, between the time that we turned in the final copy of this book to the publisher in early January 2025 and when we received copyedits in August 2025, the landscape of federal AI regulation in the United States shifted dramatically.

[25] Birrer, A. & Just, N. (2024). What We Know and Don't Know about Deepfakes: An Investigation into the State of the Research and Regulatory Landscape. New Media & Society, Article 14614448241253138, pp. 1–20.

video, audio, or multimedia AI-generated content that falsely appears to be authentic or truthful and which features a depiction of an individual appearing to say or do something the individual did not say or do."[26]

Empirical research has surfaced key regulatory challenges around deepfakes. Detection is a significant problem, with respect to people's difficulty in detecting this fabricated media; a 2024 review of computer science literature on this topic revealed that across studies, participants could identify less than two thirds of deepfakes.[27] HCI research will continue to be important in addressing this problem, which is currently very challenging; for example, a study published in *Computers in Human Behavior* evaluated detection strategies such as informing participants of common deepfake artifacts and found that these strategies did not improve detection accuracy or confidence.[28]

Though technological solutions for rapid detection have been proposed as ways to mitigate potential harms of deepfake technology (which include but are not limited to manipulation of elections, undermining journalism and public safety, jeopardizing national security, and exacerbating social divisions), as legal scholars Robert Chesney and Danielle Citron note, it would be foolish to trust that technology will definitely be capable of delivering a solution scalable and reliable enough to minimize these harms.[29] Accordingly, there have been a number of proposed legal solutions that include a mix of civil and criminal liability, from outright bans to private causes of action to platform liability.[30]

At the state level in the U.S., there have also been proposed or enacted laws on this topic, often tied to specific use cases or harms.[31] Social science and HCI research has surfaced disinformation and deepfake pornography as major societal threats and regulatory challenges of deepfakes,[32] and accordingly these are common areas for legislative action, along with expansion of regulation around defamation.

For example, California, Colorado, and Texas have all enacted laws that specifically target the use of deepfakes in a window of time prior to an election.

---

[26] CO Rev Stat §1-46-102.
[27] Birrer, A. & Just, N. (2024). What We Know and Don't Know about Deepfakes: An Investigation into the State of the Research and Regulatory Landscape. New Media & Society, Article 14614448241253138, pp. 1–20.
[28] Somoray, K. & Miller, D. J. (2023). Providing Detection Strategies to Improve Human Detection of Deepfakes: An Experimental Study. *Computers in Human Behavior*, 149, Article 107917, pp. 1–8.
[29] Chesney, B. & Citron, D. (2019). Deep Fakes: A Looming Challenge for Privacy, Democracy, and National Security. *California Law Review*, 107, pp. 1753–1819.
[30] Ibid.
[31] National Council of State Legislatures. (July 10, 2025). Artificial Intelligence 2025 Legislation. Retrieved August 12, 2025, from www.ncsl.org/technology-and-communication/artificial-intelligence-2025-legislation.
[32] Birrer, A. & Just, N. (2024). What We Know and Don't Know about Deepfakes: An Investigation into the State of the Research and Regulatory Landscape. New Media & Society, Article 14614448241253138, pp. 1–20.

A California regulation ("Elections: Deceptive Audio or Visual Media")[33] prohibits distributing "materially deceptive audio or visual media" of a candidate within 60 days of an election if it is done with the intent to harm the candidate's reputation or deceive voters, and an update in 2024 ("Defending Democracy From Deepfake Deception Act")[34] imposes certain removal obligations on large online platforms during the 120 days leading up to an election, along with disclosure requirements that extend beyond that period. Texas regulations on political advertising and campaign communications[35] now make it unlawful to create or distribute a "deep fake video" intended to harm a candidate or influence an election's outcome if it is published within 30 days of an election, and Colorado's Candidate Elections Deepfake Disclosures Act[36] provides for a civil action for "improperly disclosed" deepfakes with "reckless disregard as to the deceptiveness" of communication related to a political candidate. These laws aim to protect the electoral process by penalizing the knowing use of deceptive synthetic media (deepfakes) to mislead voters close to an election, which is an area where additional HCI research into the nature and impact of deepfakes could continue to be helpful. As election cycles continue and deepfake technology evolves, more states are expected to join this regulatory push, creating a gradually expanding patchwork of AI and election laws.

Deepfakes were also an important component of President Biden's Executive Order on the Safe, Secure, and Trustworthy Development and Use of Artificial Intelligence, which included in part marching orders for various government agencies to provide recommendations, for example, "reasonable steps to watermark or otherwise label output from generative AI."[37] During the signing of the Order in October 2023, President Biden mentioned that his staff had shown him a deepfake video of himself in order to show how the technology could be used to convincingly create a presidential statement that never happened.[38] In explaining the Order's efforts toward encouraging watermarking as a technological solution, President Biden spoke of the importance of knowing that when a loved one hears your voice on the phone, "they know it's really you."[39] President Trump's new Executive Order on AI did not include any provisions addressing synthetic media or content

---

[33] Calif. AB-730, ch. 493, 2019–2020 Leg., Reg. Sess. (Cal. 2019) (codified at Cal. Elec. Code § 20010).
[34] Calif. AB-2655, ch. 261, 2023–24 Leg., Reg. Sess. (Cal 2024) (codified at Cal. Elec. Code § 20510).
[35] Texas S.B. 751, 86th Leg., R.S. (2019). (codified at Tx. Elec. Code § 255.004).
[36] Col. HB24–1147 (2024). (codified at C.R.S. §1–46-102).
[37] The White House. (October 30, 2023). Executive Order on Safe, Secure, and Trustworthy Development and Use of Artificial Intelligence. Available at: bidenwhitehouse.archives.gov/briefing-room/presidential-actions/2025/01/14/executive-order-on-advancing-united-states-leadership-in-artificial-intelligence-infrastructure/.
[38] Kang, C. & Sanger, D. E. (October 30, 2023). Biden Issues Executive Order to Create A.I. Safeguards. *The New York Times*. Available at: www.nytimes.com/2023/10/30/us/politics/biden-ai-regulation.html.
[39] Ibid.

authentication.[40] However, in May 2025 he signed into law the first federal regulation specifically addressing deepfakes; the Tools to Address Known Exploitation by Immobilizing Technological Deepfakes on Websites and Networks Act (TAKE IT DOWN Act) focuses on non-consensual intimate imagery ("revenge porn") that is posted to online platforms, including "digital forgeries."[41]

HCI research can provide approaches to aid users in better understanding and combating the problem of deepfakes in various domains. For instance, studies have shown how deepfake videos affect public perceptions and trust in news sources,[42] as well as how fabricated video content can disrupt democratic processes by undermining the reliability of recorded evidence.[43] HCI researchers and professionals have also proposed and created designs for user interfaces that increase awareness on when and how content has been manipulated.[44]

8.3 BIAS AND DISCRIMINATION

Legally, bias typically refers to a prejudice or predisposition that compromises the impartiality or fairness of a decision-maker or process. For instance, Black's Law Dictionary describes "bias" as: "A mental inclination or tendency; an inclination or preconceived opinion; a predisposition to decide a cause or an issue in a certain way that does not leave the mind perfectly open to conviction."[45] Discrimination, in turn, legally refers to differential or unfair treatment of a person (or group) based on characteristics such as race, color, religion, sex, national origin, age, or disability, in a way that deprives them of rights or opportunities afforded to others. Black's Law Dictionary describes discrimination as: "The effect of a law or established practice that confers privileges on a certain class or that denies privileges to a certain class because of race, age, sex, nationality, religion, or handicap.... The unfair treatment or denial of normal privileges to persons because of their

---

[40] The White House. (January 23, 2025). Removing Barriers to American Leadership in Artificial Intelligence. Available at: www.whitehouse.gov/presidential-actions/2025/01/removing-barriers-to-american-leadership-in-artificial-intelligence/.

[41] Pub. L. 119-12, 2025.

[42] Vaccari, C. & Chadwick, A. (2020). Deepfakes and Disinformation: Exploring the Impact of Synthetic Political Video on Deception, Uncertainty, and Trust in News. *Social Media + Society*, 6(1), pp. 1–13.

[43] Maras, M.-H. & Alexandrou, A. (2019). Determining Authenticity of Video Evidence in the Age of Artificial Intelligence and in the Wake of Deepfake Videos. *The International Journal of Evidence & Proof*, 23(3), pp. 255–262.

[44] Sherman, I. N., Stokes, J. W., & Redmiles, E. M. (2021). Designing Media Provenance Indicators to Combat Fake Media. In *Proceedings of the 24th International Symposium on Research in Attacks, Intrusions and Defenses*, pp. 324–339; Vaccari, C. & Chadwick, A. (2020). Deepfakes and Disinformation: Exploring the Impact of Synthetic Political Video on Deception, Uncertainty, and Trust in News. *Social Media + Society*, 6(1), pp. 1–13; Wu, Y. K., Sohrawardi, S. J., Gerstner, C. R., & Wright, M. (2025). Understanding and Empowering Intelligence Analysts: User-Centered Design for Deepfake Detection Tools. In *Proceedings of the 2025 CHI Conference on Human Factors in Computing Systems*, pp. 1–26.

[45] Garner, B. A. (Ed.). (2019). *Black's Law Dictionary* (11th ed.). Thomson Reuters.

race, age, sex, nationality, religion, or handicap."[46] In other words, discrimination is the outward manifestation of bias in the form of actions, policies, or practices that treat people differently, usually unfairly, based on characteristics such as race, gender, disability, or other protected attributes. It involves measurable, tangible behavior such as denying someone a job or service due to their membership in a particular group.

In technology contexts, bias can inadvertently produce results that systematically disadvantage certain groups or perspectives, which often stems from unrepresentative data, flawed assumptions in algorithm design, or other systemic factors present in training data, the techniques or processes used to create the technology, or the context in which the technology is applied. Bias also reflects systemic inequalities and societal biases embedded within data and organizational cultures.[47] For instance, AI systems inadvertently embody ableist assumptions, such as speech recognition tools that struggle with atypical speech or interfaces that ignore screen-reader compatibility. Ableism becomes embedded in datasets and models when developers fail to include people with disabilities in research and testing.[48]

There is also a significant body of research demonstrating bias in machine learning contexts due to underlying training data that reflects existing societal bias. For example, studies have shown how facial recognition systems perform significantly worse on darker-skinned individuals than lighter-skinned individuals,[49] which leads to higher misidentification rates that can have severe consequences such as false arrests.[50] Research has also illustrated the existence and impacts of racial bias in health care algorithms, leading to less resources expended for Black patients compared to similarly sick White patients.[51] Unsurprisingly, based on what we know about human bias in employment decisions from decades of resume audit studies,[52] hiring algorithms can also reflect bias based on attributes such as race and gender.[53] Beyond predictive models, generative AI has also been heavily criticized for bias and

---

[46] Ibid.
[47] Buolamwini, J. & Gebru, T. (2018). Gender Shades: Intersectional Accuracy Disparities in Commercial Gender Classification. In Friedler, S. A. & Wilson, C. (Eds.), *Proceedings of Machine Learning Research* 81, pp. 77–91.
[48] Mankoff, J., Kasnitz, D., Camp, L. J., Lazar, J. & Hochheiser, H. (2024). AI Must Be Anti-Ableist and Accessible. *Communications of the ACM* 67(12), pp. 40–42.
[49] Bulowami, J. & Gebru, T. (2018). Gender Shades: Intersectional Accuracy Disparities in Commercial Gender Classification. *Proceedings of Machine Learning Research* 81, pp. 1–15.
[50] Hill, K. (2020, June 24). Wrongfully Accused by an Algorithm. *The New York Times*. Available at: www.nytimes.com/2020/06/24/technology/facial-recognition-arrest.html.
[51] Obermeyer, Z., Powers, B., Vogeli, C., & Mullainathan, S. (2019). Dissecting Racial Bias in an Algorithm Used to Manage the Health of Populations. *Science*, 366(6464), pp. 447–453.
[52] Bertrand, M. & Mullainathan, S. (2004). Are Emily and Greg More Employable Than Lakisha and Jamal? A Field Experiment on Labor Market Discrimination. *American Economic Review*, 94(4), pp. 991–1013.
[53] Chen, Z. (2023). Ethics and Discrimination in Artificial Intelligence-Enabled Recruitment Practices. *Humanities and Social Sciences Communications*, 10(1), pp. 1–12.

stereotypes in its results; for example, a 2024 HCI paper revealed that text-to-image systems repeatedly presented "reductive archetypes" for disabilities.[54]

Many of these contexts for which HCI research can be helpful in identifying and understanding the impact of bias have direct policy implications. For example, Asplund et al. audited housing ads served to social media users to verify if they complied with the Fair Housing Act. The audits found differential treatment based on race and gender with respect to the housing ads.[55]

It is unsurprising that discrimination has been a priority in AI regulation, given the large amount of public attention to this topic with respect to high-profile cases such as the previous examples. It is well established that bias is a problem in AI systems, and these systems are also being deployed in incredibly high-stakes contexts, such as health care, employment, and law enforcement. The U.S. also has an existing and complex body of regulation to protect individuals from unfair treatment based on protected characteristics such as race, gender, or disability – for example, the Civil Rights Act of 1964,[56] the Americans with Disabilities Act,[57] and the Fair Housing Act.[58]

Currently, AI bias and discrimination may be addressed by a patchwork of existing antidiscrimination statutes, consumer protection laws, and data privacy regulations. There are a number of proposed or enacted laws at the state level that attempt to mitigate the potential discriminatory impacts of AI. These often focus on specific (typically high risk) contexts. For example, Illinois amended their Human Rights Act[59] to prohibit an employer in the context of employment decisions from *"us[ing] artificial intelligence that has the effect of subjecting employees to discrimination on the basis of protected classes."* New Hampshire also prohibits state agencies from using AI in "classifying persons based on behavior, socio-economic status, or personal characteristics resulting in unlawful discrimination."[60]

Additionally, the AI Executive Order enacted in October 2023 called out how irresponsible uses of AI can deepen discrimination and biases in justice, health care, and housing.[61] It offered guidance to landlords and federal employees, addressed

---

[54] Mack, K. A., Qadri, R., Denton, R., Kane, S. K. & Bennett, C. L. (2024). "They Only Care to Show Us the Wheelchair": Disability Representation in Text-to-Image AI Models. In *Proceedings of the ACM CHI Conference on Human Factors in Computing Systems*, pp. 1–23.

[55] Asplund, J., Eslami, M., Sundaram, H., Sandvig, C. & Karahalios, K. (2020, May). Auditing Race and Gender Discrimination in Online Housing Markets. In *Proceedings of the International AAAI Conference on Web and Social Media 14*, pp. 24–35.

[56] Civil Rights Act of 1964, P.L. 88–352, 78 Stat. 241 (codified at 42 U.S.C. § 1971 et seq. (2006)).

[57] Americans with Disabilities Act of 1990, Pub. L. No. 101–336, 104 Stat. 327 (codified at 42 U.S.C. §§ 12101–12213).

[58] Fair Housing Act, Title VIII of the Civil Rights Act of 1968, Pub. L. No. 90–284, 82 Stat. 73 (1968) (codified at 42 U.S.C. §§ 3601–3619, 3631).

[59] 775 ILCS 5/ (2024).

[60] N.H. Rev. Stat. § 5-D:3 (2024).

[61] The White House. (October 30, 2023). Executive Order on Safe, Secure, and Trustworthy Development and Use of Artificial Intelligence. Available at: bidenwhitehouse.archives.gov/briefing-room/presidential-actions/2025/01/14/executive-order-on-advancing-united-states-leadership-in-artificial-intelligence-infrastructure/.

algorithmic discrimination through training and technical assistance, and recommended best practices in the criminal justice systems for fairness in, for example, use of AI in sentencing and predictive policing.[62]

HCI professionals may also be responsible for recognizing and addressing bias, requiring them to conduct intentional design, diverse representation, and continuous monitoring to ensure AI models serve all users equitably.[63] Datasets would also benefit from broader representation to help AI systems learn varied speech patterns, movement patterns, and interaction methods.[64] Continuous user testing with a diversity of stakeholders also has the potential to highlight functionality gaps, spurring more equitable model improvements.

8.4 GENERATIVE AI AND INTELLECTUAL PROPERTY

Intellectual property law has a long history of facing challenges due to new technology. For example, digital technology and the Internet forced significant changes to copyright law, including the creation of the Digital Millennium Copyright Act (see Chapter 6). As of 2025, there are a number of significant emerging legal issues at the interaction of IP and artificial intelligence, especially with the emergence of generative AI, which can create original content such as text, images, audio, or video. How these issues play out could have an impact on HCI, both in terms of how people interact with AI and the legal rights of the people who build it and/or whose content contributes to it. This landscape is still rapidly evolving, but here are three major challenges that are likely to be significant in the context of generative AI.

8.4.1 AI Protection

One critical question for AI and IP is that of protection for AI and its outputs. For example, who owns the rights to the works that are created by generative AI systems? Is it the human who designed or trained the system? Is it the system itself? Is it the user who requested or interacted with the system? Or is it someone else? These questions may depend on a number of factors, such as the level of human involvement, control, and creativity in generating the works; the purpose and context of using them; and the applicable laws and regulations in different jurisdictions. In the U.S., the Copyright Office and the courts[65] have generally held

---

[62] Ibid.
[63] Mankoff, J., Kasnitz, D. Camp, L. J., Lazar, J., & Hochheiser, H. (2024). AI Must Be Anti-Ableist and Accessible. *Communications of the ACM*, 67(12), pp. 40–42.
[64] Kacorri, H., Dwivedi, U., Amancherla, S., Jha, M., & Chanduka, R. (2020). IncluSet: A Data Surfacing Repository for Accessibility Datasets. In *Proceedings of the 22nd International ACM SIGACCESS Conference on Computers and Accessibility*, pp. 1–4.
[65] Cetacean Community v. Bush, 386 F.3d 1169 (9th Cir. 2004); Naruto v. Slater, 888 F.3d 418 (9th Cir. 2018).

that only human authors can claim copyright protection for their works and that AI-generated works are not eligible for such protection.[66] In other countries, the laws and policies vary widely, and there is currently no international consensus or harmonization on this issue.

With respect to patents, in the U.S., current law and practice do not allow inventions created solely by AI systems to be patented, because they require a human inventor to be named and credited. The U.S. Patent Act defines an inventor as "the individual or, if a joint invention, the individuals collectively who invented or discovered the subject matter of the invention."[67] Previous case law has defined "individual" in U.S. law to be understood as a human being.[68] However, AI systems can likely be used as tools to assist human inventors in the process of invention, without affecting the patent eligibility of the resulting inventions.

8.4.2 AI Infringement (Input)

Another issue, one that has created a great deal of debate following increased attention to generative AI, is whether using unlicensed content in training data for generative AI systems constitutes copyright infringement. For example, if an AI system uses images or text from websites or databases that do not have proper licenses or permissions for using them, is this infringement? Numerous ongoing lawsuits are likely to have significant implications for the future of generative AI and the rights of content creators and copyright owners. Many of these lawsuits are class action cases, and plaintiffs include large companies such as Getty Images,[69] well-resourced creators including George R. R. Martin and John Grisham,[70] and smaller content creators and artists.[71] Defendants include Stability AI, OpenAI, Midjourney, Microsoft, and Meta. For example, in December 2023, the *New York Times* filed a lawsuit against OpenAI and Microsoft for copyright infringement, claiming that millions of

---

[66] U.S. Copyright Office. 2023. Copyright Registration Guidance: Works Containing Material Generated by Artificial Intelligence. A Rule by the Copyright Office, Library of Congress on 03/16/2023. Federal Register: The Daily Journal of the United States Government. Available at: www.federalregister.gov/documents/2023/03/16/2023-05321/copyright-registration-guidance-works-containing-material-generated-by-artificial-intelligence.

[67] 35 U.S.C. § 100.

[68] Mohamed v. Palestinian Authority. 566 U.S. 449 (2012).

[69] Getty Images (US), Inc. v. Stability AI, Inc., 1:23-cv-00135 (D. Del.); Brittain, B. (February 7, 2023). Getty Images lawsuit says Stability AI misused photos to train AI. *Reuters*. Available at: www.reuters.com/legal/getty-images-lawsuit-says-stability-ai-misused-photos-train-ai-2023-02-06/.

[70] Authors Guild v. OpenAI Inc., 1:23-cv-08292 (S.D.N.Y.); David, E. (September 21, 2023). George R. R. Martin and other authors sue OpenAI for copyright infringement. The Verge. Available at: www.theverge.com/2023/9/20/23882140/george-r-r-martin-lawsuit-openai-copyright-infringement.

[71] Andersen v. Stability AI Ltd., 3:23-cv-00201 (N.D. Cal.); Brittain, B. (December 1, 2023). Artists take new shot at Stability, Midjourney in updated copyright lawsuit. *Reuters*. Available at: www.reuters.com/legal/litigation/artists-take-new-shot-stability-midjourney-updated-copyright-lawsuit-2023-11-30/.

their articles were used to train chatbots such as ChatGPT that now directly compete with the news outlet as an information source.[72] The outcomes of such lawsuits will likely involve, in part, whether use of content for training AI systems constitutes fair use. For example, in a notable U.S. decision in June 2025, a district court judge found that Anthropic's training of its Claude model on lawfully purchased, digitized books constituted fair use, finding the use "exceedingly transformative," though left unresolved whether copying from pirated sources would also qualify as fair use.[73] Together, these proceedings underscore that whether AI training constitutes fair use will likely vary case by case.

In the meantime, uncertainty on this point could potentially be impacting smaller AI developers and even researchers without extensive legal resources; HCI research on how understanding (or lack of understanding) of fair use (explained in more detail in Chapter 6) has revealed that uncertainty can result in chilling effects for technology use.[74] Additionally, it is worth noting that there are complex ethical issues regarding, for instance, consent, economic impacts, and attribution with respect to AI training data that, though outside the context of copyright law, will continue to be important for AI developers and researchers to grapple with in the coming years.[75]

8.4.3 AI Infringement (Output)

The output of generative AI could also potentially infringe the intellectual property rights of existing protected works – that is, if an AI system uses a large dataset of copyrighted content to learn how to create new content, it may produce *outputs* that are substantially similar to its training data, without permission or attribution. For example, the *New York Times* case also claims that OpenAI and Microsoft's AI tools create output that "recites Times content verbatim, closely summarizes it, and mimics its expressive style."[76] In the context of copyright law, the standard for infringement set by federal law is that "anyone who violates any of the exclusive rights of the copyright owner" is liable.[77] The USPTO has further clarified that if the creator or owner of an AI system could be liable for direct or contributory infringement if they "take sufficient action" to cause the AI's infringement (through programming,

---

[72] The New York Times Company v. Microsoft Corporation, 1:23-cv-11195 (S.D.N.Y.).
[73] Bartz v. Anthropic PBC, No. 3:24-cv-05417 (N.D. Cal. 2025).
[74] Fiesler, C. & Bruckman, A. S. (2014, February). Remixers' Understandings of Fair Use Online. In *Proceedings of the ACM CSCW Conference on Computer Supported Cooperative Work & Social Computing*, pp. 1023–1032.
[75] Jiang, H. H., Brown, L., Cheng, J., Khan, M., Gupta, A., Workman, D., Hanna, A., Flowers, J. & Gebru, T. (2023). AI Art and Its Impact on Artists. In *Proceedings of the AAAI/ACM AIES Conference on AI, Ethics, and Society*, pp. 363–374.
[76] The New York Times Company v. Microsoft Corporation, 1:23-cv-11195 (S.D.N.Y.).
[77] 17 U.S.C. § 501(a).

data inputs, or otherwise) or that if an AI system had more autonomy, the creator or owner might be vicariously liable.[78]

Additionally, with respect to patent law, an AI system itself could potentially infringe on a patent. However, it may be difficult for patent holders to find out if an AI system violates their patent because AI developers typically keep their methods secret. But in theory, one developer could take legal action against another based on how their models function. With respect to trademarks, the Lanham Act allows trademark owners to sue "any person" who uses their mark without permission.[79] So though AI software itself cannot be held liable, the people who use it for trademark infringement could be. Courts also have a history of adapting trademark laws to account for new technological situations, such as online infringement and counterfeiting, where people use others' marks to trick consumers (e.g., by manipulating web search results).[80] Concerns that have been raised are, for example, whether chatbots could confuse brand names in ways that humans might not (e.g., NIKE v. NIKF shoes), or whether product recommendations from chatbots could be manipulated in ways that could influence brand reputation.[81]

Finally, related to the previous discussion regarding deepfakes, it is possible that some use cases for deepfakes such as voice cloning, deceptive advertising, and nonconsensual pornography that involve exploiting specific individuals' identities could be regulated under state-level right of publicity laws. These laws, which vary from state to state, allow individuals to control and profit from commercial uses of their identity, such as name, image, or voice. Some legal scholars have argued for expansion of right of publicity laws to protect anyone whose identity has been misappropriated (not just celebrities), to extend beyond explicitly commercial uses, and/or to be implemented at the federal level.[82]

Overall, these ongoing debates around intellectual property and AI are important for HCI researchers and practitioners to attend to because they will shape how AI systems are designed, deployed, and shared, as well as how people use them and are impacted by them. HCI research, particularly as related to societal impact and technical topics around issues such as consent and transparency, is also likely to be important in this context moving forward.

---

[78] USPTO. (2020, October). Public Views on Artificial Intelligence and Intellectual Property Policy. Available at: www.uspto.gov/sites/default/files/documents/USPTO_AI-Report_2020-10-07.pdf.
[79] 15 U.S.C. § 1114.
[80] USPTO. (2020, October). Public Views on Artificial Intelligence and Intellectual Property Policy. Available at: www.uspto.gov/sites/default/files/documents/USPTO_AI-Report_2020-10-07.pdf.
[81] Curtis, L. & Platts, R. (2023). How AI Chatbots Could Change Trademark Law. *International Trademark Association.* Available at: www.inta.org/perspectives/features/how-ai-chatbots-could-change-trademark-law/.
[82] Jones, F. (2024). Tune in or Tune out: AI Developments Urges Federal Proposal for Voice Protection in Right of Publicity. *University of Denver Sports & Entertainment Law Journal* 28, pp. 31–65; Spitz, A. (2024). "It Wasn't Me": Rethinking the Right of Publicity in the Context of AI-Generated Content. In *Boston College Intellectual Property and Technology Forum*, pp. 1–16.

8.5 WHAT'S NEXT?

The constantly evolving landscape of AI technology is likely to necessitate adaptive policy approaches as we move forward, including an understanding of both risks and benefits, broader societal impacts, and strategies for mitigating harm. Currently, our understanding of the socio-technical aspects of this emerging technology is not yet sufficient to definitively determine the best approaches for addressing these aspects, with regulation or otherwise – which points to the importance of more evidence-based knowledge.[83] HCI research has the potential to contribute greatly to the development of legal frameworks in this space. Conversely, new statutes, regulations, and case law may influence the work being done related to AI within HCI.

AI systems often differ from traditional software with respect to interaction norms, particularly due to their ability to learn from data, adapt in real time, and sometimes provide outputs or recommendations that even designers and developers cannot fully predict. Can existing legal frameworks address this, or are new legal frameworks needed? Can HCI professionals proactively promote explainability and transparency through various aspects of UX design, as well as with the incorporation of user testing with diverse populations to identify potential unfairness or exclusion, or will new legal rules require it? We expect that future regulations will create additional requirements for transparency, bias auditing, or privacy protections that will require careful, human-centered implementation.

---

[83] Birrer, A. & Just, N. (2024). What We Know and Don't Know about Deepfakes: An Investigation into the State of the Research and Regulatory Landscape. New Media & Society, Article 14614448241253138, pp. 1–20.

9

Dark Patterns

9.1 INTRODUCTION

For over two decades, HCI researchers and practitioners have been talking about persuasive computing: using data and persuasion to help computer users make "good" behavioral changes and choices, such as obeying speed limits, improving "healthy" food intake, or reducing energy consumption.[1] However, the ability to present choices in a way that is persuasive may lead to interfaces that are designed specifically to deceive, to get users to give up personal information or make purchasing decisions that they otherwise would not normally do if information was presented more neutrally. These interfaces designed to be deceptive may covertly manipulate users in the task flows, overtly tweak user interfaces, and value monetary benefits over users. A range of these techniques have popularly been termed as "dark patterns" or "deceptive patterns." Dark (or deceptive) patterns can be defined broadly as user interface choices *"where design choices subvert, impair, or distort the ability of a user to make autonomous and informed choices in relation to digital systems."*[2] Interfaces that are designed to mislead and stop a user from making an autonomous and informed choice may have implications for consumer rights law. According to Sin et al.:

> *From a behavioral science perspective, dark patterns are designed to prompt consumers to evoke System 1 thinking rather than a more deliberate and thoughtful System 2 thinking by exploiting cognitive biases like scarcity bias or social proof.... Some may argue that dark patterns are nothing more than just behaviorally driven marketing strategies, sometimes known as "behavioral marketing," that are geared toward persuasion, not deception.... Admittedly, not all persuasive marketing are necessarily dark patterns. We consider those that are deceptive and do not have consumers' best interest in mind to be dark patterns.*[3]

---

[1] Fogg, B. J. (2002). *Persuasive Technology: Using Computers to Change What We Think and Do (Interactive Technologies)*. Waltham, MA: Elsevier.

[2] Gray, C. M., Santos, C. T., Bielova, N., & Mildner, T. (2024, May). An Ontology of Dark Patterns Knowledge: Foundations, Definitions, and a Pathway for Shared Knowledge-Building. In *Proceedings of the CHI Conference on Human Factors in Computing Systems*, pp. 1–22.

[3] Sin, R., Harris, T., Nilsson, S., & Beck, T. (2025). Dark Patterns in Online Shopping: Do They Work and Can Nudges Help Mitigate Impulse Buying? *Behavioural Public Policy*, 9(1), pp. 61–87.

Dark patterns are, in concept, not new. There have always been obvious examples, such as the "preselected option" tactic: for example, an airline website asks a user if they want to select an upgraded seat, and the upgrade is preselected (along with a large "continue" button, while a smaller, less obvious link would allow the user to continue without an upgrade). Or when an e-commerce site adds an item to your checkout cart without a user noticing it in the form of a service plan, or an additional add-on (both previous examples might be categorized as "Design Elements that Lead to Unauthorized Charges" in the FTC hierarchy described later in the chapter). Or when the default settings in an interface or website are such that they disadvantage the user (say, in terms of opt out privacy settings).[4] Professional organizations such as the Association for Computing Machinery have in the past added a charitable donation to the checkout process for annual membership renewal without first asking users.[5] Even subtle dark patterns may influence users to change their behavior, such as when a shopping website inaccurately displays to a user that there are only one or two pairs of shoes left in their size, causing an impulse purchase due to nervousness about low supply when in reality there are plenty of shoes available in that size.[6] Or when a company, for cancelling a service, has a "cancellation procedure [that] is clearly not as easy to use as the initiation method."[7] The prevalence of dark patterns is increasing, as one recent study that the FTC was involved with, of 642 websites and mobile apps, found that three-quarters of them had at least one dark pattern and a majority of them had multiple dark patterns.[8] Along with the growth in the use of dark patterns, consumer complaints are also increasing, so therefore it is important to (1) understand what dark patterns are from an HCI point of view, and (2) examine the legal framework for dark patterns in the U.S.

9.2 TYPES OF DARK PATTERNS

There is a large body of HCI literature related to dark patterns.[9] The literature is generally divided into studies that try to understand the different types of dark

---

[4] Gray, C. M., Santos, C. T., Bielova, N., & Mildner, T. (2024, May). An Ontology of Dark Patterns Knowledge: Foundations, Definitions, and a Pathway for Shared Knowledge-Building. In *Proceedings of the CHI Conference on Human Factors in Computing Systems*, pp. 1–22.
[5] Brignull, H. (2018). Deceptive Patterns: User Interfaces Designed to Trick People. Available at: http://darkpatterns.org/.
[6] Sin, R., Harris, T., Nilsson, S., & Beck, T. (2025). Dark Patterns in Online Shopping: Do They Work and Can Nudges Help Mitigate Impulse Buying? *Behavioural Public Policy*, 9(1), pp. 61–87.
[7] People of the State of NY v. Sirius XM Radio Inc. (2023). Available at: https://ag.ny.gov/sites/default/files/decisions/453325_2023_people_of_the_state_of_v_people_of_the_state_of_decision_order_on_188.pdf.
[8] Federal Trade Commission. (2024). FTC, ICPEN, GPEN Announce Results of Review of Use of Dark Patterns Affecting Subscription Services, Privacy. Available at: www.ftc.gov/news-events/news/press-releases/2024/07/ftc-icpen-gpen-announce-results-review-use-dark-patterns-affecting-subscription-services-privacy.
[9] Gray, C. M., Sanchez Chamorro, L., Obi, I., & Duane, J. N. (2023, July). Mapping the Landscape of Dark Patterns Scholarship: A Systematic Literature Review. In *Companion Publication of the 2023 ACM Designing Interactive Systems Conference*, pp. 188–193.

patterns, their prevalence right now online, and to measure the impact of dark patterns on consumer behavior. A newer and developing area is work on "fair patterns," or proposing solutions to dark patterns.[10] For instance, one study found that *"users exposed to mild dark patterns were more than twice as likely to sign up for a dubious service as those assigned to the control group, and users in the aggressive dark pattern condition were almost four times as likely to subscribe."*[11] Gray et al. (2024) did a comprehensive analysis of the types of dark patterns, called *"An ontology of dark patterns knowledge: Foundations, definitions, and a pathway for shared knowledge-building."*[12] In their taxonomy, they came up with five high-level dark patterns (and we encourage the reader to consult the Gray et al. paper and learn about the entire ontology of 64 patterns):[13]

(1) *Obstruction is a strategy which impedes a user's task flow, making an interaction more difficult than it inherently needs to be, dissuading a user from taking an action.*

(2) *Sneaking is a strategy which hides, disguises, or delays the disclosure of important information that, if made available to users, would cause a user to unintentionally take an action they would likely object to.*

(3) *Interface interference is a strategy which privileges specific actions over others through manipulation of the user interface, thereby confusing the user or limiting discoverability of relevant action possibilities.*

(4) *Forced action is a strategy which requires users to knowingly or unknowingly perform an additional and/or tangential action or information to access (or continue to access) specific functionality, preventing them from continuing their interaction with a system without performing that action.*

(5) *Social engineering is a strategy which presents options or information that causes a user to be more likely to perform a specific action based on their individual and/or social cognitive biases, thereby leveraging a user's desire to follow expected or imposed social norms.*

(All definitions are direct quotes from Gray et al. We also encourage the reader to check out many examples of dark patterns within each of these high-level categories, at: https://darkpatterns.uxp2.com/.)

---

[10] Potel-Saville, M. & Da Rocha, M. (2024). From Dark Patterns to Fair Patterns? Usable Taxonomy to Contribute Solving the Issue with Countermeasures. In Rannenberg, K., Drogkaris, P., &Lauradoux, C. (Eds.), *Privacy Technologies and Policy. APF 2023. Lecture Notes in Computer Science*, vol. 13888. Springer, Cham.

[11] Luguri, J. & Strahilevitz, L. J. (2021). Shining a Light on Dark Patterns. *Journal of Legal Analysis*, 13(1), pp. 43–109.

[12] Gray, C. M., Santos, C. T., Bielova, N., & Mildner, T. (2024, May). An Ontology of Dark Patterns Knowledge: Foundations, Definitions, and a Pathway for Shared Knowledge-Building. In *Proceedings of the CHI Conference on Human Factors in Computing Systems*, pp. 1–22.

[13] Ibid.

Certainly, there are dark patterns which include a combination of these classes. For instance, CNN recently did a news story about how a combination of social engineering and sneaking was being used online by political campaigns to manipulate older people with dementia into giving donations to political campaigns without them realizing it.[14]

Another ontology that is likely to have a significant impact on legal rules (because it originated in an agency that has/will have enforcement power over dark patterns) appears in a 2022 report from the Federal Trade Commission titled "Bringing Dark Patterns to Light." The types of dark patterns as defined by the FTC are:

1. **Design Elements that Induce False Beliefs** (*"advertisements deceptively formatted to look like independent, editorial content ... countdown timers on offers that are not actually time-limited, claims that an item is almost sold out when there is actually ample supply, and false claims that other people are also currently looking at or have recently purchased the same product."*)[15]

2. **Design Elements that Hide or Delay Disclosure of Material Information** (*"hiding or obscuring material information from consumers, such as burying key limitations of the product or service in dense Terms of Service documents that consumers don't see before purchase ... trick[ing] people into paying hidden fees, buri[ing] mention of fees later in the application process in an un-bolded itemization sandwiched between more prominent, bolded paragraphs ... 'drip pricing', in which firms advertise only part of a product's total price to lure in consumers, and do not mention other mandatory charges until late in the buying process ... fees that are either hidden entirely or not presented until late in the transaction .... Also problematic are disclosures made with poor color contrast, such as a white-text disclosure on a yellow background."*)[16]

3. **Design Elements that Lead to Unauthorized Charges** (*"tricking someone into paying for goods or services that they did not want or intend to buy, whether the transaction involves single charges or recurring charges ... [or] when a company deceptively offers a free trial period, but then, unbeknownst to the consumer, the trial is followed by a recurring subscription charge if the consumer fails to cancel ... [or making] it hard for consumers to cancel subscription services, resulting in ongoing recurring charges."*)[17]

---

[14] CNN (2024, October). How Elderly Dementia Patients are Unwittingly Fueling Political Campaigns. Available at: www.cnn.com/interactive/2024/10/politics/political-fundraising-elderly-election-invs-dg/.

[15] Federal Trade Commission. (2022). Bringing Dark Patterns to Light, p. 4. Available at: www.ftc.gov/system/files/ftc_gov/pdf/P214800%20Dark%20Patterns%20Report%209.14.2022%20-%20FINAL.pdf.

[16] Ibid.

[17] Ibid.

4. **Design Elements that Obscure or Subvert Privacy Choices** (*"consumers may be unaware of the privacy choices they have online or what those choices might mean. This may result in a significant deviation from consumers' actual privacy preferences ... dark patterns that subvert consumer privacy preferences often take the form of a purported choice offered to consumers related to their data, except that choice is illusory and presented in a way that nudges consumers toward increased data sharing ... through user interfaces that: (1) do not allow consumers to definitively reject data collection or use; (2) repeatedly prompt consumers to select settings they wish to avoid; (3) present confusing toggle settings leading consumers to make unintended privacy choices; (4) purposely obscure consumers' privacy choices and make them difficult to access; (5) highlight a choice that results in more information collection, while greying out the option that enables consumers to limit such practices; and (6) include default settings that maximize data collection and sharing."*)[18]

A well-known recent example from the 2020 Trump Campaign for President website included a preselected box so that any donation would be a recurring weekly donation,[19] which would likely be categorized under "Design Elements that Lead to Unauthorized Charges." There are additional potential categories of misleading interfaces, such as those that use social cues to pressure users to make decisions by making them feel guilty and/or empathy or other emotions[20] and again, we encourage the reader to examine the many types of dark patterns mentioned within the Gray et al. (2024) paper.[21]

9.3 LEGAL RULES FOR DARK PATTERNS

Legal rules related to dark patterns exist in statutes, regulations, and case law. Because of the Federal Trade Commission's jurisdiction over unfair or deceptive business practices, they are the agency at the Federal level most likely to

---

[18] Federal Trade Commission. (2022). Bringing Dark Patterns to Light, p. 15. Available at: www.ftc.gov/system/files/ftc_gov/pdf/P214800%20Dark%20Patterns%20Report%209.14.2022%20-%20FINAL.pdf.

[19] Goldmacher, S. (April 3, 2021). New York Times: How Trump Steered Supporters into Unwitting Donations. Available at: www.nytimes.com/2021/04/03/us/politics/trump-donations.html. Note, according to that NYT article, "In the final two and a half months of 2020, the Trump campaign, the Republican National Committee and their shared accounts issued more than 530,000 refunds worth $64.3 million to online donors."

[20] Alberts, L., Lyngs, U., & Van Kleek, M. (2024). Computers as Bad Social Actors: Dark Patterns and Anti-Patterns in Interfaces that Act Socially. *Proceedings of the ACM on Human-Computer Interaction*, 8(CSCW1), pp. 1–25.

[21] Gray, C. M., Santos, C. T., Bielova, N., & Mildner, T. (2024, May). An Ontology of Dark Patterns Knowledge: Foundations, Definitions, and a Pathway for Shared Knowledge-Building. In *Proceedings of the CHI Conference on Human Factors in Computing Systems*, pp. 1–22.

have broad jurisdiction over dark patterns, and so the FTC is often viewed as being at the center of legal action related to dark patterns. One of the three strategic, top-level goals of the FTC is to "Protect the public from unfair or deceptive acts or practices in the marketplace"[22] and the FTC is given jurisdiction to enforce that goal: *"Unfair methods of competition in or affecting commerce, and unfair or deceptive acts or practices in or affecting commerce, are hereby declared unlawful.... The Commission is hereby empowered and directed to prevent persons, partnerships, or corporations ... from using unfair methods of competition in or affecting commerce and unfair or deceptive acts or practices in or affecting commerce."*[23] It is important to note that most states have a state-level equivalent of an FTC Act.[24] For those seeking inspirational ideas from outside of the U.S., the EU has taken a number of steps against dark patterns, and we suggest that the reader consult Brenncke's recent paper.[25] Legal rules related to dark patterns can be found in (1) case law where courts have interpreted the FTC's existing jurisdiction over unfair and deceptive acts, (2) Federal statutes such as ROSCA, (3) the new Federal regulation from the FTC related to negative marketing, (4) state-level consumer protection statutes, and (5) the Colorado regulation that is specific to dark patterns.

9.3.1 *Case Law*

As an example of how the FTC might approach dark patterns, the FTC has recently been litigating against Amazon, Inc., claiming that Amazon:

> violated Section 5(a) of the Federal Trade Commission Act (FTC Act), 15 U.S.C. § 45(a), and Section 4 of the Restore Online Shoppers' Confidence Act (ROSCA), 15 U.S.C. § 8403. The FTC alleges that Amazon tricked, coerced, and manipulated consumers into subscribing to Amazon Prime by failing to disclose the material terms of the subscription clearly and conspicuously and by failing to obtain the consumers' informed consent before enrolling them. The FTC also alleges that Amazon did not provide simple mechanisms for these subscribers to cancel their Prime memberships.[26]

The FTC calls this investigation the "Dark Patterns Investigation."[27] This case is generally at the beginning of the litigation process, and has already survived Amazon's

---

[22] FTC. *Privacy and Security*. Retrieved January 2, 2025, from www.ftc.gov/about-ftc.
[23] 15 U.S.C. § 45(a)(1–2).
[24] Butler, H. N. & Wright, J. D. (2011). Are State Consumer Protection Acts Really Little-FTC Acts. *Florida Law Review*, 63, pp. 163–192.
[25] Brenncke, M. (2024). Regulating Dark Patterns. *Notre Dame Journal of International & Comparative Law*, 14(1), pp. 39–79.
[26] Fed. Trade Comm'n v. Amazon.com, Inc., No. 2:23-CV-00932-JHC, 2024 WL 2723812 (W.D. Wash. May 28, 2024).
[27] Ibid.

request for a motion to dismiss.[28] A trial in this case is scheduled for Fall 2026, after what is expected to be a lengthy period of discovery.

State Attorney Generals have also been involved in litigation about political campaigns (or specifically, about an amalgamated group called "WinRed") using dark patterns to pre-check boxes for ongoing political donations and making it very hard to undo that feature. See *Seagull v. WinRed, Inc.*[29] and *WinRed, Inc. v. Ellison*,[30] although it's important to note that so far, the case law is more about the Federalism aspects of attorney generals getting involved in enforcing election law, rather than getting involved in the details of the dark patterns specifically.

There has also been case law in *People of the State of NY v. Sirius XM Radio Inc.*, related to patterns that are a combination of online and non-online methods. For instance, a NY court ruled that SiriusXM violated the *Restore Online Shoppers' Confidence Act* ("ROSCA") because:

> *Respondents [SiriusXM] allow for a customer to sign up to a subscription without interacting with a live agent but require that a customer do just that in order to cancel. Given the inevitable wait times that come with a live customer service agent, and the again undisputed fact that Respondent's agents first go through an evaluation and offer process with the customer before proceeding to cancel, their cancellation procedure is clearly not as easy to use as the initiation method.*[31]

It is interesting to note that in a concurrence in the 7th circuit case *Domer v. Menard, Inc.*, involving whether terms and conditions that are hard to find due to dark patterns can still be enforced, Judge Hamilton, in his concurrence, called for more usability testing to better understand the nature of dark patterns:

> *Because user-interface design is technical and empirically testable, it should be possible for judges or juries to evaluate evidence as to whether real-life consumers are on fair notice that they have agreed to a long list of legal terms every time they complete a purchase online or download a new application on their devices. At heart, the way a reasonable consumer responds to a particular user interface is a factual issue.*[32]

9.3.2 Federal Statutes

At the Federal level, there is already a statute that relates to one specific aspect of dark patterns in commerce: the negative option feature. *"The FTC uses the phrase*

---

[28] Fed. Trade Comm'n v. Amazon.com, Inc., No. 2:23-CV-00932-JHC, 2024 WL 2723812 (W.D. Wash. May 28, 2024).
[29] Seagull v. WinRed, Inc., No. X07HHDCV226154527S, 2023 WL 4322714, at *4 (Conn. Super. Ct. June 28, 2023).
[30] WinRed, Inc. v. Ellison, 59 F.4th 934, 936 (8th Cir. 2023).
[31] *People of the State of NY v. Sirius XM Radio Inc.* Available at: https://ag.ny.gov/sites/default/files/decisions/453325_2023_people_of_the_state_of_v_people_of_the_state_of_decision_order_on_188.pdf, p. 16.
[32] Domer v. Menard, Inc., 116 F.4th 686, 706–07 (7th Cir. 2024).

'negative option marketing' broadly to refer to a category of commercial transactions in which sellers interpret a customer's failure to take an affirmative action, either to reject an offer or cancel an agreement, as assent to be charged for goods or services."[33] The Restore Online Shoppers' Confidence Act ("ROSCA"), enacted in 2010, prohibits the

> ... charge or attempt to charge any consumer for any goods or services sold in a transaction effected on the Internet through a negative option feature (as defined in the Federal Trade Commission's Telemarketing Sales Rule in part 310 of title 16, Code of Federal Regulations), unless the person –
>
> (1) provides text that clearly and conspicuously discloses all material terms of the transaction before obtaining the consumer's billing information;
> (2) obtains a consumer's express informed consent before charging the consumer's credit card, debit card, bank account, or other financial account for products or services through such transaction; and
> (3) provides simple mechanisms for a consumer to stop recurring charges from being placed on the consumer's credit card, debit card, bank account, or other financial account.[34]

While dark patterns are not mentioned per se in the FTC Act, and some have argued that the FTC should promulgate a specific regulatory process to specifically describe and broadly address all types of dark patterns,[35] the FTC has previously done enforcement work related to dark patterns. Multiple states, however, do have statutes and/or regulations related to consumer protection which specifically mention dark patterns.

9.3.3 FTC Regulation Related to Negative Option Marketing

On November 15, 2024, the FTC issued a final rule which they refer to as the "Negative Option" Rule but is also informally known as the "Click-to-Cancel" rule. "*A negative option, in contrast [to an installment contract], merely determines whether a seller may continue to send, and charge for, goods or provide services without the consumer's further action.*"[36] As the FTC describes in the rule,

---

[33] Federal Trade Commission. (2009). Negative Options: A Report by the staff of the FTC's Division of Enforcement. Available at: www.ftc.gov/sites/default/files/documents/reports/negative-options-federal-trade-commission-workshop-analyzing-negative-option-marketing-report-staff/p064202negativeoptionreport.pdf.
[34] 15 U.S.C. § 8403.
[35] Wilson, L. (2023). Is There Light at the End of the Dark-Pattern Tunnel? *George Washington Law Review*, 91(4), pp. 1048–[xviii].
[36] Federal Trade Commission. (2024). Negative Option Rule. Available at: www.federalregister.gov/documents/2024/11/15/2024-25534/negative-option-rule.

"the Commission has repeatedly stated billing consumers without consumers' express informed consent is an unfair act under the FTC Act" but also notes that "ROSCA, however, does not prescribe specific steps marketers must follow to comply with these provisions and is limited to online transactions."[37] The new rule fills that gap, however, it is important to note that the rule is promulgated under the FTC Act, not ROSCA. This rule went into effect on January 14, 2025, and covered entities had until May 14, 2025, to comply.

> Among other things, this final Rule (1) prohibits misrepresentations of any material fact made while marketing using negative option features; (2) requires sellers to provide important information prior to obtaining consumers' billing information and charging consumers; (3) requires sellers to obtain consumers' unambiguously affirmative consent to the negative option feature prior to charging them; and (4) requires sellers to provide consumers with simple cancellation mechanisms to immediately halt all recurring charges.[38]

While this is only one portion of the final rule, the requirements for easy cancellation include:

(a) *Simple mechanism required for cancellation.* In connection with promoting or offering for sale any good or service with a Negative Option Feature, it is a violation of this Rule and an unfair or deceptive act or practice in violation of section 5 of the FTC Act for the Negative Option Seller to fail to provide a simple mechanism for a consumer to cancel the Negative Option Feature; avoid being Charged, or Charged an increased amount, for the good or service; and immediately stop any recurring Charges.

(b) *Simple mechanism at least as simple as consent.* The simple mechanism required by paragraph (a) of this section must be at least as easy to use as the mechanism the consumer used to consent to the Negative Option Feature.

(c) *Minimum requirements for simple mechanism.* At a minimum, the Negative Option Seller must provide the simple mechanism required by paragraphs (a) and (b) of this section through the same medium the consumer used to consent to the Negative Option Feature....[39]

9.3.4 Related State Consumer Protection Statutes

Many states have added legal rules related to dark patterns into their consumer protection statutes. For instance, Connecticut mentions the following in their consumer protection statute:

---

[37] Ibid.
[38] www.federalregister.gov/documents/2024/11/15/2024-25534/negative-option-rule#sectno-reference-425.6.
[39] Ibid.

"Consent" means a clear affirmative act signifying a consumer's freely given, specific, informed and unambiguous agreement to allow the processing of personal data relating to the consumer. "Consent" may include a written statement, including by electronic means, or any other unambiguous affirmative action. "Consent" does not include (A) acceptance of general or broad terms of use or a similar document that contains descriptions of personal data processing along with other, unrelated information, (B) hovering over, muting, pausing or closing a given piece of content, or (C) agreement obtained through the use of dark patterns.[40]

Very similar text describing how consent cannot be obtained legally using a dark pattern, appears in the consumer protection, trade/fraud, or privacy statutes of Florida,[41] New Jersey,[42] Texas,[43] Rhode Island,[44] Nebraska,[45] New Hampshire,[46] Delaware,[47] Minnesota,[48] and Montana.[49]

California also has similar statutory text but related to genetic data:

"Express consent" means a consumer's affirmative authorization to grant permission in response to a clear, meaningful, and prominent notice regarding the collection, use, maintenance, or disclosure of genetic data for a specific purpose. The nature of the data collection, use, maintenance, or disclosure shall be conveyed in clear and prominent terms in such a manner that an ordinary consumer would notice and understand it. Express consent cannot be inferred from inaction. Agreement obtained through use of dark patterns does not constitute consent.[50]

A definition for a dark pattern exists in CA Civil Code: "*'Dark pattern'* means a user interface designed or manipulated with the substantial effect of subverting or impairing user autonomy, decisionmaking, or choice, as further defined by regulation."[51]

And dark patterns are also mentioned in a California statute called the California Age-Appropriate Design Code Act (CAADCA).[52] The CAADCA forbids businesses that provide online services, products, or features which are likely to be accessed by children from: "*Use[ing] dark patterns to lead or encourage children to provide personal information beyond what is reasonably expected to provide that online service ... to forego privacy protections, or to take any action that the business knows,*

---

[40] Conn. Gen. Stat. Ann. § 42–515.
[41] Fla. Stat. Ann. § 501.702.
[42] N.J. Stat. Ann. § 56:8–166.4.
[43] TX BUS & COM § 541.001.
[44] R.I. Gen. Laws Ann. § 6–48.1–2.
[45] Neb. Rev. Stat. Ann. § 87–1102.
[46] N.H. Rev. Stat. Ann. § 507-H:1.
[47] Del. Code Ann. tit. 6, § 12D-102.
[48] Minn. Stat. Ann. § 325O.02.
[49] Mont. Code Ann. § 30–14-2802.
[50] Cal. Civ. Code § 56.18.
[51] Cal. Civ. Code § 1798.140(l).
[52] Cal. Civ. Code §§ 1798.99.28–1798.99.40.

or has reason to know, is materially detrimental to the child's physical health, mental health, or well-being."[53]

It is important to note that the legal question of whether the prohibition of dark patterns is constitutional, is part of an ongoing case, *NetChoice, LLC v. Bonta*, and based on a recent preliminary injunction,[54] it is advisable for the reader to double-check when they read this paragraph, whether the prohibition in the CAADCA against using dark patterns to collect data from children, is still good law.

9.3.5 Example: Colorado Regulation on Dark Patterns

In terms of fleshing out the legal definition of dark pattern, clarifying what is acceptable and what isn't, and providing specifics, Colorado currently has the most detailed regulation related to dark patterns (and possibly the only regulation which is specifically focused on dark patterns). Put another way, only Colorado's regulation is at the granular, widget level, providing specific guidance on sizing, color, number of clicks, dialog process, and text narrative that can be understood and applied by UX practitioners. This regulation, titled: "User Interface Design, Choice Architecture, and Dark Patterns"[55] (see Box 1) is very useful because it is (as far as we know) the only regulation which fleshes out different types of dark patterns and provides examples. *We therefore believe that in the future, it will become very persuasive authority in court cases.*

BOX 1

1. *Consent choice options should be presented to Consumers in a symmetrical way that does not impose unequal weight or focus on one available choice over another such that a Consumer's ability to consent is impaired or subverted.*
   a. *Example: One choice should not be presented with less prominent size, font, or styling than the other choice. Presenting an "I accept" button in a larger size than the "I do not accept" button would not be considered equal or symmetrical. Presenting an "I do not accept" button in a greyed-out color while the "I accept" button is presented in a bright or obvious color would not be considered equal or symmetrical.*
   b. *Example: If multiple choices are offered to a Consumer, it should be equally easy to accept or reject all options. Presenting the option to "accept all" when offering a Consumer, the choice to Consent to the use of Sensitive Data for multiple purposes without an option to "reject all" would not be considered equal or symmetrical.*

---

[53] Cal. Civ. Code §§ 1798.99.31(b)(1)–(8).
[54] NetChoice, LLC v. Bonta, 770 F. Supp. 3d 1164 (N.D. Cal. 2025). Be aware that there is another case with the same plaintiff and defendant about a different CA statute.
[55] 4 CCR 904-3:7.10, alternatively cited as 4 CO ADC 904-3.

2. Consent choice options should avoid the use of emotionally manipulative language or visuals to unfairly, fraudulently, or deceptively coerce or steer Consumer choice or Consent.
   a. Example: One choice should not be presented in a way that creates unnecessary guilt or shames the user into selecting a specific choice. Presenting the choices "I accept, I want to help endangered species" vs "No, I don't care about animals" may be considered unfairly emotionally manipulative.
   b. Example: The explanation of the choice to Consumers should not include gratuitous information to emotionally manipulate Consumers. Explaining that a mobile application "helps save lives" when asking for Consent to collect Sensitive Data for Targeted Advertising may be considered deceptively emotionally manipulative if the Targeted Advertising is not critical to the lifesaving functionality of the application.
3. A Consumer's silence or failure to take an affirmative action should not be interpreted as acceptance or Consent.
   a. Example: A Consumer closing a pop-up window which requests Consent without first affirmatively selecting the equivalent of an "I accept" button should not be interpreted as Consent.
   b. Example: A Consumer navigating forward on a webpage after a Consent choice has been presented without selecting the equivalent of an "I accept" button should not be interpreted as affirmative Consent.
   c. Example: A Consumer continuing to use a Smart TV without replying "I accept" or "I consent" in reply to a verbal request for Consent should not be interpreted as affirmative Consent.
4. Consent choice options should not be presented with a preselected or default option.
   a. Example: Checkboxes or radio buttons should not be selected automatically when presented to a Consumer.
5. A Consumer should be able to select either Consent choice option within a similar number of steps. A Consumer's ability to exercise a more privacy-protective option shall not be unduly longer, more difficult, or time-consuming than the path to exercise a less privacy-protective option.
   a. Example: Consumers should be presented with all choices at the same time. Presenting an "I accept" button next to a "Learn More" button which requires Consumers to take an extra step before they are given the option of an "I do not accept" button could be considered an unnecessary restriction.
   b. Example: Describing the choice before Consumers and placing both the "I accept" and "I do not accept" buttons after a "select preferences" button would not be considered an unnecessary restriction.
6. A Consumer's expected interaction with a website, application, or product should not be unnecessarily interrupted or intruded upon to request Consent.

a. *Example: Consumers should not be interrupted multiple times in one visit to a website to Consent if they have declined the Consent choice offered when they arrived at the page.*
b. *Example: Consumers should not be redirected away from the content or service they are attempting to interact with because they declined the Consent choice offered, unless Consent to process the requested data is strictly necessary to provide the website or application content or experience.*
c. *Example: Consumers should not be forced to navigate through multiple popups which cover or otherwise disrupt the content or service they are attempting to interact with because they declined the Consent choice offered.*
7. Consent choice options should not include misleading statements, omissions, affirmative misstatements, or intentionally confusing language to obtain Consent.
a. *Example: Choices should not be driven by a false sense of urgency. A countdown clock displayed next to a Consent choice option which states "time is running out to Consent to this data use and receive a limited discount" where the discount is not actually limited by time or availability would be considered creating a false sense of urgency.*
b. *Example: Choices should avoid the use of double negatives when describing Consent choice options to Consumers.*
c. *Example: Consent choice options should not be presented with confusing or unexpected syntax. "Please do not check this box if you wish to Consent to this data use" would be considered confusing syntax.*
d. *Example: The language used for choice options should logically follow the question presented to the Consumer. Offering the options of "Yes" or "No" to the question "Do you wish to provide or decline Consent for the described purposes" would be considered an illogical choice option. The choice options "provide" and "decline" would be considered to logically follow the same question.*
8. The vulnerabilities or unique characteristics of the target audience of a product, service, or website should be considered when deciding how to present Consent choice options.
a. *Example: A website or service that primarily interacts with Consumers under the age of 18 should consider the simplicity of the language used to explain the choice options or the way in which cartoon imagery or endorsements might unduly influence their choice.*
b. *Example: A website or service that primarily interacts with the elderly should consider font size and space between buttons to ensure readability and ease of interaction with design elements.*
9. User interface design and Consent choice architecture should operate in a substantially similar manner when accessed through digital accessibility tools.

> A. Example: If it takes two clicks for a Consumer to Consent through a website, it should take no more than two actions for a Consumer using a digital accessibility tool to complete the same Consent process.
> B. In addition to the principles included in this part 4 CCR 904-3, Rule 7.09(A), Controllers may consider statutes, administrative rules, and administrative guidance concerning Dark Patterns from other jurisdictions when evaluating the appropriateness of the user interface or choice architecture used to obtain required Consent.
> C. Controllers shall not use an interface design or choice architecture to obtain required Consent that has been designed or manipulated with the substantial effect of subverting or impairing user autonomy, decision making or choice, or unfairly, fraudulently, or deceptively manipulating or coercing a Consumer into providing Consent.
> 1. The principles outlined in 4 CCR 904-3, Rule 7.09(A) and (B) are factors to be considered when determining if a consent interface design or choice architecture has been designed or manipulated with the substantial effect of subverting or impairing user autonomy, decision making or choice, or unfairly, fraudulently, or deceptively manipulating or coercing a Consumer into providing Consent.
> D. Consent obtained in violation of this part 4 CCR 904-3, Rule 7.09(C) may be considered a Dark Pattern, as defined in C.R.S. § 6-1-1303(9).
> E. The fact that a design or practice is commonly used is not, alone, enough to demonstrate that any particular design or practice is not a Dark Pattern.
> F. Consent obtained through Dark Patterns does not constitute valid Consent in compliance with C.R.S. §§ 6-1-1303, 6-1-1306, and 6-1-1308.

It is important to note that while California does not have a separate statute or regulation related to dark patterns, there is a section of the CCPA regulation (discussed in Chapter 4), which specifically addresses dark patterns:[56]

> (5) *Easy to execute.* The business shall not add unnecessary burden or friction to the process by which the consumer submits a CCPA request. Methods should be tested to ensure that they are functional and do not undermine the consumer's choice to submit the request. Illustrative examples follow.
> (A) Upon clicking the "Do Not Sell or Share My Personal Information" link, the business shall not require the consumer to search or scroll through the text of a privacy policy or similar document or webpage to locate the mechanism for submitting a request to opt-out of sale/sharing.

---

[56] Cal. Code Regs. tit. 11, § 7004.

(B) A business that knows of, but does not remedy, circular or broken links, or non-functional email addresses, such as inboxes that are not monitored or have aggressive filters that screen emails from the public, may be in violation of this regulation.
(C) Businesses that require the consumer to unnecessarily wait on a webpage as the business processes the request may be in violation of this regulation.
(b) A method that does not comply with subsection (a) may be considered a dark pattern. Any agreement obtained through the use of dark patterns shall not constitute consumer consent. For example, a business that uses dark patterns to obtain consent from a consumer to sell their personal information shall be in the position of never having obtained the consumer's consent to do so.
(c) A user interface is a dark pattern if the interface has the effect of substantially subverting or impairing user autonomy, decisionmaking, or choice. A business's intent in designing the interface is not determinative in whether the user interface is a dark pattern, but a factor to be considered. If a business did not intend to design the user interface to subvert or impair user choice, but the business knows of and does not remedy a user interface that has that effect, the user interface may still be a dark pattern. Similarly, a business's deliberate ignorance of the effect of its user interface may also weigh in favor of establishing a dark pattern.

9.3.6 Pending Bill in the U.S. Congress

While many of the legal rules related to dark patterns are currently existing at the state level, a bill at the Federal level has been introduced to essentially regulate dark patterns, called the DETOUR (Deceptive Experiences To Online Users Reduction) Act. It was introduced in the U.S. Senate in the 2019–2020 session of the U.S. Congress as S. 1084 and H.R. 8975, in the 2021–2022 session of the U.S. Congress as S. 3330 and H.R. 6083), and most recently in the 2023–2024 term (introduced on July 27, 2023, as Senate Bill 2708, with two Republican cosponsors and two Democratic cosponsors) and referred to the Committee on Commerce, Science, and Transportation. It is unknown whether the bill will be introduced again in the 2025–2026 Congress (as of press time, it had not been re-introduced in the current session). While the phrase "dark pattern" isn't used anywhere in the bill, Section 3 of the version of the bill introduced most recently in 2023, which describes dark patterns without using the term, states DETOUR Act, S. 2708, 118th Congress, (2023):

(a) Conduct prohibited. – It shall be unlawful for any large online operator –
(1) to design, modify, or manipulate a user interface on an online service with the purpose or substantial effect of obscuring, subverting, or impairing user autonomy, decision making, or choice to obtain consent or user data;
(2) to subdivide or segment consumers of online services into groups for the purposes of covered research, except with the affirmative express consent of each user involved; or

(3) to design, modify, or manipulate a user interface on an online service, or portion of a user interface or online service, that is directed to a child or teen with the purpose or substantial effect of causing, increasing, or encouraging compulsive usage, including using video auto-play functions initiated without the consent of a user.

Other aspects of the DETOUR Act in Section 3 relate to the collection of user data as a part of ongoing research:

(b) Duties of large online operators. – Any large online operator that engages in any form of covered research based on the activity or data of the users of the large online operator shall do each of the following:

(1) Disclose to its users on a routine basis, but not less than once each 90 days, the general purpose of any such covered research to each user whose user data is or was subject to or included in any covered research during the previous 90-day period.

(2) Disclose to the public on a routine basis, but not less than once each 90 days, any covered research with the purposes of promoting engagement or product conversion being currently undertaken, or concluded since the prior disclosure.

(3) Present the disclosures described in paragraphs (1) and (2) in a manner that is –

(A) clear, conspicuous, context-appropriate, and easily accessible; and

(B) not deceptively obscured.

(4) (A) Subject to subparagraph (B), remove and delete all user data obtained from affected users in the course of covered research if the large online operator –

(i) determines (or determines that it has reason to believe) that the affirmative express consent required under this section from such users was not acquired; and

(ii) is unable to obtain within 2 business days of such determination the affirmative express consent required under this section.

(B) If unable to remove and delete user data pursuant to subparagraph (A), discontinue the covered research.

(5)(A) Establish a process by which a user may choose to opt out of covered research at a later date from when the user previously provided affirmative express consent for such research.

(B) Subject to subparagraph (A), following the decision of a user to opt out, stop collecting, processing, or transferring any data from such user for the purposes of the covered research.

The act would authorize the National Institutes of Standards and Technology (NIST) to take a leading role in fleshing out what this means:

(a) In general. – Not later than 540 days after the date of the enactment of this Act, the Director of the National Institute of Standards and Technology shall, acting through the Information Technology Laboratory of the National Institute

of Standards and Technology, conduct research to develop and disseminate consensus-based resources consistent with subsection (b) that provide recommendations for user interface and user experience design that support user autonomy, choice, and decision making in providing user consent for online services.
(b) Content of resources. – The resources developed under subsection (a) shall –
(1) involve methodology for usability testing to identify usability problems by collecting quantitative and qualitative data to determine the ability of users to navigate options to achieve the specified goals of user autonomy, choice, and decision making in user interface and user experience design;
(2) include examples or demonstrations of user interface design that may restrict the user autonomy, choice, or decision making of a user; and
(3) include methodology to evaluate the ability to identify default settings that impair user autonomy.

And the potential enforcement would fall under the jurisdiction of the Federal Trade Commission:

A violation of section 3 or a regulation promulgated under this Act shall be treated as a violation of a rule defining an unfair or deceptive act or practice under section 18(a)(1)(B) of the Federal Trade Commission Act (15 U.S.C. 57a(a)(1)(B)).

As would the regulatory rulemaking under this act:

(4) REGULATIONS. – Not later than two years after the date of enactment of this Act, the Commission shall promulgate regulations under section 553 of title 5, United States Code, that –
(A) establish rules for the registration, formation, and oversight of independent review boards, including standards that ensure effective independence of such boards from improper or undue influence by a large online operator; and
(B) using the resources produced by the Director of the National Institute of Standards and Technology under Section 4 as guidance, define conduct that does not have the purpose or substantial effect of –
(i) obscuring, subverting, or impairing user autonomy, decision-making, or choice; or
(ii) causing, increasing, or encouraging compulsive usage for a child or teen, such as –
(I) de minimis user interface changes derived from testing consumer preferences where such changes of design elements are not done solely to obtain affirmative express consent or user data;
(II) algorithms or data outputs outside the control of a large online operator or the affiliates of such operator; and
(III) establishing default settings that provide enhanced privacy protection to users or otherwise enhance the autonomy and decision-making ability of such users.

9.4 WHAT ARE THE NEXT STEPS?

In many ways, the HCI community has already begun to research dark patterns and provide detailed analyses about the different types of dark patterns. Given that enhanced legal regulation of dark patterns is already happening in many states and has started to happen at the Federal level, it is suggested that the HCI community work now to inform this increased regulation, taking hints from the DETOUR Act which is currently under consideration in the U.S. Senate. The DETOUR Act would direct NIST to take actions which, whether or not the DETOUR Act has passed, are well within the ability of the HCI community, to develop resources which shall:[57]

> (1) involve methodology for usability testing to identify usability problems by collecting quantitative and qualitative data to determine the ability of users to navigate options to achieve the specified goals of user autonomy, choice, and decision making in user interface and user experience design; (2) include examples or demonstrations of user interface design that may restrict the user autonomy, choice, or decision making of a user; and (3) include methodology to evaluate the ability to identify default settings that impair user autonomy.

These all seem like research questions that could be investigated right now, to speed along the implementation of the DETOUR Act, if passed. That would be a valuable contribution and would be an example of the HCI community being proactive in using research to inform policy, rather than being reactive.[58]

Other ways to help move forward understanding of dark patterns would be to increase education on dark patterns both within HCI education and legal education. For instance, content on dark patterns could be included in courses on contracts (typically a 1L class) and/or consumer law (typically an elective in 2L or 3L). A more challenging question would be what the next steps are to take within HCI practice related to dark patterns. So far, research seems to point to dark patterns being effective in manipulating user behavior. Professional societies, such as ACM and UXPA, may want to add content to their codes of conduct, or codes of ethics, about the use of dark patterns. Perhaps consumer advocates may want to increase advocacy by filing lawsuits against businesses that use dark patterns to trick consumers. Since the use of dark patterns is increasing, and the complaints about dark patterns are increasing, we can expect that the number of legal rules related to dark patterns will also increase, but as suggested by Judge Hamilton of the 7th Circuit, it is important to have sufficient user testing and HCI expertise involved in this area.

---

[57] ibid
[58] Hochheiser, H. & Lazar, J. (2007). HCI and Societal Issues: A Framework for Engagement. *International Journal of Human-Computer Interaction*, 23(3), pp. 339–374.

10

Voting Interfaces and U.S. Law

10.1 INTRODUCTION

Voting is a fundamental tenet of democracy,[1] yet the process of voting is surprisingly complex, subject to all sorts of controls, biases, manipulations, and mistakes. Though the root of this complexity is often policy around voting, it can also be related to technology, humans, or both. NIST described human factors issues in voting as "the process of the voter casting a ballot as intended and, to a lesser extent, the interaction of the poll worker with the voting system."[2] Though there are many aspects of voting which are fraught (including who has the right to vote, purging voter rolls, deadlines for registering to vote, voter ID requirements, whether convicted felons can vote, which level of government controls voting, whether changes to voting rules require preclearance from the federal government, whether provisional ballots are allowed, etc.), our focus in this chapter will be much narrower: on the technology-based interfaces/mechanisms often used for voting, and the legal rules specifying the user experience of electronic technologies used for voting. Even into the 1990s, the typical voting experience was primarily mechanical (e.g., punch cards and levers), but did not involve voters interacting with electronic devices.

Because vote margins in elections between two candidates are often very narrow, many parts of the voting process are the subject of hot debate. Why? Because minor changes in the process or mechanisms can cause a 1% to 2% shift in the voting results, which can be enough to change the outcome of the election. The potential changes in outcomes are often much larger than that when interfaces are modified through a user-centered design process, often by a large margin, such as 10% to 20%. As an example, redesigning a checkout process at an e-commerce website

---

[1] In this article, Douglas argues that voting is not always treated as a right: Douglas, J. A. (2008). Is the Right to Vote Really Fundamental? *Cornell Journal of Law & Public Policy*, 18, pp. 143–202.
[2] Laskowski, S. J., Autry, M., Cugini, J., Killam, W., & Yen, J. (2004). Improving the Usability and Accessibility of Voting Systems and Products. US Department of Commerce, National Institute of Standards and Technology. Available at: https://tsapps.nist.gov/publication/get_pdf.cfm?pub_id=906168.

can "convert" more of the shopping carts into actual transactions that have been completed.[3] Based on the documented impact of interface changes, and the fact that there is evidence that one particular voting interface element – placement on the ballot – can impact voting outcomes (e.g., the candidate or party listed first may have a slight advantage),[4] one can easily imagine the interest in how minor changes in a voting interface can lead to an increased number of votes. Furthermore, it is estimated that usability problems in both paper and electronic ballots may lead to at least 1 percent of votes being cast incorrectly, meaning that the user's vote was not recorded as they intended.[5] And there can even be mechanical malfunctions in the voting interface, such as touch screens in voting machines which are miscalibrated, meaning that even if a user touched the screen in the correct coordinates, such an "offset" might cause the user's vote to be miscounted.[6] Moreover, voters must rely on the voting interface itself to verify their selections, yet another way that the voting interface impacts outcomes.

Yet, given all the interface aspects of the voting experience, the HCI community has not had an ongoing and successful track record in being involved with the design and evaluation of voting interfaces, unlike in other areas such as accessibility and privacy. Interfaces for voting (and ballot design) were not a strong focus area from the HCI community until the U.S. 2000 General Election, when these issues of ballot design came to the forefront.[7] But even since that 2000 election, where the controversy focused on voting interfaces and ballot design, the HCI community has found involvement in and ongoing influence on voting interfaces to be especially challenging, as described over fifteen years ago, *"involvement in debates over controversial topics such as electronic voting can invite critical responses, seemingly iron-clad technical and scientific arguments may be overridden by political concerns, and diverging opinions within the HCI community may preclude the development of consensus viewpoints."*[8]

There are many political and sociocultural reasons why the HCI community may have limited involvement in voting interfaces and legal issues as compared to other HCI-related topics. While the HCI community is often proactive in informing

---

[3] Bias, R. G. & Mayhew, D. J. (Eds.). (2005). *Cost-Justifying Usability: An Update for the Internet Age.* Elsevier.

[4] Koppell, J. G. & Steen, J. A. (2004). The Effects of Ballot Position on Election Outcomes. *The Journal of Politics,* 66(1), 267–281; Blom-Hansen, J., Elklit, J., Serritzlew, S., & Villadsen, L. R. (2016). Ballot Position and Election Results: Evidence from a Natural Experiment. *Electoral Studies,* 44, pp. 172–183.

[5] de Jong, M., van Hoof, J., & Gosselt, J. (2007). User Research of a Voting Machine: Preliminary Findings and Experiences. *Journal of Usability Studies,* 2(4), pp. 180–189.

[6] Mascher, A. L., Cotton, P. T., & Jones, D. W. (2010). Vote-O-Graph: A Dishonest Touchscreen Voting System. In *ACM CHI'10 Extended Abstracts on Human Factors in Computing Systems,* pp. 3205–3210.

[7] Hochheiser, H. & Lazar, J. (2007). HCI and Societal Issues: A Framework for Engagement. *International Journal of Human Computer Interaction,* 23(3), pp. 339–374.

[8] Ibid.

technology design, in the voting arena, the research is often reactive and too late to have an influence on the observed problem in the current election.[9] Furthermore, the HCI community is often not used to the head-on conflict with other areas of computing that voting interfaces bring[10] and is not used to the intense lobbying pressures that exist in voting.[11]

Nevertheless, the interfaces of electronic voting systems are undeniably an HCI/user experience issue.[12] Voting can be challenging from a user experience point of view because it is an irregular experience. Unlike using your desktop, laptop, tablet, or smartphone, which you use on a daily basis, voting occurs only rarely, or *"episodically after long hiatuses."*[13] It has been noted that one challenge of voting interfaces is that *"voters have both strong mental models and imprecise memories of the details of the interaction."*[14] Also, because in-person voting is not considered a state or federal holiday where everyone receives the day off, for most people, voting often takes place while on the way to work in the morning, or while coming home from work in the evening, or at another point during the day while there are time pressures to be elsewhere. So perhaps there is a "hidden" performance requirement that users/voters be able to successfully cast a ballot within a certain period of time, for example, five minutes.[15]

---

[9] Hochheiser, H. & Lazar, J. (2007). HCI and Societal Issues: A Framework for Engagement. *International Journal of Human Computer Interaction*, 23(3), pp. 339–374.

[10] As a side note, one of the authors had the experience of giving testimony to the Maryland state legislature about a bill related to voting interfaces for people with disabilities, which was followed by a professor from another university, focused on security, who said, "everything that he just said is wrong." That is not the typical experience of the HCI researcher or practitioner giving testimony for a legislature.

[11] Lazar, J., Abascal, J., Barbosa, S., Barksdale, J., Friedman, B., Grosslags, J., Gulliksen, J., Johnson, J., McEwan, T., Martínez-Normand, L., Michalk, W., Tsai, J.; van der Veer, G., von Axelson, H., Walldius, A., Whitney, G., Winckler, M., Wulf, V., Churchill, E. F., Cranor, L., Davis, J., Hedge, A., Hochheiser, H., Hourcade, J. P., Lewis, C., Nathan, L., Paterno, F., Reid, B., Quesenbery, W., Selker, T., & Wentz, B. (2016). Human–Computer Interaction and International Public Policymaking: A Framework for Understanding and Taking Future Actions. *Foundations and Trends in Human–Computer Interaction*, 9(2), pp. 69–149.

[12] Summers, K. & Langford, J. (2015). The Impact of Literacy on Usable and Accessible Electronic Voting. In *Universal Access in Human-Computer Interaction. Access to the Human Environment and Culture: 9th International Conference, UAHCI 2015, Held as Part of HCI International 2015*, Los Angeles, CA, USA, August 2–7, 2015, Proceedings, Part IV 9, pp. 248–257.

[13] Lazar, J., Abascal, J., Barbosa, S., Barksdale, J., Friedman, B., Grosslags, J., Gulliksen, J., Johnson, J., McEwan, T., Martínez-Normand, L., Michalk, W., Tsai, J.; van der Veer, G., von Axelson, H., Walldius, A., Whitney, G., Winckler, M., Wulf, V., Churchill, E. F., Cranor, L., Davis, J., Hedge, A., Hochheiser, H., Hourcade, J. P., Lewis, C., Nathan, L., Paterno, F., Reid, B., Quesenbery, W., Selker, T., & Wentz, B. (2016). Human–Computer Interaction and International Public Policymaking: A Framework for Understanding and Taking Future Actions. *Foundations and Trends in Human–Computer Interaction*, 9(2), pp. 69–149.

[14] Ibid.

[15] Laskowski, S. J., Autry, M., Cugini, J., Killam, W., & Yen, J. (2004). *Improving the Usability and Accessibility of Voting Systems and Products*. US Department of Commerce, National Institute of Standards and Technology. Available at: https://tsapps.nist.gov/publication/get_pdf.cfm?pub_id=906168.

In many U.S. jurisdictions, voting happens during even-numbered years: for instance, in 2020 and 2024, for the U.S. Presidential General Election, all U.S. representatives, and 1/3 of U.S. Senate seats, and in 2022, for all U.S. representatives, and another 1/3 of U.S. Senate seats. Most states and local jurisdictions try to make their local elections (for state legislatures, governors, etc.) fit this "every other year" pattern, although some have elections in odd-numbered years, and there are also "special elections" (e.g., when an elected government official dies in office). When there are elections, most jurisdictions have a primary election earlier in the year before the general election. On average, a voter who votes in all elections gets to vote once a year, but that voting is clustered in even-numbered years. Most voters will never have the opportunity to vote more than twice in a single year. So, voting is an irregular user experience, where users are not likely to remember how to use the exact interfaces and mechanisms for voting. Furthermore, as Bederson et al. (2003) describe:

> Unlike just about every other system in our society, voting systems must be usable by every citizen at least 18 years old. This includes the elderly, disabled, uneducated, and poor users. It also includes individuals who for whatever reason, have opted out of using electronic machinery – those who go into a bank and see a teller (instead of using an Automatic Teller Machine), don't scan their own groceries, and pay for gasoline with cash.[16]

So voting mechanisms must be usable by everyone of legal voting age, as well as usable with no training and with no recent usage, which is an especially challenging set of requirements for a good user interaction experience.[17] Yet those tasked with making decisions about which voting mechanisms will be used are generally concerned more with cost than any other factor and often have no training in usability.[18] All of these reasons contribute to the fact that the user interaction experience of voting remains poor. It is necessary to understand the history of voting mechanisms in the U.S. to help understand why this is such a complex and challenging area for the HCI community.

10.2 LEGAL HISTORY OF VOTING PROCEDURES AND MECHANISMS

Part of what makes voting so complex is that there are multiple levels of government in the U.S. involved with voting, including counties, states, and the federal

---

[16] Bederson, B. B., Lee, B., Sherman, R. M., Herrnson, P. S., & Niemi, R. G. (2003). Electronic Voting System Usability Issues. In *Proceedings of the SIGCHI Conference on Human Factors in Computing Systems*, pp. 145–152.

[17] Summers, K., Chisnell, D., Davies, D., Alton, N., & McKeever, M. (2014). Making Voting Accessible: Designing Digital Ballot Marking for People with Low Literacy and Mild Cognitive Disabilities. In *2014 Electronic Voting Technology Workshop/Workshop on Trustworthy Elections (EVT/WOTE 14)*.

[18] Bederson, B. B., Lee, B., Sherman, R. M., Herrnson, P. S., & Niemi, R. G. (2003). Electronic Voting System Usability Issues. In *Proceedings of the ACM SIGCHI Conference on Human Factors in Computing Systems*, pp. 145–152.

government, and these levels often make different choices when it comes to methods and interfaces for voting.[19] This complexity is not accidental: It goes all the way back to the U.S. Constitution, which gives each state control over the times, places, and manner for its elections, *"The Times, Places and Manner of holding Elections for Senators and Representatives, shall be prescribed in each State by the Legislature thereof; but the Congress may at any time by Law make or alter such Regulations, except as to the Places of chusing [choosing] Senators."*[20]

The U.S. Supreme Court, in the 2023 *Allen v. Milligan*[21] case, confirmed the role of the states in controlling elections, even in tense areas such as reapportionment, and even if the state laws have a discriminatory effect:

> *The Fifteenth Amendment – and thus §2 [of the Voting Rights Act] – prohibits States from acting with a "racially discriminatory motivation" or an "invidious purpose" to discriminate. Id., at 61–65 (plurality opinion). But it does not prohibit laws that are discriminatory only in effect.*

However, in another recent U.S. Supreme Court case, *Moore v. Harper*,[22] the justices decided on the issue of whether state legislatures had complete control over voting (the "independent legislature" theory being pushed by some on the right), or whether voting laws passed by the legislature were still subject to courts and constitutions. The Decision noted that the question being evaluated was:

> *…whether the Elections Clause insulates state legislatures from review by state courts for compliance with state law.*

And responded with saying:

> *We hold that it does not. The Elections Clause does not insulate state legislatures from the ordinary exercise of state judicial review…When a state legislature carries out its constitutional power to prescribe rules regulating federal elections, the "commission under which" it exercises authority is two-fold. The Federalist No. 78, at 467. The legislature acts both as a lawmaking body created and bound by its state constitution, and as the entity assigned particular authority by the Federal Constitution. Both constitutions restrain the legislature's exercise of power…State courts retain the authority to apply state constitutional restraints when legislatures act under the power conferred upon them by the Elections Clause. But federal courts must not abandon their own duty to exercise judicial review.*

---

[19] Lazar, J., Abascal, J., Barbosa, S., Barksdale, J., Friedman, B., Grossklags, J., Gulliksen, J., Johnson, J., McEwan, T., Martínez-Normand, L., Michalk, W., Tsai, J.; van der Veer, G., von Axelson, H., Walldius, A., Whitney, G., Winckler, M., Wulf, V., Churchill, E. F., Cranor, L., Davis, J., Hedge, A., Hochheiser, H., Hourcade, J. P., Lewis, C., Nathan, L., Paterno, F., Reid, B., Quesenbery, W., Selker, T., & Wentz, B. (2016). Human–Computer Interaction and International Public Policymaking: A Framework for Understanding and Taking Future Actions. *Foundations and Trends® in Human–Computer Interaction*, 9(2), pp. 69–149.

[20] U.S. Const. art. I, § 4, cl. 1.

[21] Allen v. Milligan 599 U. S. 1 (2023).

[22] Moore v. Harper 600 U. S. 1 (2023).

So, while the states do have the jurisdiction to determine all aspects of elections, the state legislature itself does not have complete control, as it is still subject to the checks and balances of the courts and the relevant state constitution.

10.2.1 Voting Rights Act

The fact that states had control over the manner of voting led to some states systematically excluding people of color from voting, within the "Jim Crow" framework of discrimination. The mechanisms of exclusion (such as asking potential voters to count the number of marbles in a jar), discrimination, and violence led to the passing of the Voting Rights Act of 1965 into law.[23]

We generally do not think of interfaces as discriminating based on race; however, eliminating racism in *procedures* is a core part of the Voting Rights Act:

> *(a) No voting qualification or prerequisite to voting or standard, practice, or procedure shall be imposed or applied by any State or political subdivision in a manner which results in a denial or abridgement of the right of any citizen of the United States to vote on account of race or color*[24]

While we tend to think of the Voting Rights Act of 1965 as focusing primarily on protecting voters based on race, it also included language designed to protect the voting rights of people with disabilities:

> *Any voter who requires assistance to vote by reason of blindness, disability, or inability to read or write may be given assistance by a person of the voter's choice, other than the voter's employer or agent of that employer or officer or agent of the voter's union.*[25]

In 1965, the Voting Rights Act did not require that accessible mechanisms be available for voting, and it did not protect the secret ballot of voters with disabilities. However, it is important to note that this early protection for people with disabilities came before any of the well-known federal disability rights laws – the Americans with Disabilities Act (1990), the Rehabilitation Act of 1973, or the Architectural Barriers Act (1968). A later statute, the Voting Accessibility for the Elderly and Handicapped Act (1984), focused on *"improving access for handicapped and elderly individuals to registration facilities and polling places for Federal elections,"*[26] but again did not focus on the voting mechanisms or the voting interfaces.[27] Additionally, in 1984, most voting was still being done using mechanical devices or on paper. However, there *were* hints along the way that the user experience of voting could be problematic.

---

[23] 52 U.S.C. § 10301.
[24] Ibid.
[25] 52 U.S.C. § 10508.
[26] 52 U.S.C. § 20101.
[27] See Waterstone, M. (2003). Constitutional and Statutory Voting Rights for People with Disabilities. *Stanford Law and Policy Review*, 68, pp. 1491–1550, for a discussion of how these statutes did not provide for the right to a private and independent vote for people with disabilities.

10.2.2 1984 Report from NIST

The federal Election Campaign Act Amendments of 1979 (signed into law on January 8, 1980), required that:

> The Federal Election Commission, with the cooperation and assistance of the National Bureau of Standards, shall conduct a preliminary study with respect to the future development of voluntary engineering and procedural performance standards for voting systems used in the United States. The Commission shall report to the Congress the results of the study, and such report shall include recommendations, if any, for the implementation of a program of such standards (including estimates of the costs and time requirements of implementing such a program).[28]

That report, called the "Report on the Feasibility of Developing Voluntary Standards for Voting Equipment" was issued in 1984 and described in detail many of the challenges to come with election systems in the future.[29] Note the use of the word "voluntary," which appears so frequently in discussion of voting system standards. The reason why is because, as mentioned earlier in this chapter, the U.S. Constitution gives each state the ability to determine how they run their own elections. Thus, barring some statutory and constitutional changes, any national standards for voting systems can only be "voluntary," as a national standard cannot be created.

The 1984 report defined "voting systems" as "... *any device, whether principally mechanical or electronic, which is primarily intended to record and/or tabulate individual voter choices in public elections.*"[30] At the time of the report, the primary voting interfaces were either mechanical levers or punch cards (over 85 percent),[31] and this hadn't changed by the mid-1990s.[32] While HCI researchers might not define these methods as "computing," a broader human factors researcher would definitely recognize the challenges of human interaction with these devices.

While the 1984 report focused primarily on the reliability and accuracy of potential voting systems, this report also noted the lack of research and expertise in what was then broadly called "human engineering standards":

> *Panelists stated that neither the manufacturer of voting systems nor most state and local election offices pay much attention to how the voter interacts with the various voting devices. Panelists cited evidence suggesting that not only ballot design, but the*

---

[28] PL 96–187 (HR 5010), PL 96–187, January 8, 1980, 93 Stat 1339.
[29] National Clearinghouse of Election Information of the Federal Election Commission. (1984). Voting System Standards: A report to the Congress on the development of voluntary engineering and procedural performance standards for voting systems.
[30] Ibid., p. 4.
[31] Ibid., p. 10.
[32] Bederson, B. B., Lee, B., Sherman, R. M., Herrnson, P. S., & Niemi, R. G. (2003). Electronic Voting System Usability Issues. In *Proceedings of the ACM SIGCHI Conference on Human Factors in Computing Systems*, pp. 145–152.

equipment itself, can have a great impact on minorities, minority language, handicapped, and visually impaired users. Panelists stressed that standards should encompass such matters with an emphasis on ballot design and format.[33]

The report also postulated that these human engineering standards might become political questions, potentially leading to any voluntary standards being ignored.[34]

The 1984 report accurately predicted that there was and would be very little work done in the next fifteen years on the user interaction aspects of electronic voting systems; as Roth stated in 1998, "The human use of voting equipment and voter's perceptions of the voting experience have largely been overlooked."[35]

In many ways, with one notable exception (the Roth 1998 report), the design of voting mechanisms and interfaces really did not come to the forefront of the human–computer interaction community until the 2000 U.S. Presidential Election. Interestingly, Bullock and Hood (2002) argue that the political science community also broadly ignored the mechanisms of voting, until the events of the 2000 presidential election.[36] Since then, there have been efforts from the HCI community to improve voting systems and interfaces, such as the Center for Civic Design.[37]

10.2.3 *The 2000 U.S. Presidential Election*

While there have been many criticisms of the 2000 U.S. Presidential General Election (e.g., how the Supreme Court ruled in *Bush v. Gore*),[38] we are going to focus solely on the elements of the voting interfaces that caused confusion. One of the best-known interface problems in 2000, the "butterfly ballot" from Palm Beach County, Florida, was a ballot where candidates were listed on two sides of a set of selection holes that a voter was asked to punch. Although these ballots were

---

[33] National Clearinghouse of Election Information of the Federal Election Commission. (1984). Voting System Standards: A Report to the Congress on the Development of Voluntary Engineering and Procedural Performance Standards for Voting Systems, pp. 21–22.

[34] National Clearinghouse of Election Information of the Federal Election Commission. (1984). Voting System Standards: A report to the Congress on the development of voluntary engineering and procedural performance standards for voting systems, p. 22.

[35] Roth, S. K. (1998). Disenfranchised by Design: Voting Systems and the Election Process. *Information Design Journal*, 9(1), 29–38. Roth's 1998 study comparing mechanical lever machines and punch card ballots to the direct record electronic voting machines is a notable exception to this lack of work between 1984 and 1999.

[36] Bullock, III, C. S., & Hood, III, M. V. (2002). One Person – No Vote; One Vote; Two Votes: Voting Methods, Ballot Types, and Undervote Frequency in the 2000 Presidential Election. *Social Science Quarterly*, 83(4), pp. 981–993.

[37] Center for Civic Design. (2024). Available at: https://civicdesign.org/.

[38] Balkin, J. M. (2001). Bush v. Gore and the Boundary Between Law and Politics. *The Yale Law Journal*, 110(8), pp. 1407–1458; Chemerinsky, E. (2000). Bush v. Gore was Not Justiciable. *Notre Dame Law Review*, 76, p. 1093; Klarman, M. J. (2001). Bush v. Gore Through the Lens of Constitutional History. *California Law Review*, 89(6), pp. 1721–1765 are some examples of the criticisms of that SCOTUS decision within legal scholarship.

in paper format because a voter was only supposed to select one candidate, these selection holes can be thought of as being conceptually like radio buttons (where only one option can be selected, whereas checkboxes allow for multiple selections). Six candidate teams for president were listed on the left side of the selection holes, and four candidate teams were listed on the right side of the selection holes. The core interface problem was that the first six candidates listed on the left did not match up with the first six holes; rather, the holes indicated choices that alternated from the left column to the right column. So, if a voter intended to vote for the candidate team of Al Gore and Joe Lieberman, which was the second candidate team listed on the left, if they punched the second hole, they actually would be voting for Pat Buchanan.[39] Researchers have estimated that due to this flaw in the voting mechanisms, more than 3,000 voters mistakenly voted for Pat Buchanan instead of Al Gore, which is more than George W. Bush's margin of victory.[40] In addition, for the eighteen counties in Florida which used the two-column format, the rate of overvoting was five times higher than in those counties that used a one-column ballot.[41]

The column layout was one of two major problems that voters faced with the voting mechanisms. Some of the voting mechanisms required that the voter physically punch a hole out of the ballot, known as "punch card ballots." In the 2000 presidential election, it was estimated that 32.1 percent of voters were utilizing punch card technologies.[42] When the holes are not completely punched out, this can lead to confusion in determining the voter's intent. Given that manual dexterity is not a requirement for voting, it is unclear why these types of voting machines were used so widely, since they may add hidden requirements for voting. Furthermore, Buchler et al. determined that the use of punch card voting leads to minority voters more frequently not having their votes counted as intended, compared to nonminority voters.[43] Later research by Byrne et al. (2007) found that punch card ballots have among the highest error rates; however, age of voter also played a role (surprisingly, older voters made fewer errors using the punch card ballot than younger voters).[44]

---

[39] Agresti, A. & Presnell, B. (2002). Misvotes, Undervotes and Overvotes: The 2000 Presidential Election in Florida. *Statistical Science*, 17(4), pp. 436–440.
[40] Wand, J. N., Shotts, K. W., Sekhon, J. S., Mebane, W. R., Herron, M. C., & Brady, H. E. (2001). The Butterfly Did It: The Aberrant Vote for Buchanan in Palm Beach County, Florida. *American Political Science Review*, 95(4), pp. 793–810.
[41] Agresti, A. & Presnell, B. (2002). Misvotes, Undervotes and Overvotes: The 2000 Presidential Election in Florida. *Statistical Science*, 17(4), pp. 436–440.
[42] Buchler, J., Jarvis, M., & McNulty, J. E. (2004). Punch Card Technology and the Racial Gap in Residual Votes. *Perspectives on Politics*, 2(3), pp. 517–524.
[43] Ibid.
[44] Byrne, M. D., Greene, K. K., & Everett, S. P. (2007, April). Usability of Voting Systems: Baseline Data for Paper, Punch Cards, and Lever Machines. In *Proceedings of the ACM SIGCHI Conference on Human Factors in Computing Systems*, pp. 171–180.

10.2.4 Help America Vote Act

The challenges in the 2000 election led to the passage of the Help America Vote Act (often known simply as HAVA).[45] HAVA had many different components, but the ones most relevant to HCI were providing funding to states for *"improving, acquiring, leasing, modifying, or replacing voting systems and technology and methods for casting and counting votes"*[46] A specific goal of HAVA was, *"… to replace punch card voting systems or lever voting systems (as the case may be) in qualifying precincts within that State with a voting system (by purchase, lease, or such other arrangement as may be appropriate) that--(A) does not use punch cards or levers.…"*[47]

While HAVA didn't (and couldn't) require what type of voting system jurisdictions should move to, a majority of the new voting systems introduced and adopted were electronic. HAVA also created the Election Assistance Commission to "serve as a national clearinghouse and resource for the compilation of information and review of procedures with respect to the administration of federal elections …,"[48] which, among other tasks, included that, "the Commission shall provide for the testing, certification, decertification, and recertification of voting system hardware and software by accredited laboratories"[49] as well as the creation of voluntary guidelines.[50] One component of HAVA which specifically mentioned human–computer interaction was:

> Not later than 1 year after October 29, 2002, the Commission, in consultation with the Director of the National Institute of Standards and Technology, shall submit a report to Congress which assesses the areas of human factor research, including usability engineering and human-computer and human-machine interaction, which feasibly could be applied to voting products and systems design to ensure the usability and accuracy of voting products and systems, including methods to improve access for individuals with disabilities (including blindness) and individuals with limited proficiency in the English language and to reduce voter error and the number of spoiled ballots in elections.[51]

10.2.5 The 2004 NIST Report

The NIST report on human factors in voting systems was published in 2004. For anyone interested in the post-2000 viewpoint on the user interaction issues of voting, this report is a required read, as it is the lead-up to the Voluntary Voting System Guidelines (VVSG), among other things. The report takes basic HCI concepts and

---

[45] 52 U.S.C. § 20901 et. seq.
[46] 52 U.S.C. § 20901(b)(1)(f).
[47] 52 U.S.C. § 20902(a)(2).
[48] 52 U.S.C. § 20922.
[49] 52 U.S.C. § 20971.
[50] 52 U.S.C.A. § 21101(a).
[51] 52 U.S.C. § 20983.

contextualizes them within voting. For instance, in the scenario where the voter has selected one candidate but either changes their mind or has selected that candidate in error, the report describes how different voting systems at that time would: (1) allow the voter to make the change without noting it; (2) display a dialog box asking the voter to confirm that indeed they are attempting to change that candidate selection; or, (3) require that the voter first unselect the first candidate before selecting another one.[52]

The 2004 report notes some basic performance requirements related to the user interface that have not changed over time, including the ability to cast a single vote in a winner-take-all race or multiple votes in a multimember election, the ability to modify votes selected before actually casting the ballot, preventing overvotes, and notifying voters if they have undervoted (not voted for the maximum number of candidates allowed in a given race or not voted for all races).[53]

The 2004 report also had ten recommendations related to the interaction design aspects of voting (shortened here for brevity): (1) Develop voting system standards for usability; (2) Specify the complete set of user-related functional requirements for voting products in the voting system standards; (3) Avoid low-level design specifications and very general specifications for usability; (4) Build a foundation of applied research for voting systems and products to support the development of usability and accessibility standards; (5) Tailor existing interface standards for accessibility to voting systems for review and testing; (6) Develop ballot design guidelines based on recent research from the visual design communities; (7) Develop a set of guidelines for facility and equipment layout and documentation and training materials; (8) Encourage vendors to incorporate a user-centered design approach into their product design and development cycles; (9) Develop a uniform set of procedures for testing voting systems for accessibility conformance; and (10) Develop a valid, reliable, repeatable, and reproducible process for usability conformance testing of voting products against the standards described in recommendation (1) with agreed-upon usability pass/fail requirements.[54]

The Election Assistance Commission, which came out of HAVA, is likely best known for voluntary guidelines, which are now known as the Voluntary Voting System Guidelines (VVSG).[55] Version 1 of VVSG was approved in 2005[56] and the

---

[52] Laskowski, S. J., Autry, M., Cugini, J., Killam, W., & Yen, J. (2004). *Improving the Usability and Accessibility of Voting Systems and Products*. US Department of Commerce, National Institute of Standards and Technology, p. 19. Available at: https://tsapps.nist.gov/publication/get_pdf.cfm?pub_id=906168.

[53] Ibid., p. 17.

[54] Laskowski, S. J., Autry, M., Cugini, J., Killam, W., & Yen, J. (2004). *Improving the Usability and Accessibility of Voting Systems and Products*. US Department of Commerce, National Institute of Standards and Technology, p. ii. Available at: https://tsapps.nist.gov/publication/get_pdf.cfm?pub_id=906168.

[55] U.S. Election Assistance Commission. (2024). Voluntary Voting System Guidelines. Available at: www.eac.gov/voting-equipment/voluntary-voting-system-guidelines.

[56] U.S. Election Assistance Commission. (2013). Voluntary Voting System Guidelines version 1. Available at: www.eac.gov/sites/default/files/eac_assets/1/6/VVSG.508compliant.2013.03.15.pdf.

current version of VVSG is version 2.0.[57] See Section 10.3.2 of this chapter for more information about the VVSG.

10.3 CURRENT LEGAL REQUIREMENTS

10.3.1 Help America Vote Act

The U.S. federal statute that has the greatest impact today on voting is the HAVA. Title III of the HAVA specifically mentions requirements related to usability which must be in voting systems used for federal elections and includes that voting systems must:

> (i) *permit the voter to verify (in a private and independent manner) the votes selected by the voter on the ballot before the ballot is cast and counted;*
> (ii) *provide the voter with the opportunity (in a private and independent manner) to change the ballot or correct any error before the ballot is cast and counted (including the opportunity to correct the error through the issuance of a replacement ballot if the voter was otherwise unable to change the ballot or correct any error); and*
> (iii) *if the voter selects votes for more than one candidate for a single office--*
>> (I) *notify the voter that the voter has selected more than one candidate for a single office on the ballot;*
>> (II) *notify the voter before the ballot is cast and counted of the effect of casting multiple votes for the office; and*
>> (III) *provide the voter with the opportunity to correct the ballot before the ballot is cast and counted.*[58]...
>
>> (A) *be accessible for individuals with disabilities, including nonvisual accessibility for the blind and visually impaired, in a manner that provides the same opportunity for access and participation (including privacy and independence) as for other voters;*
>> (B) *satisfy the requirement of subparagraph (A) through the use of at least one direct recording electronic voting system or other voting system equipped for individuals with disabilities at each polling place*[59]...
>
>> *Shall provide alternative language accessibility pursuant to the requirements of section 10503 of this title.*[60]

---

[57] U.S. Election Assistance Commission. (2021). Voluntary Voting System Guidelines version 2.0. Available at: www.eac.gov/sites/default/files/TestingCertification/Voluntary_Voting_System_Guidelines_Version_2_0.pdf.
[58] 52 U.S.C. § 21081(a)(1)(A)(i-iii).
[59] 52 U.S.C. § 21081(a)(3)(A-B).
[60] 52 U.S.C. § 21081(a)(4).

It is important to note that HAVA, in subsections A and B prior, was the first voting-related federal statute to require accessible voting mechanisms, rather than focusing only on accessible polling places or allowing for another individual to assist the voter with a disability. However, HAVA's requirement is for at least one accessible machine per polling place, not for all machines in a polling place to be accessible.[61] Nor does HAVA require that any ballots produced by the majority of voting machines in the polling place be identical to the ballots produced by the accessible voting machine. So under HAVA, the scenario can exist where, for instance, 98 percent of ballots cast in a polling place use optical scan ballots where voters fill in the bubbles on paper, and 2 percent of voters with print-related disabilities need to use a computerized ballot marking device which creates ballots with a different shape and format, and so the ballots of the voters with disabilities are easy to identify and possibly to trace back to the individual who voted.[62]

10.3.2 Voluntary Voting System Guidelines

As mentioned in previous sections, any standards for voting systems can only be voluntary guidance, not mandatory, due to the provisions in the U.S. Constitution. HAVA led to the development of the Voluntary Voting System Guidelines, known as VVSG and currently in Version 2.0. These guidelines are voluntary, as emphasized by the EAC on their website, "*While the Help America Vote Act (HAVA) mandates the EAC to develop and maintain these requirements, adhering to the VVSG is voluntary except in select states that require it by law.*"[63]

Version 2.0 of VVSG is 326 pages long,[64] so it's not possible to provide all of the relevant information within this chapter; however, the reader is pointed to VVSG Principle 8 – Robust, Safe, Usable, and Accessible.[65] Within principle 8 is included

---

[61] Some courts have said that the ADA cannot be used as an argument to require all voting machines in a polling place to be accessible, for instance, Am. Ass'n of People with Disabilities v. Harris, 647 F.3d 1093 (11th Cir. 2011).

[62] This exact scenario has happened in multiple years of elections in Maryland, where the state uses optical scan ballots, as well as an accessible ballot marking device for people with print disabilities, which creates ballots that look completely different from the optical scan ballots. Ironically, Maryland is the only state which has specific statutory text outlawing segregating balloting for people with disabilities: *(f) A voting system selected, certified, and implemented under this section shall:(1) provide access to voters with disabilities that is equivalent to access afforded voters without disabilities without creating a segregated ballot for voters with disabilities* Md. Code Ann., Elec. Law § 9–102. For more information, read: Lazar, J. (2019). Segregated Ballots for Voters with Disabilities? An Analysis of Policies and Use of the ExpressVote Ballot Marking Device. *Election Law Journal: Rules, Politics, and Policy*, 18(4), pp. 309–322.

[63] U.S. Election Assistance Commission. (2024). Voluntary Voting System Guidelines. Available at: www.eac.gov/voting-equipment/voluntary-voting-system-guidelines.

[64] U.S. Election Assistance Commission. (2021). Voluntary Voting System Guidelines version 2.0. Available at: www.eac.gov/sites/default/files/TestingCertification/Voluntary_Voting_System_Guidelines_Version_2_0.pdf.

[65] Ibid., p. 169

what might be considered human factors guidance on screen size, noting that screens should be anti-glare, have a minimum diagonal display size of 12 inches, and a minimum display resolution of 1920 × 1080 pixels[66] and should not give off more than three flashes in any one-minute period.[67] Requirements for accessibility of voting devices incorporate the Section 508 standards for accessibility, which were updated in 2017.[68]

Principle 5 of VVSG 2.0 – equivalent and consistent voter access – requires that all interaction methods of using a voting system (for instance, if a blind voter uses audio output instead of seeing the screen) must provide a consistent experience and provide equivalent information. *"Instructions, warnings, messages, notifications of undervotes or overvotes, and contest options must be presented to voters in [all] the display formats and interaction modes."*

There are broad suggestions for using HCI best practices, as well as more specific ones. For instance, VVSG 2.0 broadly highlights user-centered design:

The manufacturer must submit a report providing documentation that the system was developed following a user-centered design process.

The report must include, at a minimum:

1. *a listing of user-centered design methods used;*
2. *the types of voters and election workers included in those methods;*
3. *how those methods were integrated into the overall implementation process; and*
4. *how the results of those methods contributed to developing the final features and design of the voting system.*[69]

There is also more specific guidance for manufacturers to perform usability testing involving a diverse set of voters and election workers and report the results using the Common Industry Format (CIF) for Usability Test Reports.[70]

10.3.3 The Uniformed and Overseas Citizens Absentee Voting Act

It is important to note that voting can take place in three general timeframes: (1) at the polling place on election day; (2) using the same voting mechanisms during a period of early voting; or (3) via absentee/mail-in voting. The most traditional way to vote is in person, on election day. VVSG specifically notes that their guidelines are designed primarily for in person, election day voting:

---

[66] Ibid., p. 170.
[67] Ibid., p. 170.
[68] Ibid., p. 174.
[69] U.S. Election Assistance Commission. (2021). Voluntary Voting System Guidelines version 2.0, p. 72. Available at: www.eac.gov/sites/default/files/TestingCertification/Voluntary_Voting_System_Guidelines_Version_2_0.pdf.
[70] Ibid., pp. 169–177.

> There has been a growing trend to provide flexibility for voters to vote early and in-person at vote centers or at home using remote ballot marking applications. These innovative methods of voting provide additional paths to voting independently and privately for voters including those with disabilities.... These additional election systems require network access to synchronize voter records, access remote ballot marking applications, and transmit unofficial election results. The measures taken to securing these systems falls outside the scope of VVSG 2.0. However, the benefits and risks associated with the use of these technologies was carefully considered when developing the Guidelines, whereas the associated and requirements were created developed to ensure that the voting system is isolated from these additional election systems.[71]

In terms of early voting, typically the same voting mechanisms used on election day are used for early voting, the main difference being that early voting is only available at selected locations, not the widely available number of polling places used on election day. Voters may need to travel a longer distance to get to an early voting site, which is inconvenient. Yet, from an HCI point of view, the early voting experience is nearly identical to the election day experience. The only difference is that there are often fewer time pressures on the voter during early voting (since the voter chooses which day to go during the early voting period), lessening the stress and time pressure.[72]

Absentee and mail-based voting often use different mechanisms and different interfaces for voting than election day voting or early voting (specific rules are set by each state). It's important to note that at press time, eight states (i.e., California, Colorado, Hawaii, Nevada, Oregon, Utah, Vermont, and Washington) primarily use all-mail voting, where voters are automatically mailed a ballot, and only limited in-person voting is available.[73] For voters in other states, there is a process to request a mail-in ballot.

An absentee ballot, as the term is known, is simply a mail-in ballot which is not automatically sent but must be requested (some states allow you to permanently request mail-in ballots, rather than requiring that you request it each election). Some states set no conditions on who can request an absentee mail-in ballot; as long as you request an absentee ballot by the required deadline, you receive one.

---

[71] U.S. Election Assistance Commission. (2021). Voluntary Voting System Guidelines version 2.0, p. 12. Available at: www.eac.gov/sites/default/files/TestingCertification/Voluntary_Voting_System_Guidelines_Version_2_0.pdf.

[72] Summers, K., Langford, J., Rinn, C., Stevenson, J., Rhodes, E., Lee, J., & Sherard, R. (2017). Understanding Voting Barriers to Access for Americans with Low Literacy Skills. In *Design, User Experience, and Usability: Understanding Users and Contexts: 6th International Conference, DUXU 2017, held as part of HCI International 2017*, Vancouver, BC, Canada, July 9–14, 2017, *Proceedings, Part III 6*, pp. 294–312. Springer International Publishing.

[73] Available at: https://ballotpedia.org/All-mail_voting. Note that Utah will move away from all-mail voting starting in 2029. Also note that Kuhlmann and Lewis analyzed the impact of all-mail voting states on turnout by people with disabilities and found that in the five states that at the time had all-mail voting, voter turnout by people with disabilities was six points higher than in states without.

10.3 Current Legal Requirements

For instance, in Maryland, there are no criteria to meet; as long as you submit an application for an absentee ballot that is received by election officials at least seven days before the election, you receive an absentee ballot.[74] Alabama, on the other hand, limits absentee ballots to voters who meet criteria such as: (1) The voter will be absent from the county on Election Day, (2) the voter is ill or has a disability that prevents a trip to the polling place, (3) the voter is a registered voter living outside the country, such as a member of the armed forces, a voter employed outside the United States, a college student, or a spouse or child of such a person, (4) the voter is an appointed election officer or poll watcher at a polling place other than his or her regular polling place, or (5) the voter works a required shift of ten hours or more that coincides with polling hours.[75]

Rules for absentee/mail-in voting are generally set by each state, and typically involve paper ballots, rather than any type of electronic mechanisms, although people with disabilities have been successfully fighting for the right to use electronic, accessible mechanisms for absentee voting.[76] Before the recent COVID-19 pandemic, mail-in balloting was not widely popular unless you were out of the country or serving in the military. These are two situations where there is a federal statute that overrides any state-level rules on mail-in/absentee balloting: The Uniformed and Overseas Citizens Absentee Voting Act (UOCAVA)[77] is a federal statute which sets minimum requirements for states in providing access to voting for their citizens who are overseas or serving in the military:

Each State shall –

(1) *permit absent uniformed services voters and overseas voters to use absentee registration procedures and to vote by absentee ballot in general, special, primary, and runoff elections for Federal office;*

(2) *accept and process, with respect to any election for Federal office, any otherwise valid voter registration application and absentee ballot application from an absent uniformed services voter or overseas voter, if the application is received by the appropriate State election official not less than 30 days before the election*[78]

What is notable about UOCAVA in terms of voting mechanisms is that it requires that voters have the right to choose mail or electronic means for the overseas voting:

---

[74] Available at: https://ballotpedia.org/Election_administration_in_Maryland#Absentee_voting.
[75] Available at: https://ballotpedia.org/Election_administration_in_Alabama#Absentee/mail-in_voting.
[76] While a comprehensive listing of these cases is outside of the scope of this chapter, key precedents include Nat'l Fed'n of the Blind v. Lamone, 813 F.3d 494 (4th Cir. 2016) and Hindel v. Husted, 875 F.3d 344 (6th Cir. 2017). Instructions from states on accessible absentee ballots include www.ncsbe.gov/voting/help-voters-disabilities/accessible-absentee-voting for North Carolina, www.ohiosos.gov/elections/voters/voters-with-disabilities/Votingfaqs/ for Ohio, and https://absenteeballot.elections.ny.gov/home/accessible for New York.
[77] 52 U.S.C. 20301–20304.
[78] 52 U.S.C. § 20302(a).

(6) In addition to any other method of registering to vote or applying for an absentee ballot in the State, establish procedures –

(A) for absent uniformed services voters and overseas voters to request by mail and electronically voter registration applications and absentee ballot applications with respect to general, special, primary, and runoff elections for Federal office in accordance with subsection (e);

(B) for States to send by mail and electronically (in accordance with the preferred method of transmission designated by the absent uniformed services voter or overseas voter under subparagraph (C) voter registration applications and absentee ballot applications requested under subparagraph (A) in accordance with subsection (e); and

(C) by which the absent uniformed services voter or overseas voter can designate whether the voter prefers that such voter registration application or absentee ballot application be transmitted by mail or electronically;

(7) in addition to any other method of transmitting blank absentee ballots in the State, establish procedures for transmitting by mail and electronically blank absentee ballots to absent uniformed services voters and overseas voters with respect to general, special, primary, and runoff elections for Federal office in accordance with subsection (f)[79]

Because U.S. federal law is supreme over state law, UOCAVA means that an electronic means of voting is required to be offered for voters who qualify under UOCAVA, by either being overseas or in the military. That does not mean that an electronic option must necessarily exist for citizens who are living in a state and who simply prefer to vote without going to a polling place. A recent federal court decision in Alabama highlights that disparity. The court said, "*Alabama law does not allow domestic voters to submit electronic absentee ballots; they must use paper ballots. Only certain military and overseas voters can vote electronically.*"[80]

10.3.4 *State Laws on Voting Mechanisms*

As mentioned previously in this chapter, states have the primary jurisdiction in deciding the *"Times, Places and Manner of holding Elections."* State election law is currently a fast-moving area, with hundreds of new voting-related bills introduced every year across the various state legislatures, and with many of them being signed into law by the respective state governors. Many of these efforts, such as restrictions on voting registration, tougher ID requirements, postelection auditing, and purging voter rolls, or efforts to make it tougher to vote or to scare people from voting

---

[79] 52 U.S.C. § 20302(a)(6).
[80] Nat'l Fed'n of Blind of Alabama v. Allen, No. 2:22-CV-721-CLM, 2023 WL 2533049 (N.D. Ala. March 15, 2023).

(e.g., criminalizing minor infractions), are outside of the scope of HCI/UX (and therefore outside of the scope of this chapter). The major state statutes and regulations relating to voting mechanisms, generally relate to one of three areas:

1. limiting or expanding mail-in voting (e.g., by requiring that you have an excuse to request to absentee ballot);
2. limiting or expanding early voting, the number of polling places on election day, or the hours that you can vote on election day, and/or;
3. changing the type of voting machine that is required, or is primarily used (e.g., switching from/to optical scan ballots, direct recording electronic devices, ballot marking devices, etc.).

While members of the HCI community may have strong feelings about laws relating to the first two areas, only laws relating to area three are firmly in the province of HCI and thus should always involve input from the HCI community. Because of the fast-moving nature of these new state statutes and regulations, it is suggested that readers consult an up-to-date resource online with coverage across all states, such as https://ballotpedia.org/, https://verifiedvoting.org/, or www.brennancenter.org.

10.4 HOW CAN THE HCI COMMUNITY CONTRIBUTE TO THIS DISCUSSION?

As mentioned earlier in this chapter, the HCI community has had limited impact on voting interfaces, with little research into and even less development of voting interfaces.[81] Voting, due to the strong political structure, needs to have unbiased, empirical research influencing design choices made by jurisdictions in terms of what voting interfaces are used and how they are implemented. Yet there is very little of that research coming out focusing on the HCI aspects of voting. To have more of an impact on voting, the amount of HCI research and development being done in the area of voting should greatly increase. There are many potential topics, including:

- Researching existing voting interfaces and developing new voting interfaces for making voting easier to use for diverse voters (users with perceptual, motor, and/or cognitive disabilities; users across the age spectrum; and voters with lower literacy, civic literacy, and/or English proficiency)
- Research aimed at understanding how various voting interface choices impact the outcomes of elections

---

[81] With notable exceptions such as the Transparent Voting Interface documented in Gilbert, J. E., Laurenceau, I., & Louis, J. (2021). A Study of Ballot Anomaly Detection with a Transparent Voting Machine. *ACM Interactions*, 28(6), pp. 56–61.

- Research aimed at better understanding the intersection of voting security and voting usability and ways to enhance both security and usability
- Research into remote electronic and online voting

To help provide the growth and support for increased research into HCI and voting, community structures will need to be built. This includes:

- Workshops, journal special issues, and perhaps even a SIG on HCI and voting
- Awards that highlight effective research and development into HCI and voting
- Training for researchers on how to effectively engage your research with policymakers, politicians, and equipment manufacturers, for instance, how to word your HCI research to effectively communicate to those in the policy and legal communities,[82] such as "how to respond to a regulatory rulemaking."

10.5 SUMMARY

While there are many aspects and influences on voting, ensuring effective interface mechanisms for voting is especially important. Because of the infrequent nature of voting, voters don't have the benefit of learning how to use the voting mechanism from election to election. Furthermore, voting mechanisms continue to change. After the 2000 presidential election, many states moved toward direct recording electronic (DRE) voting machines, which used touchscreens and had audio options for people with print-related disabilities. However, there was a backlash against these machines because they did not provide a paper trail, and many states in the early-to-mid 2010s switched back to optical scan paper ballots. From 2008 through 2014, approximately 25% of voting precincts nationwide used only DREs with no paper verification trails for all voters, but by 2022, less than 5% used the DREs with no paper verification trails.[83] During that same time period from 2008 to 2022, the percentage of voting precincts using hand-marked paper ballots and ballot marking devices rose from 31% to over 67%. So even without a major usability debacle in a national election, the mechanisms and interfaces used by voters in elections continue to change, and so there is still an opportunity for the HCI community to engage in meaningful and impactful research and development on voting interfaces.

---

[82] For suggestions on translating research into policy impact, see Lazar, J. (2014). Engaging in Information Science Research that Informs Public Policy. *Library Quarterly*, 84(4), pp. 451–459.

[83] Data from verifiedvoting.org.

11

International Laws, Treaties, and HCI

11.1 WHAT IS AN INTERNATIONAL TREATY?

The concept of international laws or treaties between multiple nations can be traced back thousands of years. While older treaties often negotiated territory and border disputes or the end to armed conflicts, newer treaties and international laws cover a wider range of issues, from the rights of children, women, and people with disabilities to environmental protocols. Sometimes international laws, treaties, or policies are intended to impact a particular state or region (such as the European Union), but with the global tentacles of business and technology, they can end up having more of an international impact. The terms international treaty or international convention are interchangeable terms used to represent an agreement at the international level between various countries.[1] These agreements form the basis of what can be considered international law. Treaties can be established between individual countries or can be multilateral, such as those involving the United Nations. While much of the international law that impacts the U.S. is in the form of a treaty, there are also international laws that impact HCI in the U.S., such as the GDPR, which will be discussed later. Because the focus of this book is on U.S. law, the reason why only certain treaties and international laws are discussed in this chapter relates to their direct relevance or strong influence on U.S. law and HCI.

While the United Nations has been involved with hundreds of treaties, the international, multilateral treaties are the highest profile, for example, the Convention on the Prevention and Punishment of the Crime of Genocide, the International Convention on the Elimination of All Forms of Racial Discrimination, International Covenant on Civil and Political Rights, and the Convention on the Rights of Persons with Disabilities, to name a few.[2] While these major conventions do not specifically mention ICT (information and communications technologies) in their name, some of

---

[1] Legal Information Institute. *International Conventions*. Retrieved September 23, 2022, from www.law.cornell.edu/wex/international_conventions.

[2] United Nations. *International Law and Justice*. Retrieved September 22, 2022, from www.un.org/en/global-issues/international-law-and-justice.

them indirectly impact technology. One such U.N. convention, the World Intellectual Property Organization Convention, was signed in 1967 and amended in 1979.[3] It is fair to say, simply by that timeline, that ICT was not the original intent of that treaty, but only because of the context and timeline. IP law today, in general, is impacted by technology, as many innovations that fall under legal protections are technology related.

11.2 U.S. ADOPTION OF INTERNATIONAL TREATIES

Treaties that have been signed and ratified by the U.S., and result in a form of international law, are enacted through legislation or by the U.S. President through Executive Agreements.[4] An executive agreement does not mean that the U.S. has ratified a treaty. And, a signed agreement does not mean a binding agreement, unless it has been ratified by Congress. Within the U.S., an international convention is not viewed as legally binding simply because it exists. The 2008 U.S. Supreme Court case of *Medellin v. Texas* affirmed that international law by way of an international convention is binding law in the U.S. if the U.S. Congress passes legislation to make the convention binding.[5] The U.S. enters into more than 200 international agreements and treaties each year.[6] The U.S. Department of State maintains a list of "Treaties in Force" for the United States.[7] This is a much more wide-ranging list of treaties that include treaties with individual nations and multilateral treaties that include the United States and more than one other nation. It includes lower-stakes, more obscure agreements as well as more high-profile agreements. For example, included in the list is a 1963 agreement between the U.S. and Austria regarding financing educational exchange programs[8] and more historically significant agreements such as the 1947 agreement regarding the location of the United Nations.[9]

11.3 RATIFICATION AND THE IMPACT ON BINDING NATIONAL LAW

The U.S. is engaged with policy on a range of issues around the world; however, the U.S. Senate sometimes avoids ratifying U.N. treaties that relate to topics that

---

[3] World Intellectual Property Organization. (1967). *Summary of the Convention Establishing the World Intellectual Property Organization (WIPO Convention)*. Retrieved September 23, 2022, from www.wipo.int/treaties/en/convention/summary_wipo_convention.html.

[4] Epps, V., Cerone, J., & Roth, B. (2019). *International Law*, 6th ed. Carolina Academic Press, p. 13

[5] 552 U.S. 491 (2008).

[6] U.S. Department of State. *Treaties and International Agreements*. Retrieved October 2, 2022, from www.state.gov/policy-issues/treaties-and-international-agreements/.

[7] U.S. Department of State. Treaties in Force. Retrieved September 22, 2022, from www.state.gov/treaties-in-force/.

[8] U.S. Department of State. *Treaties in Force, A List of Treaties and Other International Agreements of the United States in Force on January 1, 2020* (January 1, 2020), www.state.gov/wp-content/uploads/2020/08/TIF-2020-Full-website-view.pdf, p. 30

[9] Ibid., p. 487.

in any way are politically controversial within the U.S. For example, the U.S. was actively involved in the negotiations prior to United Nations Convention on the Law of the Sea (UNCLOS); however, the United States has not ratified the current version of UNCLOS, even though it actively participated in the 1994 modifications to the treaty, citing concerns over the deep seabed mining provisions.[10] The ratification of the UNCLOS treaty has broad bipartisan support within the U.S., but not enough momentum to move it successfully through the U.S. Congress. Another example is the lack of U.S. ratification of the 1979 Convention on the Elimination of Discrimination Against Women (CEDAW).[11] This convention covers a broad swath of rights ranging from women's rights to the right to vote to reproductive rights, and the reproductive rights issue (primarily where it pertains to abortion) has been the primary reason for its political opposition in the United States.[12]

11.4 THE IMPACT OF INTERNATIONAL TREATIES ON HCI

International treaties, whether ratified by the U.S. or an influential international bloc (such as the EU), can have a varying degree of impact on HCI. Of the many international treaties, there are those treaties which are indirectly related to HCI and treaties that have a direct impact on HCI. When looking at treaties that could be indirectly related to HCI, consider treaties such as the International Covenant on Civil and Political Rights, or the International Convention on the Elimination of All Forms of Racial Discrimination. These do not immediately convey a strong relationship to HCI, yet if you look closer at those treaties, the International Covenant on Civil and Political Rights deals with free speech, and it is easy to then make the connection to HCI and design that enables or hinders freedom of speech. It is possible to imagine how the design of systems could relate to the support or restriction to civil and political rights, with the use of social media platforms that are often used in the debates and pursuits of civil and political rights. On the other hand, the connection to design and racial discrimination is also becoming clearer, most recently in regard to AI[13] (refer to Chapter 8 for more on artificial intelligence and HCI).

---

[10] U.S. Department of State. *Law of the Sea Convention*. Retrieved September 10, 2022, from www.state.gov/law-of-the-sea-convention/.

[11] United Nations. *International Law and Justice*. Retrieved September 22, 2022, from www.un.org/en/global-issues/international-law-and-justice.

[12] Baldez, L. (2014). Why the United States Has Not Ratified CEDAW. In *Defying Convention: US Resistance to the UN Treaty on Women's Rights* (Problems of International Politics, pp. 152–182). Cambridge: Cambridge University Press. doi:10.1017/CBO9781107775565.006.

[13] Hong, J. W. & Williams, D. (2019). Racism, Responsibility, and Autonomy in HCI: Testing Perceptions of an AI Agent. *Computers in Human Behavior*, 100, 79–84.

11.4.1 *Convention on the Rights of Persons with Disabilities (CRPD)*

Considering international treaties that directly relate to HCI, there is the U.N. Convention on the Rights of Persons with Disabilities, which was adopted in 2006, going into effect in 2008, for the 182+ countries which have ratified the CRPD.[14] There is also an optional protocol to the CRPD which adds procedures for submitting and investigating violations.[15] The U.S. remains the only permanent member of the U.N. Security Council to have signed but not yet ratified the CRPD, failing to reach enough votes in the U.S. Senate, despite the CRPD having many similarities to the Americans with Disabilities Act of 1990 (ADA), of which there is bipartisan support in the U.S.[16] It is important to note that the CRPD adopted what is technically a human rights model[17] (some would argue a social model of disability[18] versus a medical model) which means that there is a right not only against discrimination but also to equal rights that can be enforced and asserted by people with disabilities.[19] By contrast, the ADA requires a person to prove with medical evidence that they deserve the rights afforded to them, relying on a very "medical" approach versus a social approach to disability[20] or a human rights approach to disability. Unlike the ADA, the CRPD also extends the definition of equality in that the outcome or end result is critical – in other words, societal accommodations or modifications may be necessary.[21] Yet another difference is found in the ADA's reliance on people with disabilities bringing a complaint or a request for an accommodation versus the CRPD approach that emphasizes universal design or a more proactive, broad approach to inclusion.[22] One of the primary reasons for the CRPD's failure to be ratified in the U.S. Senate is the result of then Senators Rick Santorum of Pennsylvania and Mike Lee Lee of Utah, who brought the claim that ratification of the CRPD would infringe on U.S. sovereignty and parental rights, particularly in the area of education.[23] There is still bipartisan support for the CRPD (just as there was with the ADA), even though the U.S. has not yet successfully ratified the convention.

---

[14] United Nations Treaty Collection. Chapter 4: *Human Rights*. (December 13, 2006). https://treaties.un.org/Pages/ViewDetails.aspx?src=TREATY&mtdsg_no=IV-15&chapter=4&clang=_en.

[15] Ferrajolo, O. (2017). Optional Protocol to the Convention on the Rights of Persons with Disabilities. In *The United Nations Convention on the Rights of Persons with Disabilities: A Commentary*, pp. 703–729. Springer International Publishing.

[16] Kanter, A. S. (2019). Do Human Rights Treaties Matter: The Case for the United Nations Convention on the Rights of People with Disabilities. *Vanderbilt Journal of Transnational Law*, 52(3), pp. 577–609.

[17] Stein, M. A. (2007). Disability Human Rights. *California Law Review*, 75(95), pp. 75–121.

[18] Lawson, A. & Beckett, A. E. (2021). The Social and Human Rights Models of Disability: Towards a Complementarity Thesis. *The International Journal of Human Rights*, 25(2), pp. 348–379.

[19] Kanter, A. S. (2019). Let's Try Again: Why the United States Should Ratify the United Nations Convention on the Rights of People with Disabilities. *Touro Law Review*, 35(1), pp. 301–333.

[20] Ibid.

[21] Ibid., pp. 301–333.

[22] Ibid.

[23] Ibid.

11.4 The Impact of International Treaties on HCI

There is some dispute as to whether the CRPD envisioned a Human Rights or Social model of disability,[24] but either model would have a broader impact on U.S. technology than the narrower medical model as applied under the ADA in the U.S. With much of work, life, and pleasure being interconnected with the Web and other types of information technology, the accessibility and usability of that technology for people with disabilities is essential. Within the U.S., it has primarily been court precedent and federal government rulemaking which have been the focus for accessible technology requirements, less than in statutes. The rights afforded by the CRPD would remove any lack of clarity regarding the rights of people with disabilities regarding ICT.[25] In particular, CRPD article 9 (section g and h) focuses on accessibility to information and communications technology:[26]

1. To enable persons with disabilities to live independently and participate fully in all aspects of life, States Parties shall take appropriate measures to ensure to persons with disabilities access, on an equal basis with others, to the physical environment, to transportation, to information and communications, including information and communications technologies and systems, and to other facilities and services open or provided to the public, both in urban and in rural areas. These measures, which shall include the identification and elimination of obstacles and barriers to accessibility, shall apply to, inter alia:
   a) Buildings, roads, transportation and other indoor and outdoor facilities, including schools, housing, medical facilities and workplaces;
   b) Information, communications and other services, including electronic services and emergency services.
2. States Parties shall also take appropriate measures:
   a) To develop, promulgate and monitor the implementation of minimum standards and guidelines for the accessibility of facilities and services open or provided to the public;
   b) To ensure that private entities that offer facilities and services which are open or provided to the public take into account all aspects of accessibility for persons with disabilities;
   c) To provide training for stakeholders on accessibility issues facing persons with disabilities;
   d) To provide in buildings and other facilities open to the public signage in Braille and in easy to read and understand forms;

---

[24] Lawson, A. & Beckett, A. E. (2021). The Social and Human Rights Models of Disability: Towards a Complementarity Thesis. *The International Journal of Human Rights*, 25(2), pp. 348–379.

[25] Mantegna, J. (2013, July). *United Nations Accessibility and Information Technology*. Available at: https://abilitymagazine.com/united-nations-accessiblity-and-assistive-technology/.

[26] United Nations. *Convention on the Rights of Persons with Disabilities: Article 9–Accessibility*. (January 24, 2007). www.un.org/development/desa/disabilities/convention-on-the-rights-of-persons-with-disabilities/article-9-accessibility.html.

e) To provide forms of live assistance and intermediaries, including guides, readers and professional sign language interpreters, to facilitate accessibility to buildings and other facilities open to the public;
f) To promote other appropriate forms of assistance and support to persons with disabilities to ensure their access to information;
g) To promote access for persons with disabilities to new information and communications technologies and systems, including the Internet;
h) To promote the design, development, production and distribution of accessible information and communications technologies and systems at an early stage, so that these technologies and systems become accessible at minimum cost.

Article 21 has a focus on freedom of expression:[27]

> States Parties shall take all appropriate measures to ensure that persons with disabilities can exercise the right to freedom of expression and opinion, including the freedom to seek, receive and impart information and ideas on an equal basis with others and through all forms of communication of their choice, as defined in article 2 of the present Convention, including by:
>
> a) Providing information intended for the general public to persons with disabilities in accessible formats and technologies appropriate to different kinds of disabilities in a timely manner and without additional cost;
> b) Accepting and facilitating the use of sign languages, Braille, augmentative and alternative communication, and all other accessible means, modes and formats of communication of their choice by persons with disabilities in official interactions;
> c) Urging private entities that provide services to the general public, including through the Internet, to provide information and services in accessible and usable formats for persons with disabilities;
> d) Encouraging the mass media, including providers of information through the Internet, to make their services accessible to persons with disabilities;
> e) Recognizing and promoting the use of sign languages.

Both of these aspects of the CRPD directly impact HCI, and while the U.S. has not yet ratified the CRPD, there are so many significant technology partners around the world who have ratified the CRPD, it is impossible to say that it does not impact HCI in the U.S. Yet another example of how a treaty such as the CRPD might connect to HCI is illustrated in the topic of accessible gaming, with gaming having connections to accessibility, leveraged for educational purposes, utilized for

---

[27] United Nations. *Convention on the Rights of Persons with Disabilities: Article 21– Freedom of Expression.* (January 24, 2007). https://social.desa.un.org/issues/disability/crpd/article-21-freedom-of-expression-and-opinion-and-access-to-information.

rehabilitative methods, and directly related to recreation and sports. So, this topic then has implications to CRPD to Article 9 (Accessibility), Article 24 (Education), Article 26 (Habilitation and Rehabilitation), and Article 30 (Participation in Cultural Life, Recreation, Leisure, and Sport).[28]

11.4.2 International Covenant on Civil and Political Rights (ICCPR)

Another international treaty, the International Covenant on Civil and Political Rights (ICCPR), does not address the modern Internet, but it does address access to information, which would equal the modern use of the Internet – however, it is important to note that the U.S. has not ratified this treaty.[29] It is still important to mention within the context of U.S. HCI because many technology- or web-based products do not have a clear delineation at national borders due to their widespread use. While this treaty should be revised to reflect changes with ICT, the ratification of such a treaty would address things such as human rights protections online, in particular, Articles 19 and 25:[30]

Article 19

1. Everyone shall have the right to hold opinions without interference.
2. Everyone shall have the right to freedom of expression; this right shall include freedom to seek, receive and impart information and ideas of all kinds, regardless of frontiers, either orally, in writing or in print, in the form of art, or through any other media of his choice.
3. The exercise of the rights provided for in paragraph 2 of this article carries with it special duties and responsibilities. It may therefore be subject to certain restrictions, but these shall only be such as are provided by law and are necessary:
   (a) For respect of the rights or reputations of others;
   (b) For the protection of national security or of public order (ordre public), or of public health or morals.

Article 25

Every citizen shall have the right and the opportunity, without any of the distinctions mentioned in article 2 and without unreasonable restrictions:

(a) To take part in the conduct of public affairs, directly or through freely chosen representatives;

---

[28] Chakraborty, J. (2017). How Does Inaccessible Gaming Lead to Social Exclusion. *Disability, Human Rights, and Information Technology.* The University of Pennsylvania Press, Philadelphia, pp. 212–223.
[29] Land, M. K. & Aronson, J. D. (2018). *New Technologies for Human Rights Law and Practice.* Cambridge University Press, p. 234.
[30] United Nations. *International Covenant on Civil and Political Rights.* (December 16, 1966). www.ohchr.org/en/instruments-mechanisms/instruments/international-covenant-civil-and-political-rights.

(b) *To vote and to be elected at genuine periodic elections which shall be by universal and equal suffrage and shall be held by secret ballot, guaranteeing the free expression of the will of the electors;*

(c) *To have access, on general terms of equality, to public service in his country.*

11.4.3 Marrakesh Treaty

Intellectual property laws such as copyright laws enacted by countries around the world often also have international implications. Like the impact of the GDPR, copyright laws can also impact U.S. technology companies. One such example in 2021 was the French fine of $593 million levied against Google related to search engine content.[31] Of more direct impact is the Marrakesh Treaty, which was established by the World Trade Organization (WTO), has been in force since 2013, and is legally binding in the U.S.[32] This international agreement has had implications for U.S. technology, particularly in connection to the protection of copyright works and implications for IP law, by permitting published works to be created in an accessible format for people with disabilities where previously restrictive national copyright laws would have prevented such technology-enabled access.[33] This has had specific implications for companies and organizations involved with e-books, including libraries.[34] Aside from the Marrakesh Treaty, in the U.S., the Chafee Amendment to U.S. copyright law has also permitted alternative accessible copies of print materials to be created for people with disabilities.[35] Two key aspects of the Marrakesh Treaty as it relates to technology are the exemption in national copyright laws when creating accessible formats of materials and the cross-border flow of such formats. Article 11 of the Marrakesh Treaty covers the topic of "fair use," which is of particular relevance to the accessibility of digital content. It refers to the Intellectual Property (IP) law concept of fair use:[36]

> Article 11
>
> *General Obligations on Limitations and Exceptions*
>
> *In adopting measures necessary to ensure the application of this Treaty, a Contracting Party may exercise the rights and shall comply with the obligations that*

---

[31] Schechner, S. *Google Fined $593 Million in France Over Treatment of News Publishers.* (July 13, 2021), www.wsj.com/articles/google-fined-593-million-in-france-over-treatment-of-news-publishers-11626164911.

[32] Stamm, A. & Hsu, Y. (2021). The Marrakesh Treaty's Impact on the Accessibility and Reproduction of Published Works, 65. *TechTrends*, 5, pp. 692–695.

[33] Ibid.

[34] Helfer, L. R., Land, M. K., & Okediji, R. (2020). *Copyright Exceptions Across Borders: Implementing the Marrakesh Treaty*, p. 336.

[35] Lingane, A. & Fruchterman, J. (2003). The Chafee Amendment: Improving Access to Information. *Information Technology and Disabilities Journal*, 9(1), p. 1.

[36] World Intellectual Property Organization. *Marrakesh Treaty to Facilitate Published Works for Persons Who are Blind, Visually Impaired, or Otherwise Print Disabled.* (September 30, 2016). www.wipo.int/wipolex/en/text/301016.

that Contracting Party has under the Berne Convention, the Agreement on Trade-Related Aspects of Intellectual Property Rights and the WIPO Copyright Treaty, including their interpretative agreements so that:

(a) *in accordance with Article 9(2) of the Berne Convention, a Contracting Party may permit the reproduction of works in certain special cases provided that such reproduction does not conflict with a normal exploitation of the work and does not unreasonably prejudice the legitimate interests of the author;*

(b) *in accordance with Article 13 of the Agreement on Trade-Related Aspects of Intellectual Property Rights, a Contracting Party shall confine limitations or exceptions to exclusive rights to certain special cases which do not conflict with a normal exploitation of the work and do not unreasonably prejudice the legitimate interests of the rightholder;*

(c) *in accordance with Article 10(1) of the WIPO Copyright Treaty, a Contracting Party may provide for limitations of or exceptions to the rights granted to authors under the WCT in certain special cases, that do not conflict with a normal exploitation of the work and do not unreasonably prejudice the legitimate interests of the author;*

(d) *in accordance with Article 10(2) of the WIPO Copyright Treaty, a Contracting Party shall confine, when applying the Berne Convention, any limitations of or exceptions to rights to certain special cases that do not conflict with a normal exploitation of the work and do not unreasonably prejudice the legitimate interests of the author.*

National law defines and further clarifies some of the scope of this aspect of copyright law. There again is the case of tension or differences between national law and international law. Some countries (e.g., India and Israel[37]) have a broader approach to this, including all disabilities, and not only print disabilities. The question of entities that are allowed to create materials in accessible format and are covered under this treaty is addressed in Article 2(c) of the treaty,[38]

(c) "'authorized entity' means an entity that is authorized or recognized by the government to provide education, instructional training, adaptive reading or information access to beneficiary persons on a non-profit basis. It also includes a government institution or non-profit organization that provides the same services to beneficiary persons as one of its primary activities or institutional obligations."

One could imagine that some national governments may authorize or recognize entities that are not authorized or recognized by other national governments. Refer to Chapter 6 for a more in-depth discussion of the impact of IP law on HCI.

---

[37] Ncube, C. B., Reid, B. E., & Oriakhogba, D. O. (2020). Beyond the Marrakesh VIP Treaty: Typology of Copyright Access-Enabling Provisions for Persons with Disabilities. *The Journal of World Intellectual Property*, 23(3–4), pp. 149–165.

[38] World Intellectual Property Organization. (September 30, 2016). *Marrakesh Treaty to Facilitate Published Works for Persons Who are Blind, Visually Impaired, or Otherwise Print Disabled.* www.wipo.int/wipolex/en/text/301016.

11.5 INTERNATIONAL LAWS THAT IMPACT HCI IN THE U.S.

11.5.1 General Data Protection Regulation

The General Data Protection Regulation (GDPR) is the name for an EU law that is not a treaty and has not been ratified by the U.S. However, unlike many laws passed in a particular nation, this law directly impacts organizations based in any country across the world, as long as that organization collects data or targets anyone within the EU.[39] Because of the global nature of most technology platforms and e-commerce, this law ends up having an international reach because of those parameters. It details how data is collected, stored, protected, and used and how consent of individuals whose data may be collected must work.[40] U.S. websites and systems that are used internationally or have EU clients must now consider these privacy and data collection requirements in their design and redesign. Under the GDPR, any website or system that has customers in the EU is required to follow the requirements regarding data collection and privacy. The Territorial Scope portion (Article 3) makes it clear that the processing of data does not have to be within the European Union:[41]

> *Territorial scope*
> *This Regulation applies to the processing of personal data in the context of the activities of an establishment of a controller or a processor in the Union, regardless of whether the processing takes place in the Union or not.*
>
> *This Regulation applies to the processing of personal data of data subjects who are in the Union by a controller or processor not established in the Union, where the processing activities are related to:*
> *the offering of goods or services, irrespective of whether a payment of the data subject is required, to such data subjects in the Union; or*
> *the monitoring of their behaviour as far as their behaviour takes place within the Union.*
>
> *This Regulation applies to the processing of personal data by a controller not established in the Union, but in a place where Member State law applies by virtue of public international law.*

11.5.2 Digital Services Act

In July 2022, the EU approved a new law focused on "illegal" content online, called the Digital Services Act.[42] This is also not a treaty and has not been ratified by the

---

[39] Ibid.
[40] Ibid.
[41] European Union. *General Data Protection Regulation (GDPR)*. (2016/679). https://gdpr-info.eu/art-3-gdpr/.
[42] European Commission. *The Digital Services Act Package*. Retrieved October 1, 2022, from https://digital-strategy.ec.europa.eu/en/policies/digital-services-act-package.

U.S. This law regulates sites that promote child sexual abuse, terrorist content, or hate speech; sites that profile and target children based on categories of personal data; and sites that use "dark pattern" design.[43] The so-called "dark patterns" refers to the concept where an interface design is deceptive and manipulative, with a perfect example being a subscription where the "unsubscribe" button is designed to be small and difficult to find versus the other visual options available.[44] Article 67 of this EU law focuses on dark patterns:[45]

> *Dark patterns on online interfaces of online platforms are practices that materially distort or impair, either on purpose or in effect, the ability of recipients of the service to make autonomous and informed choices or decisions. Those practices can be used to persuade the recipients of the service to engage in unwanted behaviours or into undesired decisions which have negative consequences for them. Providers of online platforms should therefore be prohibited from deceiving or nudging recipients of the service and from distorting or impairing the autonomy, decision-making, or choice of the recipients of the service via the structure, design or functionalities of an online interface or a part thereof. This should include, but not be limited to, exploitative design choices to direct the recipient to actions that benefit the provider of online platforms, but which may not be in the recipients' interests, presenting choices in a non-neutral manner, such as giving more prominence to certain choices through visual, auditory, or other components, when asking the recipient of the service for a decision.*
>
> *It should also include repeatedly requesting a recipient of the service to make a choice where such a choice has already been made, making the procedure of cancelling a service significantly more cumbersome than signing up to it, or making certain choices more difficult or time-consuming than others, making it unreasonably difficult to discontinue purchases or to sign out from a given online platform allowing consumers to conclude distance contracts with traders, and deceiving the recipients of the service by nudging them into decisions on transactions, or by default settings that are very difficult to change, and so unreasonably bias the decision making of the recipient of the service, in a way that distorts and impairs their autonomy, decision-making and choice. However, rules preventing dark patterns should not be understood as preventing providers to interact directly with recipients of the service and to offer new or additional services to them. Legitimate practices, for example in advertising, that are in compliance with Union law should not in themselves be regarded as constituting dark patterns. Those rules on dark patterns should be interpreted as covering prohibited practices falling within the scope of this Regulation to the extent that those practices are not already covered under Directive 2005/29/EC or Regulation (EU) 2016/679.*

---

[43] Ibid.
[44] Ravenscraft, E. (July 29, 2020). *How to Spot – and Avoid – Dark Patterns on the Web.* Available at: www.wired.com/story/how-to-spot-avoid-dark-patterns/.
[45] European Parliament. *Regulation (EU) 2022/2065 of the European Parliament and of the Council of 19 October 2022 on a Single Market For Digital Services and amending Directive 2000/31/EC (Digital Services Act).* (October 19, 2022). https://eur-lex.europa.eu/legal-content/EN/TXT/HTML/?uri=CELEX:32022R2065.

Refer to Chapter 9 for more discussion of legal issues regarding dark patterns and design. If the reach of the GDPR to U.S. companies and their technology is a point of comparison, it is likely that the Digital Services Act will also impact U.S. technology and companies.

11.6 TECHNOLOGY AND INDIRECT INTERNATIONAL IMPACT

As evidenced by some of the European laws mentioned, including the GDPR and Digital Services Act, there are times when U.S.-based technology companies are impacted by internal laws that are not directly connected to the U.S. For example, in 2018 the European Union implemented a significant data privacy and security law across its member states.[46]

Another example of technology-related laws enacted in one country impacting U.S.-based companies that offer services and products internationally is the Data Security Law and Personal Protection Law that went into effect in China in November 2021.[47] The data policy regulates, among other things, data activities that could "harm the national security of the People's Republic of China," and this concept of state review and control of data transactions is one reason the U.S.-based LinkedIn recalled its Chinese operations in 2021.[48] The question of whether local laws can extend their territorial reach beyond their borders and receive international jurisdiction is met with disagreement by nations around the world, however, data protection is one subject where countries seem to less strongly protest the international requirements of local or regional laws such as the GDPR.[49] It is clear that cybersecurity data threats are a global concern, and all countries could benefit from a treaty related to data and technology systems security. As a result of the digital threats from international cybercriminals or nations as a form of cyber warfare, there have been increasing calls for a so-called "Digital Geneva Convention," including from the World Economic Forum in 2017, recognizing the cyber arms race that is happening, and the need to protect civilians as they use web-based technology, much like the necessity to protect civilians during times of war.[50] This concept could probably be expanded to state that a more comprehensive convention on ICT and the international community is likely long overdue.

---

[46] Wolford, B. *What is GDPR, the EU's new data protection law?* Retrieved September 30, 2022, from https://gdpr.eu/what-is-gdpr/.

[47] National People's Congress. (June 10, 2021). *Data Security Law of the People's Republic of China*. Available at: www.npc.gov.cn/englishnpc/c23934/202112/1abd88297889460ecab270e469b13c39c.shtml.

[48] Weise, K. & Mozur, P. *LinkedIn to Shut Down Service in China, Citing 'Challenging' Environment* (October 14, 2021), www.nytimes.com/2021/10/14/technology/linkedin-china-microsoft.html.

[49] Ryngaert, C. & Mistale, T. (2020). Symposium on the GDPR and International Law: The GDPR as Global Data Protection Regulation? *American Journal of International Law*, 114(5), pp. 7–8.

[50] World Economic Forum. (December 29, 2017). *Why We Urgently Need a Digital Geneva Convention*. Available at: www.weforum.org/agenda/2017/12/why-we-urgently-need-a-digital-geneva-convention/.

Yet another example of international laws and regulations impacting U.S. technology would be the Restriction on the use of certain Hazardous Substances (or RoHS) laws that have been enacted in the EU, China, Japan, and Korea to restrict hazardous components (such as lead, mercury, and PBBs) from being used in the production of electronic equipment.[51] While the U.S. (except for certain states, such as California, New Jersey, Illinois, Indiana, Minnesota, New York, Rhode Island, and Wisconsin) does not have RoHS regulations, the impact of such international regulations ultimately also impacts U.S. technology companies.[52] This is another example of an indirect connection to HCI, specifically HCI efforts related to sustainability.[53]

If products will not be sold in Europe or U.S. states or countries with such regulations, the U.S. technology companies do not need to comply, however, the reality is that companies do not want to be restricted to sales in those locations, and it is not practical to design and manufacture multiple versions of technology components – some which are compliant and others which are not. While there is not one comprehensive international law that covers all areas of ICT, and the U.S. has not ratified some international treaties that impact ICT, the mesh of international treaties that are in force as well as the indirect reach of regional international laws do impact U.S. technology and technology companies.

---

[51] NIST. (2021, February). *Compliance FAQs: RoHS*. Available at: www.nist.gov/standardsgov/compliance-faqs-rohs.
[52] Ibid.
[53] Bates, O., Thomas, V., Remy, C., Nathan, L. P., Mann, S., & Friday, A. (2018, April). The Future of HCI and Sustainability: Championing Environmental and Social Justice. In *Extended Abstracts of the 2018 CHI Conference on Human Factors in Computing Systems*, pp. 1–4.

Index

9/11 Commission, 5
11th circuit, 56
21st Century Communications and Video
  Accessibility Act (CVAA), 61–62, 67,
  187–188
5G networks, 196–197

absentee ballot, 244–245
absentee voting, 244–246
accessibility, digital technologies and content. *See*
  digital accessibility
ACM. *See* Association for Computing
  Machinery (ACM)
ACM Publications Policy on Research Involving
  Human Subjects and Participants,
  127–128, 133
ACPA. *See* Anti-Cybersquatting Consumer
  Protection Act (ACPA)
ADA. *See* Americans with Disabilities Act (ADA)
administrative agencies, 5, 15
  judicial deference. *See* judicial deference
  judicial review, 8
  rules, 7
administrative law, 4–5, 14
  judicial deference, 5
    Auer deference, 7
    Chevron deference, 5–6, 44, 189
    Skidmore deference, 7
  rulemaking process by, 7–8
Administrative Procedure Act (APA), 7–8
administrative rulemaking, 7
  exempted, 7
  formal, 7
  informal, 7–8
adversarial system of law, 3
agile, 23
Agreement on Trade-Related Aspects of Intellectual
  Property Rights (TRIPS), 164, 257
AI. *See* artificial intelligence (AI)

AIA. *See* Leahy-Smith America Invents Act (AIA)
Air Carrier Access Act, 6, 40, 41, 47–48, 52
airport kiosks, 48
Alaska Constitution, 97
algorithmic bias, 108
Americans with Disabilities Act (ADA), 34, 41,
  48–49, 242, 252, 253
  CRPD v., 252
  nexus theory of, 41–43
  Online Accessibility Act, 67, 69
  Title I (employment), 41, 49, 58–60
  Title II (state and local governments), 6, 49, 65
  Title III (public accommodations), 6, 40, 41,
    49, 53–58, 65
    effective communications requirement
      under, 6, 41, 43–44, 54, 65
    nexus between web accessibility and,
      41–43, 54, 65
amicus curiae, 43
Anti-Cybersquatting Consumer Protection Act
  (ACPA), 168
APA. *See* Administrative Procedure Act (APA)
appellate courts, 8, 9–11, 12, 20, 139
appellate process, 9–11
Architectural Barriers Act (ABA) of 1968, 70
artificial intelligence (AI), 27, 112, 133, 137,
  198–201, 211
  autonomous-vehicle (AV), 200
  bias and discrimination, 204–207
  Blueprint for an AI Bill of Rights, 201
  deepfakes, 200, 201–204, 210
  definition, 198
  Executive Order on Safe, Secure, and
    Trustworthy Artificial Intelligence,
    201, 203
  generative. *See* generative AI
  human-centered, 199
  patents of, 208
  and privacy laws, 108

263

Artificial Intelligence Act, 108
Asplund, J., 206
Association for Computing Machinery (ACM), 27, 135, 155, 158, 213
  ASSETS Conference, 27
  CHI conference, 22, 27
  FaccT, 28
  SIGCHI, 22, 27
  SIGSAC, 22
  Symposium on Computer Science and Law, 29
Attribution (BY) CC license, 156
autonomous-vehicle (AV), 200

Bederson, B. B., 233
Belmont Report, 116, 118, 127, 135
Berne Convention for the Protection of Literary and Artistic Works, 149, 152, 257
bias, AI, 204–207
big data research, 129–132
Bill of Rights, 4, 8, 74, 85
  Blueprint for an AI Bill of Rights, 201
Biometric Information Privacy Act (BIPA), 106
BIPA. *See* Biometric Information Privacy Act (BIPA)
Bluebook, 18, 19
Blueprint for an AI Bill of Rights, 201
born-accessible model, 47
  accessibility in procurement process, 37
  content/application/technologies, building, 37–38
  evaluation of accessibility, 38–39
    automated accessibility testing tool, 38
    manual inspections, 38
    usability testing, 38
  people with disabilities in design/development, involvement of, 36–37
Brandeis, Louis, 74
British Statute of Monopolies of 1623, 138
Bruckman, A., 113, 130
Bullock, III, C. S., 237
butterfly ballot, 237–238
Byrne, M. D., 238

CAADCA. *See* California Age-Appropriate Design Code Act (CAADCA)
California Age-Appropriate Design Code Act (CAADCA), 221–222
California Consumer Privacy Act (CCPA) of 2020, 84–85, 98–99, 100, 101, 102
  centralizing enforcement authority, 106
  on dark patterns, 225–226
California Privacy Protection Agency (CPPA), 99
California Privacy Rights Act (CPRA), 99
Calo, Ryan, 199
Canada, human subjects research regulation in, 126

Candidate Elections Deepfake Disclosures Act, 203
CASE Act of 2020, 161
case citation, 15–17
case law, 33, 34, 49, 53, 85, 139, 149, 198, 208
  copyrights, 159–160
  dark (deceptive) patterns, 217–218
  human subjects research, 120
  patents, 142–144
  privacy, 86–87
  trademarks, 168–170
CBP. *See* U.S. Customs and Border Protection (CBP)
CCPA. *See* California Consumer Privacy Act (CCPA) of 2020
CDA. *See* Communications Decency Act (CDA) of 1996
CEDAW. *See* Convention on the Elimination of Discrimination Against Women (CEDAW)
certification mark, 164
CFAA. *See* Computer Fraud and Abuse Act (CFAA)
Chafee Amendment, 256
chatbots, 198, 209, 210
Chesney, Robert, 202
Chevron deference, 5–6, 44, 189
CHI (Computer–Human Interaction), 22, 27
Chief Digital Accessibility officer, 39
Children's Internet Protection Act (CIPA), 91–92
Children's Online Privacy Protection Act (COPPA), 95
CIPA. *See* Children's Internet Protection Act (CIPA)
Circuit Courts of Appeals, 11–13
circuit split, 11, 19, 42
Citron, Danielle, 202
civil law, 2, 13
Clinton, Bill, 152
Code of Federal Regulations, 17, 18, 132
Colorado Privacy Act (CPA), 99, 100
Commerce Clause, 178–179
common law, 2, 13, 14, 33, 74, 142, 149, 159, 163, 170
The Common Rule, 111, 113, 114, 117, 120, 122, 123, 124, 126, 128, 129, 134
  §46.101, 117
  §46.102, 117
  §46.111, 118
  direct remedy for violation of, lack of, 120
  enforcement of compliance, 121–122
  and IRBs. *See* institutional review boards (IRBs)
  private rights of action, lack of, 120, 132
  suing for injury, 121
  violation of, 124, 132
  wrongful termination, 122

Commonwealth Court, 10
Communications Act of 1934, 176, 182, 188, 189, 194
  Section 255, 196
Communications Decency Act (CDA) of 1996, 183–186
Computer Fraud and Abuse Act (CFAA), 176
Computer Matching and Privacy Protection Act of 1988, 93–94
Connecticut Data Privacy Act (CTDPA), 100–101
Consolidated Appropriations Act of 2023, 46, 47
constitutional law, 4
Convention on the Elimination of Discrimination Against Women (CEDAW), 251
Convention on the Rights of Persons with Disabilities (CRPD), 252–255
cookie banners, xii
COPPA. *See* Children's Online Privacy Protection Act (COPPA)
Copyright Act, 147, 157
Copyright Act of 1790, 148, 151
Copyright Act of 1831, 151
Copyright Act of 1909, 151
Copyright Act of 1976, 148–149, 151
Copyright Alternative in Small Claims Enforcement (CASE) Act of 2020, 161
Copyright Term Extension Act, 151–152, 155
copyrights, 30, 136, 137–138, 147, 163, 256
  Berne Convention for the Protection of Literary and Artistic Works, 149, 152, 257
  CASE Act of 2020, 161
  case law, 159–160
  Chafee Amendment, 256
  circumvention, 152–154
  copyrightable subject matter, 148
  duration of, 151
  enforcement and remedies, 160–162
  exclusive rights, 148–149, 151
  federal law, 147–148
    Copyright Act, 147, 157
    Copyright Act of 1790, 148, 151
    Copyright Act of 1831, 151
    Copyright Act of 1909, 151
    Copyright Act of 1976, 148–149, 151
    Copyright Term Extension Act, 151–152
    DMCA, 152–154
    fair use doctrine, 147, 149–151, 155, 159, 209
    Statute of Anne, 147–148
  and HCI, 162
  idea-expression distinction, 148
  infringement, 150, 154, 159, 160–161, 186–187
    generative AI systems, 208–210
  licensing, 155
    Creative Commons, 155–157

exclusive license, 155
FOSS, 157
nonexclusive license, 155, 158
open source, 157–158
terms of service (TOS), 158–159
Marrakesh Treaty, 256–257
notice-and-takedown system, 154, 186, 187
red flag knowledge, 186
Title 17 of U.S. Code, 147
United States Copyright Office, 139, 147, 152, 154, 157, 161, 207
court opinions, 15
court reporters, 17
court rulings, 20
court system, 8–9
Courts of Appeals. *See* appellate courts
COVID-19 pandemic, 15, 29
  web accessibility during, 43
CPA. *See* Colorado Privacy Act (CPA)
CPPA. *See* California Privacy Protection Agency (CPPA)
CPRA. *See* California Privacy Rights Act (CPRA)
Cranor, Lorrie, 29
Crawford, K., 130
Creative Commons (CC) licenses, 155–157
criminal law, 13–14, 184
Crowdsourcing and Citizen Science Act of 2017, 129
CRPD. *See* Convention on the Rights of Persons with Disabilities (CRPD)
CTDPA. *See* Connecticut Data Privacy Act (CTDPA)
CVAA. *See* 21st Century Communications and Video Accessibility Act (CVAA)
cyberspace, 199
cybersquatting, 168, 169

damages, 13, 64, 88, 113, 145, 160, 161, 162, 170
dark (deceptive) patterns, xii, 77, 259
  definition, 212–213
    in CA Civil Code, 221
  fair patterns, 214
  false beliefs, 215
  forced action, 214
  FTC
    jurisdiction over, 216–217
    types of dark patterns, 215–216
  HCI community and, 229
  hiding/delay disclosure of material information, 215
  interface interference, 214
  legal rules of, 216–217
    CAADCA, 221–222
    California statutes, 221–222
    case law, 217–218

dark (deceptive) patterns (cont.)
  CCPA, 225–226
  Colorado regulation, 222–226
  Connecticut statutes, 220–221
  DETOUR Act, 226–228, 229
  federal statutes, 218–219
  FTC regulation to negative option marketing, 219–220
  state consumer protection statutes, 220–222
  U.S. Congress, pending bill in, 226–228
  negative option marketing, 219–220
  obstruction, 214
  privacy choices, obscuring/subverting, 216
  sneaking, 214
  social engineering, 214
  social engineering and sneaking, combination of, 215
  types of, 213–216
  unauthorized charges, 215, 216
deceptive practices, xi, 94
  Facebook, 95–96
  Federal Trade Commission Act of 1914, 94–97, 167
Declaration of Helsinki (1964), 125, 126, 127
Declaration of Independence, 1, 2
deepfakes, 200, 201–204, 210
  detection, 202
  and Executive Order on Safe, Secure, and Trustworthy Artificial Intelligence, 203
  state laws, 202–203
deference. *See* judicial deference
Department of Homeland Security, 5
Department of Justice (DOJ)
  Antitrust Division, 188
  "Dear Colleague" letter, 50–51, 62
  effective communications requirement and, 6, 43–44, 54
  guidance for state and local government websites, 52
design patents, 136, 140
DETOUR (Deceptive Experiences To Online Users Reduction) Act, 226–228, 229
digital accessibility, 31, 32, 33–35, 70
  airport kiosks, 48
  assistive technology and, 59, 60
  barriers, 31–32, 59, 69
  born-accessible design, 36–39, 47
  Chief Digital Accessibility officer, 39
  compliance monitoring, 39
  in computing course, 69
  core legal theories of, 40
    effective communications requirement of ADA, 43–44

nexus theory of ADA, 41–43
organizational type, 40–41
definition, 35–36
future accessibility requirements to manufacturers/technologies creators, 67–68
future legal questions, 65–69
lawsuits and settlement agreement, 64–65
legal procedures and remedies, 64–65
legal rules, 44
  ADA, 48–49. *See also* Americans with Disabilities Act (ADA)
  Air Carrier Access Act, 47–48
  CRPD article 9, 253–254
  CVAA, 61–62
  Marrakesh Treaty Article 11, 256–257
  Section 504 of Rehabilitation Act, 61
  Section 508 of Rehabilitation Act, 44–47
  Title I (employment) of ADA, 58–60
  Title II (state and local governments) of ADA, 50–53, 65
  Title III (public accommodations) of ADA, 53–58, 65
management of, 39–40
Maryland statutes, 62–64
nuisance lawsuit, future limit to, 68
Online Accessibility Act, 67, 69
overview of, 35
regulatory impact analysis, 69
Section 508 coordinators, 39
state laws about, 62–64
user feedback, 39
web accessibility. *See* web accessibility
Websites and Software Applications Accessibility Act, 65–66
Digital Geneva Convention, 260
Digital Millennium Copyright Act (DMCA), 147, 152–154, 207
  Section 512, 154, 186–187
  Section 1201, 152–154, 161
Digital Rights Management laws, 29
Digital Services Act, 258–260
direct recording electronic (DRE) voting machines, 248
disability rights law, 33–34. *See also* Americans with Disabilities Act (ADA); Rehabilitation Act
discretionary jurisdiction, 11
discrimination
  AI, 204–207
  CEDAW, 251
  employment. *See* Title I (employment) of ADA
  GINA, 80, 81
district courts, 9, 11, 12, 13, 20, 57

Index

DMCA. *See* Digital Millennium Copyright Act (DMCA)
DOJ. *See* Department of Justice (DOJ)
domain names as trademark, 167–168, 169

early voting, 244
ECPA. *See* Electronic Communications Privacy Act (ECPA) of 1986
educational records, privacy of, 85, 90–91
EEOC. *See* Equal Employment Opportunity Commission (EEOC)
effective communications requirement of ADA, 6, 41, 43–44, 54, 65
Eldred, Eric, 155
Election Assistance Commission, 239, 240
Election Campaign Act Amendments of 1979, 236
Elections Clause, 234
electronic communications data, privacy of, 83, 92
Electronic Communications Privacy Act (ECPA) of 1986, 83, 92, 176
Employee Retirement Income Security Act, 81
employment application process, technology in, 59–60
employment discrimination. *See* Title I (employment) of ADA
en banc hearing, 56
End-User License Agreements (EULAs), 105–106
enforcement. *See* law enforcement and remedies
English Statute of Peace Act, 74
Equal Employment Opportunity Commission (EEOC), 59, 60
E-rate program (Schools and Libraries Program), 183
ergonomics, 21
EULAs. *See* End-User License Agreements (EULAs)
European Electronic Communications Code, 177
European Union (EU)
   Artificial Intelligence Act, 108
   Digital Services Act, 258–260
   European Electronic Communications Code, 177
   EU-US Data Privacy Framework, 177–178
   GDPR. *See* General Data Protection Regulation (GDPR)
EU-US Data Privacy Framework, 177–178
exclusive copyright license, 155
Executive Agreements, 250
executive branch, 2, 4
Executive Order on Protecting Americans' Sensitive Data from Foreign Adversaries (2021), 14

executive orders, 14, 206
executive power, 2
exempted rulemaking, 7
exhaustion requirement, 58–59
eye tracking technology, 24–25

Fair Credit Reporting Act (FCRA) of 1970, 83
Fair Information Practice Principles (FIPPs), 87–88
fair use doctrine, copyrights, 147, 149–151, 155, 159, 209
   Marrakesh Treaty Article 11, 256–257
fake phishing website, xiii
Family Educational Rights and Privacy Act (FERPA), 85, 90
FCC. *See* Federal Communications Commission (FCC)
FCRA. *See* Fair Credit Reporting Act (FCRA) of 1970
federal administrative agencies. *See* administrative agencies
Federal Circuit, 9
Federal Communications Commission (FCC), 176, 178, 179, 181, 188, 189, 191, 194
federal courts, 2, 9, 11
   case citation, 16
   jurisdiction process in, 12
federal funding, 50, 54, 61, 90
federal laws, 8, 9, 20, 42, 123, 137. *See also* specific federal law
   copyrights, 147–154
   digital accessibility. *See* digital accessibility, legal rules
   human subject research. *See* human subjects research, laws, rules, and regulations of
   patents, 140–142
   privacy. *See* privacy, federal laws
   trademarks, 163–165
Federal Policy for the Protection of Human Subjects. *See* The Common Rule
Federal Register, 7, 88
Federal Trade Commission (FTC), xi, 188, 213, 217
   "Click-to-Cancel" rule, 219–220
   corporate advertising guidelines, 97
   dark patterns
      jurisdiction over, 216–217
      types of, 215–216
   guidelines for privacy-by-design, 104
   HCI issues in, xii–xiii
   negative option marketing, 219
      regulation to, 219–220
   privacy and security website, 96–97

Federal Trade Commission Act of 1914, 94–97, 167, 219
   COPPA, 95
   enforcement actions, 96
   GLBA, 95
   investigating complaints and negotiating settlements under, 95–96
   issuing regulations and rules under, 95
   Section 5, 94–97
federalism, 2
FERPA. See Family Educational Rights and Privacy Act (FERPA)
Fiesler, Casey, 153
Fifth Amendment, 85
FIPPs. See Fair Information Practice Principles (FIPPs)
First Amendment, 85, 93, 179–180, 183, 184
forced action, 214
Foreign Intelligence Surveillance Act of 1978, 92
formal rulemaking, 7
FOSS. See Free and Open Source Software (FOSS)
Fourteenth Amendment, 71, 85–86
Fourth Amendment, 82, 85, 86, 92, 180–181
Free and Open Source Software (FOSS), 157
freedom of expression, 85, 185, 197
   CRPD article 21, 254
freedom of press, 93
freedom of speech and religion, 85, 179–180, 184
FTC. See Federal Trade Commission (FTC)

GDPR. See General Data Protection Regulation (GDPR)
General Data Protection Regulation (GDPR), xiii, 27, 72, 79, 83–84, 102–103, 105, 108, 256, 258, 260
   Article 7, 103
   Article 7(3), 72
   Article 25, 104, 109
generative AI, xv, 198, 205
   and IP, 207
      AI infringement, 208–210
      AI protection, 207–208
genericide, trademarks, 166
genetic information, privacy of, 75, 80–81
Genetic Information Nondiscrimination Act (GINA) of 2008, 80, 81
GINA. See Genetic Information Nondiscrimination Act (GINA) of 2008
GLBA. See Gramm-Leach-Bliley Act (GLBA)
GPS information privacy, 79–80
Gramm-Leach-Bliley Act (GLBA), 95
Gray, C. M., 214
Grimmelman, James, 168
Gulliksen, Jan, 29

HAVA. See Help America Vote Act (HAVA)
Hayes, Gillian, 128
HCI. See human–computer interaction (HCI)
HCI community, 129, 130, 133, 231, 232, 233, 237, 247
HCI International, 28
HCI research, 28–29
   ethics, 112–113, 135
   Amy on risks associated with, 113–114
   exempt research, 119
   human subjects research. See human subjects research
   patent law impact on, 146–147
   U.S. legal basics to, 19–20
health information, privacy of, 89–90
   genetic information, 75, 80–81
Health Insurance Portability and Accountability Act (HIPAA) of 1996, 82, 83, 89–90
   de-identified health information, 90
   Expert Determination section, 90
   identifiable health information, 89–90
   Privacy Rule, 89–90
   Safe Harbor test, 90
Help America Vote Act (HAVA), 239, 241–242
   Title III, 241
high-risk AI systems, 108
HIPAA. See Health Insurance Portability and Accountability Act (HIPAA) of 1996
Hood, III, M. V., 237
Huh-Yoo, J., 118
Human Rights Act, 206
human subjects, 28
   definition, 117
human subjects research, 111–114
   Amy on risks associated with, 113–114
   ethics, 112–113
   Facebook emotional contagion study, 113–114
   informed consent, 115, 116, 120, 123, 124, 125, 129
   laws, rules, and regulations of
      ACM Publications Policy on Research Involving Human Subjects and Participants, 127–128, 133
      Belmont Report, 116, 118, 127, 135
      in Canada, 126
      clinical trail's in low- and middle-income countries, 127
      The Common Rule. See The Common Rule
      criticisms of, 133–135
      Declaration of Helsinki (1964), 125, 126, 127
      direct remedy for violation of, lack of, 120
      Florida law, 124
      ICCPR, 125–126
      international regulations, 125–128
      IRBs, 118–120
      IRBs review, 127, 131–132

Louisiana law, 124
Maryland law, 123
Massachusetts law, 124
National Research Act, 116
New Hampshire law, 124
New York law, 123–124
in Norway, 126
Nuremberg Code, 114–115, 120, 125
private rights of action, lack of, 120
remedies and case law, 120–122
state law, 123–125
suing for the actual injury, 121
in Taiwan, 126–127
Virginia law, 123
regulatory challenges, 128
online research and big data, 129–132
participatory research methods, 128–129
Stanley Milgram's obedience experiment, 116
Tuskegee syphilis experiments, 115
unethical experiments, 115–116
University of Minnesota research, 131–132
human–computer interaction (HCI), 21, 81
authority and organizations in, 26–28
cognitive aspects of, 24
disciplines and waves of, 25–26, 29
eye tracking technology, 24–25
first wave of, 25
fourth wave of, 25–26
infrastructure problem in, 26
and law, policy, 29–30
observational user data, 24–25
origin of, 21–22
people with disabilities (PWD) and, 32–33
    See also digital accessibility
prototyping, 23
second wave of, 25
"Think Aloud" method, 24
third wave of, 25
usability testing/user testing, 24
user centered design, 23
user diary, 24

ICCPR. *See* International Covenant on Civil and Political Rights (ICCPR)
ICDPA. *See* Iowa Consumer Data Protection Act (ICDPA)
IDEA. *See* Individuals with Disabilities Education Act (IDEA)
identifiable health information, 89–90
identifiable private information, definition, 117
Individuals with Disabilities Education Act (IDEA), 51
informal rulemaking, 7–8
injunctive relief, 64, 145, 160, 170

in-person voting, 243–244
inquisitorial system of law, 3
institutional review boards (IRBs), 28, 118, 122, 128, 129, 132, 133, 134
    approvals, 118, 129
    limitation of, 131–132
    local, 119
    oversight, 134
    private, 119–120
    review of, 127
        exempt research, 119
    risk evaluation, 118–119
    tribal, 125, 129
intellectual property (IP), 30, 136, 171–172, 186.
    See also copyrights; patents; trademarks
    copyrights, 136, 137–138, 147–162
    definition, 136
    generative AI and, 207–210
    Intellectual Property Clause in U.S. Constitution, 138
    international treaties and agreements, 139–140
    legal rules, 138–140
    Locke on, 139
    Marrakesh Treaty, 256–257
    patents, 136, 137–138, 140–147
    publicity rights, 137
    software and user interface protection, 137–138
    statutes and regulations of, 139
    trade secrets, 137
    trademarks, 136, 163–171
    types of, 136–137
    World Intellectual Property Organization Convention, 250
INTERACT, 27
interface interference, 214
Internal Revenue Code, 81
International Convention on the Elimination of All Forms of Racial Discrimination, 251
International Covenant on Civil and Political Rights (ICCPR), 125–126, 251, 255–256
international laws and treaties, 249–250
    CEDAW, 251
    Digital Geneva Convention, 260
    RoHS, 261
    HCI, impact on, 251
        CRPD, 252–255
        Digital Services Act, 258–260
        GDPR, 258. *See also* General Data Protection Regulation (GDPR)
        ICCPR, 251, 255–256
        Marrakesh Treaty, 256–257
        International Convention on the Elimination of All Forms of Racial Discrimination, 251
        IP, 139–140

international laws and treaties (cont.)
    LGPD, 105
    POPIA, 105
    privacy, 102–103
    ratification of, 250–251
    technology, impact on, 260–261
    UNCLOS, 251
    United Nations, 249–250
    U.S. adoption of, 250
International Telecommunication Union
        (ITU), 191–192
Internet Corporation for Assigned Names and
        Numbers (ICANN), 168
Iowa Consumer Data Protection Act (ICDPA), 101
Iowa Privacy Act (IPA), 101–102
IP. *See* intellectual property (IP)
IPA. *See* Iowa Privacy Act (IPA)
IRBs. *See* institutional review boards (IRBs)
ITU. *See* International Telecommunication
        Union (ITU)

judicial branch, 2, 4
judicial deference, 5, 44, 50
    Auer deference, 7
    Chevron deference, 5–6, 44, 189
    Skidmore deference, 7
judicial power, 2
judicial precedent, 3–4
jurisdiction, 9, 11, 12, 17, 19, 20, 33, 46, 50, 60, 71,
        74, 78, 79, 95, 106, 107, 108, 109, 119, 121,
        123, 124, 140, 177, 179, 191, 194, 200, 207,
        216–217, 228, 233, 235, 239, 246, 247, 260
    discretionary, 11
    federal courts, process in, 69
    personal, 13
    subject matter, 12
    Supreme Court, process in, 13
jury and trials by jury, 3

Lanham Act of 1946, 164–165, 167, 170, 210
law enforcement and remedies, xi, xii, 48, 60, 75,
        85, 86, 92, 93, 99, 100, 193, 194, 219
    Common Rule, 121–122
    copyrights, 152, 160–162
    Federal Trade Commission Act of 1914, 96
    patents, 144–145
    Section 508, 46, 47
    telecommunications, 196
    trademarks, 165, 166, 169, 170–171
law of the horse, 199
Leahy-Smith America Invents Act (AIA), 142
legal research and sources, 17–19
legislative branch, 2, 4, 5
legislative power, 2

legislative rules, 7
Lei Geral de Proteção de Dados (LGPD), 105
Lessig, Lawrence, 155, 199
Lexis/Nexis, 18, 19
LGPD. *See* Lei Geral de Proteção de Dados
        (LGPD)
Locke, John, 139

machine learning (ML), 108, 112, 205
mail-based voting, 244–246
Marrakesh Treaty, 256–257
Maryland digital accessibility statutes, 62–64
memorandums, 14
Metcalf, J., 130
Mickey Mouse Protection Act, 151
multifactor authentication (MFA), 78
municipal broadband, 195

National Commission for the Protection of
        Human Subjects of Biomedical and
        Behavioral Research, 116
National Information Infrastructure Protection
        Act (NIIPA) of 1996, 176
National Institutes of Standards and Technology
        (NIST), 227, 229
    human factors in voting systems (2004), 239–241
    Report on the Feasibility of Developing
        Voluntary Standards for Voting
        Equipment (1984), 236–237
National Research Act, 116, 117
National Telecommunications and Information
        Administration (NTIA), 188
natural rights, 1
Necessary and Proper Clause, 178
negative option marketing, 219
    FTC regulation to, 219–220
network neutrality, xviii, 188–190
nexus theory, 41–43
NIIPA. *See* National Information Infrastructure
        Protection Act (NIIPA) of 1996
Ninth Amendment, 85
No Derivatives (ND) CC license, 156
Non-Commercial (NC) CC license, 156
nonexclusive copyright license, 155, 158
nonpracticing entities (NPEs), 145
Norman, Donald, 23
Norway, human subjects research regulation
        in, 126
notice of proposed rulemaking (NPRM), 7, 50
NTIA. *See* National Telecommunications and
        Information Administration (NTIA)
NTIA Organization Act, 188
Nuremberg Code, 114–115, 120, 125
Nuremberg War Trials of 1949, 114

obstruction, 214
Office of Human Research Protections (OHRP), 117, 121
Online Accessibility Act, 67, 69
online research, 129–132
open-source software license, 157–158

P3P (privacy standard), xi
participatory research methods, 128–129
Patent Act, 140–141, 208
Patent Act of 1836, 141
Patent Act of 1852, 141
patents, 136, 137–138, 140, 163
   of AI systems, 208
   AIA, 142
   case law, 142–144
   design, 136, 140
   enforcement and remedies, 144–145
   federal law, 140–141
      U.S.C. Title 35, 141–142
   and HCI, 145–147
   infringement, 144–145, 146, 147
      of AI systems, 210
   Patent Act, 140–141, 208
   Patent Act of 1836, 141
   Patent Act of 1852, 141
   plant, 140
   thickets, 146
   trolling, 145, 146
   types of, 136, 140
   United States Patent and Trademark Office (USPTO), 139, 140, 141, 163, 164, 165, 166, 209
   utility, 136, 140
people with disabilities (PWD), HCI and, 32–33
   accessibility. *See* digital accessibility
   CRPD, 252–255
   voting, 235, 242
      in Maryland, 242
Personal Information Protection Law, 82
personal jurisdiction, 13
photos privacy, 79–80
physical accessibility, 33
plant patents, 140
POPIA. *See* Protection of Personal Information Act (POPIA)
PPA. *See* Privacy Protection Act (PPA) of 1980
privacy, xi, xii, xiii, xv, xvii, 1, 27, 30
   of AI, 200
   benefits and risks of sharing personal information, 75
   case law, 86–87
   companies and organizations policies on, 75

   concerns, 71, 77, 78, 79
      photos and GPS information, 79–80
   definition, 76
   evolution of, 74–76
   federal laws, 97, 104, 106
      CIPA, 91–92
      Computer Matching and Privacy Protection Act of 1988, 93–94
      ECPA, 83, 92
      FCRA, 83
      FERPA, 85, 90–91
      Fifth Amendment, 85
      FIPPs, 87–88
      Fourteenth Amendment, 71, 85–86
      Fourth Amendment, 82, 85
      FTC Act of 1914, 94–97
      HIPAA, 82, 83, 89–90
      Ninth Amendment, 85
      PPA, 93
      Privacy Act of 1974, 83, 87–88
      Standards for Privacy of Individually Identifiable Health Information (Privacy Rule), 89–90
      warrant for unreasonable searches and seizures, 86–87, 180–181
   of genetic information, 75, 80–81
   from HCI perspective, 76–77
      centralizing and decentralizing privacy settings, 106–107
      challenges for HCI researchers/developers/practitioners in designing systems and, 72–73
      co-creating privacy requirements by users, 77
      high level security, 78–79
      legal requirements, 109
      paradigms, 82
      photos and GPS information, 79–80
      privacy impact assessment, 79
      privacy laws, 78, 103–106
      privacy mode, 80
      privacy-by-design principles, 78
      usability testing, 77
   information social networking, 76
   international laws, 102–103
      GDPR. *See* General Data Protection Regulation (GDPR)
      LGPD, 105
      POPIA, 105
   from legal perspective, 82–87
      AI and privacy laws, 108
      centralizing enforcement authority, 106
      legal procedures/remedies, 106–110
      technology/societal evolution and privacy laws, 107

privacy (cont.)
  online privacy laws, 106
  penumbra, 86
  reasonable expectation of, 86
  The Right to Privacy (Warren & Brandeis), 74
  state laws, 97–98
    BIPA, 106
    CCPA, 84–85, 98–99, 100, 101, 102
      centralizing enforcement authority, 106
    CPA, 99, 100
    CPRA, 99
    CTDPA, 100–101
    IPA, 101–102
    UCPA, 102
    VCDPA, 100
  Supreme Court on right to principle as constitutional principle, 71, 74–75
  in telecommunication services, 175
  Westin's definition of, 74
Privacy Act of 1974, 83, 87–88, 93
privacy by default, 109
privacy labels, xi
Privacy Protection Act (PPA) of 1980, 93
privacy-by-design approach, 78, 96, 103, 109
  Article 25 of GDPR on, 104
  FTC guidelines for, 104
private information, definition, 117
procedural rules, 7
procurement process, 26, 34, 37
protected health information (PHI), 89–90
Protection of Personal Information Act (POPIA), 105
prototyping, 23
public accommodations. *See* Title III (public accommodations) of ADA
Public Health Service Act, 81
publicity rights, 137
punch card ballots, 238

quasi-legislative authority, 5

Rader, E., 118
REAL ID Act, 5
regulation, 1, 4, 5, 6, 7, 8, 14, 17, 18, 19, 33, 40, 41, 43, 44, 45, 47, 48, 49, 50, 51, 52, 53, 57, 58, 62, 65, 73, 79, 84, 94, 96, 97, 99, 103, 104, 166, 199, 200, 201, 202, 203, 206, 207, 211, 247, 261. *See also* specific regulation
  dark (deceptive) patterns, 219–220, 222–226, 229
  FTC, xii
  GDPR, 27, 72, 79, 83–84, 102–103, 104, 105, 108, 109, 256, 258, 260
  human subject research. *See* human subjects research

of IP, 139
telecommunications. *See* telecommunications, laws, statutes, and regulations
Trade Regulation Rules, 95
Regulation (EU) 2016/679, 83, 88, 104
regulatory impact analysis, 69
Rehabilitation Act, 34, 47, 60, 70
  Section 504, 50, 61
  Section 508, 6, 34, 40, 41, 44–47, 50, 52, 63
research, definition, 117
Research Ethics Boards (REBs), 126
Restore Online Shoppers' Confidence Act (ROSCA), 219, 220
Restriction on the use of certain Hazardous Substances (RoHS) laws, 261
RoHS laws. *See* Restriction on the use of certain Hazardous Substances (RoHS) laws
ROSCA. *See* Restore Online Shoppers' Confidence Act (ROSCA)
Ross, Annie, 33

SCA. *See* Stored Communications Act (SCA)
Section 504 of Rehabilitation Act, 50
Section 508 of Rehabilitation Act, 6, 34, 40, 41, 44–47, 50, 52, 63, 70, 243
  Strengthening Digital Accessibility and the Management of Section 508 of the Rehabilitation Act, 47
sensitive personal information, 99
separation of powers, 2
service marks, 164
Share Alike (SA) CC license, 156
Shepherd's United States Citations, 19
SIGCHI (SIG Special Interest Group on Computer–Human Interaction), 22, 27
SIGSAC (Social and Behavioral Computing), 22
sneaking, 214
social engineering, 214
Sonny Bono Copyright Term Extension Act, 151
sovereign immunity, 14–15
Standards for Privacy of Individually Identifiable Health Information (Privacy Rule), 89–90
stare decisis, 3–4, 6, 11, 19
state and local government discrimination. *See* Title II (state and local governments) of ADA
state court system, 9
state laws, 8, 20, 147, 170. *See also* specific state law
  deepfakes, 202–203
  digital accessibility, 62–64
  human subjects research, 123–125, 134
  privacy, 97–102
  on voting mechanisms, 246–247

Statement of Interest, 43
Statute of Anne, 139, 149
  copyrights, 147–148
statutes, 3–4, 5, 7, 8, 13, 14, 18, 19, 26, 33, 34, 40, 41, 43, 44, 45, 47, 48, 49, 50, 51, 53, 54, 57, 59, 60, 61, 62, 64, 65, 70, 126, 148, 163, 247, 253. See also specific statute
  dark (deceptive) patterns, 218–219, 220–222
  GINA, 80
  implementation through administrative law, 5–7
  of IP, 139
  Maryland digital accessibility, 62–64
  telecommunications. See telecommunications, laws, statutes, and regulations
statutory citation, 17
Stored Communications Act (SCA), 92
Strengthening Digital Accessibility and the Management of Section 508 of the Rehabilitation Act, 47
subject matter jurisdiction, 12
substantive rules, 7
Superior court, 10
Supreme Court, 2, 5, 9, 11, 85, 139, 178
  deference to administrative agencies
    Auer deference, 7
    Chevron deference, 5–6, 44, 189
    Skidmore deference, 7
  jurisdiction process in, 13
  on right to principle as constitutional principle, 71, 74–75
  writ of certiorari, 13

Taiwan, human subjects research regulation in, 126–127
technology design and HCI/UX, 1
telecommunications, 173–174. See also digital accessibility
  5G networks, 196–197
  broadband services, 174–175
    as information service, 189–190
    municipal, 195
  definition, 182
  in education, 194
  enforcement, 196
  E-rate program (Schools and Libraries Program), 183
  ethnographic methods, 177
  FCC. See Federal Communications Commission (FCC)
  future legal questions, 196–197
  and HCI, 190, 195, 196–197
  indirect services, 174
  international policy and standards, 191–192
  ITU, 191–192

ITU Human Factors standards, 191–192
ITU-T Recommendations, 191
laws, statutes, and regulations, 62, 176–178, 193–196
  CDA, 183–186
  CFAA, 176
  Commerce Clause of U.S. Constitution, 178–179
  Communications Act of 1934, 176, 182, 188, 189, 194, 196
  compliance with local laws, 175–176, 177
  CVAA, 187–188
  ECPA, 176
  First Amendment of U.S. Constitution, 179–180
  Fourth Amendment of U.S. Constitution, 180–181
  intersection of HCI with, 174–176
  Necessary and Proper Clause of U.S. Constitution, 179
  NIIPA, 176
  provider liability and content moderation protection, 183–186
  safe harbor protection, 186–187
  Section 230 of CDA, 183–186
  Section 512 of DMCA, 186–187
  state regulation, 194–195
  Telecommunications Act of 1996, 176, 177, 181–183, 184, 194
  third-party doctrine, 181
net neutrality, xviii, 188–190
over-the-top (OTT) services, 174
privacy and security features, 175
telegraph and telephone services, 176
two-factor authentication (2FA), 175
USF, 182
W3C, 192–193
Telecommunications Act of 1996, 176, 177, 181–183, 184, 194
terms of service (TOS), copyright license, 158–159
"Think Aloud" method, 24
Third Amendment, 85
third-party doctrine, 181
Title I (employment) of ADA, 41, 49, 58–60
  violation of, 59
Title II (state and local governments) of ADA, 6, 49, 65
Title III (public accommodations) of ADA, 6, 40, 41, 49, 53–58, 65
  effective communications requirement under, 6, 41, 43–44, 54, 65
  nexus between web accessibility and, 41–42, 54, 65
  circuit courts of appeals, 42–43
trade dress, 138, 144, 167, 170

Index

trade secrets, 137
Trademark Act of 1905, 164
trademarks, 136, 163
  application procedures, 165–166
  case law, 168–170
  certification mark, 164
  cybersquatting, 168, 169
  definition, 164
  descriptive terms as marks, 165, 169
  distinctiveness of, 165, 171
  domain names, 167–168, 169
  enforcement and remedies, 170–171
  federal law, 163–164
    Commerce Clause of U.S. Constitution, 163
    Lanham Act of 1946, 164–165, 167, 170, 210
    Trademark Act of 1905, 164
  genericide, 166
  and HCI, 171
  infringement, 164, 167, 168, 169, 170, 171
    of AI systems, 210
  international agreements on, 164
  likelihood of confusion issue, 165, 169
  loss, 166
  service marks, 164
  trade dress, 138, 144, 167, 170
  UDRP, 168
  unfair competition laws, 167, 170
  United States Patent and Trademark Office (USPTO), 139, 140, 141, 163, 164, 165, 166, 209
  use in commerce, 165, 170
trial courts, 8, 9, 11, 20
Tri-Council Policy Statement, 116, 126

UCPA. *See* Utah Consumer Privacy Act (UCPA)
UDHR. *See* Universal Declaration of Human Rights (UDHR)
UDRP. *See* Uniform Domain-Name Dispute-Resolution Policy (UDRP)
UNCLOS. *See* United Nations Convention on the Law of the Sea (UNCLOS)
unfair competition, 163, 195
unfair competition laws, 167, 170
Uniform Domain-Name Dispute-Resolution Policy (UDRP), 168
Uniformed and Overseas Citizens Absentee Voting Act (UOCAVA), 245–246
United Nations Convention on the Law of the Sea (UNCLOS), 251
United States Copyright Office, 139, 147, 152, 154, 157, 161, 207
United States Patent and Trademark Office (USPTO), 139, 140, 141, 163, 164, 165, 166, 209

Universal Declaration of Human Rights (UDHR), 71, 125
  ICCPR, 125–126
Universal Service Fund (USF), 182
unreasonable searches and seizures, 85, 180–181
Unruh Civil Rights Act, 34
UOCAVA. *See* Uniformed and Overseas Citizens Absentee Voting Act (UOCAVA)
U.S. Circuits, 11–13
U.S. Code, 17, 19
  Section 202, 189
  Title 17, 147
  Title 35, 141–142
U.S. Congress, 5, 250
  administrative agencies, 5
  Communications Act of 1934, 176, 182, 188, 189, 194, 196
  Copyright Term Extension Act, 151–152
  Crowdsourcing and Citizen Science Act of 2017, 129
  enacting law, 3
  Necessary and Proper Clause, 179
  REAL ID Act, 5
U.S. Constitution, 2, 4, 5, 8, 9, 13, 14, 44, 140, 148, 151, 234, 236, 242
  Article I, 163
  Commerce Clause, 163, 178–179
  Copyright Clause, 151
  Fifth Amendment, 85
  First Amendment, 85, 93, 179–180, 183, 184
  Fourteenth Amendment, 71, 85–86
  Fourth Amendment, 82, 85, 86, 92, 180–181
  Intellectual Property Clause, 138
  Necessary and Proper Clause, 178, 179
  Ninth Amendment, 85
  Seventh Amendment, 3
  Third Amendment, 85
U.S. court system, 8–9, 10
U.S. Customs and Border Protection (CBP), 171
U.S. law
  adversarial system of law, 3
  basis of, 2
  Circuits impact on, 11–13
  constitutional law, 4
  history of, 1–3
  judicial precedent, 3–4
  U.S. legal structure, 1–3
usability testing, 24, 48, 218, 228, 229, 243
  in digital accessibility, 38
  of privacy, 77
user-centered design, 23, 103, 230, 243
User Interface Design, Choice Architecture, and Dark Patterns, 222
USF. *See* Universal Service Fund (USF)

USPTO. *See* United States Patent and Trademark Office (USPTO)
Utah Consumer Privacy Act (UCPA), 102
utility patents, 136, 140

VCDPA. *See* Virginia Consumer Data Protection Act (VCDPA)
Virginia Consumer Data Protection Act (VCDPA), 100
Voluntary Voting System Guidelines (VVSG), 239–241, 242–243
  Version 2.0, 242–243
Voting Accessibility for the Elderly and Handicapped Act (1984), 235
voting and voting interfaces, 53, 230–232, 248
  absentee and mail-based, 244–246
  absentee ballot, 244–245
  and ballot issues during 2000 General Election, 231, 237–238
  butterfly ballot, 237–238
  challenges of, 232
  direct recording electronic (DRE) voting machines, 248
  early, 244
  Election Assistance Commission, 239, 240
  HAVA, 239, 241–242
  HCI community and, 247–248
  human engineering standards, 236–237
  in-person, 243–244
  optical scan ballots, 242
  primary, 236
  procedures and mechanisms, 233–235
  punch card ballots, 238
  Report on the Feasibility of Developing Voluntary Standards for Voting Equipment (1984), 236–237
  state laws, 246–247
  UOCAVA, 245–246
  Voting Rights Act of 1965, 235
  VVSG, 239–241, 242–243
Voting Rights Act of 1965, 235
voting systems, 236
VVSG. *See* Voluntary Voting System Guidelines (VVSG)

W3C. *See* World Wide Web Consortium (W3C)
Warren, Samuel, 74
WCAG. *See* Web Content Accessibility Guidelines (WCAG)
WCAG2ICT, 37–38, 45
web accessibility, 6, 54. *See also* digital accessibility
  ADA. *See* Americans with Disabilities Act (ADA)
  during Covid-19 pandemic, 43
  Online Accessibility Act, 67, 69
  overlay problem in, 39
  Section 508 of Rehabilitation Act. *See* Section 508 of Rehabilitation Act
  Title III of ADA. *See* Title III (public accommodations) of ADA
  WCAG, 34–36, 37–38, 41, 45, 48, 52, 57, 58, 65, 70
  WCAG2ICT, 37–38, 45
  Websites and Software Applications Accessibility Act, 65–66
web browser certificate warnings, xiii
Web Content Accessibility Guidelines (WCAG), 34–36, 37–38, 41, 45, 48, 52, 57, 58, 65, 70
  WCAG2ICT, 37–38, 45
Websites and Software Applications Accessibility Act, 65–66
Westlaw, 18, 19
willful blindness, 186
WIPO Copyright Treaty, 152, 257
Wiretap Act, 83, 92
wiretap laws, xiii
World Intellectual Property Organization (WIPO), 136
World Intellectual Property Organization Convention, 250
World Trade Organization (WTO), 256
World Wide Web (WWW), 191
World Wide Web Consortium (W3C), 192–193
writ of certiorari, 13
Wu, Tim, 188

For EU product safety concerns, contact us at Calle de José Abascal, 56–1°,
28003 Madrid, Spain or eugpsr@cambridge.org.

www.ingramcontent.com/pod-product-compliance
Lightning Source LLC
LaVergne TN
LVHW021653060526
838200LV00050B/2333